*Discrete and Dynamic
Decision Analysis*

Discrete and Dynamic Decision Analysis

J. T. Buchanan

Department of Operational Research
University of Strathclyde, Glasgow

JOHN WILEY & SONS

Chichester · New York · Brisbane · Toronto · Singapore

Library of Congress Cataloging in Publication Data:

Buchanan, J. T.
  Discrete and dynamic decision analysis.

  Includes bibliographies and index.
  1. Decision-making—Mathematical models.
I. Title.
HD30.23.B82   658.4′033   81-16066
                                        AACR2

ISBN 0 471 10130 3 (cloth)
ISBN 0 471 10131 1 (paper)

British Library Cataloguing in Publication Data:

Buchanan, J. T.
  Discrete and dynamic decision analysis.
  1. Decision-making
  I. Title
  658.4′03   HD30.23

  ISBN 0 471 10130 3 (cloth)
  ISBN 0 471 10131 1 (paper)

Photo Typeset by Macmillan India Ltd. Bangalore

Printed at The Pitman Press, Bath.

To the three Margarets—my wife Meg, mother Margaret, and grandmother Peggy—and the two Johns—my father John and grandfather Jack

Contents

Preface

The first texts on decision analysis and sequential decisionmaking appeared over twenty years ago and since then the subject–matter has found its way into numerous university and other courses, as well as exercising an influence on the research into and application of the 'decision sciences'. Recently, several professional and specialist journals have devoted entire issues to the use of decision analysis and the scope for further application. Sequential decisionmaking, although attracting considerable research interest and of obvious applicability, has suffered from a lack of wide application through practical difficulties of computation. This is now a very active research area and, taken together with contemporary enhancements in computing hardware, could soon lead to more common implementations of these models.

Material from this field of study can be successfully presented over the spectrum from the essentially non-technical appreciation (which can define the scope and content of the subject) to the mathematically dense treatise (which by virtue of its powerful abstractions can present in a compact form the central results). This book has developed from lectures given to undergraduate and postgraduate students at the Universities of Manchester and Strathclyde. These students have been from a variety of fields but mainly from operational research, mathematics, computer science, business and administration (including such subjects as accountancy), various engineering specialisms, economics and other social sciences. Although the students from more numerate backgrounds tend to have an advantage in tackling problems where manipulation and calculation are involved, it is my experience that all students can have difficulty in the interpretation and formulation of decision problems. Thus, although the level of mathematics assumed in the book is restricted, there is an ample challenge to students equipped well beyond this modest level.

Apart from a few exercises (which are identified in the text) no knowledge of the calculus is assumed. The second chapter is a self-contained presentation on probability, which even students with some background in this subject may find contains unfamiliar material. The only skill which is called on later in the book deals with conditional probabilities (taken from Chapter 2) and probability processing (from Chapter 5). Some familiarity with the rudiments of matrices is assumed from Chapter 8 onwards (covering part of the sequential decisionmaking material). In particular, matrix multiplication and the calculation of a matrix inverse (of small size) is needed. The solution of (small) sets of simultaneous linear equations is also a feature of these later chapters.

Our aim in the text is to demonstrate methods for the structuring and resolution of decision problems. As part of these processes we are concerned with problems of measurement, and these problems are studied in the second and third chapters. The use of these measurements in resolving decision problems, and in particular the use and evaluation of information, is the subject of the next three chapters. These cover the material conventionally referred to as *decision analysis* or statistical decision theory. The *discrete* structures used in these sections are effectively restricted to single decision problems or a short sequence of related decision problems. For the resolution of sequential problems (e.g. multi-time period problems) an alternative structure is needed, and our concern in the latter half of the book is with the use of these models. This subject-matter is commonly referred to as *dynamic* programming and since all of these structures are again discrete, I have chosen **Discrete and Dynamic Decision Analysis** as an honest, if long, title.

The material is developed via solutions of a small set of examples, where the description of a particular example increases in complexity as our skills are enhanced. A few algebraic demonstrations are given, but we avoid the use of a theorem/proof format and closely tie any algebra to at least one numerical example. Exercises given at the end of each chapter are overwhelmingly devoted to the formulation and numerical solution of decision problems.

A more detailed preview of the book's layout is to be found at the end of Chapter 1 where the subject-matter is referenced via concepts which have appeared in that chapter.

Given our mathematical prerequisites and the nature of the development of the material, the book can be useful for a range of courses. Dependent on selectivity and speed of progress, it can form the basis of a two-term undergraduate or one-term postgraduate course. Our examples are essentially business oriented and thus have an appeal to the range of students already mentioned in the second paragraph.

For an opportunity to teach this material and helpful encouragement to publish it I am grateful to Doug White, Professor of Decision Theory at the University of Manchester. I should like to thank the Universities of Manchester and Strathclyde for permission to use material from examination papers, and in particular I am grateful to my ex-colleagues at Manchester for permission to use questions written by them, but seen by me during my period as External Examiner. Finally, may I thank Joan Cawte and Anne Cleugh for their efficient secretarial assistance in the preparation of the manuscript. Neither my handwritten nor my 'typed' drafts could confuse them.

Glasgow   IAIN BUCHANAN

Chapter 1

Initiation and Motivation

1.1 Introduction and Examples

In this chapter we introduce via examples some of the concepts and problems to be studied more thoroughly in the following chapters. For our purposes a decision problem is defined as arising when a choice must be made from a set of alternative actions, e.g. a diner must make a selection from a menu, a government must decide which type of nuclear reactor it will opt for, or an investor must allocate his available funds to a subset of options drawn from the very wide range of possible portfolios he could construct. The problem could of course be resolved by recourse to intuition, or by making one draw from a hat where each alternative is written on a piece of paper—if that is possible. Whilst producing a resolution of the ambiguity facing the decisionmaker these mechanisms have little to recommend them to the decision analyst, although the second method (with suitable modifications) has merit in certain circumstances. Before specifying some of the complications which give rise to the interest in a decision problem, we look first at some simple illustrations.

Example 1.1

Consider the case of a man contemplating a change of car. The garage where he will exchange his car sells cars which can be said to be either 'good buys' or 'bad buys'. The net cost of exchange and running a good buy for one year is reckoned to be $1200, while the net cost of a bad buy for the same length of time is $1600. If the man's present car is kept rather than exchanged then the running cost for the coming year is $1400. Given that the owner is interested in minimizing his running costs for the coming year, what ought his course of action to be? There is no real problem if the cars in the garage are immediately identifiable as good or bad buys, and it is therefore assumed that the true quality of any car is not revealed until it is taken into ownership—surely an assumption borne out by experience?

We can summarize the outcomes for all possible cases in Table 1.1.

Example 1.2

A company director has five alternative investment plans for the coming year, and the net profit accruing from each alternative is a function of the rate of

2

Table 1.1 Net costs in dollars for Example 1.1

| | | Decision | |
		Keep	Exchange
True condition of	Good	1400	1200
potential exchange	Bad	1400	1600

inflation over that year. No one alternative is uniformly best, i.e. has the greatest net profit regardless of the inflation rate. Which alternative ought the director to pursue? To add numerical substance to this problem, suppose we have to consider only two possibilities for the inflation rate, namely high or low, and the net profits for each plan under each inflation rate are as given in Table 1.2.

Table 1.2 Profits in millions of dollars for Example 1.2

| | | Investment plan | | | | |
		a_1	a_2	a_3	a_4	a_5
Inflation	High	1.5	2	5	3	3
rate	Low	6	3	2	5	3.5

Example 1.3

You are offered the option of entering into a gamble which depends on the outcome of one toss of a coin, e.g. if the coin falls heads you win a prize, but if it falls tails you pay a penalty. Do you take up this option? Again we may summarize the ingredients of the problem as in Table 1.3.

Table 1.3 Outcomes for Example 1.3

| | | Action | |
		Accept gamble	Reject gamble
Outcome of	Heads	Win prize	*Status quo*
coin toss	Tails	Pay penalty	*Status quo*

Example 1.4

Consider an extension of Example 1.2 where the director has a succession of planning decisions to take, say one per year for the next ten years. The profit resulting from the decision in the first year will constrain to a certain extent the alternative plans which the company can consider feasible for the second year, and so on. The ability of the company to sustain certain alternatives depends on the outcome of previous decisions, and these outcomes are not entirely within the company's control since they depend on the inflation rate. This problem therefore cannot be viewed merely as ten independent problems of the type described in Example 1.2. How does the director cope with this sequence of problems?

Example 1.5

A shop sells a commodity which can either be in high or low demand. It has been observed that a week of high demand is more likely to be followed by another week of high demand than by a week of low demand, and demand is even more likely to remain high if advertising of the commodity is carried out. This publicity runs for one week at a time and is, of course, only provided at a price. Advertising also helps enhance the chances of raising demand from a low to a high level, but in none of these cases is it possible to predict with certainty what level of demand will manifest itself. Given that there are profits associated with the different demand levels, how does the shop cope with the problem of deciding whether to advertise or not, and how much should it be willing to pay for such advertising?

There are characteristics common to all these examples. In each case the specification of a chosen alternative by the decisionmaker does not necessarily determine the outcome. There are features in the environment of each problem which the decisionmaker cannot control. In Example 1.1 the net cost involved in taking the exchange option depends on whether the new car turns out to be a good or a bad buy, whereas the option of keeping the present car does determine the net cost (of $1400). For the problem of Example 1.2 the net profit as a result of a given choice of investment plan will not be known until the inflation rate manifests itself. In Example 1.3 the decision to enter into the gamble does not determine the eventual outcome, since this depends on the result of the coin toss. For Example 1.4 the net effect of a sequence of decisions will depend on the sequence of inflation rates in the ten years under consideration. Similar remarks apply to Example 1.5.

This uncertainty as to the conditions prevailing when decisions are taken is a recurrent theme in our study, and an important part of our analysis concerns itself with the measurement of this uncertainty and the subsequent use of these measurements. The term *state of nature* is commonly used to denote the variable whose value together with the choice of alternative action determines the outcome for the decisionmaker. Thus, in Example 1.1 the state of nature is the true condition of the potential exchange, whilst in Example 1.2 it is the forthcoming inflation rate. For Example 1.3 it is the result of the coin toss. Examples 1.4 and 1.5 give rise to difficulties because of the manner in which the uncertainty makes an impact on the evolution of the problem. The outcome of a present decision will determine what the next decision *problem* in the sequence is going to be, and the outcome from that problem in turn dictates the succeeding problem. For example, in the commodity demand problem it is not known when considering the advertising option in the third week where demand has been low in the previous week, what the demand will be for week three, and thus what the problem will be in week four. Given that the problem has to be seen as one large, say twenty-week, problem where the shop would like as large a profit as possible, the difficulties of coping with the interactive nature of the decisions are obvious.

1.2 Remarks on Example 1.1

Given the information of Example 1.1, how can we argue for a choice of action? One approach which uses only the information of the table of net running costs is to evaluate each decision in terms of the worst possible outcome that can follow from that decision. Thus, if the exchange option is taken, the new car could prove to be a bad buy and the resulting costs would be $1600. If the decision is to retain the present car then the running costs are known to be $1400. Comparing these costs shows that the option to keep the present car has the better 'worst possible consequence'.

Again for Example 1.2 the worst possible outcomes for each alternative are profits of 1.5, 2, 2, 3 and 3 million dollars for plans a_1 to a_5, respectively. The best of these is the 3 millions given by both a_4 and a_5. The analysis here leads to a choice of investment plan which has a guaranteed minimum profit greater than that guaranteed by any other plan. The actual profit could of course be greater than this minimum depending on the inflation rate which turns up.

Quite apart from the fact that in many problems additional information about the states of nature may be available (or can be sought), this type of argument is regarded by some analysts as controversial or even unscientific. We postpone until Chapter 4 a more detailed examination of this and other criteria which use only the information of the table, but note that this criterion is in some ways a pessimistic or conservative one in that it selects alternatives purely on the basis of the worst possible consequence.

The major component of our studies is devoted to problems where we have some quantitative information about the states of nature. This information can have come from a variety of sources, some of which will be illustrated in the following paragraphs, but the use of this information is the same once it is encoded in a standard format. For Example 1.1 if the decisionmaker has some information on the proportion of good and bad buys in the garage then this could influence the decision he would take. For example, if the garage were known to sell 90 % good buys and 10 % bad buys, the preferred alternative for the author would be to opt for the exchange. If the proportions were reversed, the author's preference would be to keep the present car. The reader may well react differently to these possibilities, and the author's preferences are only offered as one solution rather than the solution.

Information of this type is clearly relevant but need not be the only type of data which can influence choice. It is possible, usually at a price, to acquire extra information say, in this case, about the oil consumption of the potential exchange. Although low oil consumption may be strongly associated with a good buy, it will not be an infallible guide, just as high or medium oil consumption will not be a sure sign of a bad buy. For instance, suppose 60 % of all good buys have low oil consumption while 20 % have medium consumption, and for bad buys 30 % have medium consumption and 40 % have high consumption. On being told the oil consumption of a potential exchange how should the decisionmaker react, and how does he decide whether or not to pay for a test to be done in the first place?

As an alternative, or in addition to the consumption test, the decisionmaker may have the option of allowing an expert to road test the potential exchange, and on the basis of this road test the expert verdict on the condition is given. It is widely observed that expert advice is never free, often useful, but inevitably fallible. How then can the decisionmaker accommodate in his analysis this extra information, giving due recognition to the fallibility of tests and experts, and reflecting the costs involved in their use?

1.3 Remarks on Example 1.2

For the investment problem whose data is summarized in Table 1.2, there is no one action which is best under both a high and a low rate of inflation. If the inflation rate were to be high then a_3 yields the largest net profit, while a_1 produces the largest profit under a low rate of inflation. Although there is no clear cut best plan, it is possible to eliminate some of the five plans from further consideration. Comparing a_2 and a_4 it is seen that the former has a net profit which is inferior to that of the latter regardless of the inflation rate. Plan a_2 should not be followed since superior profits can be obtained from following a_4, even though nothing more is known about the inflation rate in prospect. A comparison of a_4 and a_5 demonstrates the superiority of a_4, since again the profits from a_4 are at least as large as those to be obtained from following a_5, and may indeed be larger depending on the inflation rate which turns up. From these observations it is thus possible to reduce the set of alternatives from five to three. No further reduction is possible using this type of argument, since for any pair of plans from the remaining three, one will have a superior profit under a low rate of inflation and the other a larger profit under a high rate.

Lack of certainty about the forthcoming inflation rate gives the interest to this problem. Although the rate is an uncertain quantity, it is likely that the director will have opinions about what the rate is going to be. These opinions will be a distillation of a variety of facts, reports, prejudices and judgements relevant to the determination of the inflation rate, e.g. his opinion on current and future wage bargaining, price control legislation, and electoral uncertainties. The end result is inevitably a subjective assessment that, for example, a high rate of inflation is more likely than a low one, or perhaps that the high and low rates are equally likely. In Chapter 2 we study the problem of systematically encoding in a quantitative manner such qualitative judgements. The end product of this process is a numerical synopsis of the decisionmaker's judgements on the relative likelihoods of the states of nature. Such a potent construction is not made without some effort, and the nature of this, together with the assumptions necessary to make it viable, will be of concern to us.

Given that our decisionmaker has accorded, say, equal likelihood to the high and low rates for our problem, how might this information be used to establish a selection of one plan over another? Recall that we have eliminated two of the options and are effectively examining a problem with the three options summarized in Table 1.4.

Table 1.4 The data for Example 1.2 after removal of
the dominated actions

| | | Investment plan | | |
		a_1	a_3	a_4
Inflation	High	1.5	5	3
rate	Low	6	2	5

There are many circumstances which may make option a_4 look preferable. For instance, the company may currently have assets worth \$5 million, and the director is in favour of steady predictable growth. Plan a_4 offers substantial profit regardless of the state of nature which may turn up, whereas a_1 will lead to a more speculative advance, resulting in a small growth or a (perhaps) uncontrollably large one.

On the other hand an ambitious company may be convinced of the merits of a very rapid growth and look more favourably on the undeniably 'riskier' a_1 option.

These considerations are on the basis of equally likely high and low inflation rates, and the response of either company may well be different under different expectations about the forthcoming inflation rate.

For the case where the investment options are of a different order of magnitude, e.g. the entries of the table are in tens of thousands of dollars rather than millions, then the riskier option a_1 may well recommend itself to a decisionmaker who preferred the option a_4 in the problem with the larger profits at stake (assuming the information about the inflation rate has remained the same). The profits are a smaller fraction of the company's assets, and represent a relatively small amount of growth. Such behaviour is not easily explained only in terms of the money values and relative likelihoods of the states of nature. The outcomes themselves are being assessed as to their desirability, in admittedly somewhat intangible terms. The decisionmaker's perception and evaluation of the possible outcomes is central to the resolution of this problem, and we return to this topic in Chapter 3. The study essentially involves a characterization of the decisionmaker's attitude to risk.

In reality any investment plan will have several implications for a company, besides the profit which it can generate. For instance, external credit may be taken up or money invested internally, employees may be hired or fired, market shares may increase or decrease. Comparison between outcomes is no longer on the basis of one quantity. Instead, a number of attributes have to be considered when contemplating the desirability or otherwise of a particular outcome. For the single attribute case (e.g. net profit) it is natural to assume that the preference between two outcomes will be resolved purely in terms of the magnitude of the profit, i.e. a profit of 3 million is inferior to a profit of 6 million. The outcomes can be ranked by considering their associated profits. For the multi-attribute case we have raised, this ranking (if it can be achieved) is considerably less straightforward. How does the decisionmaker rate, say, a profit of 3 millions, increase in workforce of 5000 and market share of 0.25 against an outcome where the profit is 4 millions, the workforce is to be reduced by 3000 and the market share is 0.2? Presumably he prefers a higher profit for the increased opportunities it can bring, would rather avoid a reduction in workforce because of the problems it can bring by way of dispute, low morale, bad image, etc., and would like as large a market share as possible. Under these assumptions neither of the outcomes described presents itself as obviously better than the other, although the decisionmaker may have a preference. This is not established by consideration of one attribute in isolation, but rather by consolidating the various factors in some way. Our investigation of the complexities of the measurement processes for both the single and multi-attribute cases is postponed until Chapter 3.

Just as in Example 1.1, the decisionmaker will have the option (at some cost) of obtaining extra information relevant to the assessment of the possible inflation rate. For example, Professors of Economics will, for the appropriate fee, provide their own individual forecasts of what the inflation rate prospects are, and the decisionmaker is faced with the problem of deciding which, if any, forecaster(s) he is going to hire. The prediction of a Professor is, of course, subject to error (else he would not have remained a Professor) and the decisionmaker has the problem of evaluating and reacting to this fallibility. If the forecaster is relatively new to the business, or has been adept at covering his tracks, there will be little or no record of his past performance in this role. The assessment of fallibility then takes on a subjective tone, rather like the determination of the relative likelihood of the inflation rate.

Forecasters may differ in their ability to predict correctly the forthcoming inflation rate, and indeed some forecasters may be better at recognizing an impending high rate than a low one. For example, Professor A will correctly predict a high rate of inflation (when this is indeed going to be the case) 85% of the time, but his predictions of a low rate are correct only 60% of the time, while Professor B has a consistent 75% record of correct forecasts, regardless of the forthcoming rate. The choice of forecaster to hire will depend on the director's initial evaluation of the future inflation rates, the effect of using the forecasts from the Professor(s), and the cost of obtaining the forecast(s).

The method of analysis for these problems where the uncertainties can be adequately quantified will be returned to in Chapter 4, and the use and value of information is the study of Chapter 5.

1.4 Remarks on Example 1.3

What are we to do when faced with the ubiquitous coin-tosser of Example 1.3? Perversity, or a very strong will, would be needed to keep such a character from our pages, and his inclusion is justified to the extent that he presents a decision problem whose abstraction need not be circumscribed with doubts about the validity of any simplifications, or the discrepancy between problem and statement. The paucity of data in the statement is intended to stimulate introspection about what would constitute an acceptable gamble. Playing with a 'fair' coin, would a prize of ten times the penalty tempt you into playing? e.g. where the prize is \$10 and the penalty \$1? What if the prize were \$1000 and the penalty \$100, or the prize were \$10 000 and the penalty \$1000? Would any of your answers be different if the coin were tossed and the outcome determined not once but say five times? Given that you would play a single game for a prize of \$10 and a penalty of \$1, how large an entry fee would you be willing to pay? What if the fairness of the coin were in doubt? For example, you may know it to be loaded in favour of heads (and even know the corresponding 'odds' on a head falling), or you may have no information given to you about any potential bias. In the second case you are allowed to make a number of tosses of the coin—at a cost of course—before deciding to take the gamble or not. How do you react? Would you rather pay for ten trial tosses of the coin before the decision, or is it preferable to pay for the trial tosses one at a time, and stop after a number of your choosing? A problem of this type is analysed extensively in Chapter 6.

1.5 Remarks on Examples 1.4 and 1.5

For Example 1.4 the problems remarked on with respect to Example 1.2 are compounded and extended by virtue of the sequential nature of the problem. The central difficulty is the decisionmaker's inability to control exactly the evolution of the problem over time. A decision taken in the first year does not determine exactly the condition of the company at the beginning of year two when the next decision is due. The inflation rate in year one, together with the option taken, will specify the profit for that year. Thus, at the beginning of year one the director may not even be able to stipulate the set of options from which he will choose in year two, since this set is a function of the profit in year one. Given that the time horizon for the problem is ten years, how is the decisionmaker to react?

No criterion has yet been suggested for this problem, but the natural one is to think in terms of accumulating the profits over the years, and pursuing a large total profit. The sequence of profits is not 'controllable' and account must be taken of this in any analysis. As a variant to this problem, consider one where some of the profits may be negative—in other words losses can be made. The magnitude of these losses may be such as to threaten the company's existence, since assets may be consumed in meeting the losses. Survival rather than profit may then be the dominant motive in making decisions, and the director's problem is correspondingly modified.

Adding yet another complication to the problem, suppose the director is interested in selling off the company, but only when the assets have reached a certain level. He is keen for this to be achieved in as short a time as possible, but of course must avoid bankruptcy. Given all the investments open to him each year, how does he go about realizing his goal? How does his ambition to sell out in the shortest time possible prejudice the survival of the company? Might he be better advised to pursue a longer time-scale, with a greater assurance of success? A problem of this type is offered in Chapter 10 as an exercise.

The shop in Example 1.5 faces a set of future demands which cannot be controlled, but can certainly be influenced. This influence (via advertising) is not cost-free, and the effect of the advertising depends on the existing level of demand, e.g. advertising helps sustain a high level of demand and increases the chances of a change from low to high demand. If the shop is interested in a maximum profit over, say, five weeks, what should its advertising policy be? How would this differ from the policy to be used if the time-span of the problem were to be increased to thirty weeks, or one hundred weeks?

The key to the analysis of situations where decisions interact over time lies in looking at the relationship between the initial problem and the subproblems derived as a part of this problem. Thus, the five-week problem is seen as one week longer than the four-week problem, which in turn is one week longer than the three-week problem . . . . This observation is less than revolutionary, but together with one key insight, consecrated in the form of a Principle, it is sufficient to allow our problems to be cast in a mathematical form. The resultant equations can then be analysed and/or solved to provide the appropriate strategy for the sequential problem, as in Chapter 7.

The arithmetic effort involved in solving these sequential problems is intimately related to the length of the time horizon for the problem, i.e. the number of decisions to be taken. Thus, the thirty-week problem is considerably more work than the five-week one, and the one hundred-week problem more work again. Although our problem is sufficiently small scale to allow these computations to be performed if desired, for more realistic cases the work involved could be stretching our resources, or patience. Fortunately, problems with a sufficiently long time horizon can be approximated as being of infinite duration! At first sight this may seem less than helpful, but as our study of Chapter 9 will show, the numerical effort in solving these problems can be considerably less than that of a large, but finite, time horizon. For practical purposes the solution to the infinite time horizon case can be taken as an approximation to the finite horizon case, and can indeed be shown to be appropriate under certain circumstances.

1.6 Concluding Comments and a Preview of the Forthcoming Chapters

These remarks on our five examples and some variants thereof provide a motivation for and an initiation into the contents of the chapters to follow. Before attempting an analysis of decision problems, we investigate the measurement procedures designed to cope with some of the difficulties which emerged in our early remarks. Our first concern in Chapter 2 is to develop a vocabulary and a numerical measure which can cater for the uncertainties inherent in our decision problems, e.g. a quantification of the 'reliability' of the oil consumption test of Example 1.1, the 'relative likelihood' of inflation rates and 'fallibility' of forecasts in Example 1.2, and the 'odds' in the gamble of Example 1.3. (The structure underlying the sequential problems could then also be developed but we choose to postpone this until Chapter 8, where it is close to the material which uses the results of this development.)

Armed with this we proceed in Chapter 3 to an investigation of the problem of evaluating outcomes, for example the uncertain profits of Example 1.2. We examine the assumptions necessary for this method to work, and offer some interpretations of the results which emerge. The majority of this chapter is devoted to problems where we have a single attribute outcome (e.g. profit) but some very brief and less formal attention is paid to multi-attribute outcomes and their associated difficulties.

Only after all this do we turn to the analysis and solution of decision problems in Chapter 4. The early sections of that chapter relate to criteria which operate only on tables of outcomes, with no additional information about the states of nature. Later in the chapter we enter into the mainstream of the work with an investigation of decision problems where we do use information about the states of nature, in the first instance without the complicating possibility of the purchase of extra information (e.g. forecasts). As a step on the way to the solution of problems where extra information is available, we study in Chapter 5 the implications for our assessments of such information. The proper use and value of information is then the subject of the later sections of that chapter.

As a link between the two major sections of the book, and also as a reinforcement of some of the earlier ideas, we turn in Chapter 6 to decision trees. This device essentially gives a diagrammatic rendering of the decision problem, as well as illustrating the Principle central to our analysis of sequential problems. In Chapter 7 we solve the advertising problem and others, demonstrating the Principle and the computations associated with these sequential problems. A concise treatment of a theoretical tool useful in these problems follows in Chapter 8, and the remaining chapters are devoted to an analysis of problems akin to those of Examples 1.4, 1.5 and their variants.

Chapter 2

Uncertainty and its Measurement

2.1 Introduction

Decisionmaking under uncertainty has exercised the minds of men for centuries and attempts at a formal (i.e. mathematical) analysis of the problems faced can be traced back to at least as early as the latter half of the seventeenth century. The early workers in this field recognized the conceptual and practical importance of the uncertainty measurement and outcome eyalution which we have already mentioned in the previous chapter. In part they were motivated by the desire to solve real problems, or at least to explain observed behaviour.

The coin-tossers, dice-rollers and card-players who adorn the pages of the elementary probability and statistical textbooks are only the latest in a long line of gamblers who have provided the setting for an analysis of uncertainty. We are interested in the quantification of the chance element as an aid to choosing actions, although in this chapter we concentrate only on the problem of quantification and leave the use of the resultant data until later.

The intrinsically non-deterministic nature of many phenomena has long been a source of fascination, and our everyday vocabulary abounds with words which allude to this characteristic, e.g. 'risk', 'chance', 'random', 'likelihood'. Sometimes an assessment of the uncertainty is implied, either in a qualitative manner, as in 'A is more likely than B', or perhaps quantitatively, as in 'playing the odds'. Gambling with its associated 'odds', 'stakes', and 'payoffs' offers a rich vein of examples which illustrate some of the salient features of decision problems. Our use of these problems does not necessarily reflect any predilection on the author's part. Rather, they provide a problem statement which is succinct and easily assimilated.

Although 'odds' is the commonest term associated with quantification in gambling, this ubiquity disguises the quite distinct differences in the use of the term. For example, the game of roulette has odds which are fixed for every play of the wheel. In horse racing the odds given by the bookmaker are explicit, but are likely to change during the time before the race, and reflect things other than the bookmaker's assessment of each particular horse's winning chances. On the author's only visit to a racecourse he noticed that the board giving information on the forthcoming race and the horses participating showed not only the current odds but also the total money staked on each horse. The shifting odds were automatically calculated on the basis of the money being taken in by the tellers. As a footnote the author made a modest profit from this particular racecourse. The method followed is not outlined in this text.

Bookmakers often quote odds for events other than horseracing, e.g. boxing matches, tennis tournaments, football leagues and even political elections, and it is not uncommon for the odds offered by different bookmakers for the same event to be different. Some gambles are entered into by punters without any explicit statement of odds, e.g. national lotteries, pools competitions and insurance. The appearance of such an upright activity as insurance amidst the murky pastimes of punters may surprise some readers, but to the detached eye of the decision analyst these ventures have much in common, and as a setting for the study of the second measurement problem outlined in Chapter 1, the insurance purchase decision is admirable.

Given our analytic intent the randomness inherent in the decision problems will have to be described using a language more precise than that normally associated with gambling (and normally absent in any explicit form in insurance decisions).

Our concern in quantifying the uncertainty associated with the state of nature operating at the time of choosing an action is to provide a means of evaluating the merits of alternative actions. Our description of the potential realization of the state of nature must therefore be exhaustive, given that all contingencies are to be met, and simultaneously exclude ambiguity. Thus, for Example 1.1 it is sufficient to have only two grades of car, namely good buy and bad buy. A car in the garage can be one and only one of these types. For a more complicated version of this problem it may be reasonable to distinguish say five grades of car, ranging from very bad buy through bad buy, mediocre, good buy to very good buy. Our table of outcomes replacing Table 1.1 would then have five rows (but still two columns), giving a monetary value to every possible action–state pair. The level of discrimination between categories is not a problem which will concern us here. In practical problems a variety of considerations will have to be taken into account by the analyst in deciding on an appropriate state description scheme. Such secondary decisions (deciding about the decision problem) are deemed beyond our scope.

In Example 1.2 we have again spoken of only two possible inflation rates, although the extension to a more refined state description is obvious, as will be seen later in this chapter.

2.2 Some Comments

It is an empirically verifiable fact that in coin-tossing experiments the proportion of heads will, 'in the long run', appear to stabilize around some fraction. We assume that the coin does not land on its edge or disappear down a drain, i.e. at each toss the result is either a head or a tail. These two events exhaust all the possibilities we wish to consider and are obviously mutually exclusive. Figure 2.1 illustrates the cumulative data for over 2000 repetitions of a coin-tossing experiment. Note the scale of the axis which gives the proportion of heads. The

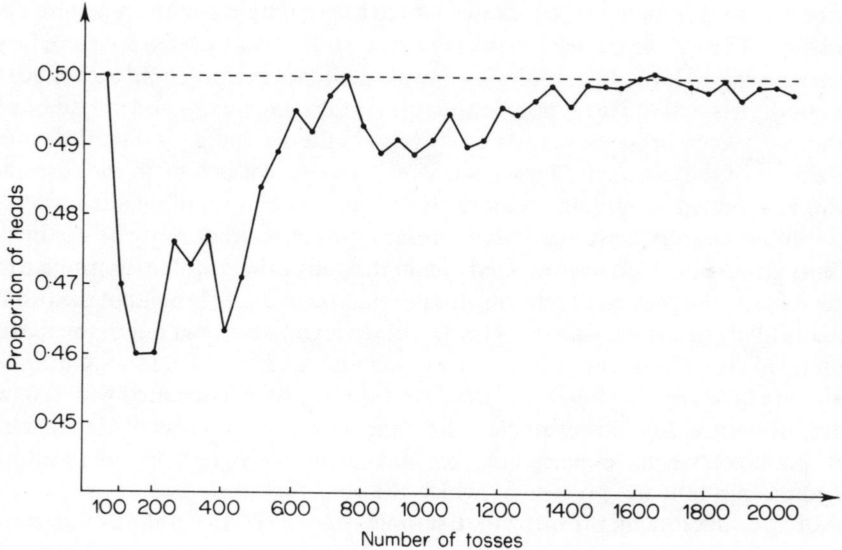

Figure 2.1 Proportion of heads versus number of tosses in a coin-tossing experiment

proportion of heads is plotted after every fifty tosses. From the data point at 1450 tosses onwards the proportion has kept in the range 0.497 up to 0.501. By the 2000th toss we have had 995 heads. The behaviour of the ratio beyond the 2000th toss is, of course, unknown. It could, for instance, drop to 995/3000 by the 3000th toss (if we had 1000 tails in a row), or increase to 1995/3000 by the 3000th toss, if we had 1000 heads in a row. Alternatively, the ratio could gravitate towards, say, 0.4, and make small oscillations about that value for a thousand tosses.

At the 2000th toss none of these possibilities can be ruled out. Given that the coin is 'fair' these possibilities would be greeted with a degree of surprise, if not suspicion. There is no logical or mathematical reason to prohibit these results, so our reaction to them must be a function of our experience of and expectations for such an experiment.

The ratio is thus a measure of the likelihood we associate with a particular event. For a set of circumstances where we do not have any established notion of the likelihood (e.g. we are told only that the coin is biased) then such a ratio might well be taken to define the relevant likelihood. For Figure 2.1 the ratio is of course changing during the course of the experiment, and although it would appear to be converging to a number (slightly below) 0.5 we have no means of finding this limiting value. Even given that we have experimented with the coin of Example 1.3, or have been given assurances about the value of the ratio, recall that the decision problem facing us relates, in the first instance, to a single toss of the coin and is *not* concerned with a number of tosses.

For Example 1.1 the uncertainty as to the state of nature (i.e. condition of the potential exchange) is expressed in a different manner. Out of the number of cars

14

in the garage, a certain quantity are known to be good buys and the remainder are bad buys. Thus, if the garage has twenty cars on offer, of which ten are good buys, then ten are bad buys. In considering one of these cars as a potential exchange the assumption is that the car is not identifiable (at that stage) as a good or bad buy to either customer or salesman. Alternatively, if the garage does know the true condition of the car then it presents it without malice or favour to the customer (who is assumed to remain temporarily in ignorance of its true state).

In either case the customer has no reason to believe that any one car of the twenty is more likely to be presented to him than any other car. No discrimination intervenes in the process of selecting his potential exchange. Ten out of the twenty equally likely options result in his being offered a good buy; ten out of the twenty equally likely options result in his being offered a bad buy. These weightings or ratios are taken as a reasonable measure of the likelihood associated with the two states of nature. For this example, where the 'repeated experiment' approach is not possible, we have been able to make some progress by invoking an assumption about the process by which the car is selected.

For the investment problem of Example 1.2, where the unknown state of nature is the forthcoming rate of inflation, neither of the above approaches would seem to be applicable. To be sure, there will be historical information about the past prevalence of high and low rates of inflation, but unlike the coin-tossing example few people would necessarily subscribe to definition based on historical frequency. We are interested only in the instances of high and low inflation rates (suitable defined), so there are two states of nature, but is it reasonable to assume that these states will therefore be equally likely to be 'selected'? It is possible that with appropriately defined ranges for these descriptions the decisionmaker of Example 1.3 could accord equal likelihood to the two possibilities, but a different decisionmaker faced with the same problem could disagree with this and offer an alternative assessment. How then to generate an assessment appropriate to this problem?

Some analysts would hold that such an assessment process is not meaningful, and that quantification of uncertainty, where it is of the kind illustrated by this example, is not valid. The very obvious subjective input is disconcerting to them, and they find the (as yet unspecified) process of assigning numerical values far from satisfactory. In general the author would disagree with this disaffection for a variety of reasons. In the first place it is not at all clear how to demarcate problems into those which can be agreed as valid for analysis by relative frequency or equal-likelihood arguments, and those which are not. For instance, in the car exchange problem the mixture of cars in the garage may be the result of the production policy of the manufacturer. If the manufacturer is to change some aspect of the production process by, for example, installing more modern equipment or improving working conditions, then the proportion of bad buys in the production total will inevitably change. How does the potential purchaser use this information about the change in the process, given he is contemplating exchange, before any general information on the latest statistics of production is available? It seems a pity to abandon the decision analysis which was previously thought acceptable and relevant (when we had a production history as a source of data), because of a change in one component of the problem.

This brings us onto the second argument in favour of the subjective assessment process. For the decisionmaker the problem has not disappeared. He is still faced with having to choose an alternative from the set of options, and it could be argued that by using his subjective input, encoded in an appropriate form rather than influencing his choice in an informal, implicit and unstructured manner, the nature and extent of this influence is at least explicit and formalized. By entering into this encoding he is increasing his awareness of the problem, and highlighting those areas where the uncertainty is critical to the resolution of the problem. This is not to say that the assessment procedures of the type which we later outline can be applied with abandon to any circumstances where uncertainty looms. The development can only be obtained subject to the decisionmaker conforming to a set of rules (axioms) which limit his freedom of behaviour. These axioms on admissible behaviour apply to the decisionmaker's responses to problems in assessing likelihoods, and essentially guarantee that the decisionmaker is maintaining a coherent stance in his responses. If a decisionmaker feels he cannot comply with these restrictions (and we later argue why he should) then the desired construction of a numerical measure for the uncertainty cannot be achieved.

As a third argument for the retention of the subjective assessment idea, we note here that the other two methods (although plausible and widely accepted) are not without difficulties. These relate in the main to the interpretation of the definitions and how these assessments would have to be performed to generate the required measurements. We return to these weaknesses in the coming sections where each of the three aspects is studied in turn.

For each 'definition' we develop a little of the background and explore the weaknesses of both the definition and the relevant domain of application. We also examine some of the consequences of these definitions. Our interest is ultimately decision-oriented, and the development of the chapter is conditioned by a desire to use the results rather than develop the theory in detail or seek a resolution to the difficulties of application. The relevant properties which appear in the next section, and re-appear in subsequent sections, are summarized in Section 2.10.

2.3 Probability as a Relative Frequency

We have already observed in the coin-tossing experiment the apparent stability of the ratio of the number of heads obtained to the number of tosses performed. To broaden the scope of our concept we introduce some terms which will prove to be useful. In this 'version' of probability we have to have an unlimited series of observations from which to extract the information relevant to the determination of the numerical values. These observations are in turn the outcome (or consequence) of an *experiment*, or *trial* which we repeat without variation in those elements of the trial which are under our control. Thus, for the coin-tossing exercise a trial or experiment corresponds to one toss of the coin, and as far as possible we perform a series of tosses under substantially the same conditions, e.g.

16

we do not permit the coin to be physically damaged or subject to gusts of wind, or to land in a mudpool.

As another example consider the problem of evaluating the lifetime of an electrical component, e.g. a light bulb. This could be expressed in terms of a number of hours of continuous use before failure of the device, or (perhaps more usefully) it could be measured in terms of the number of weeks of use in a household before failure. In either situation the lifetime is an uncertain quantity. Regardless of the manufacturer's quality control his products will exhibit a variation in lifetime, and he will naturally be interested in this variability. If he wishes to quantify the characteristics of lifetime he can perform some trials where a number of bulbs from the production line are set aside and their continuous life or household-use life is examined. In either case he will strive to ensure some uniformity in the conditions under which these trials are conducted. For instance, in the continuous-use experiments he would ensure that the sample of bulbs he is using are subject to the same temperature range, variation in power supply, vibration, etc. Not to do so would be to permit the result to be potentially influenced in a manner for which he cannot make allowances. Again in the household-use trials he would seek to subject the bulbs to essentially similar treatment. If he is using real households in which to pursue his results, then some uniformity is desirable. The bulb life reported by a bachelor airline pilot (who is often away from home, and even when home may not make heavy demands on many of his lights) can be expected to be very different to that reported by an insomniacal mother of five.

The manufacturer may of course be interested in the lifetimes of his products when subject to different types of use, but in our current framework that requires each of these categories to be replicated a 'sufficient' number of times. For the continuous-use bulb life problem the manufacturer may decide to summarize the data from the set of trials by grouping the results, i.e. rather than recording the exact lifetime of each individual bulb, he would divide the possible lifetime range into a set of sub-ranges. For example, 800 hours or less, more than 800 but 850 hours or less, and so on, perhaps ending with more than 1250 hours and up to 1300 hours, and finally, more than 1300 hours. The condition of the bulbs could be monitored every 50 hours, and this would give information of this type. Out of the collection of bulbs being examined the numbers failing during each of these intervals is noted and at the end of the experiment the proportions failing in each range are calculated. This could be expressed in diagrammatic form, and would typically look like Figure 2.2, where we have numbered the ranges $r_1, r_2, \ldots, r_{12}$, i.e. r_1 corresponds to lifetimes of 800 hours or less, r_2 corresponds to lifetimes greater than 800 hours but less than or equal to 850 hours, etc.

Suppose we are using a total of n bulbs and that $n_1, n_2, \ldots, n_{12}$ are the numbers of bulbs which fail in the ranges $r_1, r_2, \ldots, r_{12}$, respectively. Obviously we have $n = n_1 + n_2 + \ldots + n_{12}$. In the coin-tossing example we saw that the relative frequency of heads was a function of the number of tosses, and with that in mind we use $RF_n(r_i)$ to denote the *relative frequency* of lifetimes in the range $r_i (i = 1, 2, \ldots, 12)$ in a total of n trials. Thus, $RF_n(r_i) = n_i/n$. From its definition

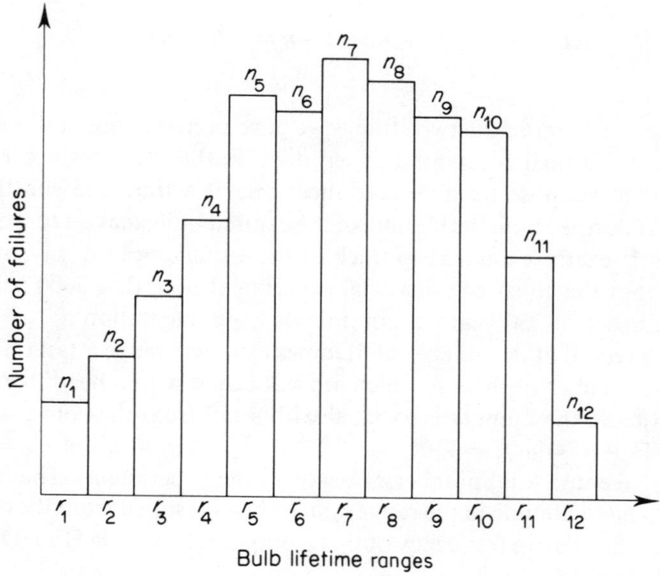

Figure 2.2 Number of failures in the set of lifetime ranges

the relative frequency is a non-negative fraction, i.e. $0 \leqslant RF_n(r_i) \leqslant 1$, for $i = 1, 2, \ldots, 12$. Note that

$$RF_n(r_1) + RF_n(r_2) + \ldots + RF_n(r_{12}) = n_1/n + n_2/n + \ldots + n_{12}/n = 1,$$

since

$$\sum_{i=1}^{12} n_i = n.$$

If we write $r_i \cup r_j$ for the event of a bulb life in either range r_i or r_j (where $i \neq j$), then

$$RF_n(r_i \cup r_j) = (n_i + n_j)/n = n_i/n + n_j/n = RF_n(r_i) + RF_n(r_j).$$

Thus, the relative frequency of these two *exclusive* events is just the sum of the relative frequencies for each event. This generalizes easily to any finite number of exclusive events, and in particular leads to

$$RF_n(r_1 \cup r_2 \cup \ldots \cup r_{12}) = RF_n(r_1) + RF_n(r_2) + \ldots + RF_n(r_{12}) = 1,$$

from above.

The set of events considered here (a lifetime in the range r_1 or r_2 or $\ldots r_{12}$) is, of course, exhaustive.

If we write $\bar{r}_i$ for the event that failure does *not* take place at a lifetime in the range r_i, then since failure must take in one of the other ranges we have

$$RF_n(\bar{r}_i) = \sum_{\substack{j=1 \\ j \neq i}}^{12} (n_j/n) = 1 - n_i/n = 1 - RF_n(r_i).$$

Consider an amalgam of the two studies we have been making in this section, in the form of a fictional compound experiment. Rather than testing a group of bulbs together, suppose we now take them one at a time and run them until failure. On failure we note the lifetime of the expired bulb, make a toss of the coin (from the first example), and keep track of these outcomes for, say, n trials. To emphasize that this must be a fictional experiment note that 2000 trials would take of the order of 230 years of continuous experimentation.

We have a record of the number of lifetimes n_i in each range r_i (set up as before) and also the number of these n_i which are associated with a head from the coin toss (say H_i) and the number associated with a tail from the coin toss (say T_i). Obviously $H_i + T_i = n_i$ ($i = 1, 2, \ldots, 12$) and $\sum_{i=1}^{12} n_i = n$. Let $n_H = H_1 + H_2 + \ldots + H_{12}$ (i.e. the total number of heads in the experiment). The number of times a bulb has a lifetime in the range r_i *and* a head resulted from the coin toss is H_i, and thus the relative frequency of this (compound) event is H_i/n. Denote this compound event by $r_i \cap H$.

A belief in any real relationship between the outcome of the coin toss and the lifetime of the bulb would be difficult to sustain. In other words, the likelihood of a head (or a tail) on a toss of the coin is *not* a function of the lifetime of the bulb that has just failed. Or again, the proportion of times that heads turns up in the coin-tossing trials is not dependent upon the lifetimes of the bulbs with whose failure times we are experimenting. Thus, the ratio H_i/n_i will not be other than minutely different from n_H/n, provided we have performed 'enough' repetitions of the experiment. In other words, we would expect the same approximate proportion of heads in each range as the proportion overall. We thus have

$$RF_n(r_i \cap H) = H_i/n = (n_i/n)(H_i/n_i) = (n_i/n)(n_H/n) = RF_n(r_i)RF_n(H).$$

The first equality follows by definition, the second by trivial manipulation, the third from our observation of the preceding paragraph and the last from the definition again.

To find the relative frequencies of events such as these both happening, we thus multiply the relative frequencies of the constituent events. Note though that this is for events which are *independent* (a concept we return to shortly).

Suppose we are able to identify two different mechanisms by which the bulb can fail, e.g. filament melt (shortened to FM) and vacuum collapse (written as VC). As well as noting the time of expiry we also note the failure mechanism, and thus build up a record of both bulb life and failure mode. Instead of the twelve mutually exclusive and exhaustive lifetime ranges and associated observations n_1, $n_2, \ldots, n_{12}$, we now have twenty-four categories—the twelve ranges and two failure modes for each range. We then have numbers n_{iFM} and n_{iVC} which record the number of failures in the range r_i due to filament melt and vacuum collapse, respectively (see Figure 2.3).

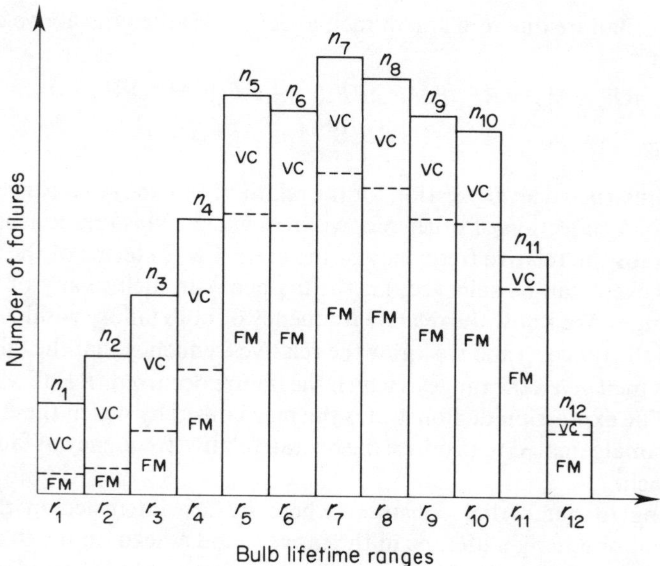

Figure 2.3 Number of failures and failure mechanisms in the set of lifetime ranges

Obviously, $n_{i\text{FM}} + n_{i\text{VC}} = n_i$. With this data we can examine events which are *conditional*. For example, given that a bulb fails in the range r_i, what is the likelihood that the failure is due to filament melt? A total of n_i bulbs fail in the range r_i and of these $n_{i\text{FM}}$ fail due to filament melt.

Writing $\text{FM}|r_i$ to denote the event of failure mode FM, *given* failure is in range r_i, we note that the relative frequency of failure due to filament melt in the range r_i is $n_{i\text{FM}}/n_i$ and we can write this as $(n_{i\text{FM}}/n)(n/n_i)$. The first term in the product is the relative frequency of failure in range r_i and filament melt as failure mode (as a proportion of the total set of failures in all periods and under both failure modes), and the second term is the reciprocal of the relative frequency of failure in the range r_i over all failures. In other words $RF_n(\text{FM}|r_i) = RF_n(\text{FM} \cap r_i)/RF_n(r_i)$.

The total number of failures due to filament melt is

$$n_{\text{FM}} = n_{1\text{FM}} + n_{2\text{FM}} + \ldots + n_{12\text{FM}},$$

and thus we have

$$n_{\text{FM}}/n = n_{1\text{FM}}/n + n_{2\text{FM}}/n + \ldots + n_{12\text{FM}}/n$$

$$= (n_{1\text{FM}}/n_1)(n_1/n) + (n_{2\text{FM}}/n_2)(n_2/n) + \ldots$$
$$+ (n_{12\text{FM}}/n_{12})(n_{12}/n).$$

In each of these products the first term is the relative frequency of failure due to filament melt, given that failure has taken place in a certain range, and the second term is the relative frequency of failure in that range. The ratio n_{FM}/n is the relative frequency of failure due to filament melt. If we write the relative frequency of failure due to filament melt as $RF_n(\text{FM})$ then the above expression leads us to

$$RF_n(\text{FM}) = RF_n(\text{FM}|r_1)RF_n(r_1) + RF_n(\text{FM}|r_2)RF_n(r_2)$$
$$+ \ldots + RF_n(\text{FM}|r_{12})RF_n(r_{12}).$$

We have constructed an expression for the relative frequency of a particular event (FM) out of a collection of other relative frequencies. This relationship gives an evaluation for the relative frequency of the event FM in terms of the manner in which this event can be achieved, i.e. the filament can melt in any of the twelve lifetime ranges. We know the relative frequency of bulb failure within each range ($RF_n(r_i)$ in the range r_i) and we know the relative frequency that the failure is due to filament melt given the range in which the failure occurred ($RF_n(\text{FM}|r_i)$ for the range r_i). The expression demonstrates the mechanism by which these quantities should be amalgamated to produce the overall relative frequency of failure due to filament melt.

Returning to our earlier construct where we are interested in the relative frequency of obtaining a lifetime in the range r_i and a head on the toss of a coin (performed after bulb failure), suppose we now examine the relative frequency of heads following a bulb failure in the range r_i. This is $RF_n(\text{H}|r_i)$ and following the formula obtained above this gives us

$$RF_n(\text{H}|r_i) = RF_n(\text{H} \cap r_i)/RF_n(r_i).$$

But $RF_n(H \cap r_i) = RF_n(\text{H})RF_n(r_i)$ and we thus have $RF_n(H|r_i) = RF_n(H)$, i.e. the relative likelihood of heads on a toss following bulb failure in the range r_i is the same as the unconditional relative likelihood of heads. The likelihood of heads is not influenced by the bulb life which preceded it. Our previous argument is confirmed in the notation we use! In such circumstances we say that the event of obtaining heads is *independent* of the lifetime of the bulb whose failure precipitated the coin toss. We remind the reader that Section 2.10 contains a summary of the properties of probabilities which we make use of in our analyses.

Having established some consequences of working with the relative frequency definition let us briefly examine some troublesome features of this method of analysis. The definition involves the notion of an (in principle) unlimited number of repetitions of an experiment, carried out either sequentially or perhaps simultaneously. Given that we make a large number of experiments in an effort to approximate the desired measurements, we cannot of course claim that the experiments are identical, only similar. In the coin-tossing problem the experiments are distinguished by their temporal succession and the coin being tossed on the 1606th toss is different from that used on the 1505th toss, since it has been tossed one hundred and one times more, and may even be different in more subtle ways. Again for the lightbulb experiment, it is obviously not the same bulb which is being run to destruction, but rather a collection of bulbs from the same production process.

For the coin-tossing experiments would not *identical* tosses of the coin generate identical results? In tossing a coin which is thought to be 'fair' and thus have equal likelihoods of heads and tails, would we not be surprised at a ratio of heads to total number of tosses which deviated by more than a small amount from one-half? In such a case we would perhaps no longer deem the coin 'fair' or maybe we would suspect the method of coin-tossing to be distorting the results. In other words, a 'proper' set of 'identical' experiments for the coin-tossing problem is one which generates an empirically determined ratio of 0.5 for the proportion of heads in the total number of tosses *for a fair coin*. Here we have a problem, since a 'fair' coin will manifest itself as having the correct proportion (approximately 0.5) of heads to the total number of tosses under a properly conducted sequence of tosses, and a sequence of tosses is known to be properly conducted (without 'undue bias') if it gives the proportion of approximately 0.5 to the number of heads out of a sufficient number of tosses of a coin, *known* to be fair. For this simplest of problems we are therefore in difficulty, either in establishing the propriety of a sequence of experiments or the probability of heads. For a problem where we have no reason to believe the coin to be fair, and therefore wish to determine empirically the probability of heads on tossing the coin, it would seem that we must commit ourselves to a sequence of tosses, observing the outcomes and striving to keep successive tosses 'essentially' the same. In the last instance it is our *judgement* of the acceptability of the conditions under which the sequence of tosses was conducted which determines the acceptability of the experimentally derived ratio. It will be appreciated that monitoring more complicated processes in an effort to ensure uniformity is correspondingly more difficult.

2.4 Probability Derived from Equal Likelihood

As an alternative approach to the encoding of uncertainties, let us return to the car exchange problem of Example 1.1. The garage has twenty examples of the model which is the potential exchange, and of these ten are good buys and ten are bad buys. The potential customer is *not* going to be the subject of a long series of purchases from the garage, a process in which he can study the relative frequency with which he receives good and bad buys. He must base any analysis solely on the information about the relative numbers of good and bad buys. The method by which any new car is selected does not discriminate between good and bad buys, e.g. the customer may be free to choose any of the twenty cars as his purchase, but he is unable to distinguish between good and bad buys in the garage. Alternatively, the garage may offer him a particular car from the set of twenty, but in doing so it acts with neither malevolence nor benevolence. In either case it is reasonable to describe each car as being equally likely to be the car which the potential customer will obtain if he proceeds with the exchange. If we are interested in the probability of the event of securing a good buy under these circumstances, then the classical approach exploits the symmetry of the problem and concludes that the appropriate probability is the ratio of the possible favourable realizations of the event (here ten) to the total number of possible events (here twenty). In other words, we examine the number of equally likely conclusions and count the proportion of those which are equivalent to the event

22

we are interested in, the ratio then giving the probability. Using GB to be the event of obtaining a good buy, and BB to be the event of obtaining a bad buy, we write $p(GB) = 10/20$, and by the same argument $p(BB) = 10/20$, where $p(GB)$ and $p(BB)$ are the probabilities of GB and BB, respectively.

Note that with this definition each probability will lie in the range zero to one, and for this example $p(GB) + p(BB) = 1$. Consider now the problem of encoding information about oil-consumption tests. It is known that out of ten good buys, six will have low oil consumption (denote by LOC), two will have medium oil consumption (MOC) and two will have high oil consumption (HOC). Out of ten bad buys there are 4, 3 and 3 in the high, medium and low consumption categories, respectively. We write

$$n(GB \cap LOC) = 6; \qquad n(GB \cap MOC) = 2; \qquad n(GB \cap HOC) = 2,$$

$$n(BB \cap LOC) = 3; \qquad n(BB \cap MOC) = 3; \qquad n(BB \cap HOC) = 4,$$

where $n(X \cap Y)$ is the number of cars which are of type X and have oil consumption Y. This data is summarized in Figure 2.4 which the reader may find useful in validating the fairly terse arguments which follow.

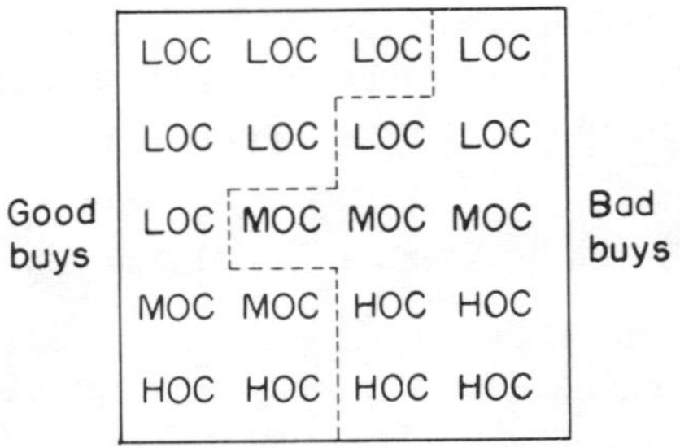

Figure 2.4 A representation of the car types and their oil consumption characteristics

Given that we are dealing with good buys, the probability of having a car with low oil consumption, written $p(LOC|GB)$ to be consistent with the notation of the last section, is given by the proportion of good buys which also exhibit low oil consumption. Thus,

$$p(LOC|GB) = n(GB \cap LOC)/n(GB) = (n(GB \cap LOC)/20)/(20/n(GB))$$

$$= p(GB \cap LOC)/p(GB),$$

where $p(X \cap Y)$ is the probability of the (compound) event of X *and* Y (for appropriate X and Y).

To find the probability of obtaining a car with low oil consumption note that both good and bad buys can demonstrate this property. Write $n(LOC)$ to be the number of cars with low oil consumption and $p(LOC)$ to be the probability of a test result of low consumption. We have

$$p(\text{LOC}) = n(\text{LOC})/20 = (n(\text{GB} \cap \text{LOC}) + n(\text{BB} \cap \text{LOC}))/20$$

$$= p(\text{GB} \cap \text{LOC}) + p(\text{BB} \cap \text{LOC})$$

$$= p(\text{LOC}|\text{GB})p(\text{GB}) + p(\text{LOC}|\text{BB})p(\text{BB}).$$

The last equality follows from applying twice the previous result involving *conditional probabilities*. When it comes to analysing decision problems we are actually more interested in the calculation and application of probabilities of the form $p(\text{GB}|\text{LOC})$. We are concerned with the implications of a test result, and what it tells us about the likelihood of good and bad buys. This is the object of our study in Chapter 5.

The reader will have noted a parallel between the relationships developed above and those of the previous section. In the next section we analyse another example which yields to this classical approach.

2.5 Another Example

As another illustration let us examine the process of deriving probabilities for the problem of rolling two distinguishable six-sided dice. Given that we have no reason to believe the dice to be loaded, each die can land in one of six ways (i.e. showing number 1 to 6 uppermost) and the pair of dice can therefore present one of 36 outcomes on a roll of the dice. Denoting by (n_1, n_2) the event of die 1 showing number n_1 and die 2 showing number n_2 (where $1 \leqslant n_1, n_2 \leqslant 6$) we can easily list all possible events:

(1,1)	(1,2)	(1,3)	(1,4)	(1,5)	(1,6)
(2,1)	(2,2)	(2,3)	(2,4)	(2,5)	(2,6)
(3,1)	(3,2)	(3,3)	(3,4)	(3,5)	(3,6)
(4,1)	(4,2)	(4,3)	(4,4)	(4,5)	(4,6)
(5,1)	(5,2)	(5,3)	(5,4)	(5,5)	(5,6)
(6,1)	(6,2)	(6,3)	(6,4)	(6,5)	(6,6)

Under our assumption of the dice being fair, we accord each of these 36 events an equal likelihood, and thus the probability of any one of them is 1/36. We find it convenient here to describe events (whose likelihood we seek) in a telegraphic rather than symbolic style. These descriptions are enclosed in parentheses when used in manipulation. In this case a 'p' preceding an expression $(\ldots)$ should be read as 'the probability of $\ldots$'.

Let us look at two exclusive events, say die 2 showing an even number or the sum of the numbers on the two dice being 2. There are 18 different ways in which the second die may show an even number, and these are given by the pairs of numbers in the 2nd, 4th and 6th columns—18 in all. Only one outcome yields a

24

sum of 2, and that is the pair $(1, 1)$. Thus,

$$p(\text{die 2 shows even } or \text{ sum } = 2) = (18 + 1)/36 = 18/36 + 1/36$$
$$= p(\text{die 2 shows even}) + p(\text{sum} = 2).$$

In general if E_1 and E_2 are any two *exclusive* events constructed for this problem we have $p(E_1 \cup E_2) = p(E_1) + p(E_2)$. The reader will easily see that for any event E, and denoting as usual the non-occurrence of E by $\bar{E}$, we have $p(E) + p(\bar{E}) = 1$. Consider another event, this time a conditional one. We seek the probability that die 1 shows 3 or less, given that the sum is greater than or equal to 7. Denote this by $p(\text{die } 1 \leqslant 3 | \text{sum} \geqslant 7)$. Of the 36 pairs, 21 give a sum greater than or equal to 7, and of these 21 six have a die 1 number which is less than or equal to 3. Thus,

$$p(\text{die } 1 \leqslant 3 | \text{sum} \geqslant 7) = 6/21 = 6/36 \times 36/21$$
$$= p(\text{die } 1 \leqslant 3 \cap \text{sum} \geqslant 7)/p(\text{sum} \geqslant 7).$$

For any two events E_1 and E_2 we have

$$p(E_2 \cap E_1) = p(E_1 \cap E_2) = p(E_2 | E_1)p(E_1).$$

We have $p(E_2 | E_1) = p(E_2)$ when E_2 is *independent* of E_1 and $p(E_1 \cap E_2) = p(E_1)p(E_2)$.

The reader should confirm these results for a particular choice of E_2 and E_1. For example, take E_2 to be the event of an even number on die 2, and E_1 to be the event of die 1 showing 5 or 6.

If we wish to calculate the probability of die 1 showing strictly less than die 2, then denoting this by $p(\text{die } 1 < \text{die } 2)$ we can construct this by exhausting all the possibilities conditional on all possible values for die 2. Thus,

$$
\begin{aligned}
p(\text{die } 1 < \text{die } 2) &= p((1,2) \cup (1,3) \cup (1,4) \cup (1,5) \cup (1,6) \cup (2,3) \cup (2,4) \cup (2,5) \\
&\quad \cup (2,6) \cup (3,4) \cup (3,5) \cup (3,6) \cup (4,5) \cup (4,6) \cup (5,6)) \\
&= p((1,2)) + p((1,3) \cup (2,3)) + p((1,4) \cup (2,4) \cup (3,4)) \\
&\quad + p((1,5) \cup (2,5) \cup (3,5) \cup (4,5)) \\
&\quad + p((1,6) \cup (2,6) \cup (3,6) \cup (4,6) \cup (5,6)) \\
&= p(\text{die } 1 < \text{die } 2 | \text{die } 2 = 2)p(\text{die } 2 = 2) \\
&\quad + p(\text{die } 1 < \text{die } 2 | \text{die } 2 = 3)p(\text{die } 2 = 3) \\
&\quad + \ldots + p(\text{die } 1 < \text{die } 2 | \text{die } 2 = 6)p(\text{die } 2 = 6).
\end{aligned}
$$

This agrees with the general form where for an event A and a set $E_1, \ldots, E_k$ of exclusive and exhaustive events

$$p(A) = p(A|E_1)p(E_1) + \ldots + p(A|E_k)p(E_k).$$

2.6 Some Difficulties With This Method

The method we have outlined in the previous two sections is sometimes known as the *equal-likelihood*, *logical*, *Laplacian* or *classical* approach. As with the relative frequency approach, this method, which relies on the assertion that certain designated events are 'equally likely', has its difficulties. Probabilities are defined here as a consequence of accepting the validity of the equally likely description, and one obvious problem is how to define 'equally likely' without recourse to the concept of probability. The early workers in this field, motivated by an interest in games of chance and thus concerned with dice-rolling, coin-tossing and card games, argued that events are equally likely if there is no 'relevant lack of symmetry' between them. Thus, for dice the apparent physical symmetry is intended to be consistent with 'fairness' in the use of the die. The die is not perfectly symmetric—after all the faces are distinguished by different numbers or collections of dots—but this asymmetry is *judged* not to be relevant. For the dice problem it may be possible to perform a sequence of rolls of the die and observe the frequency of occurrence of each face, but in no way can this be thought of as 'verifying' the probabilities derived from the classical argument. We are in the same tautologous difficulties here as for the 'fair' coin-tossing experiment.

The restricted applicability of this method is yet another weakness. It requires that we have a demarcation of the uncertainties into equally likely possibilities, and the difficulties of this have already been hinted at in the analysis of Example 1.2. For a problem with easily defined states (e.g. the die with six faces) but an acknowledged asymmetry (e.g. the die is loaded), the Laplacian argument is of no use.

2.7 Subjective Probability

As an adjunct to our two previous uncertainty analyses, consider that posed by Example 1.2, where a decision has to be taken in the face of an uncertain forthcoming rate of inflation. It is obvious that neither the relative frequency argument (relying on historical records of the occurrence of high and low inflation rates), nor the equally likely argument (relying on the description of the uncertain states possessing an appropriate symmetry) suggests itself as particularly relevant to the problem of encoding in a numerical manner the inherent uncertainty of the inflation prospects. For the examples we have used to illustrate these approaches, the probability we are seeking to define is, in a sense, a property of the system under study, albeit we are unable to render the concepts totally objective. For instance, there is a (subjective) judgement involved in the extent to which experiments in the relative frequency work are deemed to be performed under 'substantially the same conditions', and in the classical approach the judgement is concerned with the designation of events so that there is 'no relevant lack of symmetry'. The method we are about to propose declares that judgement can be taken further in the assessment of probabilities, and indeed is the basis for numerical assignment. Hence, for the inflation rate of Example 1.2 the director's 'degree of belief' in the different rates of inflation is the key to the construction of *subjective probabilities*. Note carefully that these are the property of the director, not an attribute of the inflation rate itself. Different decisionmakers will (probably) give differing assessments on the appropriate probabilities, due to discrepancies in their beliefs about the inflation rate. These differences are the result of a variety of factors, e.g. differences in their current knowledge of the situation or different interpretations of the same data. Neither of two differing assessments is necessarily incorrect as long as they maintain an internal *consistency* (or *coherence*), the form of which we examine later. We should not necessarily seek to obtain an assessment agreeable to, say, two different decisionmakers, since this is *not* what our decision problems are concerned with.

Not surprisingly, perhaps, the coherence required of our assessor is such as to give rise to quantities which satisfy the relationships we have already demonstrated for the relative frequency and equal-likelihood approaches. It should be noted here that the notion of subjective probability, and in particular its use and manipulation under the same rules as the other interpretations, is a subject of considerable controversy among statisticians, decision analysts and philosophers of science. Some would deny the existence of such a quantity, saying that the assumptions which the process makes about individuals and their perception of uncertainty are far too strong, and totally at odds with observed behaviour. Others would assert that the process is but the formal quantification of an attribute which individuals exhibit, and the process of formalization is both instructive and productive.

The strongest claim made for the subjective probability work and for the value measurement of the next chapter is that it is *conditionally normative*. In brief, this means that, given the decisionmaker agrees with the rules for the measurement process(es), then he *ought* to select the action(s) which the (as yet unspecified) procedure calculates as optimal. The probabilities are not conjured out of thin air. Rather, they reflect (indeed are deduced from) statements given by the decisionmaker about the relative likelihood of pairs of events. For example, given two events A and B, the decisionmaker can say that 'A is more likely than B', or perhaps 'B is more likely than A', or 'A and B are equally likely'. This type of assessment, common in the field of decision analysis, relies on a series of judgements such as this. These involve the *binary relationship* 'is more likely than'. Questions involving the binary relationship are posed as problems with pairs of events.

From a variety of statements like this, under the condition that they are policed to ensure the coherence we require, the numerical assessment is achieved. Given that the decisionmaker does not dispute the necessary coherence requirements, the numerical assessment (i.e. the subjective probability) is an inescapable, logical consequence of his judgements on relative likelihood. The process is not designed to be descriptive in the sense that it models observed behaviour in the face of uncertainty. It prescribes the assessment of uncertainty which ought to be used, given that the decisionmaker agrees to the policing rules. Different decisionmakers, through different responses to the primitive binary problems posed, can arrive at very divergent numerical assessments. How appropriate and valid is a mechanism which allows this to happen? Recalling our earlier remarks that the prime motivation in all this work is decision-oriented, the problem of having very different assessments from two different decisionmakers is not a real one. Given that each decisionmaker has presented a valid reflection of his (subjective) relative likelihood judgements, their influence on the decisions taken in each decisionmaker's problem will be consistent with each individual's course of action in the absence of such quantification, if we believe such action to be determined by the subjective degree of belief.

The literature on the subject reflects the variety of expositions which are possible. At the most formal end of the spectrum an axiomatic scheme can be constructed, and this scheme is rich enough to imply the existence of a numerical assessment of uncertainty (with the same properties as other probability 'types'). The axioms or assumptions which are used are in terms of a binary relationship which expresses the relative likelihood between pairs of events. Thus, for two events A and B, we write $A < B$ to mean that B is more likely to occur than A. More correctly, we understand this to mean that B is *thought* more likely to occur than A. If A and B are considered equally likely, then we write $A \sim B$. Combining these two notational devices we write $A \lesssim B$ to mean that B is at least as likely as A.

With this notation we can now state and examine some of the assumptions for subjective probability. The first assumption simply states that any two events A and B are *comparable* in terms of their relative likelihood, i.e. one and only one of the three relations holds:

$$A < B; \quad A \sim B; \quad A > B.$$

Taken at face value this requires wide-ranging powers of discrimination on the part of the assessor. For example, if A is the event 'at the next national elections the turnout will be less than 65 %', and B is the event 'I fail to obtain a good grade in my Decision Analysis paper in the final examination', then the assumptions demand that the assessor be able to nominate the more likely of these two events, or decide that they are equally likely—if these events are part of the structure of the decision problem.

Perhaps fortunately, decision problems tend to involve the assessment of probabilities of events which are less disparate in character. For instance, they may refer to future levels of inflation rate, or future demand for a new product. In either case the comparisons are about likelihoods of events which are on the same 'scale', e.g. the more likely of an inflation rate in the range 8–10 % or 11–13 %, or the more likely of sales exceeding 150 000 in the first year or being below that figure. It does not follow that the assessment of relative likelihood is necessarily rendered trivial by concentrating on problems of the type just displayed. However, the fact that the events are different in degree, rather than different in kind, does make comparison easier.

Some evaluation procedures, briefly mentioned in Section 2.8, do demand that judgements be made concerning events which are different in kind. One of the pair being compared relates to the events whose probability characteristics we are evaluating, and the other is drawn from a set of 'yardstick' objective events. Although the events are thus of a different kind the fact that one has an accessible, perhaps even physical form alleviates to some extent the mental gymnastics otherwise demanded.

A second property, that of *transitivity*, is necessary in our development of the numerical assessment. If A, B and C are three events, and if B is at least as likely as

A (i.e. $A \lesssim B$) and *C* is at least as likely as *B* ($B \lesssim C$), then our assessor is demonstrating transitivity in his judgements if he claims that *C* is at least as likely as *A* ($A \lesssim C$). Alternatively, if $A < B$ (*A* is less likely than *B*) and $B < C$ (*B* is less likely than *C*) then $A < C$ (*A* is less likely than *C*).

In the context of assessing the likelihoods of inflation rates, if a decisionmaker holds that a rate in the range 11–12% is less likely than a rate in the range 8–10%, and this in turn is less likely than a rate of more than 12%, then to be transitive he has to agree that a rate in the range 11–12% is less likely than a rate of more than 12%. Should he disagree with the third statement then he is being intransitive. Such disagreement cannot be ruled out on mathematical grounds, although we may induce a revision of his judgement by pointing out this 'incoherence'. Exercise 2.10 invites the reader to argue the case for the reasonableness of transitivity.

If the decisionmaker is faced with assessing the relative likelihood of two events *A* and *B*, and *A* is part of *B* (or *A* implies *B*)—in set-theoretic terms *A* is contained in *B*—then a third assumption is that $A \lesssim B$. For example, take *A* to be an inflation rate in the range 8–10% and *B* to be a rate in the range 8–11%. Alternatively, take *A* to be 'sales will exceed 150 000' and *B* to be 'sales will exceed 120 000'. In comparison with the two previous assumptions this seems uncontentious and likely to be observed.

These assumptions, or rules, are part of that set of assumptions which, if obeyed, will lead to the assignment of numerical values to relative likelihood, yielding probabilities of events. The actual process of encoding and policing the assessments can be done in a variety of ways and our concern in the next few paragraphs is to examine some of these methods, and finish with an exercise of evaluation.

Although it may be possible to work directly from the completed set of assumptions to a probability assessment, this is more likely to be the exception than the rule. For instance, in Example 1.2 if the director decides after the definition of high and low inflation rates (in numerical terms) that these are equally likely, then this means that his subjective judgement leads to the assessment that $p(\text{high}) = p(\text{low}) = 1/2$. Should he hold that the low rate is less likely than the high rate there is as yet no mechanism in our description to encode numerically this relative likelihood statement.

By way of comparison we are in the position of a person who is able to assess the relative weights of two bags by taking one in each hand and judging which is the heavier, or whether they are equally heavy. The reader may care to re-interpret the assumptions above in a context where the binary relation is taken to mean 'weighs less than'. In this context they appear manifestly reasonable. Although the relative weights may be fairly readily assessed, it is the case that assigning an appropriate numerical value to the weight of a bag is more demanding. In weights, as in the problem involving likelihoods, the measurement process is standardized by making comparison with and using a scale derived from a fixed (or agreed) quantity, e.g. one pound or one ton.

Before the introduction of graduated scales the weight of an object would be found by balancing the object against a collection of known weights using some suitably sensitive instrument. The standard used is not the same in all measurement of weight (or more correctly, mass), although the standards themselves can be expressed in terms of one another. Thus, for normal everyday work the household units of kilograms or pounds are adequate, but working in the field of nuclear physics it is more convenient to have as a unit the mass of some sub-atomic particle (say a neutron) and express the mass of other objects in terms of this quantity. The use to be made of the quantities concerned dictates the scale.

For work in subjective probability it is again the case that we have a base or reference scale with which we make either direct or indirect comparisons of relative likelihood. This can take a variety of forms, the two most common of which involve in one case the direct comparison of the event with an event of known probability, and in the other, events are constructed in such a way as to be equally likely. Decisionmakers with little or no acquaintance with numerical methods in general and probability in particular are often most confident coping with events which are equally likely. This is usually restricted even more to the case of two exclusive and exhaustive events, in which case equally likely means that there is a 'fifty-fifty' chance of either event happening. It is usually easier to judge that two bags are equally heavy (whether they weigh four kilograms each or one quarter of a kilo each), than to be sure of the relative weights. For example, with a bag of three kilos and another of two kilos, it is easy to detect the heavier bag. The difficulty arises when the relative weights are sought, i.e. 'the bag in my left hand weighs three kilos and that in my right weighs two kilos' or even 'the bag in my right hand is two-thirds the weight of that in my left'. And so it is found with numerical probabilities.

2.8 Probability Assignment

In this section we give a brief account of two assignment procedures, one involving a direct comparison with an objective probability, the other working with a succession of 'fifty-fifty' comparisons.

In the direct comparison method the comparability property is exploited repeatedly. For instance, consider the inflation example where numerical probabilities for the events of high and low rates of inflation are sought (and these are the only two possible cases). Suppose a decisionmaker considers low less likely than high. As the source of our objective probability we take a pointer spinning in a wheel, the entire machine designed to have no bias about the direction in which the pointer stops after being spun. The concept is illustrated in Figure 2.5.

An equal-likelihood argument leads to the conclusion that the probability of stopping in a certain subsection of the circumference of the circle is given by the ratio of the length of that subsection to the length of the circumference of the circle. Thus, for an arc AB where the straight line AB is a diameter of the circle, the probability of the pointer stopping so as to point at the arc AB is $1/2$. If AB is segmented and distributed around the circumference as in Figure 2.6, the probability remains $1/2$.

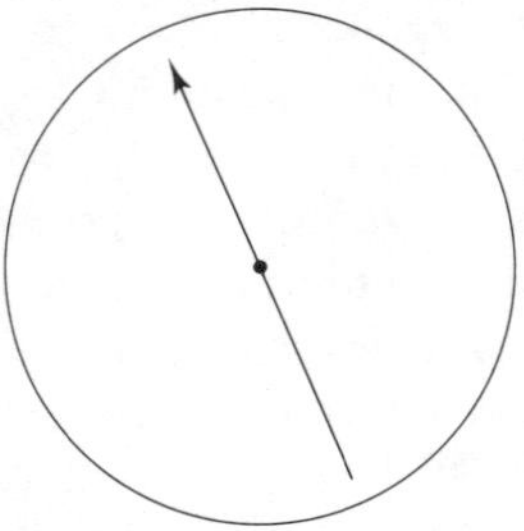

Figure 2.5 The 'probability wheel'

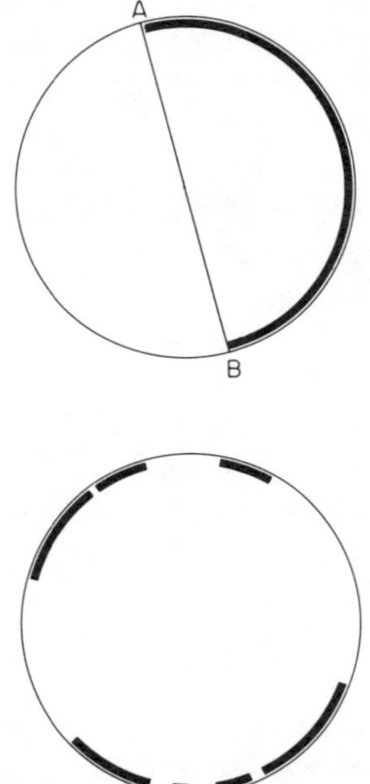

Figure 2.6 The arc *AB* is equal in length to the sum of the segments in
the other cirle

The only relevant data in the calculation of the probability of the pointer
stopping in a certain section of the circumference is the total length of the section
in question, not its distribution around the circumference.

We are going to exploit the ability of the decisionmaker to compare relative
likelihoods by offering him a succession of arc lengths *AB* until he judges that for
a particular length of arc, the pointer is as likely to stop within that length as the
inflation rate is to be high. That he will be able to decide on such a length is
guaranteed by the comparability axiom. The lengths in question need not be given
numerical values when presented to the decisionmaker, and indeed greater
success is often found by using only a visual presentation, e.g. different coloured
arcs of blue and green.

One method of dramatizing the process is to construct two fictional gambles which present the decisionmaker with the opportunity to win a prize if in one case the inflation rate is high, and in the other pointer-spinning case if the pointer stops in, say, the blue sector. The decisionmaker must choose which gamble to enter— he can only enjoy one—and we presume he will opt for the gamble with the greater likelihood of winning the prize. By manipulating the size of the blue sector the interrogator can eventually offer the decisionmaker an objective gamble involving the pointer spin which is as attractive (to the decisionmaker) as the 'gamble' on the inflation rate, assuming our rules are obeyed. The proportion of blue sector is then the appropriate probability, i.e. the probability of a high inflation rate. The existence and uniqueness of such a probability is guaranteed for us by the comparability and transitivity axioms (see Exercise 2.9).

This short description glosses over a variety of behavioural problems associated with the performance of such interrogations. Although we will not explore these problems, references to papers which do so will be given in the next section.

Among the exercises at the end of Chapter 3 are some illustrating a means of interrogation where the decisionmaker—in his own best interests—will provide a true assessment of, for example, a subjective probability. Any inclination to offer a biased answer is removed by the means with which the information is sought. Although only given for a problem trivial in scale and complexity they are indicative of the elaboration which can be used in the assessment procedures.

Having settled on an arc length, the ratio of this arc length to the circumference of the circle is the decisionmaker's (subjective) probability of a high inflation rate. Since he believed that low inflation was less likely than high, we will have $p(\text{high}) > 1/2$, say, $p(\text{high}) = 0.6$. The axioms for relative likelihood are constructed in such a way that the consequent probabilities have the same properties as the previously explored probability types. Thus, to find the subjective probability of a low rate of inflation

$$p(\text{low}) = 1 - p(\text{high}) = 0.4,$$

since high and low are exclusive and exhaustive possibilities. If the problem involved an increased number of possibilities for the rate of inflation, this could still be tackled in the same way using the probability wheel.

In a sense the decisionmaker is here nominating lengths (probabilities) which match his judgements on the relative likelihoods of particular events. For the alternative scheme the events are constructed in such a way as to be equally likely. This construction can be most easily pursued in the context of a dialogue between a decisionmaker (DM) and an analyst (A). Consider again the investment example, but this time let interest in the inflation rate prospects be more refined than just high or low. For this problem the decisionmaker is concerned about the forthcoming rate of inflation, and each of the alternative actions may lead to, say, five different conclusions depending on the rate. Table 1.2 is thus replaced by one with five rows instead of two, as in Table 2.1.

Our imaginary dialogue is interspersed with commentary (in square brackets)

Table 2.1 Profits in millions of dollars for the refined version of
the investment problem

Investment Plan

		a_1	a_2	a_3	a_4	a_5
	$>20\%$	2	1	5	2.5	3
	$14\text{--}20\%$	3	2	4	2.5	2
Inflation rate	$12\text{--}13\%$	3	1	3	4	4
	$7\text{--}11\%$	2	5	1	3	3
	$<7\%$	2	6	1	2	1

on the progress of events, and concludes with a graphical display of the decisionmaker's judgements.

A: The first thing to establish in this exercise is the range of inflation rates you think it appropriate to include in our study. In other words we need an upper and a lower limit on the rate.

DM: How do we go about finding those? Most of the forecasts in the press differ from one another. Am I to take the largest and smallest values of these as my limits?

A: No, not necessarily. Bear the forecasts in mind if you will—you can hardly erase them from your memory—but remember these numbers that you read about are, in a sense, only part of the story. The economists and forecasters are working with a lot of data, and the results they produce are summarized (perhaps not by themselves) as one figure.

DM: You mean what they nominate as the forthcoming rate of inflation is an average figure, or a most likely figure?

A: That's not always made clear. But let's not worry about the interpretation of these forecasts at the moment. What I want from you are the two end points of the range we are to investigate. It is important that these end points should include all the inflation rates you think likely to turn up.

DM: Likely?

A: Well, let's put numbers to it. Consider the upper limit of the range first. We cannot be certain that an unforeseen economic or political crisis will not occur, and one effect of such a crisis may be to precipitate a bout of very high inflation rates.

DM: I don't see that happening in the next year. All the indications are that the rate is coming down, and if it were to increase again, it wouldn't be to the very high levels of two years ago.

A: What then do you consider a sensible upper limit to consider? Say the level which you think the odds are one hundred to one against exceeding?

DM: It's rather hard to fix on a number. I mean 25% seems as reasonable as 30%, and these are pretty wild figures.

A: They weren't inappropriate two years ago.

DM: But things are more settled now, and really it would take a very unfortunate string of events to bring about a recurrence of those rates.

A: Let's not worry too much about precision. Accuracy is more important, and remember you can revise your assessments as we go along, if they make you feel too uncomfortable.

DM: Well, all right. Let's settle for 25%.

A: And at the other end of the scale?

DM: Well I know what the official target is, and it strikes me as optimistic, though we shouldn't be too far off the mark.

A: Allow yourself to be optimistic.

DM: Well if I said 5% I wouldn't like to quote odds at it being bettered. You talked of odds of one hundred to one, but really if you had asked for two hundred to one or even a thousand to one, I don't think I would be able to give an alternative figure with confidence.

A: Fine. These eventualities are not easy to evaluate, but I think you'll find that, for your problem, the analysis is not very sensitive to changes in the value of these end points. If it were then our dialogue would have to take a very different form, and we would probably find it necessary to examine the ways in which the very unlikely, but highly significant, eventualities can arise.

DM: I'll be pleased to avoid that problem.

A: We've agreed so far that the inflation rate for the coming year is most likely to be in the range 5–25%, and that any eventuality outside that range is so unlikely that we can ignore it for the present. Our next step is to investigate this range, looking at subintervals of it which you will construct in response to my prompts. There are two points to bear in mind as we proceed. In the first place this is not an attempt to trick you or highlight any flaws in your judgement. Between us we are seeking to consolidate and explicate these judgements. The procedure is not one with which you will be acquainted and you can therefore expect some mental discomfort as part of the process. Which brings me to my second point—the need to be adaptive. As the interview proceeds you may well feel inhibited in your response by virtue of your answers to some of my earlier prompts. If this is the case we merely re-start the interrogation at the appropriate point, and we can do this as often as you like.

DM: Is there any means we can use to keep track of my answers which will be meaningful to me? I appreciate that your eventual use of the data may be different, when you make the transition from response summary to probability encoding, but is there an easy visual aid for me?

A: Yes. In fact the same device can work for both of us, at least in this simple example. We will start with a line, designated to be of unit length. In fact we will draw it of a convenient size, in the knowledge that the figure will become more complicated as the analysis proceeds. At the left and right-hand ends of the line we add 5% and 25%, respectively, your two outside values for the inflation rate, giving the figure below.

5   25

Given this range, what figure for the inflation rate divides this range into two intervals of equal likelihood?

DM: I'm not sure how to answer that.

A: Let me offer you a hypothetical gamble, based on a number R for the inflation rate, where R is bigger than 5 but less than 25. This number R divides the range into two intervals, the first from 5 up to R, written $(5, R)$, and the second from R up to 25, written $(R, 25)$. When the inflation rate reveals itself, it will be in one of those two intervals. For a particular value of R I allow you to choose one of the intervals. If the inflation rate turns out to lie in the interval you have chosen then you receive a desirable prize, else you receive nothing.

DM: I think I see what you're getting at.

A: If I nominate an R value, say R equal to 20, then your choice of interval is?

DM: Easily the interval from 5 up to 20.

A: And for R equal to 10?

DM: I would choose the interval 10 up to 25.

A: What I want from you is an R value which makes the two intervals equally desirable. In terms of the gamble, you are indifferent between $(5, R)$ and $(R, 25)$. You judge these to be equally likely, else you would presumably prefer the more likely interval with the better chance of the desirable prize.

DM: I've got two problems here. The first is that I can think of several legitimate values for R. They are obviously all of approximately the same value, but no one value stands out as more significant than any other.

A: I appreciate the problem. We will concentrate on one value and if it makes the process too uncomfortable later on we can look at it again.

DM: My second problem is concerned with the R value again, though in a different way. The way I see it, if the rate turns out to be exactly R then I win regardless of which interval I have chosen.

A: You have raised a problem which I had hoped to keep obscured. Let's circumvent it in the following way. Assume the inflation rate is recorded as a whole number, for instance 12% or 8%, and has no fractional part. We are then excluding 12.5%, 8.75%, etc. but make no convention on how the fraction is deleted. Let us adopt the convention of always dividing intervals into subintervals at a point which has a fractional part, and let's make it one-half. Thus, our R is of the form $12\frac{1}{2}\%$, for example. Since the actual rate is announced as an integer, it must lie to one side or other of R, and hence your problem disappears. You can appreciate that this may result in some loss of precision, but if this is the case we can use the same process with different conventions, for example by taking our scale of inflation with increments of 0.5% and using R values which avoid the points of that scale—anything ending in 0.25 or 0.75 would do.

DM: I'm happy enough to work with whole numbers, at least until the process is more familiar. Given that I can revise my judgements I would say that a rate of 12% or less is as likely as anything in excess of that rate.

A: Fine. We will mark the point 12.5 with a vertical bar and concentrate on the intervals you have created. I notice that you avoided the use of these mid-points we just talked about. If it's easier to think in terms of those, then do so. We will continue marking the divisions we create by vertical bars on the figure, but we will not cramp the scale by writing anything other than whole numbers on it.

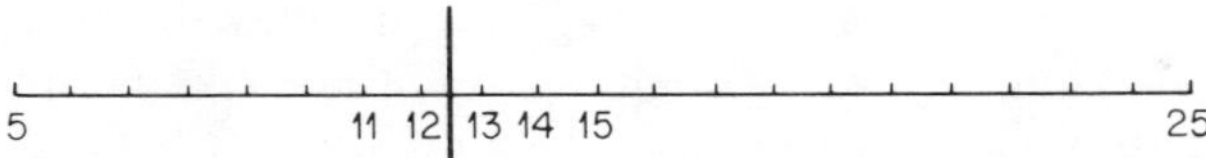

DM: Since I can see the numbers on the scale I find it easier to ignore your sophisticated devices.

A: Your next task is to concentrate on the bottom interval you have created. I want you to assume that the rate *is* going to be in the interval 5% up to 12%, and divide that interval into two equally likely parts.

DM: Well I think 10% and above seems about right.

A: And for the interval from 13 to 25%?

DM: To me this seems a more difficult question. You are saying that I have to believe the rate is in this range and under these circumstances decide on two equally likely subintervals?

A: Yes. By some mechanism you *know* the rate to be in the range 13–25%.

DM: I'd settle for the ranges 13–16% and 17–25% as equally likely.

A: If we incorporate your last two judgements into the last figure we obtain

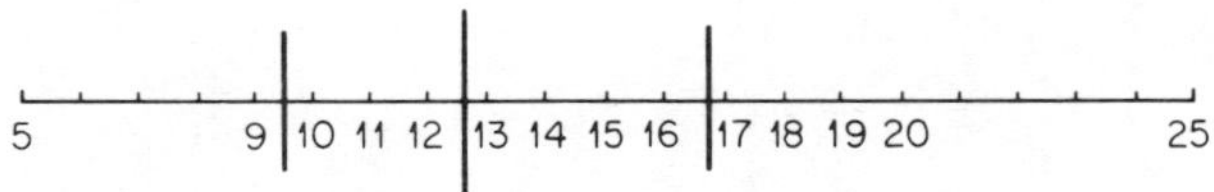

A: We now return to the lower rates and yet again ask you to nominate divisions into intervals of equal likelihood. Let's start with the 5–9% range.

DM: I'm having doubts about the end point—my choice of 5%. Are my responses not going to be influenced by the value of the end point?

A: Indeed yes. Do you wish to think again about the range?

DM: No, but it concerns me to see my own judgements displayed in this way.

A: In itself, no bad thing.

DM: Agreed. I'll stay with my present judgements and say that below 8% is as likely as 8 or 9% [the other half of the interval under consideration].

A: And for the interval from 10 to 12%?

DM: Twelve percent is as likely as the other two, although I must say that this is the first judgement where I feel slightly constrained by the restriction on only using whole numbers.

A: Don't worry, the intervals do not get any smaller! As I said, we can refine this, but let's complete this process. [The assessments are as in the figure below.]

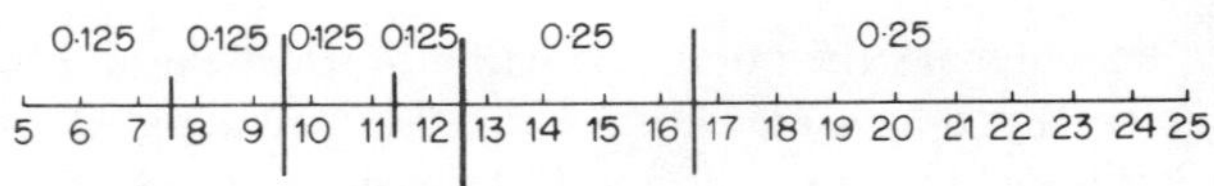

A: You'll note that I have annotated the figure with fractions reflecting your subjective assessments. As you offer judgements on further subdivisions there are implications beyond the subinterval you are currently pondering. For example, the range 8–11 % is as likely as the range 13–16 %, by your declaration, even though you were not specifically interrogated about the relationship between these ranges.

DM: Yes, I could see that coming. I was having reservations about my choice of 16 %, and was considering an alternative of 17 %.

A: Are there any other adjustments you would like to make?

DM: No. I'll settle for 17 % as my midpoint of the upper half, and think about the subdivisions for the 13–17 % and 18–25 % ranges.

A: I've constructed an amended diagram with your new assessment. [The figure below.]

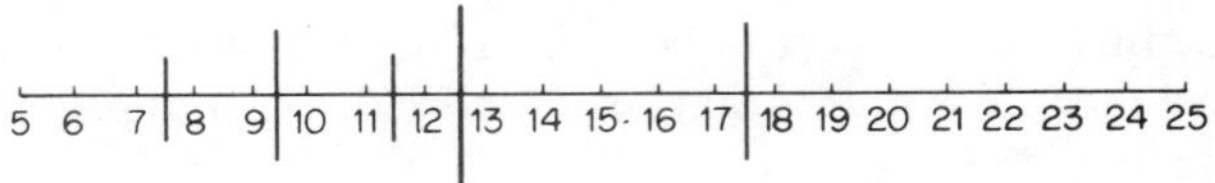

DM: For the 13–17 % interval I'll opt for 13 and 14, and 15–17 as the subdivisions, while for the last interval I think 18–20 and 21–25 are equally likely.

A: Your completed chart now looks like this

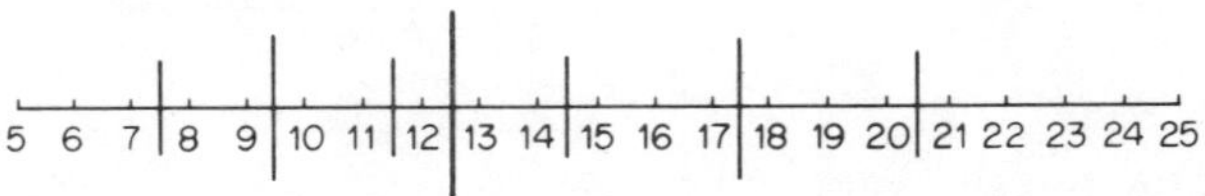

A: A consequence of our construction is that the eight intervals are judged equally likely, and hence have a (subjective) probability of 1/8 or 0.125. As you pointed out during the interrogation the increments we are working with were becoming perilously near the size of range which you were constructing, and a continuation to further interval subdivisions would have meant a re-evaluation with smaller increments, say 0.5 %, on our original interval.

DM: How do you relate these judgements to the original decision problem, and in particular to the states for that problem?

A: The most immediate answer to that uses a diagram built on the foundations of the last figure above. As we have already observed, the eight intervals are equiprobable, but we can say no more about the likelihoods of individual inflation rates, at least not without further assumption or interrogation. If we take the first resort, one simple assumption is that within an equiprobable interval all the rates are equally likely. Thus, in the interval containing rates 10 and 11% the probability of a rate of 10% (assumed equal to the probability of a rate of 11%) is $0.125/2 = 0.0625$. For the interval containing 15, 16 and 17% we have that the probability of a rate of 15% is $0.125/3 = 0.0417$ approximately. For the interval containing (only) 12% we thus have that the probability of a rate of 12% is 0.125. For the entire range of rates from 5 to 25% we can plot these values to obtain Figure 2.7.

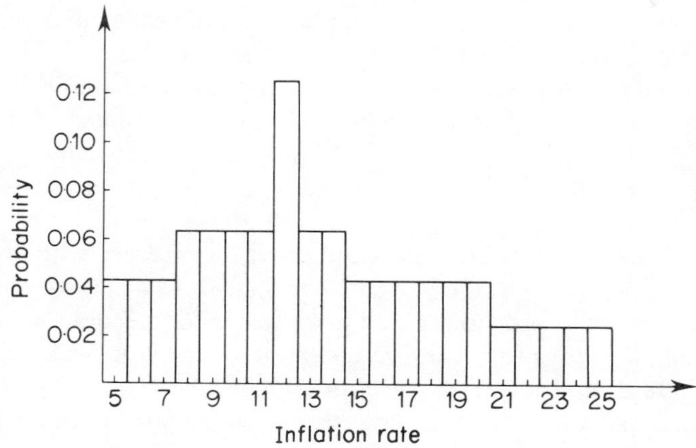

Figure 2.7 Inflation rate probabilities derived from the interrogation

A: Note that the abscissa is just the complete range in our analysis with slight alterations at both ends to ensure uniformity. If we seek likelihoods for the states of the problem given in Table 2.1 we have, for example, the probability of the inflation rate being in the range 14–20% inclusive is given by the sum of the probabilities for rates 14%, 15%, up to 20%. This is easily seen to be 0.3125.

As another example, the probability of a rate in the range 7–11% inclusive is the sum of the probabilities of the rates 7%, 8%, up to 11%, and this takes the value 0.2917 approximately.

DM: The tails of the diagram—by that I mean those parts concerned with the top and bottom end of the range—look rather strange . . .

A: . . . as a result of the assumption. We only made it to get a quick sketch of your answers. If it's important we can look at the assessment using a fine grid, and subject you to another interrogation.

DM: For the moment, I think not.

2.9 Further Reading

Since we are seeking a succinct demonstration of our two methods in the text, the description exhibits some of the qualities of a laboratory test, divorced from a real context. This is particularly true of the direct wheel method which looks more like an undergraduate psychology experiment than a method with serious application. Nevertheless, the literature provides evidence of success with (enhanced) versions of these and other methods. The paper by Spetzler and Staël von Holstein (1975) is addressed to the practical problems of application and provides a useful analysis of the features of such application. In particular they examine the type and source of bias which interviewees can exhibit, and describe the potential 'modes of judgement' which the subject uses in his or her evaluations and responses. Many of the difficulties of application are behavioural and adequate provision must be made for them in the interview process.

Tversky and Kahneman (1974) give a very readable account of behavioural (as opposed to technical) difficulties in the subjective assessment of uncertainty. Hampton, Moore and Thomas (1973) provide a wide-ranging report on subjective probability and its measurement, and supply an extensive set of references.

In general the (research) literature cited above is concerned with experimental or practical application and the associated difficulties, while books which include material on subjective probability tend to campaign for the idea that the concept is sound, and at most provide a demonstration of the type we have given.

Lindley (1971) and Raiffa (1968) both offer lucid, proselytizing accounts of decision analysis in general (and subjective probability in particular), although they are very different in style. The order in which we develop our material matches more closely that of Lindley. Another useful text for the reader with minimal technical background is the account by Aitchison (1970).

2.10 A Summary of Our Results in Probability

As promised at various points in the chapter we bring together in a terse but hopefully convenient form those properties of probability relevant to our needs. The reader is invited to compare these relatively abstract statements with their more particular realizations in Section 2.3 (relative frequency), and Sections 2.4 and 2.5 (classical definition). The exercises at the end of the chapter provide an opportunity to explore some of the properties in the context of particular examples.

For any event we write p(event) for the probability of that event. If A and B are two events then

(i) $\overline{A}$ is the event of A not occuring;

(ii) $A \cup B$ is the event of A or B;

(iii) $A \cap B$ is the event of A and B;

(iv) $A \mid B$ is the event of A given B.

Consider a set of exhaustive and mutually exclusive events $E_i (i = 1, 2, \ldots, n,$ say) and two events A and B. Then we have the following:

(a) the probability of an event is a number in the range zero to one inclusive;

(b) $p(A \cup B) = p(A) + p(B)$ if A and B are mutually exclusive; hence, $p(E_i \cup E_j)$
$= p(E_i) + p(E_j),$ if $i \neq j$;

(c) $\sum_{i=1}^{n} p(E_i) = 1$;

(d) $p(\overline{A}) = 1 - p(A)$;

(e) $p(A \mid B) = p(A \cap B)/p(B)$;

(f) if A and B are independent then $p(A \cap B) = p(A)p(B)$; equivalently, $p(A \mid B) = p(A)$;

(g) $p(A) = \sum_{i=1}^{n} p(A \mid E_i)p(E_i)$.

Exercises for Chapter 2

In these few exercises we provide an opportunity for readers to apply the ideas of probability construction and manipulation which have been developed in this chapter. As far as our forthcoming analysis is concerned the most important material relates to conditional probabilities. In fact the key result has not yet been established, but is investigated in Chapter 5. Our future analyses do not rely to any extent on the ability to use probability in other than very specific contexts. Hence, our skeletal development and minimal set of exercises. We have posed a few questions relating to the assumptions for subjective probability. In the chapters which follow we are not involved in the construction of such probability descriptions, although the examples and exercises may well use numbers which can only have come from such a source.

2.1   A box contains two black, three white and four red balls. Calculate the probability of two successive draws from the box giving

(i)   a black then a white ball;

(ii)   two red balls; and

(iii)   no red balls.

Assume in each case that the ball from the first draw is replaced. For the same events find the probabilities when the ball from the first draw is not replaced.

2.2   Two cards are drawn simultaneously from a set of four which consists of two kings, the ace of spades and the ace of hearts. What is the probability that two aces are drawn? What is the probability of the other card being an ace if one card is an ace? What is the probability of the other card being an ace if one card is the ace of spades?

2.3   Three people, A, B and C, each fire one shot at a target. Each person has a probability of hitting the target with one shot and these are 0.10, 0.30 and 0.40 for A, B and C, respectively. If one bullet is found in the target what are the probabilities that it came from A, from B and from C?

How many shots would A have to fire to give a probability of hitting of at least (i) 0.5, and (ii) 0.9?

2.4   In a game of Russian roulette the six chambers of a gun (of which only one is loaded) are spun before each pull of the trigger. What is the probability of the bullet being fired during the first three pulls of the trigger?

2.5   A machine has two subsystems which must both be functioning if the machine is to be operable. The first system consists of four components and the second of three components. For each subsystem only one component need be functioning for that subsystem to be functioning. If each component of the first subsystem has a failure probability of 0.4 and each component of the second subsystem has a failure probability of 0.5, calculate the probability that the machine is operable.

2.6   Batches of bulbs (plant not light!) can be described as either 'good' or 'bad' in quality. On being used each batch will either flower fully, partially flower or flower not at all. Out of ten 'good' batches seven will flower fully, two partially and one not at all. Out of ten 'bad' batches, two will flower fully, five partially and three not at all. In a shop where there are three 'good' batches to every one 'bad' batch (and we assume that the customer cannot discriminate between them at the time of purchase), what is the probability that one batch chosen by the customer will flower fully? What is the probability that it will not flower at all? If the customer takes home two batches, what is the probability that at least one will flower fully?

2.7   Consider the simultaneous dice-rolling experiment of Section 2.5 where we now use one fair die and one loaded die. The loaded die is known to have a probability of 1/8 for each of 1, 2, 5 or 6 showing on a single roll of the die while the probability of a 3 or a 4 is 1/4 in both cases.

On a single roll of the pair of dice what is the probability that the sum of the numbers on the two dice is less than or equal to 6? Again on a single roll of the dice what is the probability that the fair die shows a number less than or equal to that of the loaded die?

If one of the dice is chosen at random and rolled, what is the probability that it shows (i) a 3, and (ii) a number 3 or more?

Given that the total on the two dice is six what is the probability that the fair die shows 2 or less and the loaded die 3 or more? What is the probability that the fair die shows 2 or less given that the loaded die shows 3 or more and the total is 6? What is the probability that the loaded die shows 3 or more given that the total is 6?

2.8   For three events, A, B and C, use the rules of Section 2.10 to prove that

$$p(A \mid B \cap C)p(B \mid C) = p(A \cap B \mid C).$$

With reference to the previous example, take A to be the event that the fair die shows 2 or less, B to be the event that the loaded die shows 3 or more, and C to be the event that the total shown is 6. Hence, check your results for the last paragraph of Exercise 2.7.

2.9   Given that a decisionmaker's judgement of relative likelihood, i.e. the binary relation 'is at least as likely as', satisfy the comparability and transitivity conditions, why should the use of the probability wheel of Section 2.8 lead to the assignment of a subjective probability for some event, and why should this assignment be unique?

2.10 Why is transitivity a reasonable property to demand of judgements involving relative likelihood? (*Hint*: Consider three events, A, B and C, where the decisionmaker is intransitive in his judgements, with say 'A more likely than B', 'B more likely than C' and 'C more likely than A'. Construct three gambles where in the first (second, third) the decisionmaker receives a prize or not depending on whether $A(B, C)$ holds or not, where it is the same prize in all three gambles. Confront the decisionmaker with these gambles.)

Chapter 3

Utility and its Measurement

3.1 Introduction

During our remarks on Example 1.2 (Section 1.3 of Chapter 1) reference was made to the desirability of outcomes, reflecting the sense in which the money outcome is perceived. While it is almost invariably the case that decisionmakers will rank money outcomes so that the larger of two amounts is preferred, this ordinal relationship contributes little to our attack on the decision problem. Our earlier remarks displayed some of the variety of postures which could be sensibly maintained by a decisionmaker. It is our purpose in this chapter to proceed from such articulation to a suitable quantification. The process as we present it has much in common with that section of the previous chapter which dealt with the personal or subjective probabilities and their assessment.

For the version of the investment example which considers multi-attribute consequences (i.e. profit, market share and workforce size), the easy ranking normally associated with single attribute outcomes is missing. Again we can proceed from suitably coherent preferences on the decisionmaker's part to a numerical measure for the merit of the outcomes. The majority of the material of this chapter is concerned with single attribute outcomes and their evaluation. Little attention will be given to the extra difficulties associated with the multi-attribute outcomes, and only a few remarks made on methods for coping with these additional problems. No evaluation process will be attempted for multi-attribute outcomes, but reference will be made to descriptions in the literature.

The applicability of these ideas is *not* restricted to problems where the outcome (in the standard tabular form) is expressed in some units (to give a scalar outcome) or a set of units (to give a vector outcome). For instance, in Example 1.3 if the prize to be won is a three-week holiday in Mexico and the penalty is the entry fee to the gamble (expressed in dollars), our procedure is unchanged. Or again, for an example with no money outcomes, consider the problem summarized in Table 3.1. We are faced with the option at the weekend of either spending a day skiing or writing a section for a textbook. The prospective skiing conditions and weather are uncertain, although information on both is obtainable by way of a status report and forecast.

None of the outcomes has a scalar characteristic, though I suppose number of pages written is one measure for the outcome of the 'write' option. The author's preferences are for an 'enjoyable outing' over 'several pages complete', and this in

Table 3.1 Outcomes for the writer's dilemma

		Action	
		Go skiing	Write
Conditions	Good	Enjoyable outing	Several pages complete
	Bad	Unpleasant outing	Several pages complete

turn is preferred to an 'unpleasant outing'. In accordance with the principles of Chapter 2 an assessment of the relative likelihood of Good and Bad conditions can be made. This may be influenced by media reports of current and forecast weather and ski conditions, and by accounts from recent visitors to the ski area. Indeed, the assessments of fellow skiers could be taken into account.

When evaluating the alternative actions the relative likelihood of Good and Bad conditions would be significant. Faced with a very likely prospect of Good conditions the author's option would be to go skiing, while a likely prospect of Bad conditions would induce the decision to stay at home and write.

The response to likelihood assessments which are less clear cut (i.e. offer intermediate likelihoods for Good and Bad conditions), is not obvious. A forecast which would entice me to the slopes could well induce the alternative decision in a book-writing and skiing colleague who faces the same dilemma. Even if we agreed on our interpretation of the forecasts and reports—to the extent that our assessments of the conditions and weather prospects were in close agreement—it is perfectly possible that we could take different options. This divergence of decision can only be explained by our differing assessments of the merits of the outcomes in Table 3.1, but note that we still agree on the preference order. Perhaps I relish the skiing rather more, or perhaps my colleague sees more positively the promotion and financial rewards of authorship, but for some reason our perceptions of the outcomes are distinct. Neither of us is necessarily in error in our perception, although we may wish to revise them in the light of experience or information.

3.2 Expectation as a Measure

Having made some observations on Table 3.1 and, the reader will have noticed, failed to offer a solution to the problem summarized in that table, we return to problems with scalar (money) outcomes and, in most examples, 'objective' probabilities for the states of the problem.

Consider a coin-tossing gamble where we have *known* probability p of heads on a toss of the coin, and thus a probability $(1 - p)$ of tails on a toss. If we perform, say, 1000 tosses of the coin, then the number of heads we would expect in that sequence is $1000p$, and the number of tails $1000(1 - p)$. On any given sequence of 1000 tosses the actual number of heads could of course be anything from zero to 1000, but more than a small deviation from the expected number of $1000p$ is highly unlikely. For a given value of p we can in fact calculate the relevant probabilities from some elementary probability theory. If there is a reward of, say,

44

5 units for a head and a penalty of, say, 3 units for a tail, then in the course of 1000 tosses the total profit we would expect is of the order of $5 \times 1000p + (-3) \times 1000(1 - p)$. We divide this figure by 1000 to find the average profit per toss and obtain $5p + (-3)(1 - p)$. We are forming the product of outcome and probability of outcome, and sum over all (here both) outcomes. This expression is called the *expected profit* for one toss of the coin or, more generally, the *expectation* for that gamble. As we have seen, it agrees with average profit per gamble argued from a relative frequency or long-run basis. The operation of forming the expectation provides a measure, in this case for the gamble, which incorporates both the information on likelihoods (probabilities) and numbers associated with outcomes.

We have already mentioned the early interest in uncertainty, and in particular, in gambling. Much of the interest was motivated by the decision problem facing a gambler, i.e. which, if any, of a set of gambles to enter. These gambles had cash outcomes and relied on the usual mechanisms of dice, cards and coins. The probabilities could be assessed in objective terms and expectations formed for each gamble. An expectation of profit was thus a favourable gamble, and the best gamble that which offered the largest positive expectation. For the set

gamble 1:   win 10 units with probability 1/2 and lose 2 units with probability 1/2;

gamble 2:   win 12 units with probability 1/3, 9 units with probability 1/3 and lose 3 units with probability 1/3;

gamble 3:   win 6 units with probability 1/4, lose 4 units with probability 3/4;

we form the expectations

expected outcome from gamble $1 = 1/2 \times 10 + 1/2 \times (-2) = 4$;
expected outcome from gamble $2 = 1/3 \times 12 + 1/3 \times 9 + 1/3 \times (-3) = 6$;
expected outcome from gamble $3 = 1/4 \times 6 + 3/4 \times (-4) = -1\frac{1}{2}$.

The most favourable gamble in terms of expectation is thus gamble 2. Any entry fee for this gamble which is less than 6 units still leaves a net positive profit, while an entry fee of 6 or more makes the gamble unfair, i.e. there is a net expected loss.

Given the relationship between expected outcomes and average outcomes over a number of plays of the gamble, the consensus of early (eighteenth-century) writers was that a gamble with net expected profit is favourable, and should be taken. Any entry fee to the gamble should of course be included in the calculation. It is understood that this tactic applies to one occurrence of the gamble, and does not rely on the offer of a sequence of gambles for its validity. Having proposed such a rule, it was apparent that it lacked universal application. There were circumstances, real and hypothetical, where prudent decisionmakers would willingly enter a gamble offering a net expected loss when the outcomes were assessed in money terms. The most common real example was (and is) in the area of insurance. Details of this are to be found in Section 3.5 below, but the elements are easily described. On payment of a premium the insured is covered against the financial consequences of the loss of, or damage to, some asset, for instance a cargo at sea. Without insurance he will either suffer no loss (in the event of a safe journey) or some loss (partial or total) as the result of a misfortune. Given the likelihoods for the appropriate misfortunes (and there will be actuarial statistics for some of these insurance problems) it will be found that the insurance option is inferior in terms of expected money evaluation to the 'no insurance' decision. Even with allowance for the overheads which the insurance company must incorporate in its calculations, the premium asked is in excess of that determined by the expected money evaluation as fair. Knowing this the decisionmaker still insists on insurance.

As a hypothetical example consider the dilemma facing a gambler who must choose between entering a gamble with two outcomes, or accepting the offer of a sum of money for certain. Suppose the gamble involved a prize of $10 000 with probability p and no prize with probability $(1 - p)$. If we take $p = 0.5$ the gamble has an expected outcome in money terms of $5000. Given that the certain offer is for $5000, then in expected money terms the gamble and the offer are equally desirable, yet the certain offer would be more attractive to many decisionmakers. Even if the offer were reduced to, say, $4000 this offer—now inferior in expected money terms—would still have wide appeal. Such preference for options which contradict the rule of maximizing expected profit cannot be dismissed as irrational. Even with full awareness of the mechanism and rationale for expectation, the decisionmaker will persist with his previous choice.

As another example of the unsatisfactory nature of expected money assessment consider the following gamble, which gives rise to a phenomenon usually described as the St Petersburg Paradox. You are to receive a prize in a gamble, the size of the prize being determined by the length of a sequence of tails in a series of tosses of a fair coin. The coin is tossed until the first head occurs, when the process stops and your prize is awarded. If the first toss gives a head you receive a prize of $2. If the first toss gives a tail and the second a head you receive $4. Should the sequence be tail, tail and then a head your prize is $8. In general, if the first head occurs on the nth toss you receive 2^n as a prize. What entry fee would you pay for this gamble? Note that you receive at least $2 on playing the game, since the worst that can happen (from your point of view) is a head on the first toss. Since the coin is fair the probability of a head on the first toss is $1/2$. Under the assumption that successive outcomes of tosses are independent the probability of a tail on the first toss followed by a head on the second is the product of the probabilities of these two independent events, i.e. $1/2 \times 1/2$. Similarly the sequence tail, tail and then a head has probability $1/2 \times 1/2 \times 1/2$. In general the probability of the first head occurring on the nth toss is

$$1/2 \times \underbrace{1/2 \times \ldots \times 1/2}_{(n-1)} = (1/2)^n$$

Thus, the expected money payoff for the gamble is given by

$$1/2 \times 2 + (1/2)^2 \times 4 + \ldots + (1/2)^n \times 2^n + \ldots = 1 + 1 + \ldots + 1 + \ldots,$$

and this sum is infinite. What then is a reasonable entry fee? Any finite entry fee still leaves a net infinite expected payoff, yet responses to the question of an entry fee are commonly very low, e.g. \$2 up to \$8, perhaps more depending on the subject.

The probability of a large payoff is small. For example, it can be shown that the probability of receiving a payoff over \$100 is $1/2^6 = 1/64 = 0.01\,5625$, while the probability of receiving over \$1000 is $1/2^9 = 1/512 = 0.00195$ approximately. One response to the inadequacy of the expectation operation in these examples rests on the notion that the outcomes, though described as precise sums of money, are perceived by the decisionmaker in other than money terms. An accurate account of his perceptions is necessary for an understanding of the choice exercised by him in these problems. Thus, in our earlier gamble versus certain offer problem it is the author's experience that most students of decision analysis, being of modest means and stable disposition, will prefer the certainty of \$5000 to a gamble with an even chance of \$10 000 or nothing. If we change the scale of the problem by dividing the sums involved by say, one hundred, then some individuals previously in favour of the 'sure thing' will now prefer the gamble with an even chance of \$100 or nothing to the certainty of \$50. Reduce the scale even further, offering an even-handed gamble with outcomes of \$10 and nothing against a certainty of \$5, and yet more takers will commonly be found for the gamble in lieu of the sure thing. In each of these problems the gamble and the certain offer have the same expected outcome in money terms. What is changing, of course, is the scale of the problem, from one involving substantial cash sums through modest amounts to relatively small sums. Depending on his circumstances the reader may agree or disagree with my choice of adjectives, and of course may not have exhibited the sequence of reactions of this paragraph. In each case the distinct perceptions of the decisionmaker are fundamental to any analysis which attempts description or prescription.

Faced with these difficulties the early analysts sought to explain the decisions taken by reference to the general wealth of the decisionmaker. Thus, relative to the wealth of a millionaire the sums involved in the initial gamble are quite small and he might reasonably prefer the gamble to the sum for certain. For someone of more modest means the quantities involved are relatively substantial and the appeal of the sure thing is overwhelming. That same individual may of course revert to gambling in the scaled-down problems where his perceptions of the sums involved may well be akin to those of the millionaire in the original gamble. Out of this comes the notion that the perception of the incremental 'worth' of a sum of money is relative to the underlying wealth of the evaluator. The 'merit' of an extra \$1000 will be less to us if we are already millionaires than if we have more common resource levels. If we graph total wealth against perceived worth (as a function of total wealth) this argument will lead to a relationship similar to that of Figure 3.1.

Technically the function is *concave*. The gradient of the function, which reflects the marginal merit described above, is decreasing with increasing wealth. We omit for the time being any marking of scale or origin. As will be demonstrated in Section 3.5, such a function is consistent with the insurance purchase decision,

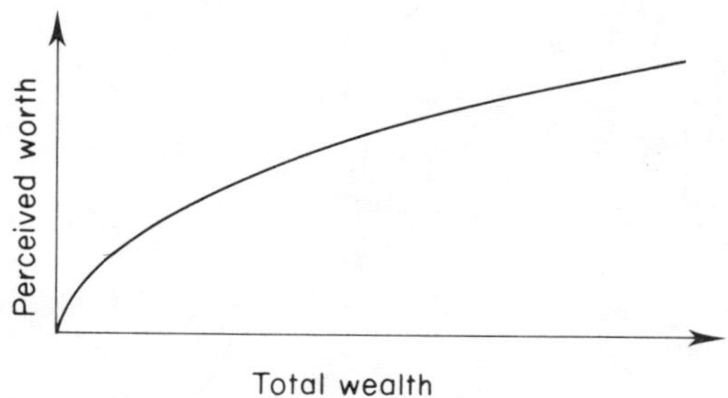

Figure 3.1 Total wealth versus its perceived worth

and the preference for a sure-thing payoff instead of a gamble with the same expected payoff in money terms. In its present form it does *not* accord with the decision to gamble for a given expected payoff (in lieu of the sure thing) for *any* value of the total wealth of the decisionmaker.

If in the St Petersburg Paradox we use such a function, say the logarithm of the total wealth as advocated by some early analysts, then, given the decisionmaker has initial wealth w, the expected outcome from the gamble is

$$(1/2)\log(w+2) + (1/2)^2 \log(w+4) + \ldots + (1/2)^n \log(w+2^n) + \ldots,$$

and regardless of the base to which the logarithm is taken, this can be shown to have a finite sum. This would seem to put us on firmer ground for an analysis of a suitable entry fee for the gamble, but unfortunately this is not yet the case. By a (technical) adjustment to the gamble of the paradox, involving a change in the payoffs as a function of the sequence of tails, we can again pose a problem where the expected outcome using our new perceived worth function is infinite.

To forestall this problem we have to make an additional assumption about the nature of our perceived worth function. A source of difficulty with functions like the logarithm above is their unboundedness. While it is certainly true that we would wish our function to reflect a greater perceived worth in larger values for the total wealth, there is an intuitive appeal (backed up in a later section by a theoretical necessity) in the concept of our needs and desires (which after all do influence the perception of worth of a given quantity of wealth) being satiated by high enough levels for total wealth. We do not deny the validity of a preference for $10 million over, say, $5 million, and the further preference for $11 million over $10 million. We have already argued for an evaluation of wealth which exhibits the 'diminishing marginal merit' property of Figure 3.1, but we now propose that such a function should not increase without bound. Any individual, regardless of energy or longevity, can count on only a finite number of achievements, can own only a finite number of paintings, read (or write) a finite number of books, ski a finite number of hills. To have a wealth of $10 million offers ample scope to indulge in these activities, and $11 million will be even less of a constraint, but the extra opportunities the extra wealth allows do not increase without limit. Figure 3.2 illustrates the nature of the perceived worth function we are arguing in favour

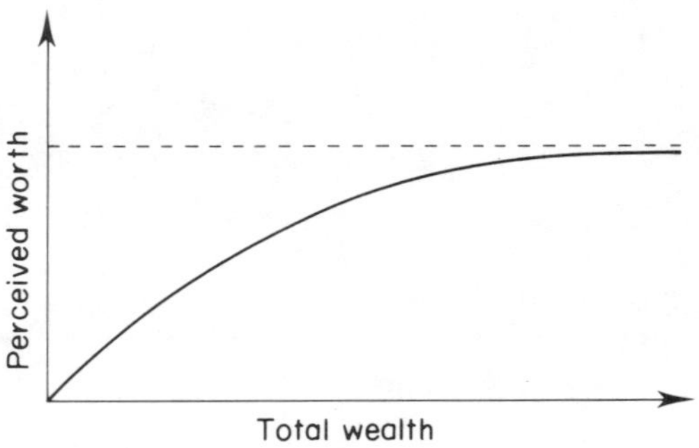

Figure 3.2 A bounded perceived worth function

of. It still exhibits the diminishing marginal merit of Figure 3.1, but now we have a finite upper limit (not yet given on a scale) for the perceived worth of any amount of total wealth. The function and the horizontal line are asymptotic, the gap between them diminishing but still extant as total wealth increases.

With such a bounded function the problems of infinite expected outcomes, as in the St Petersburg Paradox, disappear and some attempt can be made at an analysis for an appropriate entry fee to the gamble. We do not pursue this any further. Note that in both Figures 3.1 and 3.2 we have casually assumed that the perceived worth for total wealth was bounded below. The absence of this property would lead both to paradoxes akin to that shown above and to difficulties in the establishment of a theoretical framework for such a function. We return to this point in the next section which deals with the assumptions necessary for the establishment of such perceived worth functions.

The concept central to the development of this chapter is *utility*. In the section on Further Reading (Section 3.8) reference will be found to material on the history of this concept, and the major contributors to the area of study. The choice of name for the concept is slightly unhappy since it is already in use in other subject areas. This is a common problem, but in this case seems to have given rise to a more-than-usual number of misunderstandings. As in the subjective assessment of uncertainty the existence of a (subjective) assessment of worth or utility is conditional on the consistency of the decisionmaker's judgements. As before, the building block for the process is a binary relationship, but this time judgements about preference rather than relative likelihood are being sought. To parallel the development of Chapter 2 we present, with comments and criticisms, a set of assumptions (axioms) involving preference, this set being rich enough to allow the construction of a utility function which embodies in a quantitative form the decisionmaker's preference structure for the problem concerned. We next return to the insurance and gambling problems of Section 3.2 and examine the properties of utility functions consistent with certain behavioural characteristics. We then turn to the problem of assessment and, in the context of a dialogue, demonstrate one method for constructing the utility function.

3.3 Some Assumptions

In the axiomatic treatments of utility to be found in the literature (some in conjunction with subjective probability) a variety of developments are proposed. Reference to these will be found in the section on Further Reading. Our concern in this development is with the nature of the axioms and their relevance to models for decisionmaking, rather than the detailed technical aspects of the theories. The following development owes much to that of Luce and Raiffa (1957).

The binary relationship in use in this section is $\gtrsim$, where $A \gtrsim B$ is interpreted as 'A is at least as preferred as B' or equivalently 'A is preferred to B or A and B are indifferent'. Here A and B are two outcomes of interest, and the judgement is from our decisionmaker. We use $>$ for strict preference and $\sim$ for indifference between alternatives.

Comparisons are going to be made, indeed demanded, using this preference and indifference relationship. It is convenient and only slightly restrictive to envisage the entities which are the subject of interest as being either one of a set of *basic outcomes*, $O_1, O_2, \ldots, O_n$, or a 'mixture' of these as defined below. For example, the basic outcomes could be a discrete set of levels of total wealth, or a set of profit levels (as in the investment example). We denote a *mixture* (or gamble or lottery) involving these basic outcomes by $(p_1 O_1, p_2 O_2, \ldots, p_n O_n)$, where $p_i \geqslant 0$ for $i = 1, 2, \ldots, n$ and $\sum_{i=1}^n p_i = 1$ (and hence have a probability interpretation). By $(p_1 O_1, p_2 O_2, \ldots, p_n O_n)$ we mean a gamble—a single gamble—where the outcome O_i will be the prize with probability p_i (for $i = 1, \ldots, n$). One and only one basic outcome will be the prize as a result of a gamble. Details of the mechanism for randomly generating the outcome in accordance with the probability values are irrelevant as long as the constituent probabilities are clear to the decisionmaker. If the introduction of the mixture construct seems unusual or arbitrary we invite the reader to re-examine Table 2.1, representing the outcomes for the refined investment example. Given that we have a probability description of the inflation rate prospects (as in the previous chapter) then a column of that table, representing the effect of a given action, can be thought of as a mixture akin (but not identical) to that defined above. For any one action (column) one outcome (profit level) will be received and the appropriate probabilities are known. To solve the decision problem we must choose between actions, not between outcomes. In a deterministic setting, choice between outcomes is likely to be straightforward if these are scalar, e.g. profit levels. Preference between actions corresponds to preference between mixtures, and hence our interest in the concept. In fact we introduce the additional concept of mixtures of mixtures, but leave the description until the appropriate section.

The following set of assumptions is in no sense minimal, i.e. they may be more restrictive than is necessary. The descriptions of the assumptions are intended to make for an easy, informal development rather than provide the smallest set of axioms from which to construct the desired result.

50

First Assumption (*Comparability and Transitivity*)

Any two basic outcomes are comparable, as are any two mixtures. In both cases preference and indifference are transitive, e.g. if A, B and C are three basic outcomes (mixtures) where $A \gtrsim B$ and $B \gtrsim C$, then $A \gtrsim C$.

Comparability and transitivity of the basic outcomes imply that they can be ranked and we assume that this has already been done in the numbering, i.e. $O_1 \gtrsim O_2 \gtrsim \ldots \gtrsim O_n$. To make the problem non-trivial at least one of the relations must be strict preference, giving $O_1 > O_n$. Recall that we have placed no restriction on the nature of these basic outcomes. If they are simple scalar quantities representing, for example, profit in millions of dollars or market share expressed as a percentage, then a 'natural' order among them can reasonably be expected, e.g. preference in the direction of increasing profit in the first example and increasing market share in the second.

If the basic outcome is more complicated, either by virtue of being multi-attribute (and hence summarized in vector terms), or because it has no natural quantified characteristics, then comparability and transitivity are correspondingly more difficult to execute and maintain. As an example of the second type of complication consider some basic outcomes as follows:

O_1: take 3 weeks holidays in Southern Europe with guaranteed sunshine;
O_2: take no holiday but spend the time on some interesting research;
O_3: take time off work but divide it between short holidays taken locally and some house repairs and decoration.

If I contemplate a choice between O_1 and O_2 then, on the grounds that I would be invigorated and refreshed by the holiday, ready to face the demands of a new academic year, and any way my wife would really appreciate the holiday, I could choose O_1 in preference to O_2. On looking at O_2 versus O_3 I could readily argue for O_2 in preference to O_3 on the grounds that it is a more interesting and personally rewarding use of the time. In judging O_1 against O_3 I might be struck by the expense of the first option and a certain urgency in the need for repairs and decorations. I could then convince myself that O_3 is preferable to O_1. Since we already have O_1 preferred to O_2 and O_2 to O_3 I have just been *intransitive* in my preferences. This hypothetical example demonstrates one source of intransitivity in real problems, namely the underlying basis for comparison is changing between preference commitments. I am not using the same yardstick for all pairs of outcomes put before me.

In this first assumption comparability and transitivity is also demanded of judgements involving mixtures and it is to the difficulties of this requirement that we now turn. There is an example (due to the French economist Allais) which illuminates the difficulties of living up to this assumption. In this example we are posed with two decision problems, where each decision problem consists of choosing one of two gambles. Thus, we have

Decision Problem 1:   choose between
       gamble 1: $500 000 for certain,
and gamble 2: $2 500 000 with probability 0.1,
                 $500 000 with probability of 0.89, no prize with probability 0.01.

Decision Problem 2:   choose between
       gamble 3: $500 000 with probability 0.11,
                 no prize with probability 0.89,
and gamble 4: $2 500 000 with probability 0.1,
                 no prize with probability 0.9.

Since we later find it useful to argue from a diagrammatic representation of these decision problems, we present them below. Figure 3.3 corresponds to Problem 1 and Figure 3.4 to Problem 2. Our convention is to denote probabilities of events by numbers on arcs, and outcomes (in this case prizes) by numbers at nodes.

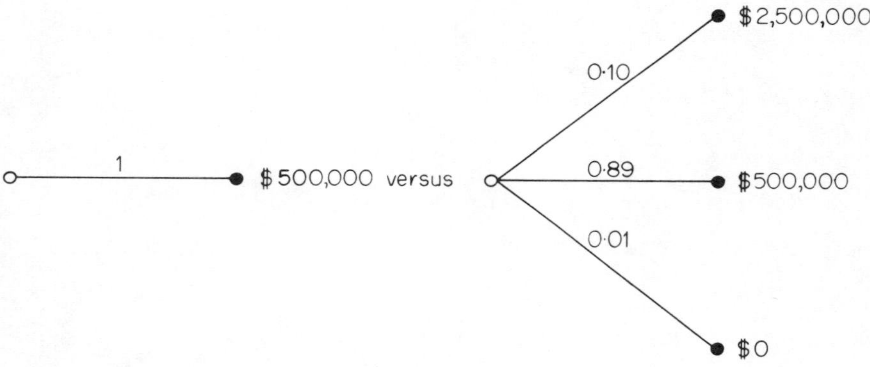

Figure 3.3 Decision Problem 1

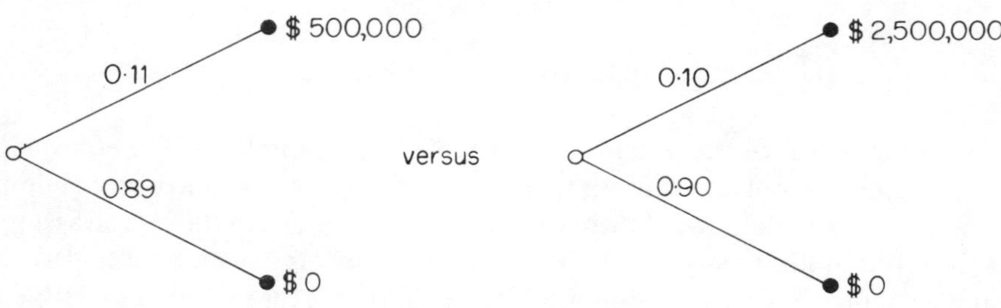

Figure 3.4 Decision Problem 2

If Decision Problem 1 is presented to a group of students, it is commonly found that gamble 1 is preferred to gamble 2. The rationale for this choice is the attraction of the certainty of half a million dollars, rather a large sum, against a 'true' gamble—gamble 2—where although even more money may be won, there is a prospect of winning nothing. Although the likelihood of this event is only one in a hundred, it still seems to encourage those presented with the problem to opt for the assured outcome of gamble 1.

In Decision Problem 2 it is commonly found that gamble 4 is preferred to gamble 3. On being asked for a reason for this choice, the decisionmaker will point out that the likelihood of a prize in the two gambles is nearly the same, and really he finds it difficult to distinguish between the two probabilities. Since the likelihood of a prize is so similar in the two gambles, he will opt for the gamble with the bigger prize, gamble 4.

As Allais pointed out, such a pair of preferences is not compatible with the axioms we need for our utility construct. To demonstrate the nature of the contradiction inherent in these options we re-draw Figures 3.3 and 3.4 as Figures 3.5 and 3.6, respectively.

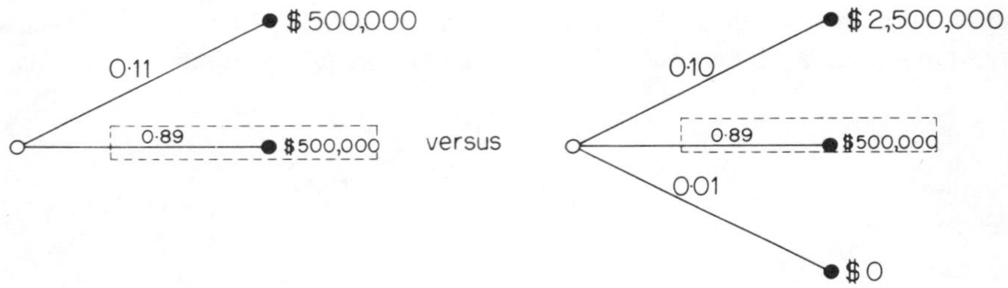

Figure 3.5 An amended representation of Decision Problem 1

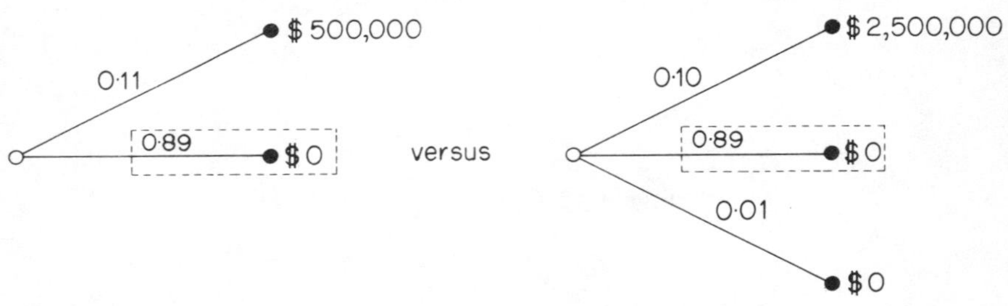

Figure 3.6 An amended representation of Decision Problem 2

We have re-drawn the certain prize of $500 000 in gamble 1 in the equivalent form where two outcomes (both prizes of $500 000) are assigned probabilities such that one and only one of them will occur. The prize of $500 000 is still assured as the result of this re-structuring. We have circled by broken lines those parts of gambles 1 and 2 which are in common, hence the device for re-drawing gamble 1.

In Figure 3.6 we have re-drawn gamble 4 to highlight the feature in common with gamble 3, and again encircled those common elements in broken lines. Our argument to demonstrate the inconsistency of preference for gamble 1 over gamble 2 together with a preference for gamble 4 over gamble 3 is technically imperfect, but the reader can correct this deficiency once the other assumptions have been given.

From Figure 3.5 we can see that a preference for gamble 1 over gamble 2 must be due to a preference for a prize of $500 000 with probability 0.11 over a 'partial' gamble where the prizes are $2 500 000 (with probability 0.10) and $0 (with probability 0.01). The preference is determined by those elements of gamble 1 and gamble 2 which are distinct. From Figure 3.6 a preference for gamble 4 over gamble 3 is (again arguing from the distinct elements of these gambles) determined by a preference for the partial gamble involving a $2 500 000 prize with probability 0.1 and no prize with probability 0.01 over the prospect of receiving $500 000 with probability 0.11. This is, of course, in contradiction to the deduction from Figure 3.5.

To be consistent the preference must be either

(a) for gamble 1 over gamble 2, and gamble 3 over gamble 4, or
(b) for gamble 2 over gamble 1, and gamble 4 over gamble 3.

The commonly held combination described above is therefore not consistent. Critics would argue that the axiom structure is inappropriate since it is not compatible with observed behaviour, although it is also possible to suggest that the decisionmaker may reverse his preference having seen this analysis. As with our subjective probability work, the reader is reminded that the final constructs or measurements are dependent upon the decisionmaker's agreement with the axioms. Our measurements and the consequent decision process are again *conditionally normative*.

Intransitivity is incompatible with the development of decision analysis as we present it. As an argument for the unreasonableness of intransitive behaviour consider the situation where a decisionmaker has stated his preference between pairs of objects drawn from the set of three objects, A, B and C, and is intransitive in his preference. Thus, he prefers, say, A to B, and he prefers B to C but his preference is for C over A. If he currently has object A in his possession we know that he prefers object C to object A, and it is reasonable to expect that he would pay some money—even if only a small sum—to have C rather than A. Obliging as we are, we take his money and give him C in lieu of A. We know of course that he prefers B to C and again are willing to give him B on payment of a sum of money (which reflects his preference for B over C) and object C. Finally, we offer him object A, which he prefers to his current possession B, and money changes hands yet again. After these three transactions he is again in possession of object A (which he started with), but is short of the three sums of money he used to exchange for the more preferred objects. The cycle can be repeated, and the unfortunate intransitive—known as a 'money pump'—spends even more of his cash. (An argument of this type can be used in our study of transitivity in the subjective probability work—see Exercise 2.10.)

Before proceeding to the second assumption we need to broaden the scope of our definition of a mixture. Our current definition of a mixture is in terms of a gamble involving basic outcomes $O_i (i = 1, \ldots, n)$, namely $M = (p_1 O_1, \ldots, p_n O_n)$. We now identify this as a *simple mixture*. We extend the definition of a mixture to include a gamble involving simple mixtures, thus

$M = (p_1 M_1, \ldots, p_m M_m)$ where each M_i is a simple mixture, and the $p_i (i = 1, \ldots, m)$ are such that $\sum_{i=1}^{m} p_i = 1$ with all $p_i \geqslant 0$.

Second Assumption (*Reduction of Mixtures*)

A mixture which is a gamble over simple mixtures is indifferent to the simple mixture where the appropriate probabilities are derived according to the ordinary rules of the probability calculus.

For example, if $M = (p_1 M_1, \ldots, p_m M_m)$, where $M_i = (q_1^i O_1, q_2^i O_2, \ldots, q_n^i O_n)$ for $i = 1, \ldots, m$, then M is indifferent to $(P_1 O_1, P_2 O_2, \ldots, P_n O_n)$, where

$$P_j = p_1 q_j^1 + p_2 q_j^2 + \ldots + p_m q_j^m \text{ for } j = 1, \ldots, n. \qquad (*)$$

Figure 3.7 clarifies the process involved in computing the probabilities for the basic outcomes.

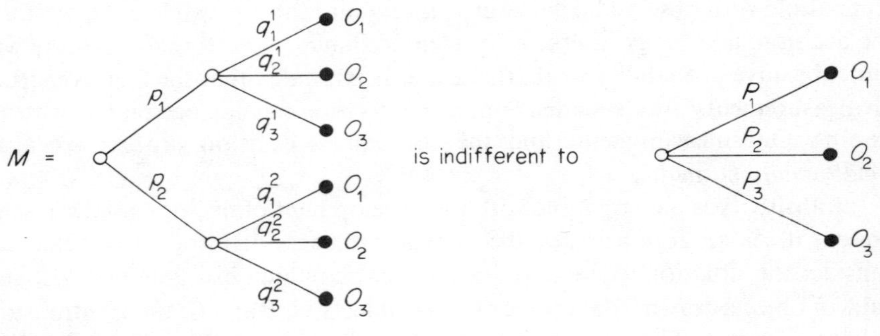

Figure 3.7 An illustration of the Second Assumption

We take $M = (p_1 M_1, p_2 M_2)$, where $M_1 = (q_1^1 O_1, q_2^1 O_2, q_3^1 O_3)$ and $M_2 = (q_1^2 O_1, q_2^2 O_2, q_3^2 O_3)$. Outcome O_1 can arise in two exclusive ways. In the first of these M_1 occurs (with probability p_1) and then O_1 turns up, which will be with probability q_1^1. Thus, O_1 turns up via this mechanism with probability $p_1 q_1^1$. Similarly, O_1 turns up via M_2 with probability $p_2 q_1^2$. Since these are exclusive mechanisms the probability of O_1 is given by $P_1 = p_1 q_1^1 + p_2 q_1^2$. Analogous expressions can be found for P_2 and P_3. The assumption states that all mixtures are reducible to simple mixtures, and that any preference judgements are unaltered by this process. We assume that the probabilities of our assumptions are appropriate for the use to which they have been put, i.e. we assume the events to be independent (thus allowing the joint occurrence to be assigned the probability which is the product of probabilities), or that any dependence is correctly described and $(*)$ above remains valid.

What can we say of the validity of the assumption? Perhaps lost among the details of the probability manipulation is the fact that the original and reduced (simple) mixtures are to be indifferent. Thus, the two-stage gamble is indifferent to the one-stage gamble with appropriate probabilities. There is thus 'no joy' in the gamble itself else the two-stage (or any multi-stage) gamble would be preferred to one with fewer stages but equivalent payoffs. Since many people do admit to enjoyment of gambling itself, divorced from the prospect of financial gain, the assumption is not universally valid. Indeed, some (mainly automated) games seem to be designed to 'prolong the agony' before payoff is achieved. In defence of the assumption, we note that in applications of decision analysis where structures such as those of M (in Figure 3.7) arise, the multi-stage nature of the formulation is not a feature of the problem which the decisionmaker can control. It will often be a modelling device to impose structure.

We have already established, via the First Assumption, that the basic outcomes can and have been ordered, i.e. $O_1 \gtrsim O_2 \gtrsim \ldots \gtrsim O_n$.

Third Assumption (*Continuity*)

Each outcome O_i is indifferent to a simple mixture involving only O_1 and O_n, i.e. there exists a unique u_i, where $0 \leqslant u_i \leqslant 1$, such that O_i is indifferent to $(u_iO_1, 0O_2, 0O_3, \ldots, 0O_{n-1}, (1-u_i)O_n)$. For convenience we write a simple mixture of this type showing only those outcomes with (potentially) non-zero probability. Thus, we would write $O_i \sim (u_iO_1, (1-u_i)O_n)$.

For the case of strict preference where we have $O_1 > O_i > O_n$, consider the mixture $(pO_1, (1-p)O_n)$ versus the basic outcome O_i. For values of p near one it seems reasonable that the simple mixture is preferable to O_i, while for p near zero the outcome O_i is preferred. Our continuity assumption demands that there is a (unique) value of $p(= u_i)$ where the simple mixture and the basic outcome are indifferent. For values of p strictly greater than this break-point the mixture is preferred, while for values below the break-point the basic outcome is preferred.

The establishment in practice of such a p value may be difficult. For instance, if we take O_1 as a penalty of \$5, O_i as a penalty of \$35 and O_n as death, the assumption asserts that (given we have $O_1 > O_i > O_n$!) there is a gamble involving an outcome of either the \$5 penalty or death such that the decisionmaker is indifferent between the penalty of \$35 and this gamble. At first sight most readers would deny the existence of any suitable p value. They would assert that the \$35 penalty is always preferable to the simple mixture, regardless of how small the probability of death. But what of the motorist faced with the choice of a 'quick and dirty' puncture repair (costing, say, \$5) or a replacement of the defective tyre (at a cost of \$35)? If we assume that the repair is known *not* to make the tyre as safe as a new replacement would be, does not the common choice of the cheap repair over the replacement imply the acceptance of the simple mixture against the basic outcome? It certainly is true that an explicit value of p is not considered, but the choice of cheap repair does indicate the acceptance of some risk, however small.

Fortunately, few problems present basic outcomes as extreme as death, and this may account for the fact that popular descriptions of this third assumption sometimes refer to it as indicating the presence of 'neither Heaven nor Hell' in the set of basic outcomes. Presumably the phrase is meant to indicate the absence of an outcome so good or so bad that we would never use it in a mixture.

Apart from the difficulties inherent in extreme outcomes, the assumptions (eventually) imply a fine degree of discrimination on the part of the decisionmaker. An example from Lindley (1971) illustrates the problem and provides a counter-argument to the criticism. Given the option of $100 for certain or a gamble where $101 is received with probability p and $0 with probability $(1-p)$, our assumptions imply the existence of a p value such that the decisionmaker is indifferent between the certain payoff and the gamble. A conventional response to this statement is the assertion that the decisionmaker cannot conceive of a p value (strictly less than 1) where he would *not* take the $100 for certain. Since the extra payoff is only $1—and that is not achieved with certainty—it is not worth the risk of receiving $0, regardless of how small is the likelihood of this event. This is shown in Figure 3.8.

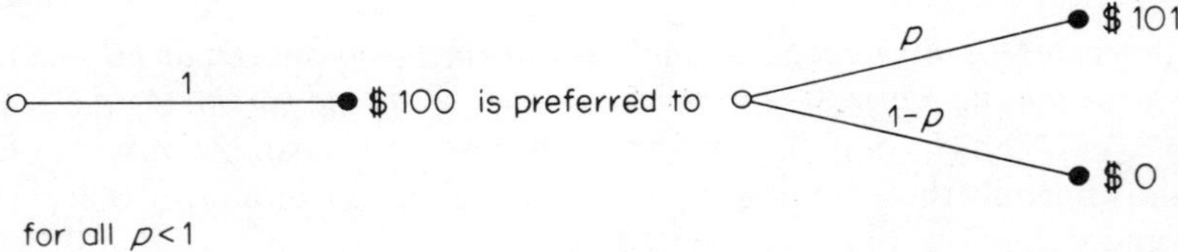

Figure 3.8 A judgement which contradicts the Third Assumption

Presumably the same decisionmaker will prefer $101 (102) for certain against a gamble offering $102 (103) with probability p (as before) and $0 with probability $(1-p)$. Hence, the preferences shown in Figures 3.9 and 3.10.

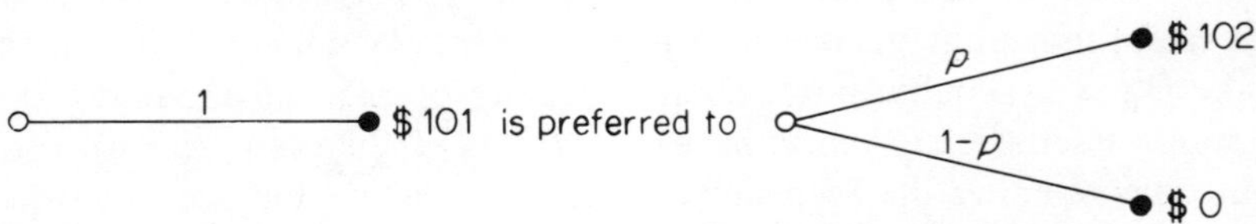

Figure 3.9 A judgement consistent with that of Figure 3.8 (for the same p), but again in contradiction to the Third Assumption

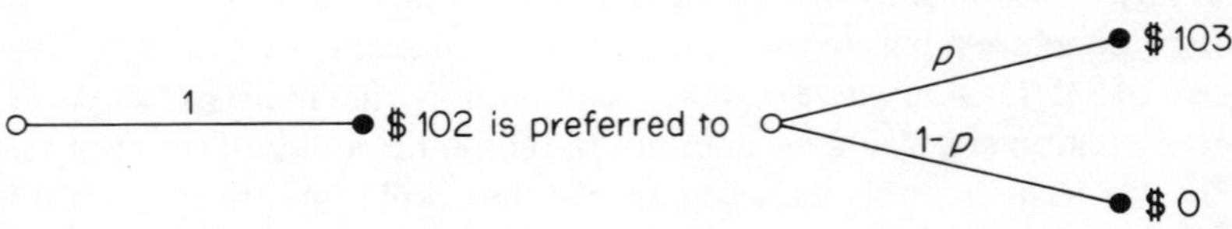

Figure 3.10 Again consistent with Figure 3.8

In each case the gamble offers only \$1 more than the certain amount, and has a non-zero probability of a zero payoff. In progressing from Figure 3.8 to Figure 3.9 the guaranteed level of the certain payoff has increased, but the gamble offers only the same enhancement. Again in going from Figure 3.9 to Figure 3.10 the certain amount is greater in the second case, so that there is more to lose by entering the gamble, and only the same potential gain of an extra dollar. Hence any p value for which the certain quantity in Figure 3.9 is preferable to the gamble will generate the same preference for certain payoff over gamble in Figure 3.10. The next portion of the argument makes repeated use of a result which is stated as the Fourth Assumption (below).

We know from Figure 3.9 that a certain \$101 is preferred to the gamble involving \$102 and zero. Therefore in Figure 3.8 if we substitute for the \$101 payoff (in the gamble) a gamble which is *not* preferred to \$101 we will find that the certain \$100 is still preferred to this two-stage gamble, shown in Figure 3.11.

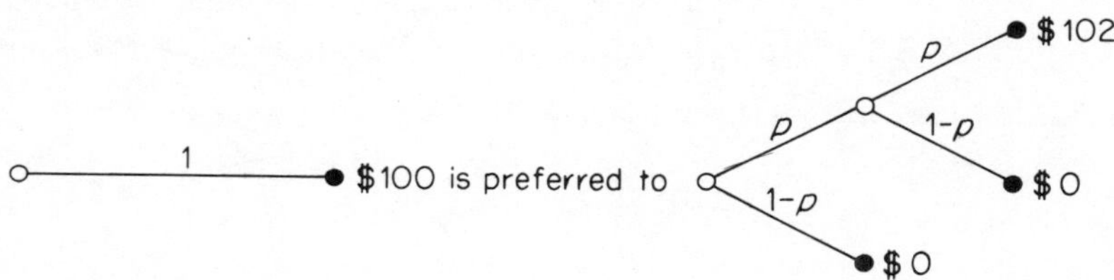

Figure 3.11 From Figures 3.8 and 3.9 (and the Fourth Assumption)

We know from the Second Assumption that this can be re-drawn as in Figure 3.12. If we now substitute for \$102 a gamble over which it is preferred we obtain Figure 3.13. Using the second assumption again this reduces to Figure 3.14. This can be continued in an obvious way to give, for example, Figure 3.15. If we take n sufficiently large, e.g. $n = 9900$ then we obtain Figure 3.16.

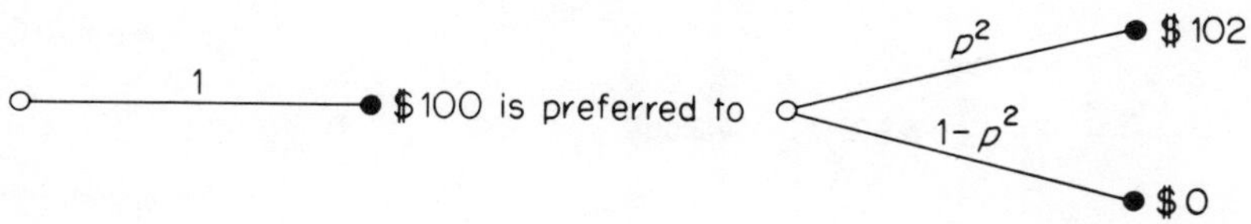

Figure 3.12 From Figure 3.11, using the Reduction of Mixtures

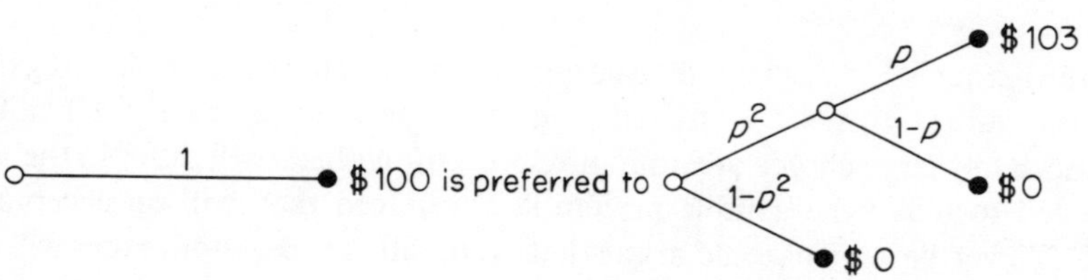

Figure 3.13 From Figures 3.10 and 3.12 (and the Fourth Assumption)

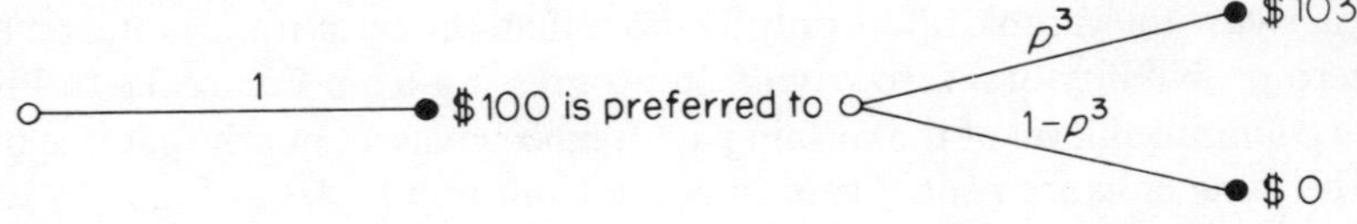

Figure 3.14 From Figure 3.13, using the Reduction of Mixtures

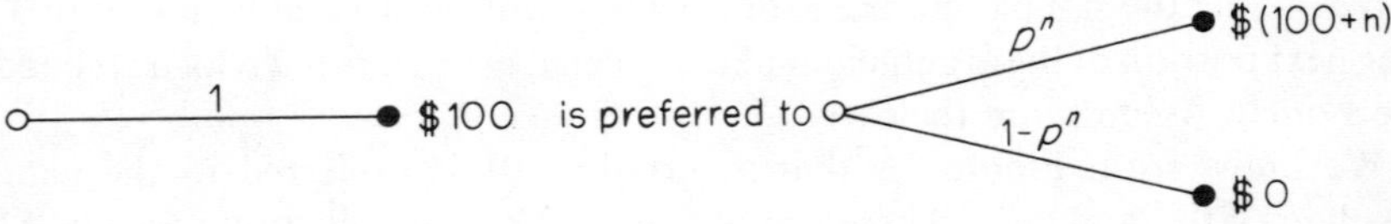

Figure 3.15 The conclusion of a succession of substitutions and reductions

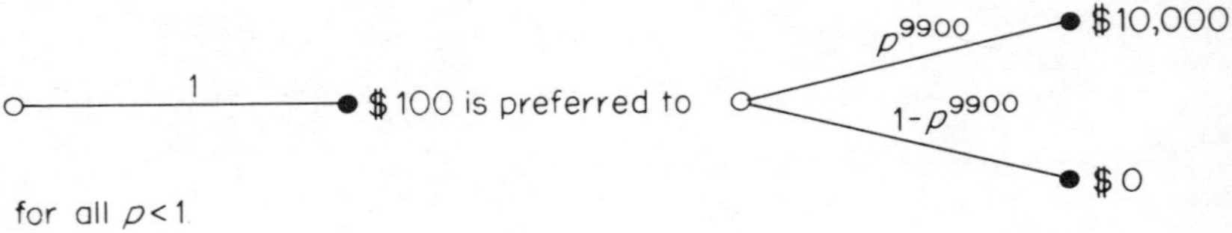

Figure 3.16 A judgement consistent with that of Figure 3.8

Now that the gamble contains a large payoff as well as the zero payoff is it still sensible to maintain that the certain \$100 is preferable? We can make p^{9900} as close to one as we like, by taking a large enough value for p (but still less than 1). For the gamble of Figure 3.17 is there no q value (short of 1) which would entice the decisionmaker away from the certain \$100?

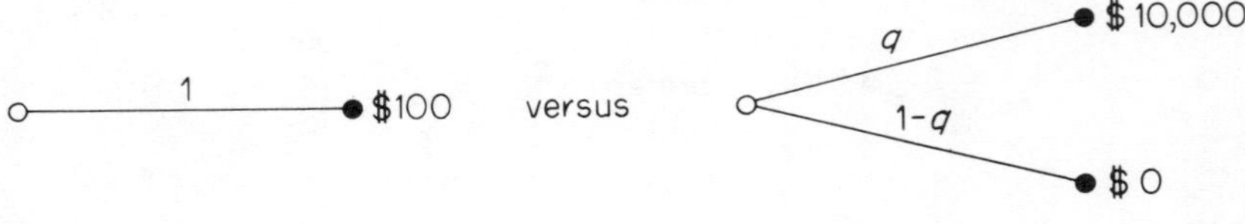

Figure 3.17

If the reader is still not willing to admit a preference for the gamble—regardless of the q value—then he is invited to extend the example even further by an appropriately large choice of n in Figure 3.15. Individuals will differ in the size of n needed to make the gamble preferable, as indeed they will on acceptable q values. Nevertheless we would argue that eventually the decisionmaker will reach a position where he can discriminate in favour of the gamble against the certain \$100, and when that position is reached he will be in contradiction of his preference shown in Figure 3.15. From this contradiction we deduce that the decisionmaker is incoherent if he insists on the preference expressed in Figure 3.8 for all $p < 1$.

The argument of the previous paragraphs has made repeated use of the

Fourth Assumption (*Substitutability*) which we now state.

In any mixture we may substitute for a basic outcome O_i that unique simple mixture $(u_iO_1, (1 - u_i)O_n)$ indifferent to O_i, the original and derived mixtures being indifferent.

In fact our substitution was not exactly of this form, but the principle is the same.

Finally, our **Fifth Assumption** (*Monotonicity*) establishes preference between simple mixtures which use only the extreme basic outcomes O_1 and O_n. *A simple mixture $(pO_1, (1 - p)O_n)$ is preferred or indifferent to $(qO_1, (1 - q)O_n)$ if and only if $p \geqslant q$.*

Between simple mixtures of this restricted type, that with the more probable 'most preferred alternative' (O_1) is to be preferred. Where the outcomes are restricted to, say, money outcomes with O_1 as \$1000 and O_n as \$10 the axiom seems reasonable. If we consider problems where the outcomes involve, for instance, death (as in the discussion after the Third Assumption) then it is possible to provide apparent counter-examples to the validity of the assumption. These can often be 'defined away' by an appropriate reconsideration of the components of the problem, and we chose not to pursue any of these problems here.

3.4 Expected Utility

We now have a rich enough set of assumptions to allow the establishment of a measure which will be our guide to an appropriate choice of action in decisionmaking under uncertainty. For a simple mixture $M = (p_1O_1, \ldots, p_nO_n)$ where we already have $O_1 \gtrsim O_2 \gtrsim \ldots \gtrsim O_n$ we can, by the Third Assumption, find for each basic outcome O_i a unique gamble involving only O_1 and O_n such that $O_i \sim (u_iO_1, (1 - u_i)O_n)$. If we substitute these gambles in M to give a multi-stage mixture M', then by the Fourth Assumption $M \sim M'$. For the sake of symmetry in the presentation we write $O_1 \sim (u_1O_1, (1 - u_1)O_n)$ and $O_n \sim (u_nO_1, (1 - u_n)O_n)$, where obviously $u_1 = 1$ and $u_n = 0$. Figure 3.18 displays both M and M'.

By the Second Assumption (on the reduction of multi-stage mixtures) M' is indifferent to the mixture $M'' = (PO_1, (1 - P)O_n)$, where $P = p_1u_1 + p_2u_2 + \ldots + p_nu_n$. M'' is illustrated in Figure 3.19.

By the use of the Third, Fourth and Second Assumptions we have thus reduced a mixture involving all basic outcomes to one involving only the most preferred and least preferred alternatives (O_1 and O_n, respectively). The role of the First

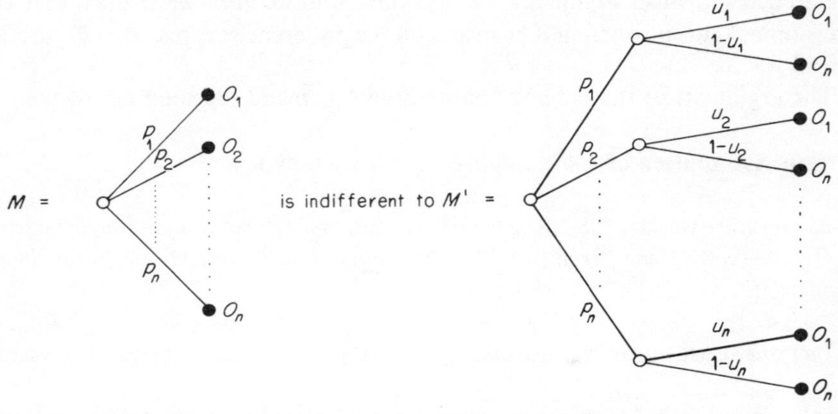

Figure 3.18 The mixture M is re-expressed as a mixture M', where the outcomes are either O_1 or O_n

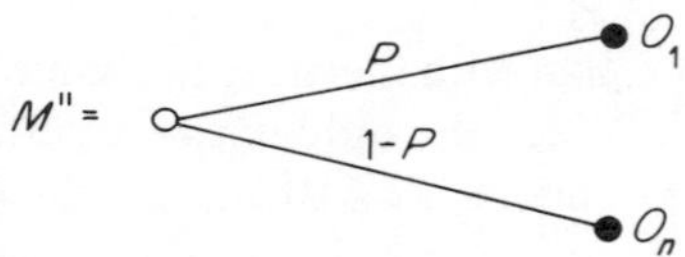

Figure 3.19 The multi-stage mixture M' of Figure 3.18 is reduced to a mixture M''

Assumption is to guarantee the uniqueness of the u_i, among other things (cf. the parallel property in the subjective probability work alluded to in Exercise 2.9).

If we have another simple mixture $N = (q_1 O_1, q_2 O_2, \ldots, q_n O_n)$, say, then similarly $N \sim N'' = (Q O_1, (1 - Q) O_n)$, where $Q = q_1 u_1 + q_2 u_2 + \ldots + q_n u_n$. If we wish to choose between M and N, then $M \succsim N$ if and only if $P \succsim Q$ (from the Fifth Assumption). Thus, we have established the following *theorem*:

If our binary relationship $\succsim$ satisfies the First to Fifth Assumptions then for each basic outcome O_i there exists a number u_i such that preference between two simple mixtures such as M and N above is reflected in the relative magnitude of the expected values $p_1 u_1 + \ldots + p_n u_n$ and $q_1 u_1 + \ldots + q_n u_n$.

Note that the same set of u_i appear in both expressions. For a simple mixture $M = (p_1 O_1, \ldots, p_n O_n)$ let us define the function $u(M) = p_1 u_1 + \ldots + p_n u_n$. We refer to such a function as a *utility function*. The set of assumptions has thus guaranteed the existence of a utility function $u(\cdot)$ such that for two simple mixtures M and N, $M \succsim N$ if and only if $u(M) \geqslant u(N)$.

Consider the gamble which gives mixture M with probability r and mixture N with probability $(1 - r)$, and denote this gamble by R. Figure 3.20 illustrates the structure of this gamble.

Now $M \sim (pO_1, (1 - p)O_n)$ and $N \sim (qO_1, (1 - q)O_n)$ for appropriate p and q so that we obtain Figure 3.21, where the second indifference follows from the

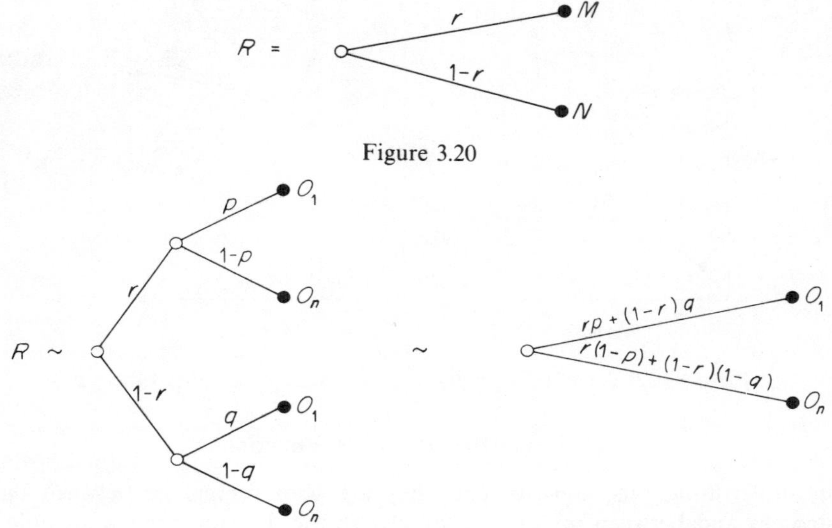

Figure 3.20

Figure 3.21 The reduction of R to a mixture involving only O_1 and O_n

reduction of the two-stage mixture to a one-stage mixture. Thus,

$$u(R) = rp + (1-r)q = ru(M) + (1-r)u(N). \qquad (\dagger)$$

This extends in an obvious way to a mixture of more than two mixtures. To find the utility (properly, the expected utility) of a gamble involving mixtures we simply form the expectation of the utilities of the constituent mixtures.

In the development given above we set $u_1 = 1$ and $u_n = 0$, and this obviously gives $0 \leqslant u_i \leqslant 1$ for $i = 2, 3, \ldots, n-1$. The two important properties of a utility function are:

(a) the maintenance of the preference order, i.e. $M \gtrsim N \leftrightarrow u(M) \geqslant u(N)$, and

(b) the expectation property ($\dagger$) above.

Given that we have constructed such a utility function $u(\cdot)$ for the problem in hand, then it is straightforward to demonstrate that the utility $u^*(\cdot)$ defined by

$$u^*(M) = au(M) + b, \quad \text{for all mixtures } M,$$

where $a > 0$ and b is any constant, also has the properties (a) and (b). In working with utility functions it is therefore important to remember that the absolute values of the numbers which emerge are unimportant. Only relative values matter. In terms of a graph displaying both $u(\cdot)$ and $u^*(\cdot)$, the effect of a different b is to set the origin at different levels on the vertical axis, while a has the effect of changing the scale along the axis. Preference (which precedes its numerical characterization in the form of a utility function) is accurately modelled by both $u(\cdot)$ and $u^*(\cdot)$. Thus, the $u(\cdot)$ displayed in the left-hand graph of Figure 3.22 and the $u^*(\cdot)$ of the right-hand graph are consistent with the same underlying preference structure, where we are characterizing preference over, say, money.

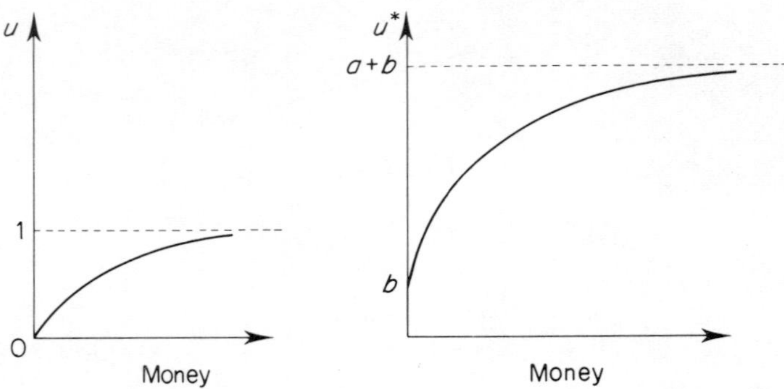

Figure 3.22 The effect of a and b on the scale of a utility function

3.5 Properties of Utility Functions

Our utility functions, consistent as they are with preference between basic outcomes and between mixtures, characterize the decisionmaker's attitude to decisionmaking under uncertainty. Presented with risky alternatives, i.e. actions where the consequence is not a function of the choice of action alone but is influenced by other uncontrollable variables, our decisionmaker is assumed to compare the alternatives and exhibit a coherent preference between them. Let us re-examine the investment example (Example 1.2) at the stage where we have eliminated dominated alternatives, i.e. the problem is that of Table 1.4, consisting of three actions and two states. In Section 3.6 we will examine a mechanism by which utility functions can be constructed, but for the moment assume that we have the decisionmaker's utility function for profit, and that it takes the form of Figure 3.23. This gives the utility for profit for all levels of profit which can be

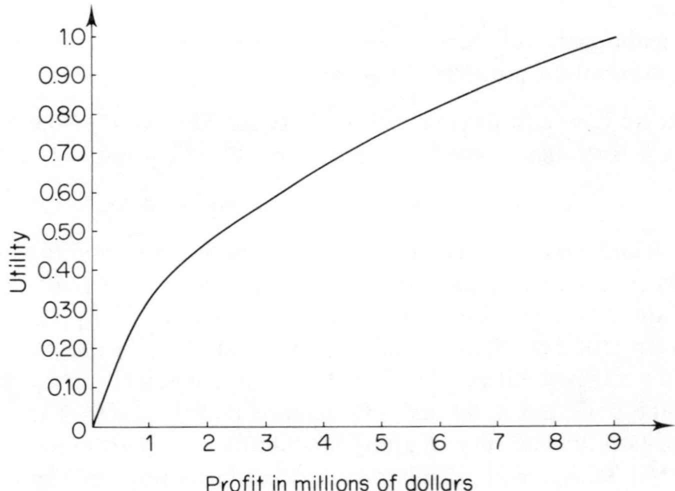

Figure 3.23 Utility function for profit, to be used in the investment example

envisaged (or are judged relevant). In fact we have chosen $u(x) = \sqrt{x}/3$ for $0 \leqslant x \leqslant 9$, where x is the profit level in millions of dollars, as giving a representative type of curve. If we have assessments for the likelihoods of high and low inflation rates of p and $(1-p)$, respectively, then denoting by $EU(a)$ the expected utility consequent to choosing action a we have

$$
\begin{aligned}
EU(a_1) &= pu(1.5) + (1-p)u(6) = 0.82 - 0.41p, \\
EU(a_3) &= pu(5) \quad + (1-p)u(2) = 0.47 + 0.27p, \\
EU(a_4) &= pu(3) \quad + (1-p)u(5) = 0.75 - 0.17p.
\end{aligned}
$$

Obviously, the action giving maximum expected utility depends on the value of p. We can in fact pursue properties of the solution over all possible p, but we leave this analysis until Chapter 4, and examine only a few cases here.

If high and low rates are equally likely, i.e. $p = 1/2$, we have $EU(a_1) = 0.62$, $EU(a_3) = 0.61$, and $EU(a_4) = 0.67$. Thus, a_4 is the action which maximizes expected utility. For a value of $p = 0.8$, we obtain $EU(a_1) = 0.49$, $EU(a_3) = 0.69$ and $EU(a_4) = 0.61$, with a_3 giving the best expected outcome.

At $p = 0.4$, when the expected money yield of a_1 ($0.4 \times 1.5 + 0.6 \times 6$) is the same as the expected money yield of a_4 ($0.4 \times 3 + 0.6 \times 5$) we have $EU(a_1) = 0.66$ and $EU(a_4) = 0.68$. Without defining the concept exactly we note that the *variability* in money terms of a_4 (about the expected money yield) is less than the variability in money terms of a_1 about the same expected money outcome. Action a_4 is that chosen by the expected utility criterion, where the utility function is constructed by consideration of preferences between pairs of actions. The actions are perceived as resulting in (or even being equivalent to) mixtures, which are combinations of basic outcomes and probabilities. The 'risks' associated with an action (and this variability can be seen as one measure of risk) are an intrinsic part of the information presented to the decisionmaker in the establishment of his utility function. They are not presented, of course, in any processed form, but are present in the raw data.

At $p = 0.29$, when the expected utilities of a_1 and a_4 are the same ($= 0.7$), the expected money outcome of a_1 is $0.29 \times 1.5 + 0.71 \times 6 = 4.7$ million, while action a_4 has an expected money yield of $0.29 \times 3 + 0.71 \times 5 = 4.42$ million. Again action a_1 has more variability (around its expected money outcome) than a_4 (has around its lower expected yield). We emphasize that the decisionmaker's preferences do not arise out of an expectation operation or any other numerical calculation. Rather, we use the end result of his preferences to demonstrate a characteristic which he has displayed in his provision of the data for the utility function.

In Figure 3.24 we reproduce the utility function of Figure 3.23 but omit the scales from the axes since they are redundant for the analysis which follows. Consider two profit levels A and B (where $A < B$) and a mixture of A and B, where these two profits are equally likely. The expected money outcome for this mixture is denoted by C, where $C = \frac{1}{2}A + \frac{1}{2}B$.

If we consider the problem in terms of expected utilities, then the expected utility of the mixture is $\frac{1}{2}u(A) + \frac{1}{2}u(B)$ which from the figure is obviously less than

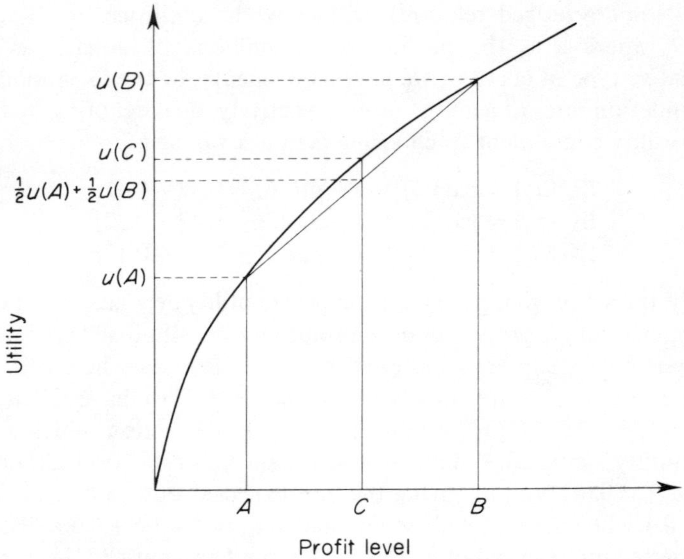

Figure 3.24 Comparison of expected money and expected utility for
a choice between C and an equally likely mixture of A and B

$u(C)$. Posed now as a decision problem with the option C for certain or a gamble with equally likely outcomes of A and B, we readily see that, while the gamble and the certain quantity have equal expected money outcomes, in terms of expected utilities the certain outcome is superior to the gamble, i.e. $u(C) > \frac{1}{2}u(A) + \frac{1}{2}u(B)$.

This characteristic of *risk aversion* is inherent in the shape of the utility function. The name follows from the avoidance of gambles (which are fair and even advantageous in expected money terms) due to the inferior expected utility measure against outcomes for certain. Figure 3.24, which features a concave function, is claimed to be typical of that exhibited by many subjects who have been interrogated on their utility functions for (typically) money outcomes. In the next section we demonstrate just such an interrogation. If the utility function exhibited by the decisionmaker is of the convex type illustrated in Figure 3.25, then an argument similar to that above will demonstrate that the decisionmaker would enter a gamble which in expected money terms is unfair, i.e. he is risk-seeking.

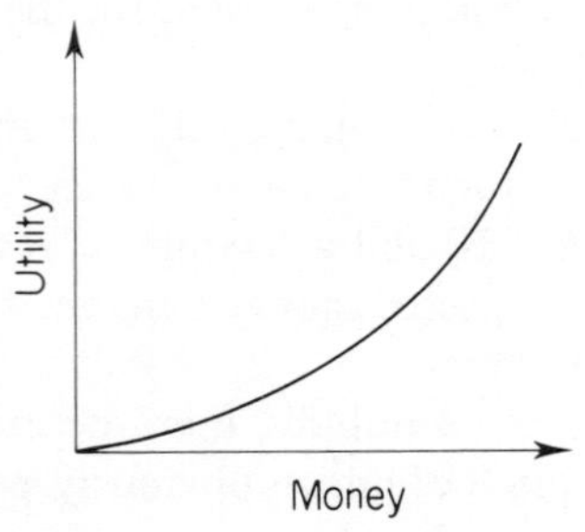

Figure 3.25 A risk-seeking (convex)
utility function

Some analysts claim that many decisionmakers exhibit a utility curve like that of Figure 3.26 which is risk-seeking in its lower sections but changes to risk-averse further up the range.

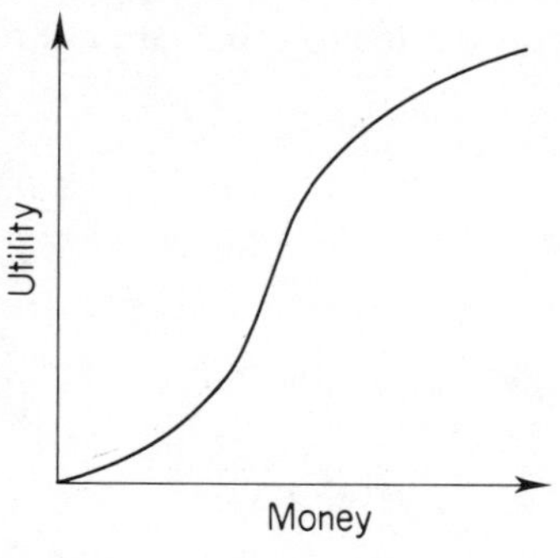

Figure 3.26 A utility function displaying risk-seeking and risk-averse characteristics in different parts of the range

Our final concern before the illustration of a utility function construction is with an analysis of the insurance purchase decision. Our decisionmaker has worldly assets of money value C which could be completely destroyed by a rather unlikely catastrophe. For a sum of c he can insure against such an event, and the data for the problem of buying insurance or not can be posed in the familiar tabular format of Table 3.2.

Table 3.2 Outcomes for the insurance purchase problem

| | | Decision | |
		Buy insurance	Do not buy insurance
Future	Catastrophe	C-c	0
	No catastrophe	C-c	C

The genuine insurance purchase problem where the item potentially being insured is only a part of the total assets of the decisionmaker can be analysed in an analogous manner. We have taken a very simple-minded version to simplify the presentation. Also missing, in the interests of simplicity, are the intermediate possibilities, where only part of the decisionmaker's assets are lost. If we denote the probability of catastrophe by p then in expected money terms the measure of the decision *not* to buy insurance is $p0 + (1 - p)C = (1 - p)C$, while the decision to buy insurance has an expected money outcome (indeed an actual money outcome) of $C - c$. We are ignoring any distinction between the continuous presence of the decisionmaker's assets (in the absence of catastrophe) and the inevitable disruption involved in their destruction and subsequent reinstatement (in the event of a catastrophe). Using real data we would find that $(1 - p)C > C - c$, i.e. $pC < c$. Since these are expected money outcomes the decision giving the larger value is to be preferred—in this case the option not to buy insurance. The presence of thriving insurance industries in most countries indicates that any purchase decision cannot be based on an analysis which uses expected money as a measure for consequence. On the assumption of a risk-averse decisionmaker an analysis of the problem based on an expected utility measure does indicate the merit of insurance purchase. Data for the analysis is included in Figure 3.27. The curvature of the concave utility function is exaggerated to produce a clearer, but not a different, result.

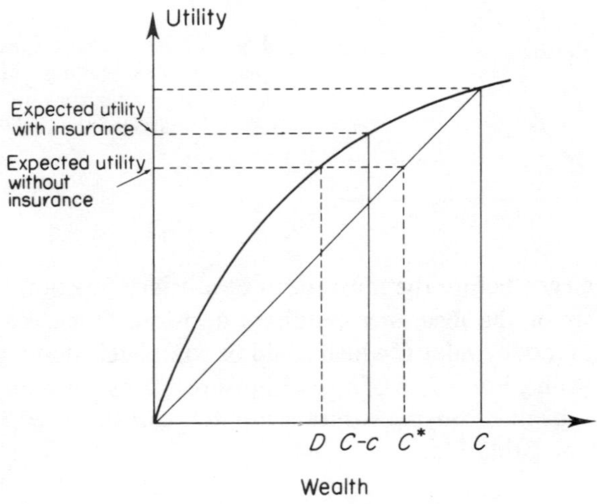

Figure 3.27 A demonstration of the compatibility of the
insurance purchase decision with risk-aversion

If we put $(1 - p)C = C^*$, say, then the order of expected money outcomes along the money axis shows the superiority of the decision not to insure (where the expected outcome is C^*) against the outcome with insurance $C - c$. We claim this ordering of expected money outcomes as a valid reflection of real data. If we measure the outcomes in expected utility terms then the expected utility from insurance, given by $u(C - c)$, is superior to the expected utility of the decision not to insure—given by $pu(0) + (1 - p)u(C)$. The utilities are weighted in the same combination as the money outcomes (i.e. p in the case of 0, $(1 - p)$ in the case of C). The effect of the risk-averse utility function of Figure 3.27 is to reverse the order of merit for the two decisions in going from the expected money to the expected utility measure.

As long as the expected utility for insurance is superior to that for no insurance, the insurance option is optimal. The size of the premium c determines the merit of the insurance decision (for a given p value). From the insurance company's point of view it is important that $C - c < C^*$ if this contract is expected to be profitable. We return to the details of this below. As c increases $C - c$ decreases until a large enough premium would make $C - c$ coincide with point D on the money axis. The reader can easily confirm that at this premium the expected utilities of insurance and no insurance are equal. For premiums in excess of $C - D$ the better decision in expected utility terms is not to insure. For a given likelihood of catastrophe (i.e. value of p) the utility function allows us to calculate the maximum premium which ought to be paid for insurance cover. It is left as an exercise to show that from the announcement of a premium to cover a given risk, the decisionmaker can calculate via his utility function the likelihood of catastrophe for which the premium requested represents an insurance option which ought to be taken.

What of the insurance company's viewpoint? There is empirical evidence in support of a 'company's' utility function—if it exists—exhibiting the same risk-averse property as that of many an individual decisionmaker. In looking at an individual as a potential customer the redress to a client whose assets are destroyed involves a sum from the company which is a relatively small proportion of the company's total wealth, W. The client's assets C are substantial to him but, if the company had to compensate him they would lose a tiny fraction of their wealth, coming nowhere near the ruin which the client would experience if he had no insurance cover.

An analysis of the company's problem of taking on an individual client therefore involves outcomes which are in the close neighbourhood of their substantial total wealth, W. In terms of a graph for their utility function we are looking at levels of wealth far removed from the origin and therefore a good distance along the axis. If this graph is of the risk-averse type then we are likely to be looking at levels of wealth where the marginal increase in utility for increasing wealth levels is relatively small and the graph—locally at least—can be reasonably approximated by a straight line. The degree of curvature of the graph is indicative of the extent to which the decisionmaker is risk-averse. We are not reneging on our previous assumption of risk-aversion on the company's part, merely assuming that it is of a small enough order for the linear approximation to allow the following argument to be sustained (and if necessary enhanced for a non-linear curve).

If the company's present wealth is W, then the decision not to take on a particular client will leave this level unchanged. If a client whose assets are of value C is accepted for a premium of c then there are two exclusive and exhaustive consequences. If no catastrophe befalls the client (and the probability for this is $(1-p)$) the wealth of the company is increased to $W + c$. If the client needs compensation in the event of the destruction of his assets (and this will happen with probability p) the company's wealth is reduced to $W + c - C$ (assuming, as normal, that the company retains the premium). These possibilities are displayed in Figure 3.28 where we have graphed our approximation to the company's utility function over the range of interest.

Again we exaggerate the distance between outcomes in the interests of an uncluttered figure. The expected money outcome from accepting the client as a risk is $(1-p)(W+c) + p(W+c-C) = W + c - pC = W^*$, say, and using real data we would find that this is greater than the expected money outcome from not taking on the client, i.e. $W + c - pC > W$, which implies $pC < c$. This is exactly the observation made in the analysis of the client's decision. From Figure

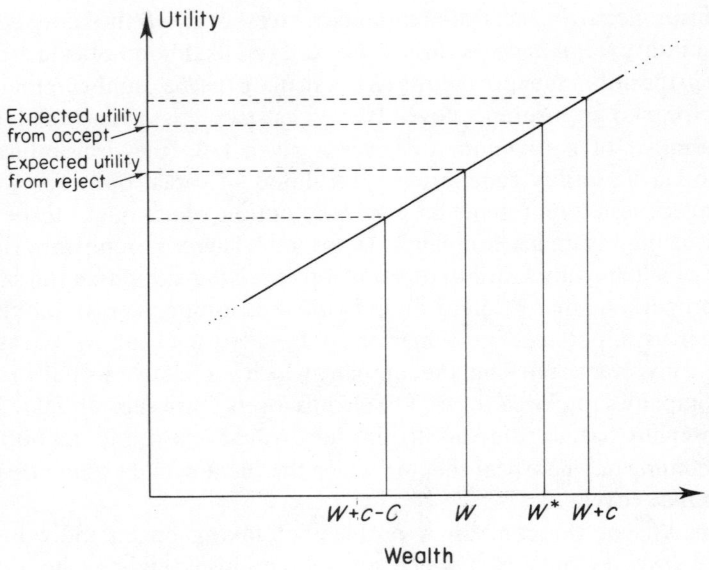

Figure 3.28 The insurance problem from the company's viewpoint

3.28 we note that in terms of expected utility the better option is to accept the client. Here the order of the alternatives is the same under the expected money and expected utility outcomes. Technically the linear approximation makes the company risk-neutral, but a small degree of curvature in an amended version of Figure 3.28 would not change our analysis. In setting the level of premium to offer a potential client the company will consider factors other than the likelihood and magnitude of the outcomes, since it has overheads (in the form of offices and staff) which must be supported out of income from premium.

3.6 Utility Assessment

Procedures for utility measurement parallel in many ways those of personal or subjective probability assessment. References will be found in the Further Reading section to material which goes beyond the unidimensional utility function we have studied to the multidimensional version, which we will touch on in the next section.

We choose to present only one method, based on the problem of Example 1.2. For that problem a given investment decision produced one of two payoffs, depending on the rate of inflation which turns up. The entries of Table 1.4 (which contains only the undominated actions) are profits in millions of dollars, and it is this which we seek to measure in utility terms. In practice it may be sounder to re-cast the problem slightly so that the outcome is not profit but, say, net worth of company, i.e. it reflects assets plus profits from investment. The numbers of Table

1.4 are then seen in a perspective which may otherwise be missing. We retain the original (profits only) entries but remain alert to their hypothetical context.

As in Chapter 2 we cast the process in the form of a dialogue between a decisionmaker (DM) and an analyst (A). Any comments are made in square brackets.

A: In looking at the investment problem where the payoffs are in millions of dollars, let's forget for the moment the actual plans which have been investigated and for which profit levels have been calculated [i.e. the contents of Table 1.2]. The first issue to settle is a range within which the profit from the next year's operation will be.

DM: Well historically we have made profits which at today's prices go from —$3 million up to $8 million. That amount of loss I don't see being repeated, and in fact a net loss is not in prospect for any likely investment. We have eliminated all options which do not yield a profit regardless of the inflation rate.

A: Did any of these have very good as well as very bad payoffs?

DM: No, they are marginal options which we may have considered further if we had had the funds for several investments, but given our limited commitment to only one investment, we produced the set which you have seen. I guess if we think about it we could find a few more.

A: For our purposes all we need is an appropriate range of possible profits. To be useful to you, in either your original or an extended problem, it must contain all possible outcomes.

DM: In that case let's look at anything from break-even [zero profit] up to $9 million.

A: Using these outer limits I'm going to ask you once again to envisage a series of fifty-fifty possibilities. This time I'm looking for a number—a profit in millions of dollars—which you regard as indifferent to a gamble involving two equally likely numbers [profits] which I nominate. As an example, let's look at the limits of your range. Presumably you would prefer a certain profit of $8 million to a situation where you are equally likely to get nothing or $9 million?

DM: Yes.

A: And you presumably would prefer an equally likely chance of nothing and 9 million to a certain profit of, say, half a million?

DM: Definitely.

A: Well what I am looking for is some intermediate number, obviously greater than one-half but less than 8, such that the fifty-fifty gamble with zero and 9 million is as attractive as the certain sum you nominate. I appreciate the difficulties inherent in this, and would only repeat one of the comments I made at the time of the probability assessment—it is not a competition or a trick. We are endeavouring to help you articulate your preferences. Revision and adaptation are allowable and indeed sensible courses of action.

DM: Fine. Well thinking out loud, if I may, we [the company] really need to avoid a very small profit this coming year. Looking ahead we can see the need for substantial internal expenditure which will have to come out of profit. It may be nice to declare substantial dividends and bonuses but the first priority is for this internal expenditure. Your 9 million is very attractive, but that zero is something we really want to avoid. My initial reaction to the figure for a guaranteed profit would be modest, say 2 million.

A: What is your response to the same type of question with equal chances of zero and two million?

DM: That 2 million came from my previous answer? It wasn't a figure you had in mind to ask?

A: Right. I'll be using your responses in my questions.

DM: The feelings I talked of earlier still apply. We dare not end the year with no profit. I would settle for half a million.

A: Now what about the bright end of the scale? The fifty-fifty gamble is with your 2 million and the 9 from the top end of the range.

DM: Anything in this range keeps us out of a crisis, and the more the merrier. I am willing to be quite bold on this one and nominate 5 million.

A: Let's use 5 and look at the two ranges where it is an end point. First the 5 up to 9 million?

DM: Let's say $6\frac{1}{2}$.

A: And the 2 up to 5 million?

DM: Three.

And so it can continue. In Table 3.3 we have summarized the responses received

Table 3.3 A set of responses (certain profits judged indifferent) to a set of gambles (involving two equally likely profits)

Number	Equally-likely chance of two profits below		Certain profit judged indifferent
1	0	9	2
2	0	2	0.5
3	2	9	5
4	5	9	6.5
5	2	5	3
6	0	0.5	0.2
7	0.5	2	1.2
8	0.5	5	2.2
9	0.2	3	1.4
10	0.2	1.2	0.6
11	0.2	6.5	1.8
12	0.5	9	3.5
13	1.2	3	1.9
14	1.2	6.5	3.2
15	3	6.5	5.5
16	0	5	1.5

so far and added possible answers to a further set of questions. The sequence of questions is structured though some variation in order is possible, and will achieve the same end product. We have previously seen how the utility function can be rescaled without prejudice to its faithful representation of preference. Thus, denoting the expected utility of profit level P millions by $u(P)$ we set $u(0) = 0$ and $u(9) = 1$. Our decisionmaker is indifferent between two millions for certain and an equal likelihood of zero and nine millions. From the second property of utility functions we thus have $u(2) = \frac{1}{2}u(0) + \frac{1}{2}u(9) = 0.5$. Every other response listed in the table can be treated in the same way. An expected utility is calculated using previously calculated values. Thus, from number 2 in the table $u(0.5) = \frac{1}{2}u(0) + \frac{1}{2}u(2) = 0.25$, and from number 3 $u(5) = 0.75$. Proceeding in this way we find $u(6.5) = 0.875$, $u(3) = 0.625$, $u(0.2) = 0.125$ and $u(1.2) = 0.375$. From number 8 we have $u(2.2) = \frac{1}{2}u(0.5) + \frac{1}{2}u(5) = 0.5$, but recall that we already have $u(2) = 0.5$. In fact, the sequence of questions is designed to produce just such 'collisions' for some points. There are a total of four responses whose expected utility is 0.5, three each where the expected utility is 0.625 and 0.375, and two each for utility levels 0.25 and 0.75. By further questioning we could produce more utility points then create more collisions, but the set above is rich enough for our demonstration.

Table 3.4 gives the utility information from each response, and the reader is encouraged to confirm those entries not already calculated above. In Figure 3.29 we plot the judgements, and fit a curve through these as best we can. The concave curve is of course a manifestation of risk-aversion on the decisionmaker's part. In fact, the curve is very close to that given by the utility function of Section 3.5, where we took $u(x) = \sqrt{x}/3$ for the sake of generating results which we could use

Table 3.4 Utility calculations based on the responses
of Table 3.3

Number	Certain profit judged indifferent	Utility
1	2	0.5
2	0.5	0.25
3	5	0.75
4	6.5	0.875
5	3	0.625
6	0.2	0.125
7	1.2	0.375
8	2.2	0.5
9	1.4	0.375
10	0.6	0.25
11	1.8	0.5
12	3.5	0.625
13	1.9	0.5
14	3.2	0.625
15	5.5	0.75
16	1.5	0.375

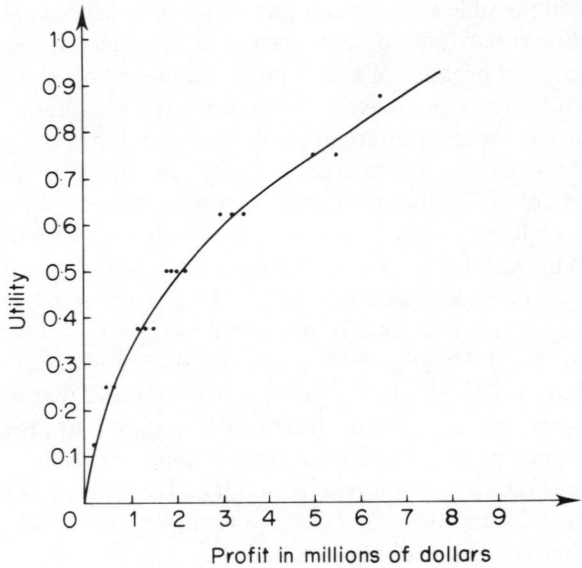

Figure 3.29 A plot of the utility function found by interrogation

in our study. The answers of our decisionmaker, while demonstrating minor variation in the exact profit level to utility assignments, nevertheless do group in a sensible and satisfying manner. If we had a response from the decisionmaker which gave rise to a point not near the curve as we presently have it (e.g. for a profit of five million an imputed utility of 0.5) then the structured sequence of questions, designed as it is to highlight inconsistencies, would make this obvious. In the presence of such a point we could go back to the original responses and examine them for any judgements the decisionmaker may wish to revise. This was not a feature of our example above, though always a possibility. If the 'rogue' points cannot be traced to some *agreed* inconsistency on the decisionmaker's part, and dismissed by a re-judgement of some of the responses, then we are in some difficulty. In this case the utility function could have some unusual property and the variation we are seeing is attributable to that, or the decisionmaker has genuinely represented his preferences and they are not such as to allow the construction of a utility function. For either reason we are not able to pursue with a decision analysis as we will come to understand it.

3.7 Multi-attribute Problems

As we have already noted for Example 1.2, a realistic version of the problem will mean consideration by the investor of more than just the profit levels consequent on a decision being taken and a rate of inflation turning up. There will be consequences (say in a production context) for market share and workforce size, among others. For our single attribute problem we commented on the easy order in which outcomes could often be placed (e.g. preference ranking corresponding to increasing profit) but for multi-attribute outcomes the comparison between outcomes is less straightforward. Some decisions may result in all consequences being bettered for all states by some other dominating options, but for non-trivial problems we will always be left with a set of actions where no dominance exists between pairs of that set. Let us restrict our discussion to the problem where the outcome is a pair of values, one for profit level and the other for market share. The pertinent points can be made using this simplest possible extension to our single-attribute problem. One approach to the problem is to attempt the construction of a utility function which essentially amalgamates the utility functions appropriate to each component attribute. The process of amalgamation is determined by the nature of the trade-offs between attributes. Thus, if we construct a utility function for profit and another for market share, a function which attempts to measure the merit of an outcome expressed as a profit level, market share pair can be arrived at in a number of different ways. The method (if any) by which constituent utility functions can be amalgamated to produce a single measure for the two-attribute problem depends on the trade-off judgements which the decisionmaker is willing to make. This statement can be put into a formal setting, as in (but distinct from) our description of the assumptions, but we evade this option. To make progress in constructing the multi-attribute utility function judgements *across* the attributes rather than *between* levels of an attribute are necessary. Thus, we need preferences or, more usefully, indifference between pairs of outcomes which are themselves two-dimensional vectors.

As a result of this process the decisionmaker may display a relationship between the attributes which gives constant trade-off rates, e.g. for an extra 1 % of market share a fall in profits of $0.1 million is worthwhile, regardless of the level of market share and profit. Alternatively, the trade-off may be dependent on the levels of attributes. For example, the trade-off of the previous sentence may only apply when market share is currently 10 % and profits 3 millions, or it may apply for a situation where market share is 10 % and any profit level. This degree of dependence (or independence) is reflected in the structure of the multi-attribute utility function.

3.8 Further Reading

In Edwards and Tversky (1967) the article by Savage (which is an excerpt from his book Savage, (1954)) gives not only an account of the early ventures into the analyses of perceived worth or utility, but some references to the subsequent history of that concept and its transformations, mainly at the hands of economists. This intermediate history is irrelevant to our needs, since the problems being addressed were not concerned with decisionmaking under uncertainty as we understand it. It is unfortunate that 'utility' should have been used to represent a variety of quite distinct concepts since at least several of the criticisms of modern utility theory are really an attack on the older meaning of the word. The modern version of utility theory, characterized by its axiomatic approach, owes much to the pioneering work of Savage (1954) and von Neumann and Morgenstern (1947), through the earliest influential twentieth-century writings are those of Ramsey (1926). These references are cited out of a sense of completeness, and the non-mathematical reader will find some of our later references more approachable.

A variety of axiomatic treatments are possible (some in conjunction with subjective probability). In Savage, and more recently in White (1976), some relationships between the developments are to be found. More approachable and very readable (but with an unobtrusive sophistication) is Luce and Raiffa (1957). Their development of the assumptions for utility is the model for our Section 3.3. Lindley (1971) is again persuasive, but Raiffa (1968) offers a more extended discussion and examples of the construction of a utility function.

Hull, Moore and Thomas (1973) offer an accessible discussion on measurement, while Johnson (1977) investigates the 'technology' of the procedures for assessment and gives an extensive set of references. Keeney and Raiffa (1976) provide a full development for multi-attribute problems with applications, while Bell, Keeney and Raiffa (1977) is a collection of papers representative of theory and applications. Edwards (1977) is concerned with the use of measurements for social decisionmaking.

Exercises for Chapter 3

As far as subsequent material is concerned, the reader should be able to calculate expectations, mainly in the form of expected money, but occasionally using expected utility. The early exercises below are designed to allow some practice at these procedures. Some of the exercises demand the use of the calculus for their solution—a prerequisite we have avoided in the text. Such exercises are starred (*), and those students equipped with the very minimal calculus needed are encouraged to attempt these questions. Students unfamiliar with exponential (e) and logarithmic (log) functions can avoid questions or parts of questions without prejudice to their understanding of forthcoming chapters.

3.1   For each of the four gambles calculate the expected money outcome and thus find that option which maximizes net expected profit per play.

gamble 1:   prizes of \$10, \$4 and \$2 with probabilities 1/4, 1/2 and 1/4, respectively; entry fee \$1.

gamble 2:   prizes of \$12 and \$2 with equal likelihood; entry fee \$2.

gamble 3:   prizes of \$10, \$5 and \$0 with equal likelihood; no entry fee.

gamble 4:   prizes of \$20, \$5 and—\$8 with probabilities 1/2, 1/4 and 1/4, respectively; entry fee \$5.

3.2   Consider the problem facing a man whose possessions (valued at \$10 000) are susceptible to accidental destruction. For a fee of f dollars he is guaranteed against any loss, and he reckons the probability of an accident to be 0.1. If the man evaluated his options in terms of the expected money criterion would he opt for insurance when the fee was \$1200? If the man had a utility function $u(x) = \sqrt{x}$ for \$x, would he opt for insurance if he evaluated his options in terms of expected utility?

What is the maximum amount the man would pay for insurance if he used the expected utility criterion?

3.3 A firm is offered a contract to develop an electronics subsystem for a new aeroplane. If the system is developed within two years the profit will be \$500 000, but if development takes longer a loss of \$2.5 million will be made. The Research and Development department of the firm assess the probability of development within two years as 0.9.

(i) If the firm has a linear utility for money ought it to take the contract, or not?

(ii) If the utility is given by $u(x) = x - 0.1x^2 + 100$ (where x is the firm's assets in millions of dollars) what will the decision be, assuming the current assets are \$3 million?

(iii) In what way is the utility function of part (ii) unusual?

3.4 A company whose assets are \$2 million must decide whether or not to enter into a research and development project whose outcome is uncertain. If the project succeeds this will increase the assets by \$1 million, but if it fails the assets are reduced to \$500 000. Find the minimal probability of project success which would lead the company to enter into the project given that the criterion used to evaluate options is

(i) expected money outcome;

(ii) expected utility with utility functions $u(x)$ as follows where x is in millions of dollars:

(a) $u(x) = \sqrt{x}$,
(b) $u(x) = x - 0.1x^2$,
(c) $u(x) = 1 - e^{-x}$,
(d) $u(x) = 1 - (\frac{1}{2})^x$.

Which of these functions is consistent with risk-aversion? Which is bounded over all non-negative x?

3.5 In insuring possessions valued at \$1000 against accidental loss (an event with a probability of 0.1) the insurance company asks for a fee of \$150. For each of the utility functions $u(x)$ given below (where x is in thousands of dollars) calculate if the insurance option is acceptable or not:

(i) $u(x) = 1 - e^{-x}$,
(ii) $u(x) = 1 - (\frac{1}{2})^x$,
(iii) $u(x) = \sqrt{x}$,
(iv) $u(x) = x - 0.1x^2$.

If the insurance company were to ask for a fee of f dollars, find for each of the utility functions above the maximum acceptable value for f.

3.6 A decisionmaker's utility function for his capital is given by $\log_{10}x$, where x is in dollars. His total capital is \$50 000 of which \$30 000 is represented by his house. What is the maximum premium that he would pay to insure his house if the probability of accident which would completely destroy the house is 0.01?

*3.7   A marketing executive is to be asked his assessment of the chance for future success of a product. In order to encourage him to state his true belief, p, the scoring rule below has been devised. If he says the chance of the product being successful is r he will receive:
   (a) 1000 $(1 - (1 - r)^2)$ dollars if the product is successful;
   (b) 1000 $(1 - r^2)$ dollars if the product is unsuccessful.
Show that if the manager is guided solely by his desires for money in this experiment and if his utility for money is linear, then he is encouraged to state his true belief (i.e. $r = p$) by this rule.

   Suppose, however, his utility for money is quadratic, i.e. $u(x) = x^2$, where x is in thousands of dollars. Show that in this case the scoring rule encourages a biased result, unless $p = 0$, $1/2$ or 1.

*3.8   For the same problem outline as Exercise 3.7 with a true belief of p and a stated belief of r, let the rewards be:
   (a) 1000 $\log_e r$ dollars if the product is successful;
   (b) 1000 $\log_e (1 - r)$ dollars if the product is unsuccessful.
Show that, if the manager's utility for money is linear, then he will always tell the truth (i.e. $r = p$).

   However if his utility for money is
$$u(x) = 1 - e^{-x},$$
where x is in thousands of dollars, and his probability p for success is $1/5$, show that he will state $r = 1/3$.

Chapter 4

Criteria for Decision

4.1 Introduction

The previous two chapters have explored the measurement problems associated with uncertainty and outcome evaluation and, with the proviso that the decisionmaker agrees with the assumptions (and can behave accordingly), we have argued for a criterion which nominates as optimal that action which maximizes expected utility (for a given decision problem). Critics of this approach point to both the problem of the acceptability of the assumptions and the characteristics of observed behaviour which contradict the goal of maximizing expected utility. In the previous chapter we attempted to meet criticisms of the assumptions. We noted the success of the utility approach in explaining observed behaviour in the case of the insurance purchase problem, and remind the reader that our concern in decision analysis is with the normative, rather than the behavioural, aspects of the problem. We are interested in (ideally) offering a prescription for optimal choice in a decision problem, not necessarily explaining observed behaviour. Given that the decisionmaker can police his preferences (and beliefs, if appropriate) in line with our assumptions then (inescapably) his optimal choice is governed by the pursuit of maximum expected utility. Inevitably a number of alternative schemes have been proposed, and it is to two of these that we now turn. Both schemes operate on only the table of outcomes (for example, Table 1.2) and are designed to assume no further information about the states of nature.

In neither case does the criterion proposed have the integrity of the maximizing expected utility rule. As prescriptions for action they are *not* the consequences of behaviour in accordance with a set of assumptions, though the measures associated with the criteria do agree with some of the assumptions of Chapter 3. We have three reasons for their inclusion. First, the description of each criterion has an air of plausibility, and matches in some ways the rationale adduced in particular decision problems. Our second reason for the inclusion rests on the use of geometric presentations during our study. This geometry re-emerges in our work on decision analysis proper and, although we could proceed through our entire analysis without recourse to graphical illustration, a number of points are particularly well suited to presentation or reinforcement in such a context. Thirdly, we wish to encourage the reader to some controlled speculation about the structure of decision problems. Although we feel the expected utility criterion to be the most satisfactory mechanism for decision analysis—and some authorities would say the *only* mechanism—it is desirable that the reader consider alternatives before being in turn convinced of our conclusions.

In preparation for the sections to follow we introduce some notation. A decision problem has an associated set of states of nature Θ and a set of actions A. For our problems these sets are both finite. The decisionmaker must choose an action $a \in A$ in the face of an unknown $\theta \in \Theta$, and the consequence of a choice of a when the true (underlying) state of nature is θ is an outcome $O(\theta, a)$. Thus, in Example 1.1 $\Theta = \{\text{Good buy, Bad buy}\}$, $A = \{\text{Keep, Exchange}\}$ and the $O(\theta, a)$ are the entries of Table 1.1. For Example 1.2 we have $\Theta = \{\text{High inflation, Low inflation}\}$ $A = \{a_1, a_2, a_3, a_4, a_5\}$ and the $O(\theta, a)$ are the entries of Table 1.2.

An action $a \in A$ is said to be *dominated* by an action $a' \in A$ if the outcome for a' is at least as good as the outcome for a for all $\theta \in \Theta$. In particular, if the outcomes are rewards then a' dominates a if $O(\theta, a') \geqslant O(\theta, a)$ for all $\theta \in \Theta$. In the case of outcomes which measure loss the inequality is obviously reversed.

If, in addition, there is a state of nature for which the outcome for a' is strictly better than the outcome for a $(O(\theta, a') > O(\theta, a)$ in the case of rewards) then a' *strictly dominates a*. An action a is *admissible* if it is not strictly dominated by any other action. An action which is not admissible is *inadmissible*.

Thus, for the investment Example 1.2, where the outcomes are as Table 1.2, a_4 strictly dominates both a_2 and a_5, making a_1, a_4 and a_3 admissible, while a_2 and a_5 are inadmissible.

4.2 The Criterion of Wald

Associated with the American statistician A. Wald is a criterion akin to that implicit in part of our remarks on Examples 1.1 and 1.2. Here each action is seen in terms of its worst outcome, so that in Example 1.1 the exchange decision could lead to a cost $1600, while the decision to keep the present car has a worst (indeed an actual) outcome of $1400. This criterion proposes that we chose an action to give us the best of these worst outcomes, so that the option to keep is optimal.

In Example 1.2 the worst outcome is that of lower profit (rather than higher loss as in Example 1.1) so that the worst outcomes for a_1 to a_5 are $1.5, $2, $2, $3, and $3 million, respectively. In looking over these actions a_4 and a_5 both yield a guarantee of at least $3 million profit, and these would be actions chosen by the Wald criterion. Had we eliminated inadmissible actions before this calculation—and this seems sensible—the Wald criterion would pick a_4 as optimal.

For a problem where the outcomes $O(\theta, a)$ are rewards (or profit) we are calculating $\min_{\theta \in \Theta} O(\theta, a)$ for each action a and then finding $\max_{a \in A} (\min_{\theta \in \Theta} O(\theta, a))$. The maximizing action(s) is optimal. Such an action is referred to as a *maximin* action.

Where the outcomes are losses the worst consequence for each action is $\max_{\theta \in \Theta} O(\theta, a)$ and the best of the worst is given by $\min_{a \in A} (\max_{\theta \in \Theta} O(\theta, a))$, i.e. that action for which the maximum is a minimum. Such an action is referred to as a *minimax* action.

Nowhere do we use information about the states of nature. Our criterion is pessimistic, since it is evaluating actions in terms of the worst consequences that can flow from them. In the case of a problem where the outcomes are rewards it finds that action with the greatest *guaranteed* payoff, while for a problem where the outcomes are losses, it finds that action for which *inevitable* losses are smallest.

Our definition and the illustrations so far have been on a table of outcomes. Given that we have a utility structure (i.e. a utility function can be constructed) the argument and definition can be (perhaps more properly) applied to that table. Thus, if we use the utility function of Section 5, Chapter 3, where $u(x) = \sqrt{x}/3$ and x is in millions of dollars, Table 4.1 gives the utility of outcomes derived from Table 1.2.

Table 4.1 Utilities for the investment problem

	a_1	a_2	a_3	a_4	a_5
θ_1	0.41	0.47	0.75	0.58	0.58
θ_2	0.82	0.58	0.47	0.75	0.62

If we denote the entries of the table by $U(\theta, a)$ as distinct from the $O(\theta, a)$ of Table 1.2, then Figure 4.1 displays the actions in a plot where the axes measure $U(\theta_1, a)$ and $U(\theta_2, a)$.

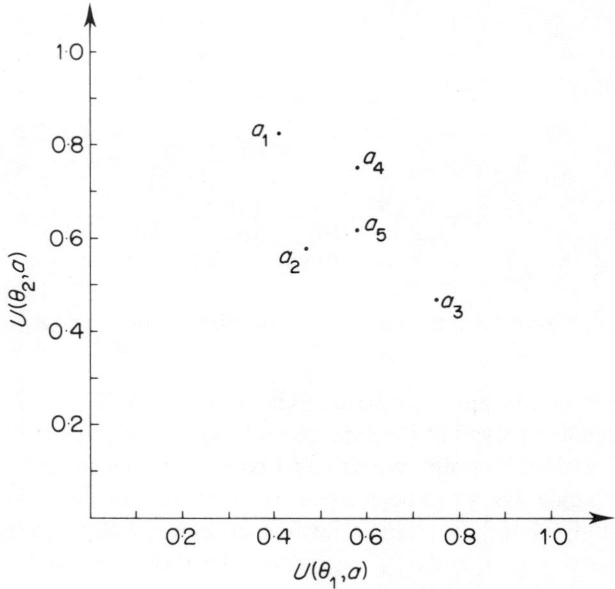

Figure 4.1 A plot of the data of Table 4.1

Consider another 'action' defined as a mixture of existing actions a_4 and a_3. Using a coin whose probability of heads is q, we make a single toss of the coin and take action a_4 if the result is a head and action a_3 if the result is a tail. If we write

$U(\theta_1, a_6)$ and $U(\theta_2, a_6)$ for the expected utilities of a_6 under states of nature θ_1 and θ_2 respectively then

$$U(\theta_1,a_6) = qU(\theta_1,a_4) + (1-q)U(\theta_1,a_3) = 0.58q + 0.75(1-q) = 0.75 - 0.17q,$$
$$U(\theta_2,a_6) = qU(\theta_2,a_4) + (1-q)U(\theta_2,a_3) = 0.75q + 0.47(1-q) = 0.47 + 0.28q.$$

If we use a fair coin ($q = 1/2$) then $U(\theta_1, a_6) = 0.67$ and $U(\theta_2, a_6) = 0.61$, while for $q = 3/4$, say, $U(\theta_1, a_6) = 0.62$ and $U(\theta_2, a_6) = 0.68$.

In Figure 4.2 these points are added to those of Figure 4.1. As q ranges between zero and one, the point corresponding to the expected outcome for a_6 will 'sweep out' the line joining a_4 and a_3. These end points correspond to the extreme cases of $q = 1$ and $q = 0$, respectively.

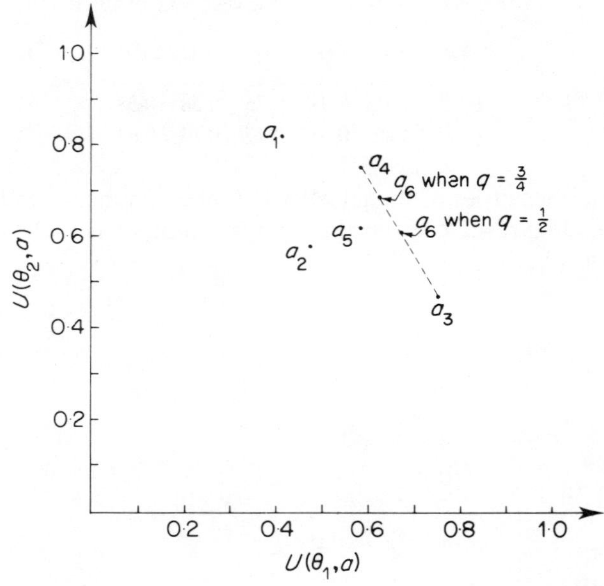

Figure 4.2 Expected utilities for mixtures of a_3 and a_4

If we extend the concept of a mixture to incorporate three 'pure' actions, say a_1, a_4 and a_3, then an analysis of the expected utilities for this mixture under θ_1 and θ_2 would show that the point in Figure 4.1 corresponding to such a mixture lies within the triangle whose verticies are a_1, a_4 and a_3. Consideration of all such mixtures would 'fill out' the triangle, i.e. to every point within the triangle can be found a mixture of a_1, a_4 and a_3 whose expected utilities are just the co-ordinates of that point (see Figure 4.3).

Extending the mixture concept even further to include all five actions (though we could exclude a_5) will give actions whose expected utilities are the co-ordinates of points within the region (quadrilateral) bounded by a_1, a_2, a_3 and a_4. Every mixture generates a point of the quadrilateral, but we note that some points of the region can be generated in several ways (see Figure 4.4).

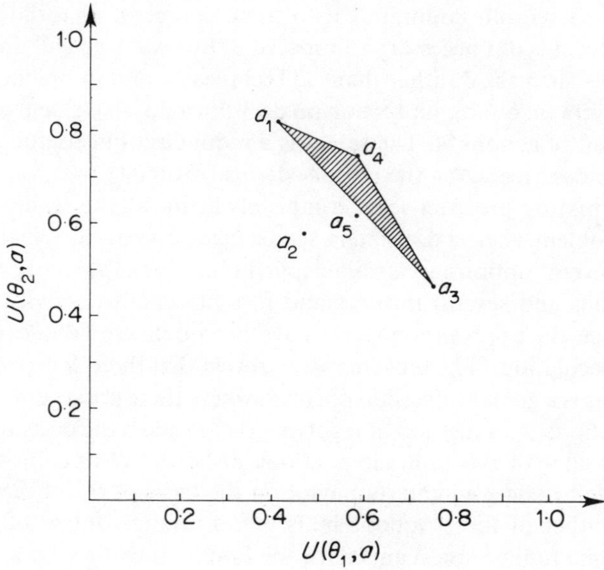

Figure 4.3 Expected utilities for mixtures of a_1, a_3 and a_4

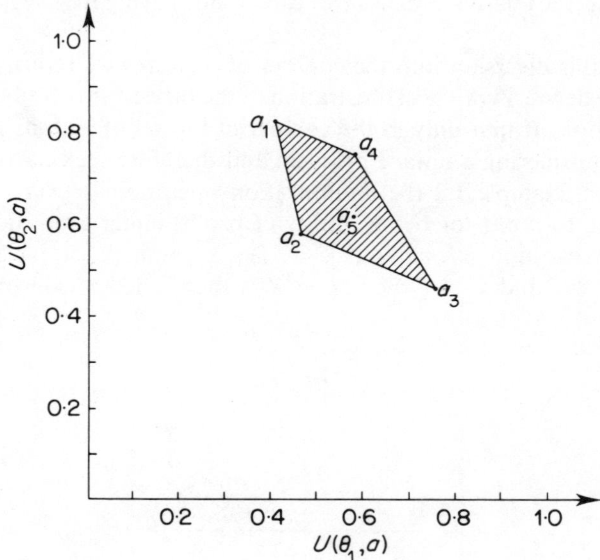

Figure 4.4 Expected utilities for mixtures of all five actions

By extending the mixture definition to include enough pure actions (here four is enough) we can construct the (quadrilateral) region, which we will call $\mathscr{A}$, out of our original set of actions A. Creations such as this, forming what is known as the *convex hull* of a set of points, have important applications in a variety of areas of mathematics. Given our commitment to some degree of pictorial presentation (and remember it is not necessary to proceed in this way) we will find it easier to work with sets such as $\mathscr{A}$ rather than A. Technically, and in practice, we always produce answers (in our major section on decision analysis) which are in terms of the original set of actions A. The set $\mathscr{A}$ is a redundant but useful construction. Some writers describe $\mathscr{A}$ as the *risk set* derived from A.

Least the mixture prospect seem completely artificial, the reader is invited to consider a problem where a decision has to be made on how to spend an evening's relaxation. Several options are available, including perhaps a concert, an opera, several cinemas and several theatres and it is possible to construct a table of outcomes once the appropriate states have been defined. (We leave this as an exercise in speculation.) The table may well reveal that there is no uniformly best option, i.e. this is a genuine decision problem where there are several (at least two) admissible actions. As a method of resolving the problem the decisionmaker may well, when faced with two admissible actions, decide to toss a coin. Alternatively, he may decide to select an entertainment on the basis of the cheapest available tickets. For either of these options he is relinquishing control of the decision process to some random mechanism. In the first he is using a coin, with known properties or properties which can be easily discovered. For the second he is committing himself to a random action where he may not know the details of the mechanism, i.e. the relative likelihood of each venue having the cheapest available tickets.

Following this diversion into the concept of mixtures we return to the Wald criterion, and derive a graphical illustration of the process involved in finding the optimal solution, at first only in the context of the set of actions A.

If we are considering a reward problem and therefore seek maximin actions, recall that for Example 1.2 the minimization operation is over two numbers corresponding to profit (or better, utility of profit) under each state of nature. Consider the two-dimensional set $X = \{(x_1, x_2): \min(x_1, x_2) \geq c\}$. Since we must have $x_1 \geq c$ and $x_2 \geq c$ the region X is the shaded region of Figure 4.5.

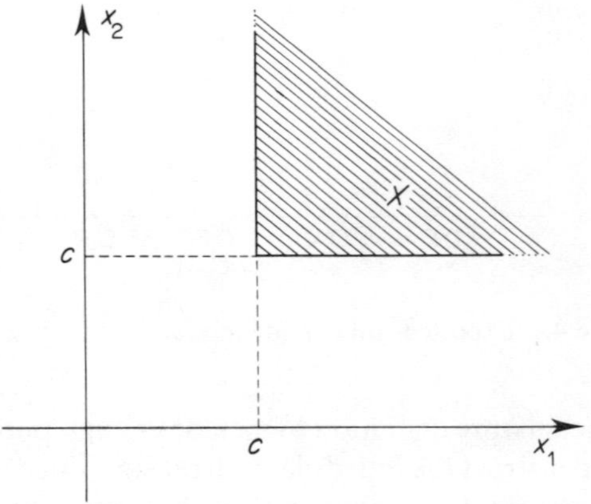

Figure 4.5 The set $X = \{(x_1, x_2): \min(x_1, x_2) \geq c\}$

The set $X^* = \{(x_1, x_2): \min(x_1, x_2) = c\}$ is then just the two sides of the region X, as in Figure 4.6.

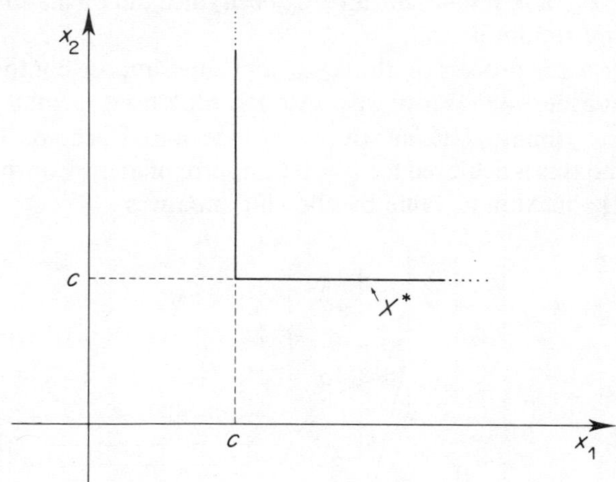

Figure 4.6 The set $X^* = \{(x_1, x_2): \min(x_1, x_2) = c\}$

Turning now to the use of this observation in the Wald criterion, we have $U(\theta_1, a)$ instead of x_1 and $U(\theta_2, a)$ instead of x_2. The first operation, for each a, is minimization over θ, i.e. choosing $\min\{U(\theta_1, a), U(\theta_2, a)\}$ (instead of $\min(x_1, x_2)$). In Figure 4.7 we have superimposed contour values for this minimum over the set of outcomes corresponding to A.

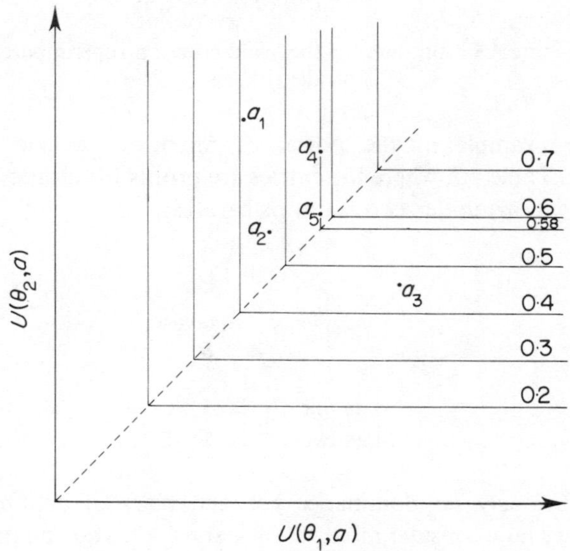

Figure 4.7 Contours for the Wald criterion superimposed
on the data of Table 4.1

Since we are seeking the maximum (over the set A) of this minimum value it is obviously found by the contour of largest value passing through a member of A. In this case it is a_4, or a_5 if it has not already been ruled out on inadmissibility. The value for the maximum is 0.58.

If we use the same process on the set $\mathscr{A}$ and superimpose contours on Figure 4.4 we arrive at Figure 4.8. Where we previously took $\max_{a \in A} (\min_{\theta \in \Theta} U(\theta, a))$ we now take $\max_{a \in \mathscr{A}} (\min_{\theta \in \Theta} U(\theta, a))$, i.e. we include mixed actions. The maximum value is 0.64 and this is achieved for $q = 0.62$ approximately. For this example we can enhance the maximum value by allowing mixtures.

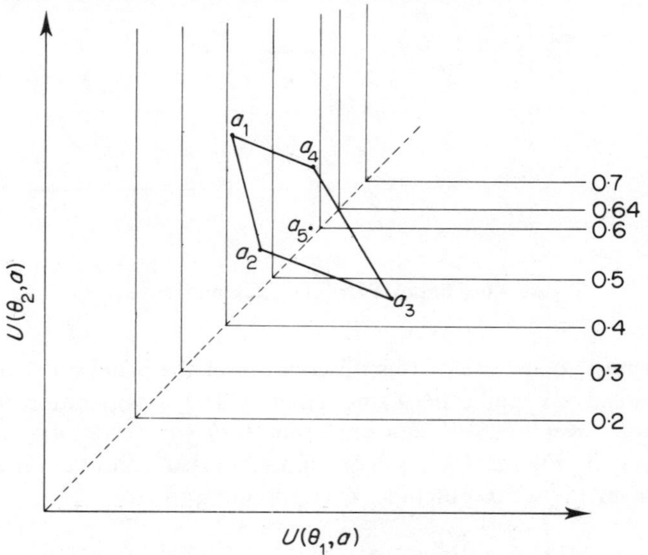

Figure 4.8 Contours for the Wald criterion superimposed on the risk set

As another example of the power of mixtures, consider the problem summarized in Table 4.2, where the entries are profits (or utilities of profits) for each of three actions under two states of nature.

Table 4.2

| | Action | | |
	A	B	C
State one	2	3	6
State two	4	2	1

There is obviously no dominance between pairs of actions and all are admissible. If we now consider mixtures of A and C then any mixture of A and C will have an expected profit which maps it into a point of the line AC, the exact point depending on the likelihood of A (or C). In Figure 4.9 the action B is now dominated by any mixed action whose expected profit corresponds to a point on the line *DE*.

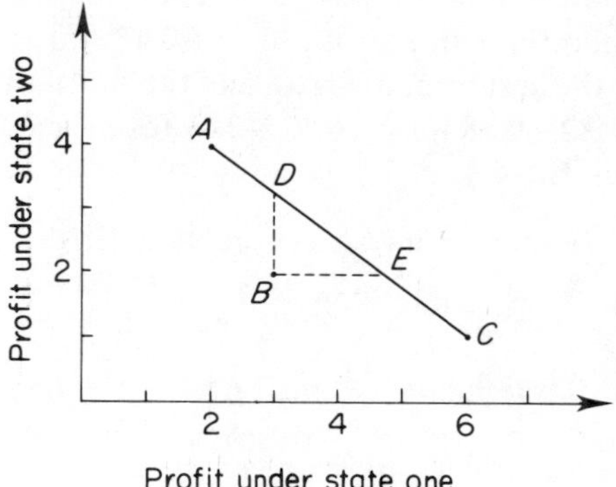

Figure 4.9 *B* is dominated by any mixture
'between' *D* and *E*

Here *B*, which was previously a maximin action (along with *A*) and, more importantly, was previously admissible, is now inadmissible! Remember that the coin toss (or equivalent) which is used in the mixture will produce a result which dictates that either action *A* or action *C* is taken. We are not analysing a problem which poses the choice of *A*, *B* or *C* a number of times, where in the case of 1000 repetitions of the problem we could take action *A* say 500 times and action *C* 500 times. As a result of the randomization we are to take either *A* or *C*, neither of which we individually prefer to *B*, and yet the Wald criterion imputes a greater value to the mixture than to the best actions chosen from the pure actions.

At least part of the motivation for the development of a criterion of this kind is the desire to avoid measurement problems associated with the states of nature. The process of utility assignment is willingly embraced but the construction of probabilities for states avoided, or in extreme cases, the possibility of such construction denied. There can be few problems for which no information on the states is available, either through research or introspection. Given this information exists, does it not make sense to exploit rather than ignore it?

4.3 The Criterion of Savage

Associated with the name of Savage is a criterion which operates rather like the minimax version of Wald's criterion. The data for this operation is not the raw data of a table of outcomes but a table processed from this original information.

The outcome from a pair of state (θ) and action (a) is no longer perceived as, say a profit $O(\theta, a)$ million dollars, or yielding a utility $U(\theta, a)$ (if this is the measure). Rather, the evaluation of the state–action pair is in terms of the shortfall from the best outcome which could have been achieved had the true state been known. Thus, for the investment problem where we are considering the utility outcomes of Table 4.1, a knowledge that the inflation rate is to be high (θ_1) determines an optimal response in the action a_3. Any other action in the face of a high rate of inflation yields a profit inferior to that of a_3. Thus, the shortfall for action a_1 is $0.75 - 0.41 = 0.34$, and for action a_2 it is $0.75 - 0.47 = 0.28$, etc. In the face of a low rate of inflation the best response is a_1, and the shortfall for the other actions is easily found e.g. $0.82 - 0.58$ for a_2, $0.82 - 0.47$ for a_3, etc. Table 4.3 gives these *regrets* derived from Table 4.1.

Table 4.3 Regrets for the investment problem, derived from Table 4.1

		a_1	a_2	a_3	a_4	a_5
Inflation	High (θ_1)	0.34	0.28	0	0.17	0.17
rate	Low (θ_2)	0	0.24	0.35	0.07	0.20

For a given state of nature (row) we find that outcome which is the best under these conditions. Thus, for a problem where the outcomes are rewards or profits (or are in utility terms) we find for a given θ, $\max_{a \in A} U(\theta, a)$ or $\max_{a \in A} O(\theta, a)$. With this quantity the regret for a state–action pair $R(\theta, a)$ is then given by $R(\theta, a) = (\max_{a \in A} U(\theta, a)) - U(\theta, a)$ or $R(\theta, a) = (\max_{a \in A} O(\theta, a)) - O(\theta, a)$. If the problem is one where we have a table of losses the best outcome under a given state of nature θ is that of minimum loss, i.e. $\min_{a \in A} O(\theta, a)$. Any other loss is in excess of this value and the regret is thus given by $R(\theta, a) = O(\theta, a) - \min_{a \in A} O(\theta, a)$. In both cases regret is a non-negative quantity. For any row (state of nature) in a regret table there is at least one zero entry, corresponding to the action(s) which is the optimal response for that state of nature. Other entries correspond to inferior actions which yield positive regret. Since regret is undesirable, actions which lead to it in undue quantities are to be avoided. The mechanism of this method is to apply the same rules to regret as Wald would for an outcome table of losses, i.e. we minimize the maximum regret (as opposed to minimizing the maximum loss). Thus, for each action a we calculate $\max_{\theta \in \Theta} R(\theta, a)$, which gives the worst consequence (measured in regret) following a choice of a. The optimal action is that which minimizes this worst consequence, i.e. $\min_{a \in A} (\max_{\theta \in \Theta} R(\theta, a))$. Thus, from Table 4.3 we have

action:	a_1	a_2	a_3	a_4	a_5
$\max_{\theta} R(\theta, a)$:	0.34	0.28	0.35	0.17	0.20

and $\min_a \max_\theta R(\theta, a)$ is found by taking action a_4, giving the minimax regret a value of 0.17.

If we parallel the construct of Figure 4.7, but recall that we are now using a minimax rule rather than a maximin one, then we can easily display contours of equal maximum regret for a two-dimensional problem as in Figure 4.10. We have also plotted the regret for the five actions from Table 4.3.

Since we seek $\min_a \max_\theta R(\theta, a)$, then that action of A which lies on the contour of smallest maximum regret is that chosen by the Savage criterion—in this case obviously a_4. If, as in Section 4.2, we allow mixtures of pure actions, then regret

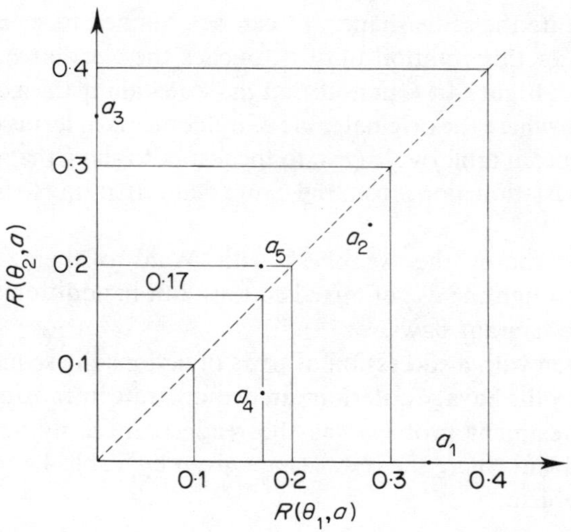

Figure 4.10 A plot of the data of Table 4.3 with
contours of the Savage function

for these mixed actions can be calculated. In fact, mixtures of the points of A in
Figure 4.10 will yield the set $\mathscr{A}^*$ in Figure 4.11.

If we seek $\min_{a \in A^*}(\max_\theta R(\theta, a))$ then this takes a value of approximately 0.132
at a mixture of a_3 and a_4 (in fact the mixture is the same as that which maximized
the minimum expected utility in section 4.2). Minimax regret has been lessened by
the use of mixtures. Examination of $\mathscr{A}^*$ in Figure 4.11 and $\mathscr{A}$ in Figure 4.4 will

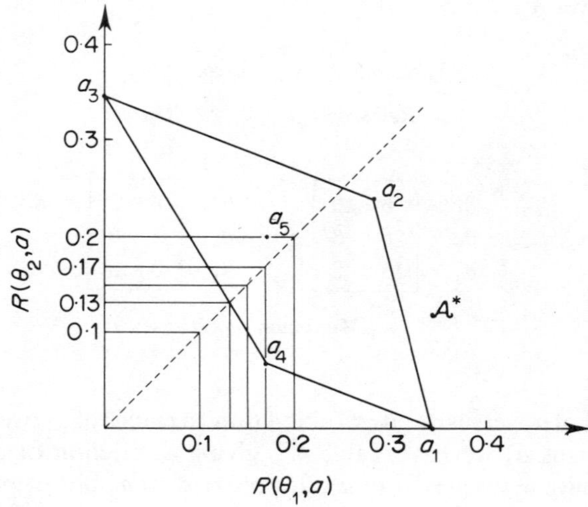

Figure 4.11 Contours of the Savage function together
with mixtures of the actions

show that these are the same shape. $\mathscr{A}^*$ can be obtained from $\mathscr{A}$ by a rotation. The translation of this rotation until it touches the axes (at a_1 and a_3) yields Figure 4.11 out of Figure 4.4 (but note that the scales along the axes are different).

For a problem where the original table of outcomes is in terms of losses (rather than a utility or profit table) we leave it to the reader to show that the regret figure is derived by translation alone from the figure demonstrating losses (see Exercise 4.6).

Thus, Savage shares the weakness with Wald of being susceptible to improvement through the use of mixed actions, but in addition to this there are two rather more flagrant flaws.

When presented with a succession of pairs of actions the sequence of optimal actions chosen by the Savage criterion can demonstrate intransitivity. This is not true for the investment problem (as the reader can easily verify). Consider, though, the problem where the rewards are given by Table 4.4 for a three-state, three-action problem.

Table 4.4 On this problem Savage is intransitive

| | | Action | | |
		a_1	a_2	a_3
	θ_1	6	10	7
State	θ_2	6	8	10
	θ_3	13	8	10

If we use Savage to solve the problem of a_1 versus a_2, then we have, as in Table 4.5, the table of rewards extracted from Table 4.4 giving the regret table and a choice of a_1 over a_2.

Table 4.5 a_1 is preferred to a_2

| | Rewards | | | Regrets | |
	a_1	a_2		a_1	a_2
θ_1	6	10	θ_1	4	0
θ_2	6	8	θ_2	2	0
θ_3	13	8	θ_3	0	5

Maximum regret 4 5

Comparison of a_2 versus a_3 gives Table 4.6 and a choice of a_2 over a_3. Finally, if we take a_1 versus a_3 we have Table 4.7, giving a selection of a_3 over a_1. In summary we have a_1 preferred to a_2, a_2 preferred to a_3 but a_3 preferred to a_1.

To illustrate the second major flaw, consider again the investment problem of Table 1.2, but with the addition of a new pure action, say a_6, which has a profit of \$8 million under a high inflation rate and one million dollars under a low rate.

Table 4.6 a_2 is preferred to a_3

	Rewards a_2	a_3		Regrets a_2	a_3
θ_1	10	7	θ_1	0	3
θ_2	8	10	θ_2	2	0
θ_3	8	10	θ_3	2	0

Maximum regret   2   3

Table 4.7 a_3 is preferred to a_1

	Rewards a_1	a_3		Regrets a_1	a_3
θ_1	6	7	θ_1	1	0
θ_2	6	10	θ_2	4	0
θ_3	13	10	θ_3	0	3

Maximum regret   4   3

This addition creates no new dominance relationships in the table. Converting this into utility terms we obtain Table 4.8, which is just Table 4.1 with the additional a_6 column. If we calculate the regret from this table of utilities we obtain Table 4.9, where the maximum regret for each action is also shown.

Table 4.8 The investment problem with an additional action

	a_1	a_2	a_3	a_4	a_5	a_6
θ_1	0.41	0.47	0.75	0.58	0.58	0.94
θ_2	0.82	0.58	0.47	0.75	0.62	0.33

Table 4.9 Regrets derived from the utilities of Table 4.8

	a_1	a_2	a_3	a_4	a_5	a_6
θ_1	0.53	0.47	0.19	0.36	0.36	0
θ_2	0	0.24	0.35	0.07	0.20	0.49

Maximum regret   0.53   0.47   0.35   0.36   0.36   0.49

The action giving the minimum of the maximum regrets is now a_3. By the addition of an action which is not itself chosen as optimal we have changed the optimal action from a_4 to a_3! This is a most unfortunate property. It complicates the problem of deciding on the relevant alternatives for inclusion in the problem since the choice of optimal action can be influenced by actions which are themselves not candidates for optimality.

4.4 The Expected Utility Criterion

As a slight diversion we have explored two criteria which operate on the table of outcomes (or table of utilities of outcomes) associated with a decision problem. Despite the superficial plausibility of the criteria they have characteristics which we cannot readily allow in our decision process, and they do not appear again in the remainder of this study. Instead, our attention returns to the use of the expected utility criterion, and in this section we examine and solve a first version of the investor's problem.

We have already seen in Section 3.5 of Chapter 3 the nature of the calculation of expected utility for the actions of the investment problem. If we have a probability p for the high inflation rate and therefore $(1-p)$ for the low rate, we have, using Table 4.1:

$$\begin{aligned}
EU(a_1) &= 0.41p + 0.82(1-p) = 0.82 - 0.41p, \\
EU(a_2) &= 0.47p + 0.58(1-p) = 0.58 - 0.11p, \\
EU(a_3) &= 0.75p + 0.47(1-p) = 0.47 + 0.28p, \\
EU(a_4) &= 0.58p + 0.75(1-p) = 0.75 - 0.17p, \\
EU(a_5) &= 0.58p + 0.62(1-p) = 0.62 - 0.04p,
\end{aligned}$$

We choose that action which maximizes expected utility and therefore $\max_{a \in A} \{EU(a)\}$. We have already seen in Chapter 3 how the maximum is given by different actions, dependent on the value for p, and we illustrate in Figure 4.12 a graph of each of the functions $EU(a)$ for $a \in A$. Each expected utility is a linear function of p, which is of course restricted to the range zero up to one.

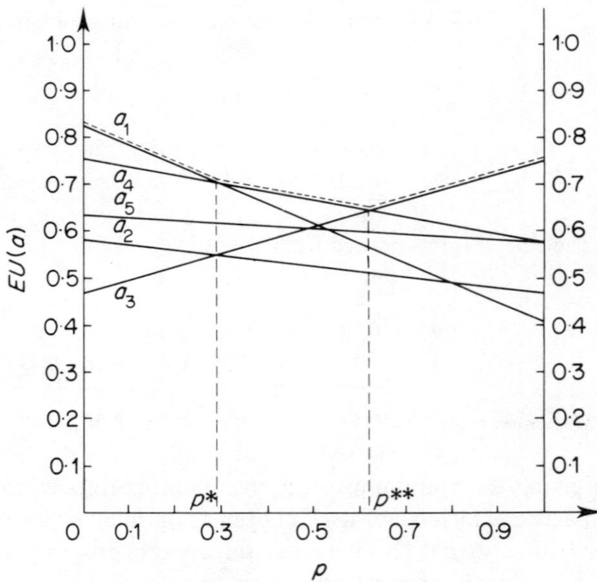

Figure 4.12 Expected utilities of the five actions plotted as linear functions of p over the range $0 \leqslant p \leqslant 1$

Since we choose a to maximize the expected utility, the maximum is given by a_1 for $0 \leqslant p \leqslant p^*$, by action a_4 for $p^* \leqslant p \leqslant p^{**}$ and by a_3 for p in the range $p^{**} \leqslant p \leqslant 1$. We can find p^* by solving $EU(a_1) = EU(a_4)$ giving $p^* = 7/24 = 0.29$, and similarly p^{**} is found by solving $EU(a_4) = EU(a_3)$ to give $p^{**} = 28/45 = 0.62$. The optimal action is given by either a_1 or a_3 or a_4 but never by a_2 or a_5. Recall that these actions are inadmissible (both being dominated by a_4). The value of the maximum expected utility as a function of p is given by the broken line in Figure 4.12.

If we plot lines of the form $pU(\theta_1, a) + (1-p)U(\theta_2, a) = c$, then as c varies these parallel lines, whose slope is determined by p, join points of equal expected utility (see Figure 4.13).

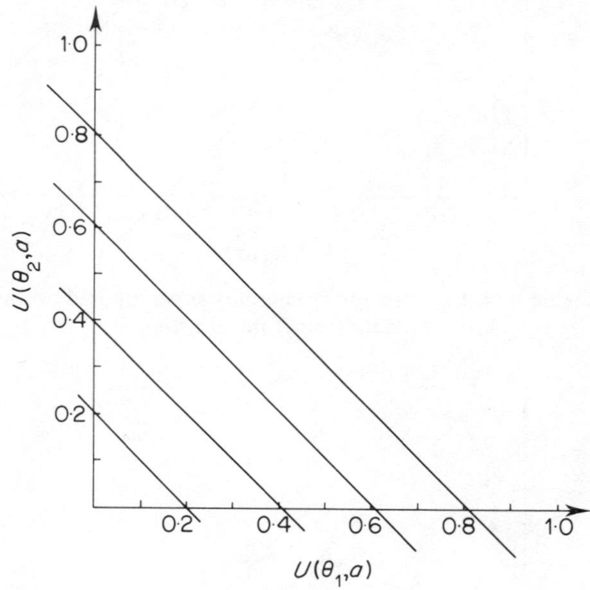

Figure 4.13 Contours of equal expected utility

If we superimpose these contours onto Figure 4.1 then we have Figure 4.14, where for this p value a_4 is obviously the optimum action.

If we form the set $\mathscr{A}$ which corresponds to the expected utilities of all mixtures of actions of A, and again superimpose the contours of equal expected utility (as in Figure 4.15) we see that the maximum expected utility is still given by a_4. No improvement has taken place due to the introduction of mixtures. We have $\max_{a \in \mathscr{A}}(EU(a)) = \max_{a \in A}(EU(a))$.

Readers familiar with linear programming will recognize that we are maximizing a linear function over a convex polyhedron and an optimal solution will always be found at an extreme point, which here corresponds to a pure action.

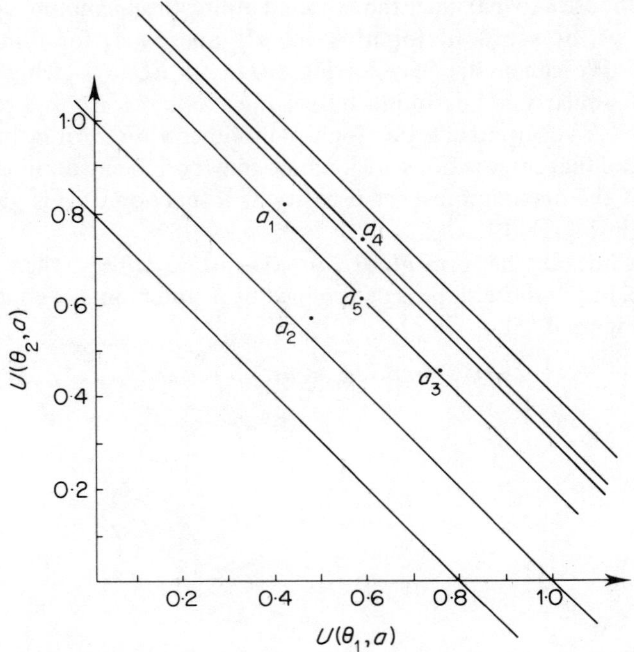

Figure 4.14 Expected utility contours superimposed on the
data from Table 4.1

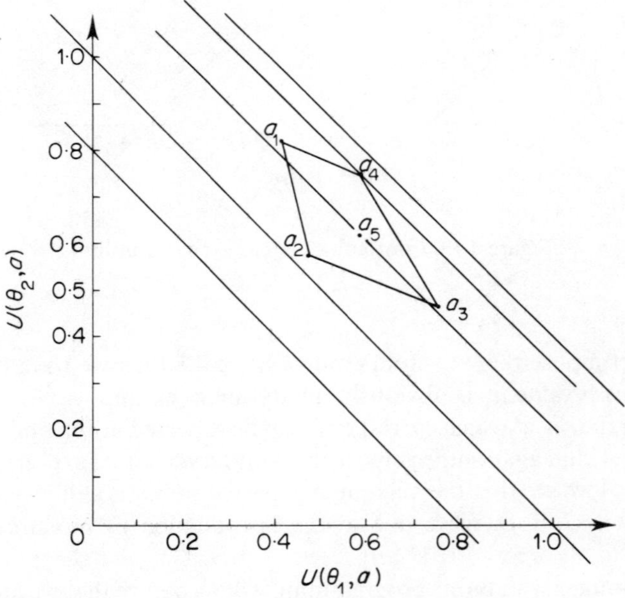

Figure 4.15 Expected utility contours superimposed on
the risk set

In fact, this property for Example 1.2 can be seen in the context of the graphical representation of Figure 4.12. If we consider only two actions, say a_4 and a_3, and define an action a^* which is a mixture of these where a_4 is taken with probability q and a_3 with probability $(1-q)$, then $U(\theta_1, a^*) = qU(\theta_1, a_4) + (1-q)U(\theta_1, a_3)$ and $U(\theta_2, a^*) = qU(\theta_2, a_4) + (1-q)U(\theta_2, a_3)$. We have

$$
\begin{aligned}
EU(a^*) &= pU(\theta_1, a^*) + (1-p)U(\theta_2, a^*) \\
&= pqU(\theta_1, a_4) + p(1-q)U(\theta_1, a_3) + (1-p)qU(\theta_2, a_4) \\
&\quad + (1-p)(1-q)U(\theta_2, a_3) \\
&= q\{pU(\theta_1, a_4) + (1-p)U(\theta_2, a_4)\} + (1-q)\{pU(\theta_1, a_3) \\
&\quad + (1-p)U(\theta_2, a_3)\} \\
&= qEU(a_4) + (1-q)EU(a_3).
\end{aligned}
$$

Consider Figure 4.16 where we have graphed $EU(a_4)$ and $EU(a_3)$ as functions of p over its allowable range. For any value of q, $EU(a^*)$ is a weighted sum of the $EU(a_4)$ and $EU(a_3)$, and over the range of p will have an expected utility given by the dotted line of Figure 4.16 (which has been drawn for a q value of $1/3$). Over the entire range of p either $EU(a_4)$ is greater than $EU(a^*)$ or $EU(a_3)$ is greater than $EU(a^*)$. These occur in the ranges $0 \leqslant p \leqslant 0.62$ and $0.62 \leqslant p \leqslant 1$, respectively. The mixture is therefore never superior to the better of the expected utilities of its pure components. Only when $EU(a_4) = EU(a_3)$ does a^* rank as an alternative optimum.

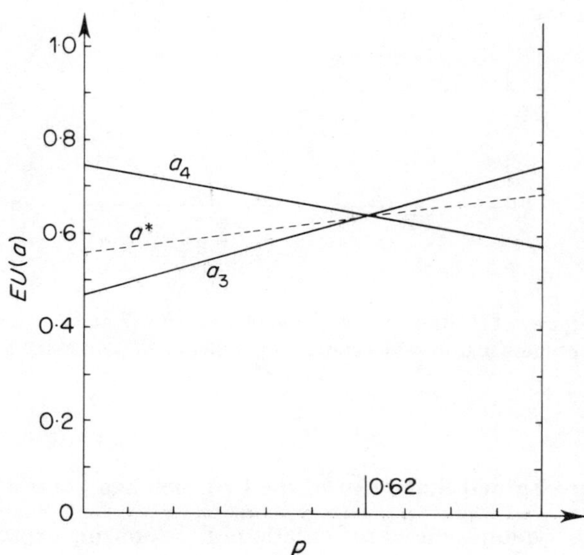

Figure 4.16 Expected utility of a^*, which is a mixture of a_3 and a_4

The variation in optimum action as a function of p (as demonstrated in Figure 4.12) can be seen again in an amended version of Figure 4.15, given as Figure 4.17. For an expected utility contour set parallel to AB the maximum expected utility is obviously attained at a_1. In fact, for any contour which is oriented between the horizontal (corresponding to $p = 0$) and the face of $\mathscr{A}$ joining a_1 and a_4 (which gives a p value of 0.29) a_1 is the action giving maximum expected utility. If the contour is parallel to the a_1, a_4 face then obviously a_1, a_4 and all mixtures of a_1 and a_4 lie on the same contour and thus these actions all give the maximum expected utility over $\mathscr{A}$. As p increases beyond 0.29, providing contours parallel to say CD, then a_4 is the action maximizing expected utility. This will be the unique optimum until p has increased enough to give contours parallel to the a_4, a_3 face. This happens for a p value of 0.62. At this unique value a_4, a_3 and all mixtures of a_4 and a_3 give the maximum expected utility. For values of p in the range of $0.62 \leqslant p \leqslant 1$ the contours will be oriented to make a_3 the unique optimum action.

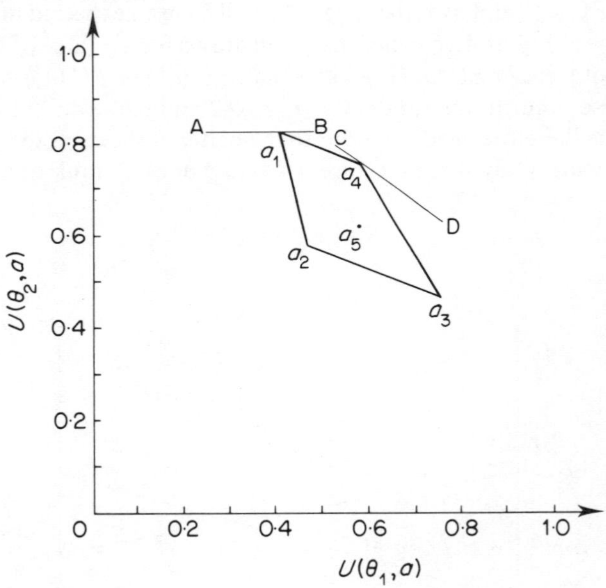

Figure 4.17 Utility contours parallel to AB will make a_1 the optimum action, while contours parallel to CD will make a_4 optimal

4.5 A More Formal Statement of the Criterion and Some Properties

In the previous section we used the criterion of maximizing expected utility to solve the simple version of the investor's problem and demonstrated some properties of this solution process. Our purpose now is to summarize in an algebraic form the process and properties we have just seen.

Consider a decision problem where we have a set of actions $A = \{a_1, \ldots, a_n\}$ one of which must be chosen in the face of an unknown state of nature, and this state will be one of the set $\Theta = \{\theta_1, \ldots, \theta_m\}$. We have a set of outcomes assessed in terms of the utility $U(\theta, a)$ for $\theta \in \Theta$ and $a \in A$. If we have a probability description for Θ, where $g(\theta_i)$ is the probability of θ_i, then obviously $g(\theta_i) \geqslant 0$ and $\sum_{i=1}^{m} g(\theta_i) = 1$. For any action $a \in A$ the expected utility of a is given by $EU(a)$, where $EU(a) = \sum_{i=1}^{m} g(\theta_i)U(\theta_i, a)$ for all $a \in A$. We thus seek the $\max_{a \in A}(EU(a))$.

The probability description $g(\theta)$ is usually known as a *prior distribution* for the state of nature. If the prior distribution is such that $g(\theta_i) > 0$ for $i = 1, \ldots, m$ then the action which maximizes the expected utility must be admissible. To prove this, assume the contrary, i.e. there exists an inadmissible action a^* which maximizes the expected utility for a prior distribution $g(\theta)$. Since a^* is inadmissible there is an action $a \in A$ such that $U(\theta_i, a) \geqslant U(\theta_i, a^*)$ for $i = 1, \ldots, m$ and $U(\theta_i, a) > U(\theta_i, a^*)$ for at least one θ_i. Then

$$EU(a) = \sum_{i=1}^{m} g(\theta_i)U(\theta_i, a) > \sum_{i=1}^{m} g(\theta_i)U(\theta_i, a^*) = EU(a^*),$$

which contradicts the optimality of a^*. Thus, for prior distributions satisfying the restriction, the optimal action is admissible.

To demonstrate the necessity of the condition on the prior distribution consider Figure 4.18. Here a_4 is inadmissible (since it is strictly dominated by a_3) but for expected utility contours which are vertical the actions a_3, a_4 and all the mixtures of them have maximum expected utility over the set shown. This contour set corresponds to $g(\theta_1) = 1$ and $g(\theta_2) = 0$.

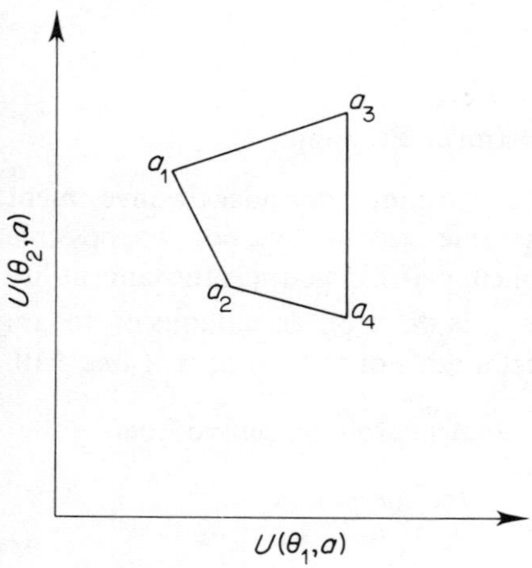

Figure 4.18 Action a_4 is strictly dominated by a_3 but has the same expected utility as a_3 when the contours are parallel to the $a_3 - a_4$ face

A mixture a^* of actions of A is specified completely by the probability q_j for taking action a_j, $j = 1, \ldots, n$, (where $\sum_{j=1}^{n} q_j = 1$). Now

$$U(\theta_i, a^*) = \sum_{j=1}^{n} q_j U(\theta_i, a_j)$$

and

$$EU(a^*) = \sum_{i=1}^{m} g(\theta_i)U(\theta_i, a^*)$$

so that

$$EU(a^*) = \sum_{i=1}^{m} g(\theta_i)\left(\sum_{j=1}^{n} q_j U(\theta_i, a_j) \right)$$

$$= \sum_{j=1}^{n} q_j\left(\sum_{i=1}^{m} g(\theta_i)U(\theta_i, a_j) \right)$$

$$= \sum_{j=1}^{n} q_j EU(a_j) \leqslant \sum_{j=1}^{n} q_j\left(\max_{a \in A} EU(a) \right)$$

$$= \max_{a} EU(a)\left(\sum_{j=1}^{n} q_j \right) = \max_{a \in A} EU(a).$$

The inequality follows since for the given prior distribution there is some optimizing action given by $\max_a EU(a)$ and this quantity is obviously greater than or equal to the expected utility for every component action a of A. This maximum is not dependent on j and can therefore be placed before the summation. We thus have that the expected utility for any mixture of A is never greater than that of the best 'pure' action (for that prior probability). In other words, a maximum expected utility can always be found from a pure action. We have seen how for some prior probability distributions mixtures can be as good as their constituent pure actions, but they are never better.

4.6 The Refined Investment Problem

To illustrate the method in a more complicated example consider the investment problem displayed in Table 2.1. For this example there are five, not two, possible values for the state of nature and five investment plans. If we apply the same utility function as before, i.e. $u(x) = \sqrt{x}/3$, where x is the profit in millions of dollars (given in Table 2.1), we can easily construct a table of utilities as in Table 4.10.

Table 4.10 Utilities for the refined investment problem, derived from Table 2.1

		Investment plan				
		a_1	a_2	a_3	a_4	a_5
	> 20%	0.47	0.33	0.75	0.53	0.58
	14–20%	0.58	0.47	0.67	0.53	0.47
Inflation rate	12–13%	0.58	0.33	0.58	0.67	0.67
	7–11%	0.47	0.75	0.33	0.58	0.58
	< 7%	0.47	0.82	0.33	0.47	0.33

We will solve this problem for the subjective prior probabilities given by our decisionmaker in the interrogation of Section 2.8. The reader can easily check that the appropriate priors are (approximately in some cases) $p(>20\%) = 0.1250$, $p(14\text{–}20\%) = 0.3125$, $p(12\text{–}13\%) = 0.1875$, $p(7\text{–}11\%) = 0.2917$ and $p(<7\%) = 0.0833$. Thus, we have $EU(a_1) = 0.1250 \times 0.47 + 0.3125 \times 0.58 + 0.1875 \times 0.58 + 0.2917 \times 0.47 + 0.0833 \times 0.47 = 0.5250$, and similarly $EU(a_2) = 0.5371$, $EU(a_3) = 0.5356$, $EU(a_4) = 0.5658$ and $EU(a_5) = 0.5417$. The action offering maximum expected utility is thus a_4. Having gone beyond two states of nature we no longer have an easy presentation of the sensitivity of the optimal solution to variation in the prior probabilities. We can, of course, find for any prior distribution the optimal action, but there is no neat visual summary of the information.

4.7 Further Reading

Our main interest in this chapter has been the further study of expectation. The two criteria of Wald and Savage are of interest since they are formal versions of rationale which are sometimes proposed as mechanisms for decision. The common ground with the expected utility criterion, in the graphical material, helps reinforce some of the underlying geometry. White (1976) takes a fairly formal look at the Wald and Savage regret criteria, as well as a number of other proposals which we have chosen to neglect.

Most of the references given at the end of Chapter 3 deal with expectation as a measure. Further references on decision analysis and its uses are given at the end of Chapter 5.

Exercises for Chapter 4

These exercises provide an opportunity for the reader to practise the application of the Wald and Savage criteria, but more importantly to understand the use of the expectation operator (normally, expected money). Particular attention should be paid to problems where the sensitivity of solutions with respect to prior probabilities is explored. This geometry re-emerges in Chapter 5.

4.1   Consider the four-action, five-state decision problem where the entries of the table are rewards.

		Action			
		a_1	a_2	a_3	a_4
	θ_1	2	1	-1	1
	θ_2	2	1	4	3
State	θ_3	0	1	1	0
	θ_4	1	1	0	0
	θ_5	0	1	2	0

Find the optimal action with respect to the Wald and Savage criteria.

4.2   For the problem with the following reward outcomes find the action which a decisionmaker would take using (i) the Wald criterion and (ii) the Savage criterion.

		Action			
		a_1	a_2	a_3	a_4
	θ_1	0	9	3	5
State	θ_2	10	0	1	2
	θ_3	5	1	1	0
	θ_4	5	0	10	5

Find also the maximum fee worth paying under each criterion to learn true state of nature with certainty. (*Hint*: Construct a new action which consists of paying fee f, and then taking best response to the state announced.)

4.3   For the following reward table determine as a function of x the optimal action under (i) the Wald criterion and (ii) the Savage criterion.

		Action			
		a_1	a_2	a_3	a_4
	θ_1	x	2	3	6
State	θ_2	3	2	2	6
	θ_3	4	2	1	1
	θ_4	6	4	9	3

4.4   For the following table of losses find the preferred actions under (i) the Wald criterion and (ii) the Savage criterion.

		Action		
		a_1	a_2	a_3
	θ_1	0	2	4
State	θ_2	1	2	1
	θ_3	2	2	3
	θ_4	3	2	2

4.5   For the four-action, four-state problem below, where the entries of the table are losses, find the actions selected by (i) the Wald criterion and (ii) the Savage criterion.

		Action			
		a_1	a_2	a_3	a_4
	θ_1	2	1	0	1
State	θ_2	2	1	4	3
	θ_3	0	1	0	0
	θ_4	1	1	0	0

Find also the maximum fee worth paying under each criterion to learn the true state with certainty.

4.6   By using a numerical illustration involving two states of nature (or otherwise) show that for a problem where the outcomes are losses the set of points generated by the regret calculation (including mixtures) is just a translation of the risk set for the problem and the translation is such that (at least) one pure action lies on each regret axis (cf. Figure 4.11).

4.7   Consider the decision problem where we have two states of nature and five actions with rewards (in millions of dollars) given by the table.

		Action				
		a_1	a_2	a_3	a_4	a_5
State	θ_1	10	6	7	5	8
	θ_2	5	7.5	6	7	7

Are any of these actions inadmissible? Using the expected money criterion find the optimal solution as a function of p, the probability for state θ_1.

Suppose our decisionmaker has a utility function $u(x) = \sqrt{(x-3)/4}$, where x is in millions of dollars. Using the expected utility criterion find the optimal solution as a function of the (prior) probability for state θ_1.

4.8   Consider the problem of an oil company which is faced with a decision on the scale of development to undertake on a newly discovered oil field. When making the development decision the size of the field is unknown, although it is known to be either small, medium or large. The table gives the net profit in billions of dollars for each of two development strategies and all three field sizes.

		Plan	
		a_1	a_2
	Small	10	10
Field	Medium	12	10
size	Large	16	20

If the prior probabilities on the field size are $p(\text{Small}) = 1/4$, $p(\text{Medium}) = 1/2$ and $p(\text{Large}) = 1/4$, which is the better option under the expected money criterion?

4.9   A farmer is concerned to minimize his crop losses over the growing season and reckons that he will use one of five plans in his operation of the farm. The actual loss made is dependent on the plan undertaken and the rainfall during a critical phase of the year. The table below gives losses in thousands of kilograms for each combination of plan and rainfall category. Note that our model considers only two categories for the state of nature, i.e. a rainfall quantity described as Dry and one described as Wet.

<table>
<tr><td></td><td></td><td colspan="5">Plan</td></tr>
<tr><td></td><td></td><td>a_1</td><td>a_2</td><td>a_3</td><td>a_4</td><td>a_5</td></tr>
<tr><td>Rainfall</td><td>Dry</td><td>1</td><td>1.5</td><td>3</td><td>2</td><td>3</td></tr>
<tr><td>category</td><td>Wet</td><td>5</td><td>3</td><td>2</td><td>3</td><td>3</td></tr>
</table>

Plot this data in a manner which shows the relationship between these (pure) plans and construct from that representation the outcomes associated with all mixtures of actions (i.e. the risk set). Which actions are admissible? If we have a probability for category Dry of p (and hence a probability $(1 - p)$ for Wet) use a second geometric representation to find as a function of p the plan(s) which minimize expected crop loss. Relate the solutions found by the two methods.

If the farmer has a utility function for crop losses given by $u(x) = 1 - x^2/36$, where x is in thousands of kilograms, find (as a function of p) the plan(s) which maximize expected utility. This utility function decreases as x increases, unlike our earlier examples. Why should that be so?

Chapter 5

Decision Problems with Information

5.1 Introduction

In the later sections of the previous chapter we solved two versions of the investment problem using the criterion of expected utility maximization. For a given prior distribution on the states of nature—here the inflation rate—we can find the optimal action. The construction of the probabilities for these inflation rates could leave the decisionmaker less than fully confident and the investor may well seek extra information about the prospects from, say, a consultant. Two features which we must recognize in the use of information are its cost and its imperfections. Any forecast which the consultant may make will be for a fee (perhaps to cover the costs which he incurs in the research for the forecast) and will be subject to error. His prediction alone is not a guarantee that the forecast rate of inflation will turn up.

Again in the car exchange problem of Example 1.1 we may have 'objective' information about the relative numbers of good and bad buys which the garage sells, and by examining the car, perhaps taking a test drive, arrive at some conclusion as to its true condition. At some cost an independent test can be made, say a measurement of the oil consumption. Data will exist on the association between oil consumption and the underlying true condition of the car, and will be such as not to identify the true state with certainty. Thus, good buys may tend to exhibit low oil consumption rather than medium or high results, but a test result of high consumption does not preclude the car from being a good buy. The buyer may be faced with a range of tests of different complexity, reliability and cost and he then faces the problem of deciding how much information to buy, bearing in mind the costs and likely benefits.

The purchase of information may be a one-off or single-stage operation, i.e. the decisionmaker decides to buy and act on the extra information or he calculates that it is not cost-effective and chooses his course of action on his prior information. Alternatively, the information purchase decision may be multi-stage. Here the decisionmaker, having purchased some information may, as a result of this extra information, decide to purchase yet more information (postponing a choice of action until the outcome of this information purchase) or he may be 'convinced enough' by the current information to elect for a course of action.

The extra information about the state of nature is often referred to as an *observation*, or the outcome of an *experiment*. If we commission a test or experiment there will be a set of possible outcomes. We denote this set by Z and a member of it by z or z_i, as appropriate. The relationship between observation and underlying state of nature is usually expressed in the form of a conditional probability, e.g. if $Z = \{z_1, z_2, z_3\}$ and $\Theta = \{\theta_1, \theta_2\}$ then we would have a set of conditional probabilities $p(z_j|\theta_i)$ for $j = 1, 2, 3$ and $i = 1, 2$. For Example 1.1 we could have z_1 corresponding to high oil consumption, z_2 to medium oil consumption and z_3 to low oil consumption. We must of course have $p(z_j|\theta_i) \geqslant 0$ and $\sum_j p(z_j|\theta_i) = 1$ for each i.

In Section 5.2 we solve the investment problem for the case where additional information is available in the form of a consultant's forecast. The solution mechanism essentially considers all possible strategies and evaluates the strategies in terms of their expected utility. From this enumeration and evaluation the optimal strategy can be found. This process can be illustrated via diagrams akin to those of Section 4.4 of Chapter 4, and the relevance of the extra information clearly seen.

For problems of even a modest size the enumeration procedure is inefficient, and in Section 5.3 we start on an alternative but equivalent solution process. This involves the direct use of prior and purchased information to produce, on amalgamation, an updated description of the likelihoods for the states of nature. The appropriate method for amalgamation is investigated and its use in the alternative solution procedure described. We re-solve the investment problem using this new method.

In Section 5.4 we return to the car exchange problem and reinforce the ideas of the previous section by its solution. The problem provides the initial setting in Section 5.5 for our investigation of the value of information. Returning to the investment problem we again look at the value of information, though here the numerical manipulation (but not the underlying idea) is complicated by virtue of the use of the utility function. The final section is concerned with the problem of multiple observations.

5.2 The Investment Problem and The Use of Forecasts

Consider again the simple version of the investor's problem where he must choose one of five actions in the face of an uncertain forthcoming rate of inflation, which may be either high (θ_1) or low (θ_2). The decisionmaker has some prior probabilities for these states, say $g(\theta_1) = p$, and hence $g(\theta_2) = 1 - p$. Using the services of a consultant he can acquire a forecast for the forthcoming rate. The consultant will give either a prediction of a high rate of inflation (denote this by z_1) or a prediction of a low rate of inflation (denote this by z_2). The prediction can, of course, be in error. We use conditional probabilities $p(z_j|\theta_i)$, for $i = 1, 2$ and $j = 1, 2$, to describe the relevant data. Given that the true forthcoming rate is high, suppose the consultant correctly predicts this 80 % of the time, and thus gives the wrong prediction 20 % of the time. Again for a forthcoming low rate suppose he correctly predicts this 60% of the time, and thus incorrectly gives a prediction of a high rate 40% of the time. We summarize this information in Table 5.1 where the entries of the table are $p(z_j|\theta_i)$.

	z_1	z_2
θ_1	0.8	0.2
θ_2	0.4	0.6

Table 5.1 Conditional probabilities of prediction given forthcoming inflation rate

Our description of these conditional probabilities has been in terms of a loosely worded historical frequency (percentage). It is not necessary that the information on the experiment be of this type, and it could equally well come from a 'logical' or subjective source.

Although we initially have a five-action problem, any optimal solution to the problem will involve only admissible actions, as we later demonstrate. The investor's problem is therefore reduced to the choice from the admissible actions $(a_1, a_3$ and $a_4)$.

If the consultant is to be hired and his advice used, the investor must decide what action to take following a given forecast. Since the consultant will only be hired if he can improve the investor's performance, the analysis of how to use the prediction must be a component of the process of appraising the forecaster's usefulness. The investor therefore must decide which action to take, given each prediction. We have two possible predictions (z_1 or z_2) and three admissible actions. The total number of distinct responses to the possible forecasts is therefore $3 \times 3 = 9$. The investor's possible responses can best be summarized in a *decision rule* or *strategy* which gives for each prediction an action to be taken, i.e. a function, say d, from Z to A. As an example of such a function we could have $d(z_1) = a_3, d(z_2) = a_1$, which means that in the event of a forecast of high inflation the investor takes action a_3, while for a forecast of low inflation he takes action a_1. Table 5.2 describes all nine strategies for this problem (numbered d_1 to d_9). Thus, $d_6(z_1) = a_3$ and $d_6(z_2) = a_4$. Let D be the set of all such strategies.

Table 5.2 The nine strategies for the investment problem

		Strategy								
d		d_1	d_2	d_3	d_4	d_5	d_6	d_7	d_8	d_9
Forecast	z_1	a_1	a_1	a_1	a_3	a_3	a_3	a_4	a_4	a_4
	z_2	a_1	a_3	a_4	a_3	a_1	a_4	a_1	a_3	a_4

For a given strategy and state of nature we can find the probabilities that each of the admissible actions will be taken. Thus, for d_1, we always take a_1 regardless of the observation, so that for θ_1 and θ_2 the *action probability* of a_1 is 1, and for a_3 and a_4 is zero. Consider strategy d_6. Here we take a_3 if z_1 is the forecast, and a_4 if z_2 is the forecast. Consulting Table 5.1 we see that for a state of nature θ_1 we have a probability of z_1 (and hence of a_3) of 0.8, while for z_2 (and thus a_4) the probability is 0.2. For the alternative state of nature θ_2 we have a probability of z_1

(and hence for a_3) of 0.4, while for z_2 (and hence a_4) the probability is 0.6. We can summarize these action probabilities for strategy d_6 thus:

$$d_6$$

	a_1	a_3	a_4
θ_1	0	0.8	0.2
θ_2	0	0.4	0.6

This construction can be repeated for all strategies giving the action probabilities of Table 5.3.

Table 5.3   The action probabilities for the nine strategies

	d_1			d_2			d_3			d_4			d_5			d_6			d_7			d_8			d_9		
	a_1	a_3	a_4	a_1	a_3	a_4	a_1	a_3	a_4	a_1	a_3	a_4	a_1	a_3	a_4	a_1	a_3	a_4	a_1	a_3	a_4	a_1	a_3	a_4	a_1	a_3	a_4
θ_1	1	0	0	0.8	0.2	0	0.8	0	0.2	0	1	0	0.2	0.8	0	0	0.8	0.2	0.2	0	0.8	0	0.2	0.8	0	0	1
θ_2	1	0	0	0.4	0.6	0	0.4	0	0.6	0	1	0	0.6	0.4	0	0	0.4	0.6	0.6	0	0.4	0	0.6	0.4	0	0	1

Recall that the table of utilities for outcomes is

	a_1	a_3	a_4
θ_1	0.41	0.75	0.58
θ_2	0.82	0.47	0.75

Consider strategy d_6. If the state of nature is θ_1, then following d_6 the investor takes a_3 with probability 0.8 (involving outcome utility 0.75) and a_4 with probability 0.2 (obtaining utility 0.58). Thus, the expected outcome from using d_6 under state of nature θ_1, which we denote by $U(\theta_1, d_6)$, is given by $0.8 \times 0.75 + 0.2 \times 0.58 = 0.72$. Similarly $U(\theta_2, d_6) = 0.4 \times 0.47 + 0.6 \times 0.75 = 0.64$.

In general we write $U(\theta, d)$ for the expected utility outcome using strategy (or decision rule) d when the state of nature is θ. Table 5.4 gives the expected utilities for all nine strategies under each state of nature. In general we are using $U(\theta,d)=\sum_j U(\theta,d(z_j))p(z_j|\theta)$ (where here $j = 1,2$). Given prior probabilities of p and $(1-p)$ for θ_1 and θ_2, respectively, we can find for any decision rule d its expected utility, denoted by $EU(d)$. Thus, $EU(d) = pU(\theta_1, d) + (1-p)U(\theta_2, d)$. As an example, $EU(d_6) = p \times 0.72 + (1-p) \times 0.64 = 0.64 + 0.08p$. All our strategies have expected utilities which are linear functions of p (compare with

Table 5.4 Expected utilities for each pair of strategy and inflation rate

	d_1	d_2	d_3	d_4	d_5	d_6	d_7	d_8	d_9
θ_1	0.41	0.48	0.44	0.75	0.68	0.72	0.55	0.61	0.58
θ_2	0.82	0.61	0.78	0.47	0.68	0.64	0.79	0.58	0.75

Section 4.4). We can plot this expected utility for each strategy for all p in the range $0 \leqslant p \leqslant 1$, to obtain Figure 5.1 (compare with Figure 4.12, but note the different vertical scale).

For a given p value we choose that strategy which maximizes expected utility, i.e. we seek $\max_{d \in D} \{EU(d)\}$, where $EU(d) = \sum_i U(\theta_i, d) g(\theta_i)$. From Figure 5.1 it is clear that optimal strategies are d_1, d_7, d_5, d_6 or d_4 (depending on the value for p). We can easily find the critical value of p where the optimal strategy changes.

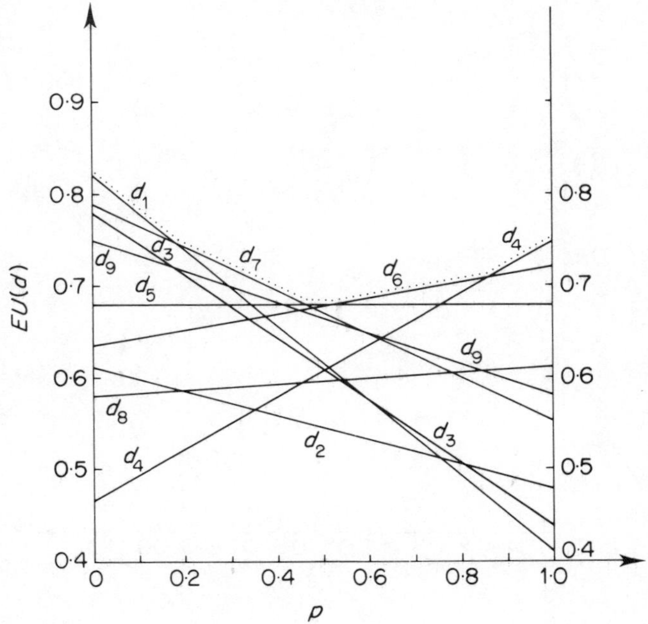

Figure 5.1 Expected utilities of the nine strategies plotted as
linear functions of p over the range $0 \leqslant p \leqslant 1$

Thus, to find the break-point between d_1 and d_7 we solve $EU(d_1) = EU(d_7)$, i.e. $0.82 - 0.41p = 0.79 - 0.24p$ to obtain $p = 3/17 = 0.18$ approximately. The reader can confirm that the successive break-points are at $p = 11/24 = 0.46$ (the changeover from d_7 to d_5), $p = 1/2$ (the changeover from d_5 to d_6) and $p = 17/20 = 0.85$ (the changeover from d_6 to d_4).

We can exploit the presence of only two values for the states of nature by plotting the $U(\theta_1, d)$ and $U(\theta_2, d)$ values for all the strategies d, as in Figure 5.2 (compare with Figure 4.14 or 4.15). In fact we have mixed the strategies to produce the convex hull of the discrete set of points from the pure set of strategies D. This is for visual effect rather than an exploration of the mixture possibilities.

If we examine, for a given prior distribution, the contours of equal expected utility then, as in Figure 4.15, we find that a maximum value will be attained at a vertex of the region, and in particular at d_1, d_7, d_5, d_6 or d_4. The particular strategy which optimizes the expected utility is, of course, dependent on the p

value, as we have seen in Figure 5.1. An argument similar to that of the final paragraph of Section 4.4 of Chapter 4 will show the sensitivity of optimal solution to p value, and give the same break-point values from Figure 5.2 as have already been calculated from Figure 5.1.

Our earlier notions of *dominance* and *admissibility* which were with respect to actions, can be extended to strategies. Thus, a strategy $d \in D$ is *dominated* by a strategy $d' \in D$ if the outcome for d' is at least as good as the outcome for d for all

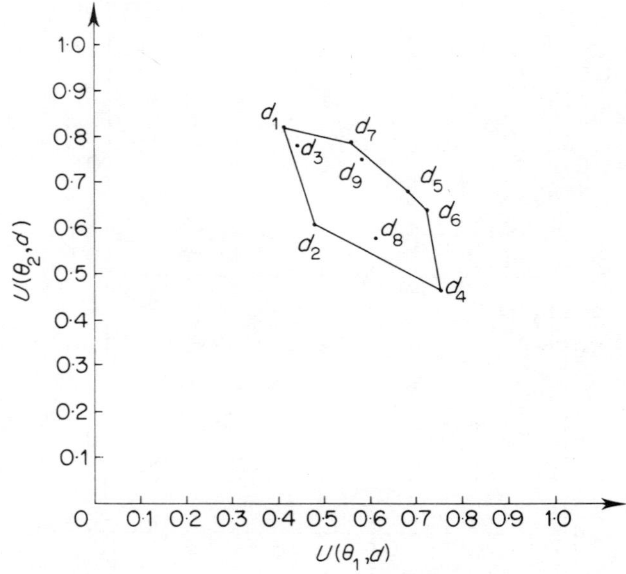

Figure 5.2 A plot of the data of Table 5.4

$\theta \in \Theta$. In the case of outcome measured in (expected) utility terms this is $U(\theta, d') \geq U(\theta, d)$ for all $\theta \in \Theta$. If, in addition, there is a state of nature for which d' has a superior outcome to that for d, then d' *strictly dominates* d. Again in utility terms this means that $U(\theta, d') > U(\theta, d)$ for at least one $\theta \in \Theta$. A strategy is *admissible* if it is not dominated by any other strategy (in the set of strategies under consideration). A strategy which is not admissible is *inadmissible*.

Thus, from Figure 5.2 (or Figure 5.1 or even Table 5.4) we see that d_7 dominates d_3 and d_2, while d_5 (and d_6) dominates d_2 and d_8. We can see from Figure 5.1 or 5.2, but not easily from Table 5.4, that d_9 is dominated by a mixture of d_7 and d_5. It is obvious from these figures that d_9 never maximizes expected utility over the set of pure strategies, for any prior distribution.

Since we have $U(\theta, d) = \sum_j U(\theta, d(z_j))p(z_j|\theta)$, then for a particular state of nature, if a strategy d assigns an inadmissible action to an observation which occurs with strictly positive probability (for that state of nature), the strategy itself is inadmissible. For example, if $d(z_i) = a$, and a is inadmissible, then there is an action $a' \in A$ such that $U(\theta^*, a') > U(\theta^*, a)$ for some θ^*. Define a new strategy d'

so that $d'(z_j) = d(z_j)$ for all j except $j = i$, and let $d(z_i) = a'$. Then

$$U(\theta^*, d') = \sum_j U(\theta^*, d'(z_j))p(z_j|\theta^*) > \sum_j U(\theta^*, d(z_j))p(z_j|\theta^*) = U(\theta^*, d).$$

Thus d is inadmissible. Only admissible actions ought to be considered in the construction of strategies, though note that (as in the investment example) use of admissible actions does not always lead to an admissible strategy, e.g. d_3, d_2 or d_8.

We have seen one method of incorporating the extra information of a forecast into the investment problem, but what can we say of the usefulness of the information? If we extract from Figure 4.12 the graph giving maximum expected utility against p value (denoted by a broken line in that diagram), extract from Figure 5.1 the graph giving maximum expected utility against p value (denoted by a dotted line in that diagram) and simultaneously plot these two piecewise linear functions as in Figure 5.3, we can offer an immediate answer to our question. Note the vertical scale (chosen for clarity of presentation).

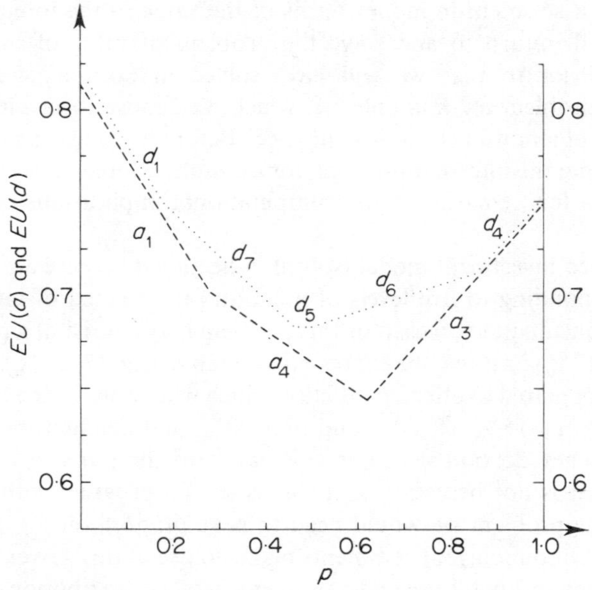

Figure 5.3 A comparison of the optimal expected utility (in the absence of extra information) with the utility to be expected using an optimal response to the extra information for the investment problem. Both functions are piecewise linear over the range of p.

We see that over part of the range of p values (in fact from 0.18 to 0.85) the expected utility from the optimum strategy using the prediction is superior to the expected utility from the optimal action (in the absence of extra information). Recall that strategy d_1 takes action a_1 (regardless of the prediction) while strategy

d_4 takes action a_3 for both predictions. Strategies d_7, d_5 and d_6 (the other members of D which can be optimal) each have different actions in response to the two possible predictions. For p values in the range $0.18 < p < 0.85$ the expected utility is enhanced by taking a strategy which does depend on the prediction. The vertical distance between the broken and the dotted lines is the difference in expected utility between using an optimal action and an optimal strategy, and the magnitude of the difference reflects the usefulness of the prediction. Thus, for $0 \leqslant p \leqslant 0.18$ and $0.85 \leqslant p \leqslant 1$ the proper use of the forecast does not enhance the expected outcomes. The investor has a prior probability for a high inflation rate which is either small enough ($p \leqslant 0.18$) or large enough ($p \geqslant 0.85$) for the prediction to be of no consequence.

What then is a reasonable consultation fee for the investor to pay, in order to receive the prediction? The value to the investor of the consultant's prediction is dependent on the investor's prior probabilities for the state of nature. The vertical gap between the two lines of Figure 5.3 is a measure of the value, but since this example has been worked using a non-linear utility function (our square root function) the assessment in money terms of the value of the forecast is slightly messy. We will return to and solve the problem of value of information in Section 5.5. Prior to that we will have solved in Section 5.4 the value of information problem for Example 1.1, which we choose to tackle without the complication of a non-linear utility function. Before investigating an alternative method of using the information from, for example, a forecast, we conclude this section with a few remarks on the computational implications of the present method.

In the refined investment model (solved in Section 4.6) there are five states of nature corresponding to five levels of inflation rate deemed of interest for the problem. A consultant's forecast for this problem may consist of a prediction for the rate (e.g. 17%) or it may be expressed as a range (e.g. $13-15\%$). Suppose the consultant is prepared to offer a prediction which will be one of the four ranges of less than 10%, $11-15\%$, $16-20\%$ and over 20%, and denote these by z_1 to z_4, respectively. They do not of course coincide with the $\theta_i (i = 1, \ldots, 5)$ of our problem, but it is not necessary that this is so. To progress with a numerical solution to the problem we would need to have $p(z_j | \theta_i)$, for $i = 1, \ldots, 5$ and $j = 1, \ldots, 4$, but our current comments make no use of this. Given that we have these conditional probabilities and a prior probability distribution for the states of nature, then our solution process can proceed as before. There is no dominance between any pair of the five actions, and they are all potential members of the strategies which we can enumerate and evaluate. For any of the four predictions we can take any of the five actions, giving a total of $5 \times 5 \times 5 \times 5 = 625$ strategies! A good proportion of these may well prove to be inadmissible on further calculation, but none can be excluded at this stage. This is a daunting amount of calculation given the modest size of the problem involved, and obviously bodes ill for the solution of more realistic applications. Fortunately, we are able to derive and use an alternative but equivalent procedure, and it is to this that we now turn.

5.3 Bayes' Theorem and the Extensive Form of Analysis

Apart from the data about outcomes (or utilities of outcomes) present in a decision problem we have prior probabilities $g(\theta)$ over the states of nature and conditional probabilities of observations (forecasts, test results) given by $p(z|\theta)$. In terms of aiding the decisionmaker the observation should discriminate between states of nature. After the announcement of a particular observation, say z_j, what can we now say about the likelihoods of the various states of nature? For example, in the simple form of the investment problem, if the consultant predicts high inflation, and prior to this the investor thought the two rates equally likely, what likelihood should he now attach to the high and low inflation rate prospects, given that the consultant is fallible?

What we are seeking is the probability for the state of nature θ given the observation z, and we denote this by $g^*(\theta|z)$. We can in fact construct this conditional probability out of the original $g(\theta)$ and $p(z|\theta)$ by use of some of the probability rules given at the end of Chapter 2. In fact we make use of rule (e) and rule (g).

Let us denote the (joint) probability of θ and z by $p(\theta \cap z)$ and the probability of z by $p(z)$. Using rule (e) we have

$$g^*(\theta_i|z_j) = p(\theta_i \cap z_j)/p(z_j). \qquad\qquad (*)$$

By another application of rule (e) we have $p(\theta_i \cap z_j) = p(z_j|\theta_i)g(\theta_i)$, while rule (g) gives us $p(z_j) = \sum_i p(z_j|\theta_i)g(\theta_i)$. Combining these two results for the numerator and denominator of $(*)$ we obtain:

$$g^*(\theta_i|z_j) = \frac{p(z_j|\theta_i)g(\theta_i)}{\sum_i p(z_j|\theta_i)g(\theta_i)} \qquad\qquad (**)$$

All the components of the right-hand side of $(**)$ are available to us and we can therefore calculate the *posterior probabilities* $g^*(\theta_i|z_j)$ of states of nature conditional on observation. This result is usually called *Bayes' Theorem* after the eighteenth-century English clergyman to whom it is attributed.

As an example consider the $p(z_j|\theta_i)$ of Table 5.1 together with a prior of $g(\theta_1) = g(\theta_2) = 1/2$. We have:

$$p(z_1) = p(z_1|\theta_1)g(\theta_1) + p(z_1|\theta_2)g(\theta_2) = 0.8 \times 1/2 + 0.4 \times 1/2 = 0.6$$

and

$$p(z_2) = p(z_2|\theta_1)g(\theta_1) + p(z_2|\theta_2) = 0.2 \times 1/2 + 0.6 \times 1/2 = 0.4.$$

Then

$$g^*(\theta_1|z_1) = p(z_1|\theta_1)g(\theta_1)/p(z_1) = 0.8 \times 0.5/0.6 = 2/3,$$
$$g^*(\theta_2|z_1) = p(z_1|\theta_2)g(\theta_2)/p(z_1) = 0.4 \times 0.5/0.6 = 1/3,$$
$$g^*(\theta_1|z_2) = p(z_2|\theta_1)g(\theta_1)/p(z_2) = 0.2 \times 0.5/0.4 = 1/4,$$
$$g^*(\theta_2|z_2) = p(z_2|\theta_2)g(\theta_2)/p(z_2) = 0.6 \times 0.5/0.4 = 3/4.$$

Thus, from a condition where the rates are equally likely before the prediction, a forecast of high inflation gives a posterior probability to high inflation of 2/3 (and inevitably a posterior probability of 1/3 to the low inflation prospect), while a forecast of low inflation gives a posterior probability to low inflation of 3/4 (and thus a posterior probability of 1/4 to the high inflation prospect). For a different prior, say $g(\theta_1) = 0.25$ and $g(\theta_2) = 0.75$, the reader can confirm that the posterior probability of high inflation given that it is forecast is 0.4, while the posterior probability for low inflation given that it is forecast is 0.9. The prior probability of 0.25 for high inflation is certainly increased by the prediction of high inflation to a posterior of 0.4, but the low inflation rate is still assessed as more likely.

The format in which the original conditional information $p(z\,|\,\theta)$ is presented allows of a compact tabular numerical scheme for proceeding from the prior to the posterior probabilities. In Table 5.5 we display a general version of the scheme which we now describe. This is followed by a recalculation of the posteriors for the simple investment problem using this new scheme.

Table 5.5 A tabular rendering of Bayes' Theorem. This is also our standard format for calculation

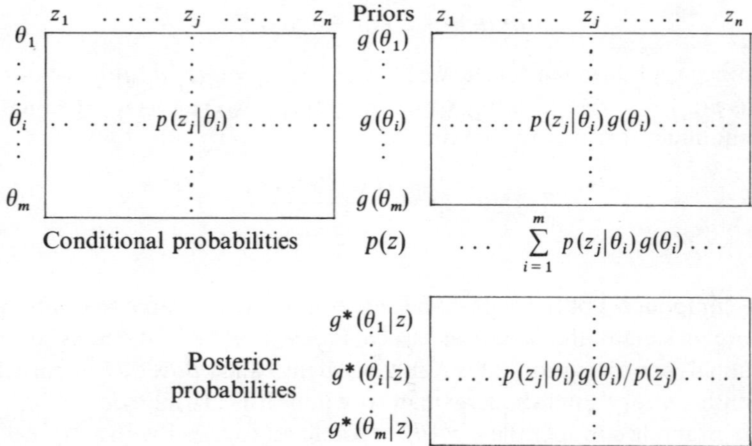

Our original information is given by the box of conditional probabilities and the priors for the states of nature. We form an intermediate box of numbers (the right-hand box) where the entries for each row of that box are just found by multiplying the corresponding entries of the same row in the conditional probability box by the prior for that row. The intermediate box is of course of the same size ($m \times n$) as the original set of conditional probabilities and gives the joint probabilities of θ and z. We then form the column sum of that intermediate box to obtain the entries of the $p(z)$ row. To find the entries of the third box, which is the $m \times n$ table of posterior probabilities, we process columns of the intermediate box. Entries of a column of the third box are found by dividing the corresponding entry in the column of the intermediate box by the column sum ($p(z)$) for that column. The reader can easily verify from the entries of Table 5.5 that we are proceeding in accordance with Bayes' Theorem.

For the data of the simple investment problem we thus have Table 5.6. The reader can confirm that our two sets of calculations have produced the same numerical results. Since we must have $\Sigma_j p(z_j) = 1$ and $\Sigma_i g^*(\theta_i|z_j) = 1$, for all j, there are some checks we can make on our arithmetic in this format.

Table 5.6 The calculation of posterior probabilities in our standard format

	z_1	z_2	Priors		z_1	z_2
θ_1	0.8	0.2	0.5		0.4	0.1
θ_2	0.4	0.6	0.5		0.2	0.3
				$p(z)$	0.6	0.4
$g^*(\theta_1|z)$					0.67	0.25
$g^*(\theta_2|z)$					0.33	0.75

Our decision problem in the face of uncertainty is to construct a strategy which gives the best expected outcome, i.e. maximum expected reward (or utility) or minimum expected loss. In Section 5.2 this was achieved by optimizing the expression for $EU(d)$ and we thus sought $\max_{d \in D} EU(d) = \max_{d \in D}\{\Sigma_i U(\theta_i, d)g(\theta_i)\}$, where $U(\theta_i, d) = \Sigma_j U(\theta_i, d(z_j))p(z_j|\theta_i)$ is the expected outcome using strategy d under state of nature θ_i. In the next paragraph we paraphrase the problem of strategy selection and demonstrate an equivalent but computationally easier process. The derivation involves the use of Bayes' Theorem.

We have

$$EU(d) = \sum_i U(\theta_i, d)g(\theta_i) = \sum_i \left(\sum_j U(\theta_i, d(z_j))p(z_j|\theta_i) \right)g(\theta_i)$$

$$= \sum_i \sum_j U(\theta_i, d(z_j))p(z_j|\theta_i)g(\theta_i) = \sum_i \sum_j U(\theta_i, d(z_j))g^*(\theta_i|z_j)p(z_j)$$

$$= \sum_j \left(\sum_i U(\theta_i, d(z_j))g^*(\theta_i|z_j) \right)p(z_j) = \sum_j EU(d(z_j)|z_j)p(z_j),$$

where we have written $EU(d(z_j)|z_j) = \sum_i U(\theta_i, d(z_j))g^*(\theta_i|z_j)$. This is the expected outcome (utility) from using strategy d, given that observation z_j occurs. Since this measure is the expected outcome (using a particular strategy) consequent to a particular observation and thus uses the posterior probabilities, it is sometimes called the *expected posterior outcome*. The reader is invited to compare this quantity with the expected measure of Section 4.5 where the actions are evaluated with respect to the prior distribution for the states of nature.

Our expected outcome for strategy d is then just the weighted sum (weighted that is by the $p(z_j)$) of the expected posterior outcomes. Each constituent expected posterior outcome involves only one response out of the optimal strategy, i.e. $d(z_j)$ for observation z_j. By reversing the order of summation in our manipulation we have accumulated all reference to the action (assigned to) $d(z_j)$ in the expected posterior outcome $EU(d(z_j)|z_j)$. Since the decision problem is to optimize $EU(d)$ over $d \in D$, we may now optimize each $EU(d(z_j)|z_j)$ independently, i.e. choose optimal $d(z_j)$.

To illustrate this process we re-solve the investor's problem where we have in Table 5.7 a restatement of the posterior probabilities and utility outcomes for the admissible actions.

Table 5.7 A restatement of the utilities and posterior probabilities for the investment problem

	a_1	a_3	a_4		z_1	z_2
θ_1	0.41	0.75	0.58	θ_1	0.67	0.25
θ_2	0.82	0.47	0.75	θ_2	0.33	0.75

$$U(\theta, a) \qquad\qquad g^*(\theta|z)$$

For a prediction of high inflation (z_1) we have posterior probabilities for θ_1 and θ_2 of 0.67 and 0.33, respectively. We thus have:

$$EU(a_1|z_1) = \text{expected posterior utility from } a_1 \text{ (given } z_1)$$
$$= 0.67 \times 0.41 + 0.33 \times 0.82 = 0.55,$$

$$EU(a_3|z_1) = \text{expected posterior utility from } a_3 \text{ (given } z_1)$$
$$= 0.67 \times 0.75 + 0.33 \times 0.47 = 0.66,$$

$$EU(a_4|z_1) = \text{expected posterior utility from } a_4 \text{ (given } z_1)$$
$$= 0.67 \times 0.58 + 0.33 \times 0.75 = 0.64.$$

The optimal response to a prediction of high inflation is a_3, giving an expected posterior utility of 0.66. Similarly from a prediction of z_2 we have:

$$EU(a_1|z_2) = \text{expected posterior utility from } a_1 \text{ (given } z_2)$$
$$= 0.25 \times 0.41 + 0.75 \times 0.82 = 0.72,$$

$$EU(a_3|z_2) = \text{expected posterior utility from } a_3 \text{ (given } z_2)$$
$$= 0.25 \times 0.75 + 0.75 \times 0.47 = 0.54,$$

$$EU(a_4|z_2) = \text{expected posterior utility from } a_4 \text{ (given } z_2)$$
$$= 0.25 \times 0.58 + 0.75 \times 0.75 = 0.71,$$

and the optimal response to z_2 is thus a_1, with an expected utility of 0.72. Recall from our calculations illustrating the process of finding posteriors that $p(z_1) = 0.6$ and $p(z_2) = 0.4$. The expected utility from our strategy is thus $0.6 \times 0.66 + 0.4 \times 0.72 = 0.68$.

This is exactly that found by our first attempt at this problem where using Table 5.4 we have $EU(d_6) = 1/2 \times 0.72 + 1/2 \times 0.64 = 0.68$, and $d(z_1) = a_3, d(z_2) = a_1$—the strategy just found.

Note that we have evaluated six expectations en route to the optimal policy, i.e. three actions after each of two observations. This compares with the nine strategies evaluated in our previous solution process. Admittedly there is more arithmetic in both processes than is summarized by these lone figures (for instance in the formulation of action probabilities for the first method and prior to posterior calculations for the second method) but they are a useful indication. For the refined investment example with four observations and five actions we have already demonstrated that this generates $5^4 = 625$ strategies for evaluation by the first method. Using the second, Bayesian method we must evaluate all of the five actions after each observation, giving a total of $4 \times 5 = 20$ expectations to be performed.

In general, for a problem with n observations and k admissible actions the first method will involve the evaluation of k^n strategies, while the second involves nk expectations and will then be much less computationally burdensome, even for modest-sized problems.

5.4 The Car Exchange Problem with Information

Using our new method of evaluating actions with respect to posterior probabilities conditional on observations, we return to the car exchange example and solve this for the two cases where extra information (from an oil consumption test) is available or not. We solve this using expected money outcomes, and make no computation of utility. The assumption of a utility function which is linear over the range of interest would lead to the same result, but note that the outcomes we are using (from Table 1.1) are losses, and the utility function would have to reflect the less desirable qualities of larger numbers. Thus, a function of the form $u(x) = a + bx$, where $b < 0$, would suffice. In fact we solve the problem in terms of losses and expected losses, and thus use our alternative nomenclature here.

Let us denote the two states of good and bad buys by θ_1 and θ_2, respectively, and the three test results of high, medium and low oil consumptions by z_1, z_2 and z_3, respectively. Our actions are a_1 (to keep the present car) and a_2 (to exchange for the car offered by the garage). In Section 1.2, where several remarks were made on Example 1.1, we postulated a plausible set of oil consumption test figures and it is these we use in this problem. Thus, $p(z_1|\theta_1) = p(z_2|\theta_1) = 0.20$ (giving $p(z_3|\theta_1) = 0.6$), while $p(z_1|\theta_2) = 0.4$, and $p(z_2|\theta_2) = p(z_3|\theta_2) = 0.3$. On the assumption of equally likely priors for good and bad buys (i.e. $g(\theta_1) = g(\theta_2) = 1/2$) our standard format for the calculation of posteriors proceeds as in Table 5.8.

Using Table 1.1 we have for observation z_1:
    expected posterior loss using $a_1 = 1400$;
    expected posterior loss using $a_2 = 0.33 \times 1200 + 0.67 \times 1600 = 1466.66$.

Table 5.8 The calculation of posterior probabilities for the car exchange problem

	z_1	z_2	z_3	$g(\theta)$	z_1	z_2	z_3
θ_1	0.2	0.2	0.6	0.5	0.1	0.1	0.3
θ_2	0.4	0.3	0.3	0.5	0.2	0.15	0.15
$p(z)$					0.3	0.25	0.45

	z_1	z_2	z_3
$g^*(\theta_1\mid z)$	0.33	0.40	0.67
$g^*(\theta_2\mid z)$	0.67	0.60	0.33

The better expected outcome (smaller expected loss) is 1400 give by a_1. For z_2:
expected posterior loss using $a_1 = 1400$;
expected posterior loss using $a_2 = 0.4 \times 1200 + 0.6 \times 1600 = 1440$.

The better expected outcome (lesser expected loss) is 1400 given by a_1. Finally, for z_3:
expected posterior loss using $a_1 = 1400$;
expected posterior less using $a_2 = 0.67 \times 1200 + 0.33 \times 1600 = 1333.33$.
The better expected outcome is 1333.33 using a_2.

Since z_1, z_2 and z_3 have probabilities of 0.3, 0.25 and 0.45, respectively, the expected outcome using this strategy is $0.3 \times 1400 + 0.25 \times 1400 + 0.45 \times 1333.33 = 1370$. Our calculations omitted units, but we now note that the strategy (of keeping the present car when the test result on the potential exchange is a high or medium consumption, and exchanging only after a result of low consumption) gives an expected loss of \$1370.

To solve this by the method of Section 5.2 would involve the enumeration of all strategies, calculation of their action probabilities and thus the expected loss for each strategy under each state of nature $(O(\theta, d))$, and eventually the expected loss for each strategy found by using the expectation of the $O(\theta, d)$ over all states of nature. Since we have three test outcomes and two responses there are $2^3 = 8$ strategies.

In the absence of a test the two actions have been shown to have expected outcomes of \$1400 (under the prior probabilities as above). Proper use of the test gives an expected saving of \$30.

Our next concern is with the solution of this problem over the entire range of priors for the case of extra test information and the solution in its absence. If we have $g(\theta_1) = p$ and hence $g(\theta_2) = 1 - p$, then the expected outcomes are $EO(a_1) = 1400$ and $EO(a_2) = 1200p + 1600(1 - p) = 1600 - 400p$. In the absence of any information the better option is that with lower expected loss, so that for any p the optimal expected outcome is given by $\min(1400, 1600 - 400p)$. Figure 5.4 displays the nature of this function of p, denoted by the broken line in that diagram.

If we use the same conditional information on the tests but use in the process the priors p and $1 - p$ for θ_1 and θ_2, respectively, we obtain Table 5.9. Now we

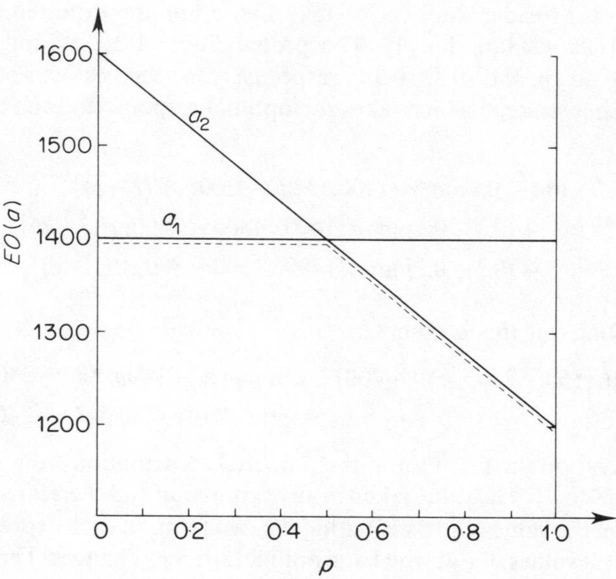

Figure 5.4 Expected outcomes for the car exchange problem
for p in the range $0 \leqslant p \leqslant 1$

Table 5.9 The calculation of posterior probabilities from arbitrary priors

	z_1	z_2	z_3	$g(\theta)$	z_1	z_2	z_3
θ_1	0.2	0.2	0.6	p	$0.2p$	$0.2p$	$0.6p$
θ_2	0.4	0.3	0.3	$1-p$	$0.4(1-p)$	$0.3(1-p)$	$0.3(1-p)$

	z_1	z_2	z_3
$p(z)$	$0.4-0.2p$	$0.3-0.1p$	$0.3+0.3p$

	z_1	z_2	z_3
$g^*(\theta_1\mid z)$	$\dfrac{p}{2-p}$	$\dfrac{2p}{3-p}$	$\dfrac{2p}{1+p}$
$g^*(\theta_2\mid z)$	$\dfrac{2(1-p)}{2-p}$	$\dfrac{3(1-p)}{3-p}$	$\dfrac{1-p}{1+p}$

have $EO(a_1\mid z_1) = EO(a_1\mid z_2) = EO(a_1\mid z_3) = 1400$ from the nature of decision a_1. For the alternative option

$$EO(a_2\mid z_1) = O(\theta_1, a_2)g^*(\theta_1\mid z_1) + O(\theta_2, a_2)g^*(\theta_2\mid z_1)$$
$$= 1200p/(2-p) + 3200(1-p)/(2-p) = (3200 - 2000p)/(2-p).$$

Given z_1 the optimum expected outcome is $\min(1400, (3200-2000p)/(2-p))$. Similarly, we have $EO(a_2\mid z_2) = ((2400p) + 4800(1-p))/(3-p) = (4800 - 2400p)/(3-p)$, so that given z_2 the expected outcome is $\min(1400, (4800 - 2400p)/(3-p))$.

Given z_3 the reader can verify that the optimum expected outcome is $\min\{1400, (1600+800p)/(1+p)\}$. The probabilities of z_1, z_2 and z_3 are $(0.4-0.2p)$, $(0.3-0.1p)$ and $(0.3+0.3p)$, respectively, so the best expected outcome (derived from a strategy which takes the optimal response to each test result) is given by

$$(0.4-0.2p)\min\{1400, (3200-2000p)/(2-p)\}$$
$$+(0.3-0.1p)\min\{1400, (4800-2400p)/(3-p)\}$$
$$+(0.3+0.3p)\min\{1400, (1600+800p)/(1+p)\}.$$

On multiplying out this becomes

$$\min\{560-280p, 640-400p\} + \min\{420-140p, 480-240p\}$$
$$+\min\{420+420p, 480+240p\}.$$

In each expression the first term is the potential contribution from a_1, while the second relates to a_2. The value taken in any expression and therefore in the sum is dependent on the value of p. By equating the two terms in each expression we can find the critical values of p at which the optimal strategy changes. Thus, in the first expression $560-280p = 640-400p$ gives $p = 2/3$, so that for $p \leqslant 2/3$ the first option (corresponding to a_1) is superior, while for $p \geqslant 2/3$ the second option is better. For $p = 2/3$ the two actions have the same expected outcome. Similarly, in the second and third expressions of the sum the break points will be found to be $3/5$ and $1/3$, respectively. Thus, for $0 \leqslant p \leqslant 1/3$ the minimum in each expression is given by the first of the two terms so that the expected outcome is

$$(560-280p)+(420-140p)+(420+420p) = 1400.$$

This corresponds to a choice of a_1 for all test outcomes (the action corresponding to the first, optimizing option in each of the expressions).

For $1/3 \leqslant p \leqslant 3/5$ the third expression is smaller in the second of its two terms while the first and second expressions are still smaller in their first terms. The expected outcome is thus $(560-280p)+(420-140p)+(480+240p) = 1460 - 180p$. This corresponds to the strategy $d(z_1) = d(z_2) = a_1, d(z_3) = a_2$.

For $3/5 \leqslant p \leqslant 2/3$ the second expression is now smaller in its second term, the first expression is still smaller in its first term, and the third continues to be smaller in its second term. Thus, the expected outcome, derived as it is from the strategy $d(z_1) = a_1, d(z_2) = d(z_3) = a_2$ has expected outcome

$$(560-280p)+(480-240p)+(480+240p) = 1520 - 280p.$$

Finally, for $2/3 \leqslant p \leqslant 1$ the optimizing strategy is $d(z_1) = d(z_2) = d(z_3) = a_2$ (all are minimized in their second terms) and the expected outcome is

$$(640-400p)+(480-240p)+(480+240p) = 1600 - 400p.$$

We have thus constructed the optimal expected outcome as a function of p, and simultaneously found the optimizing strategy. Figure 5.5 shows this piecewise linear function. If we also include in this figure the optimum expected outcome

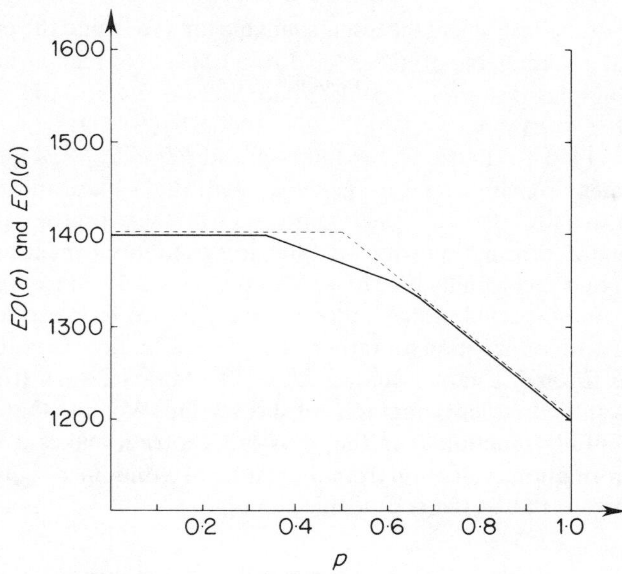

Figure 5.5 Expected outcome with optimal use of test information versus optimal expected outcome using only the prior
probabilities

with no information (taken from Figure 5.4), and denote it by the broken line,
then over part of the range of p (in fact for $1/3 \leqslant p \leqslant 2/3$) the proper use of
information results in a smaller expected loss. The vertical distance between these
functions of p is a measure of the value of the information in the oil consumption
test, and it is to a study of this and related questions that we now turn.

5.5 The Value of Information

In Figure 5.3 (for the investment problem) and Figure 5.5 (for the car exchange
problem) we have seen the effect of the proper use of information in enhancing the
expected outcome in a decision problem (for part of the range of prior
probabilities). By responding to the fallible prediction of the consultant, the
investor can increase his expected utility if the prior probability for high inflation
is in the range 0.18–0.85 – ignoring for the moment the cost of such information.
Similarly, the prospective car purchaser can decrease his expected loss by using
the oil consumption test and responding optimally to the outcome, providing
only that the prior probability of a good buy is in the range 1/3 up to 2/3, and
again ignoring the cost of the test.

For the numerical solution found in the previous section, where we took $g(\theta_1)$
$= 1/2$, the expected loss is \$1370, which represents an expected saving of \$30 on
the optimal cost without the test. In this problem it is advantageous to the
prospective purchaser to pay up to \$30 for the test to be performed (for these
particular priors). This is more formally demonstrated by the following

argument. For the case where the test is available for a fee f and the purchaser has elected to take it, the table of losses (cf. Table 1.1) should read as in Table 5.10.

Then using the posteriors calculated in Section 5.4 for this problem we have $EO(a_1|z_1) = 1400 + f$, $EO(a_2|z_1) = 1466.67 + f$, $EO(a_1|z_2) = 1400 + f$, $EO(a_2|z_2) = 1440 + f$, $EO(a_1|z_3) = 1400 + f$, and $EO(a_2|z_3) = 1333.33 + f$. The optimal strategy remains $d(z_1) = d(z_2) = a_1$ with $d(z_3) = a_2$, and the expected outcome for this strategy is $1370 + f$. Compared with the expected outcome in the absence of extra information which is 1400, it is therefore beneficial to take the test and respond accordingly if $1370 + f \leqslant 1400$, i.e. $f \leqslant 30$. Since we are dealing with money and expected money outcomes (as opposed to expected utility) the expected value of information (or rather its money evaluation) is easily found. We need not go through a table such as Table 5.10 but can work from expected outcomes as in our earlier paragraphs of this section. We note that the use of a (non-linear) utility function as in the investor's problem makes it necessary to return to information evaluation from the setting of a (modified) outcomes table, and we return to this at the end of this section.

Table 5.10 The outcomes in dollars for the car
exchange problem when a fee f is included

	a_1	a_2
θ_1	$1400 + f$	$1200 + f$
θ_2	$1400 + f$	$1600 + f$

The variation of the value of information (for the car exchange problem) as the prior p ranges over zero up to one can perhaps be more clearly seen if we graph the difference between the optimal expected outcome without information and that with proper use of the information. For a given p we are illustrating $\min\{EO(a_1), EO(a_2)\} - \min_{d \in D}\{EO(d)\}$. Thus, for $0 \leqslant p \leqslant 1/3$ the difference is zero. For $1/3 < p < 1/2$ the difference is $1400 - (1460 - 180p) = 180p - 60$, while for $1/2 \leqslant p \leqslant 3/5$ it is $(1600 - 400p) - (1460 - 180p) = 140 - 220p$. For $3/5 \leqslant p \leqslant 2/3$ the difference is $80 - 120p$, while for $p \geqslant 2/3$ it is again zero. Figure 5.6 illustrates the nature of this piecewise linear function. The maximum fee which it is worthwhile paying for the test is the \$30 already calculated (at $p = 1/2$). For $p \leqslant 1/3$ and $p \geqslant 2/3$ the test does not enhance the expected loss and consequently ought not to be taken.

We have seen the variation in value of a test with respect to changes in prior probability levels, but what of that other component of the prior to posterior calculation, namely the conditional probabilities of test outcomes? For the calculations in the case of $p = 1/2$ the oil consumption test result certainly shifted the odds of good and bad buys, increasing the likelihood of a good buy (θ_1) following a low oil consumption result (z_3) but decreasing it in the other two cases (z_1 and z_2). While influencing the probabilities, the test still leaves open the possibility of either state of nature being the true one. A perfect test would allow the decisionmaker to identify unambiguously the true state of nature, and consequently take his best option against such a state.

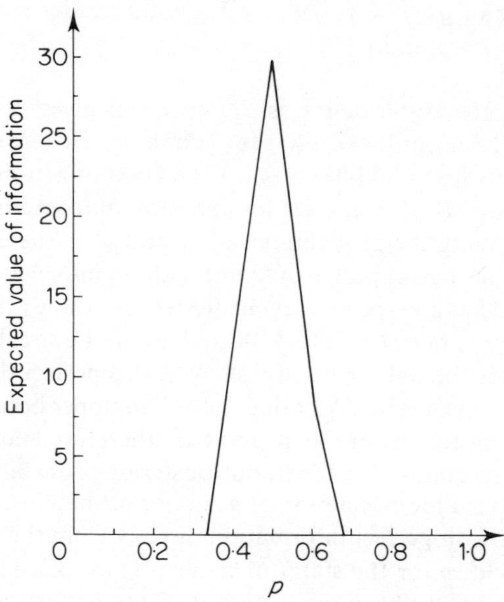

Figure 5.6 Expected value of information for
the car exchange problem, as a function of the
prior probability p

Suppose we have a perfect diagnostic for the car exchange problem, i.e. a test which signals that the car under test is a good buy if this is so, and similarly signals that a car is a bad buy if this is so. Let us denote these signals by s_1 and s_2, respectively. We thus have $p(s_1|\theta_1) = 1$ (implying $p(s_2|\theta_1) = 0$), and $p(s_2|\theta_2) = 1$ (with $p(s_1|\theta_2) = 0$). For the case where we have equally-likely good and bad buys ($p = 1/2$) the calculation of the posterior probabilities from these priors and conditionals is thus as in Table 5.11.

Not surprisingly the posterior probability of a good buy, given the signal s_1, is 1, and the probability of such a signal is $1/2$. Similarly, the posterior probability of a bad buy given the signal s_2 is 1, and the probability of such a signal is $1/2$. For the

Table 5.11 The calculation of posteriors using perfect
information

	s_1	s_2	Priors		s_1	s_2
θ_1	1	0	0.5		0.5	0
θ_2	0	1	0.5		0	0.5
				$p(s)$	0.5	0.5
$g^*(\theta_1|s)$					1	0
$g^*(\theta_2|s)$					0	1

more general case of $g(\theta_1) = p$, $g(\theta_2) = 1 - p$, the reader should confirm that $p(s_1) = p$, $p(s_2) = 1 - p$ and $g^*(\theta_1|s_1) = g^*(\theta_2|s_2) = 1$, $g^*(\theta_1|s_2) = g^*(\theta_2|s_1) = 0$.

Given signal s_1 the better action is a_2, since this gives an expected (indeed actual) loss of \$1200 against the 1400 for action a_1. Given signal s_2 the better action is a_1 with its loss of \$1400, against the 1600 of action a_2. This optimal strategy $(d(s_1) = a_2, d(s_2) = a_1)$ has an expected outcome of $0.5 \times 1200 + 0.5 \times 1400 = \$1300$ (using the probabilities of s_1 and s_2 in the expectation). If we compare this with the best expected outcome without information (\$1400) we see that the perfect test has an expected saving of \$100 (for these priors). The *expected value of perfect information* (*EVPI*) is \$100 in this case. Few realistic problems can be expected to offer the possibility of tests with this perfect discrimination, but calculation of the appropriate EVPI does afford an upper bound on the value of any test information for the problem, and may therefore allow some test to be ruled out on cost grounds alone (without posterior probability calculation).

We can in fact avoid the calculation of posterior probabilities and calculate the expected outcome with perfect information directly from the table of outcomes and prior probabilities for the states of nature. Thus, considering the table of costs for Example 1.1, we have that action a_2 is the better response against θ_1, which occurs with prior probability 0.5, and gives a loss of \$1200. Against θ_2, the better action is a_1, with a loss of \$1400, and this is incurred with the probability of θ_2 turning up, i.e. the prior probability 0.5. The expected loss for this strategy is thus $0.5 \times 1200 + 0.5 \times 1400 = 1300$, which is the same quantity as was found via the posterior probabilities.

As with less perfect information, we can analyse the perfect system where the priors are arbitrary. If the prior probabilities are $g(\theta_1) = p$ and $g(\theta_2) = 1 - p$, then taking action a_2 when θ_1 is perfectly forecast and a_1 when θ_2 is perfectly forecast gives an expected outcome of $1200p + 1400(1 - p) = 1400 - 200p$. We have already seen that the best outcome with no information has an expected outcome of $\min\{1400, 1200p + 1600(1 - p)\} = \min\{1400, 1600 - 400p\}$. Thus, the *EVPI* is given by $\min\{1400, 1600 - 400p\} - (1400 - 200p) = \min\{200p, 200 - 200p\}$. This function is displayed in Figure 5.7.

Repeating the above argument in a more formal context, we can derive an expression for the *EVPI*. For a problem with outcomes measured in utilities, the best response against a state of nature θ_i is that which gives $\max_{a \in A} U(\theta_i, a)$, and this θ_i is the true state of nature with probability $g(\theta_i)$. Under a perfect test then the expected outcome is $\sum_i g(\theta_i)\{\max_{a \in A}(U(\theta_i, a))\}$. Without information the best response is that which gives $\max_{a \in A}\{\sum_i g(\theta_i)U(\theta_i, a)\}$ so that

$$EVPI = \sum_i g(\theta_i)\left(\max_{a \in A}(U(\theta_i, a))\right) - \max_{a \in A}\left(\sum_i g(\theta_i)U(\theta_i, a)\right).$$

Problems with an outcome measure in rewards or losses can be similarly treated (see Exercise 5.14).

Returning to the investment problem, let us examine the expected outcomes with $g(\theta_1) = g(\theta_2) = 0.5$. In the absence of information the best action is a_4

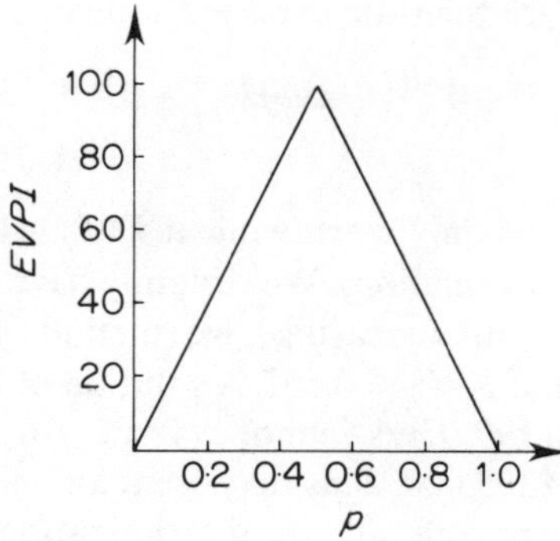

Figure 5.7 Expected value of perfect information for the car exchange problem, as a function
of the prior probability p

giving an expected utility of $0.5 \times 0.577 + 0.5 \times 0.745 = 0.661$ (to 3 decimal places). Using the services of the consultant we can see from Figure 5.3 (or Table 5.4) that the best strategy is d_5 with an expected utility of 0.678 (to 3 decimal places). The difference between the two expected outcomes with and without information is the gain in expected utility to be derived from the optimal use of the consultant's prediction. Unlike the car exchange example where the expected gain is in money terms and therefore translates directly into an upper limit on any fee for the oil consumption test, the use of a non-linear utility function for the investor's problem slightly complicates the arithmetic (but not the method) of finding an appropriate upper limit on the fee which the investor should pay for the consultant's service.

Strategy d_5 is defined as $d_5(z_1) = a_3$ and $d_5(z_2) = a_1$. Suppose the consultant's fee is f, where to be compatible with the contents of Table 1.2 this is expressed in millions of dollars! This sum then must be deducted from the profits if the consultant is used. In the following analysis we assume that d_5 remains the optimal strategy for the decision problem with information and a fee of f for this information. It is straightforward but tedious to show that this is so, and is left as an exercise for the reader (see Exercise 5.20). That part of the outcome table of interest (i.e. involving a_1 and a_3) is thus given by Table 5.12.

Recall that the posteriors are $g^*(\theta_1|z_1) = 0.67$, $g^*(\theta_2|z_1) = 0.33$, $g^*(\theta_1|z_1) = 0.25$ and $g^*(\theta_2|z_2) = 0.75$ and that $p(z_1) = 0.6$ and $p(z_2) = 0.4$. If we follow

Table 5.12 Outcomes in millions of dollars for
the optimal actions of the investment problem
when a fee f is included

	a_1	a_3
θ_1	$1.5 - f$	$5 - f$
θ_2	$6 - f$	$2 - f$

the same strategy as before then the expected utility of this is given by

$$0.6\{0.67(\sqrt{5-f}/3)+0.33(\sqrt{2-f}/3)\}+0.4\{0.25(\sqrt{1.5-f}/3)$$
$$+0.75(\sqrt{6-f}/3)\} = F(f) \text{ say.}$$

The use of the consultant is only worthwhile if $F(f) \geqslant 0.661$ (which is the best expected utility without information). We certainly have $F(0) > 0.661$, and since $F(f)$ obviously decreases with increasing f, we can find the maximum fee f worth paying from the solution of $F(f) = 0.661$. A solution of this (which we leave the reader to confirm) is $f = 0.199$. Thus, in money terms, for the consultant's services it is worth paying up to \$199 000. This may seem an unreal figure, but note the order of magnitude of the payoffs, and the discrimination about the forthcoming rate which the consultant's prediction brings (in the investor's posterior probabilities). For the solution of the investor's problem where the utility is taken as linear, the expected value of information is even greater in money terms (see Exercise 5.15).

If we had a perfect predictor for the inflation rate this would lead to a choice of a_3 when θ_1 is forecast and a_1 when θ_2 is forecast. If the fee for this perfect prediction system is f (in millions of dollars), then the expected utility in the case of equally likely priors is $0.5\sqrt{5-f}/3+0.5\sqrt{6-f}/3 = F^*(f)$, say. Now $F^*(0)$ > 0.661 (the expected outcome without information), so again we can find the maximum money which the investor should pay for such a system by solving $F^*(f) = 0.661$. This is readily achieved by eliminating square roots in $\sqrt{5-f}$ $+ \sqrt{6-f} = 3.97$ by squaring both sides of this expression and then squaring again the rationalized terms of the first operation. We find $f = 1.552$ million dollars! Thus a perfect prediction system is worth up to one and a half million dollars.

5.6 Multiple Observations

In the context of the car exchange example, where the use of money outcomes eases the evaluation of information, we examine a method of incorporating information from more than one test. Given the data from this extra 'experiment'—in fact a judgement following a road test of the prospective purchase—we evaluate the worth of this test and then examine its use in conjunction with the oil consumption test.

After taking a test drive in the prospective exchange the potential purchaser judges the car to have performed well or badly, where we denote these test outcomes by y_1 and y_2, respectively. Let us assume that the probability of judging the car's performance as good when it is in fact a good buy is 0.6, and similarly the car's performance is judged bad when it is a bad buy with probability 0.6. Thus, $p(y_1|\theta_1) = p(y_2|\theta_2) = 0.6$ and $p(y_1|\theta_2) = p(y_2|\theta_1) = 0.4$. If a decision is to be taken on the basis of the road test alone then we can easily construct the optimal strategy (when, say, $g(\theta_1) = g(\theta_2) = 0.5$). Table 5.13 demonstrates the calculation of the posteriors for this problem. Thus, $EO(a_1|y_1) = EO(a_1|y_2) = 1400$, $EO(a_2|y_1) = 1360$ and $EO(a_2|y_2) = 1440$. The better response to y_1 is a_2 and to

Table 5.13 The calculation of posteriors from
the road test outcome, using the initial priors

	y_1	y_2	Priors	y_1	y_2
θ_1	0.6	0.4	0.5	0.3	0.2
θ_2	0.4	0.6	0.5	0.2	0.3

$$p(y) \quad 0.5 \quad 0.5$$

	y_1	y_2
$g^*(\theta_1\mid y)$	0.6	0.4
$g^*(\theta_2\mid y)$	0.4	0.6

y_2 is a_1. The expected outcome for this strategy (since y_1 and y_2 'can be seen in the calculation to occur with probability 0.5 each) is $0.5 \times 1360 + 0.5 \times 1400 = 1380$.

Let us restrict the potential purchaser to four options in this problem. These are

(i) to make a decision on the basis of his prior information alone;

(ii) to take a (free) road test and make a decision using the information gleaned from that experiment (i.e. either y_1 or y_2);

(iii) to ask for the oil consumption test to be performed, for a fee of, say, \$25, and make a decision on the basis of the test outcome (i.e. one of z_1, z_2 and z_3); and

(iv) to take a road test and an oil consumption test, which in these circumstances the garage is willing to provide for \$10.

The expected outcomes for the first three options have already been evaluated and the optimal strategies derived. For (i) both actions give an expected outcome of \$1400. We have just seen that (ii) results in an expected outcome of \$1380. For (iii) the expected outcome is \$1370 plus the cost of the test (obtained using the strategy $d(z_1) = d(z_2) = a_1$, $d(z_3) = a_2$). This gives an expected cost of \$1395.

To analyse the fourth option let us assume that the results from the test drive (y_1 or y_2) and the oil consumption test (z_1, z_2 or z_3) are independent. Thus, the driver's judgement of the car's performance on the road test is independent of the oil consumption experiment outcome. Given that the car is a good buy, the probability that it returns a low oil consumption on the test and is judged to have performed well when driven is $0.6 \times 0.6 = 0.36$, the probability of a low oil consumption conditional on a good buy multiplied by the probability of a good performance on the road test conditional on a good buy. If we write $p(z_j \cap y_k \mid \theta_i)$ for the probability of oil consumption test result z_j and the road performance judgement y_k, given that the true state of the car is θ_i, then the independence assumption (which is actually plausible in this example) allows us to write $p(z_j \cap y_k \mid \theta_i) = p(z_j \mid \theta_i)p(y_k \mid \theta_i)$. Since we have three values for z_j and two for y_k there are six pairs of these 'compound' observations. Table 5.14 gives the conditional probabilities for these events and the resultant posterior probabilities for the states of nature in the standard format.

We write $g^*(\theta_i \mid z_j \cap y_k)$ for the posterior probability of state θ_i given oil

Table 5.14 The calculation of posterior probabilities when road test and oil consumption probabilities are amalgamated

	z_1y_1 z_1y_2 z_2y_1 z_2y_2 z_3y_1 z_3y_2	Priors	z_1y_1 z_1y_2 z_2y_1 z_2y_2 z_3y_1 z_3y_2
θ_1	0.12 0.08 0.12 0.08 0.36 0.24	0.5	0.06 0.04 0.06 0.04 0.18 0.12
θ_2	0.16 0.24 0.12 0.18 0.12 0.18	0.5	0.08 0.12 0.06 0.09 0.06 0.09

$$p(z \cap y) \quad 0.14\ \ 0.16\ \ 0.12\ \ 0.13\ \ 0.24\ \ 0.21$$

$$g^*(\theta_1 | z \cap y) \quad 0.43\ \ 0.25\ \ 0.50\ \ 0.31\ \ 0.75\ \ 0.57$$
$$g^*(\theta_2 | z \cap y) \quad 0.57\ \ 0.75\ \ 0.50\ \ 0.69\ \ 0.25\ \ 0.43$$

consumption z_j and road test performance y_k, and $p(z_j \cap y_k)$ for the (joint) probability of z_j and y_k. Note that this is unconditional.

For each of the six pairs we can calculate the expected loss for the actions a_1 and a_2, and choose for each compound observation that action which gives the smaller expected loss. For example, for the $z_1 y_2$ pair we have an expected outcome using a_1 of 1400 and an expected outcome using a_2 of $0.25 \times 1200 + 0.75 \times 1600 = 1500$. The better response is thus a_1. If we write $d(z_j \cap y_k)$ as the optimal response to the pair of results z_j and y_k the reader can confirm that $d(z_1 \cap y_1)$, $d(z_1 \cap y_2)$, $d(z_2 \cap y_1)$ and $d(z_2 \cap y_2)$ are all equal to a_1 (giving an expected loss of \$1400 in every case). For $z_3 y_1$ and $z_3 y_2$ the optimal response is a_2 and the expected losses are \$1300 and \$1371.4, respectively. Using the $p(z_j \cap y_k)$ entries of Table 5.14 we find that the expected loss using this strategy is $(0.14 + 0.16 + 0.12 + 0.13) \times 1400 + 0.24 \times 1300 + 0.21 \times 1371.4 = \$1370$. To this must be added the fee of \$10 for the oil test to give a total expected cost of \$1380.

In summary, our four options have optimal expected outcomes of \$1400, \$1380, \$1395 and \$1380, respectively. The two best options are therefore the road test alone and the combined road test and oil consumption test. In the case of the latter we have assumed that the potential purchaser commits himself simultaneously to both tests, and our analysis did not concern itself with the sequence in which these tests were performed. If we do consider the tests as separate then another, fifth, option opens up.

Suppose the customer can take a road test and then, on the basis of his judgement on the car's performance, decide whether or not to ask for an oil consumption test to be performed (at the same fee of \$10). The road test will result in one of two outcomes (y_1 or y_2) and in our analysis of this test at the beginning of this section we calculated the posterior probabilities for the true condition of the car given these (exclusive) outcomes. Our first analysis is of the options given that there is a good performance on the road test (y_1). The appropriate posterior probabilities for θ_1 and θ_2 are now 0.6 and 0.4, respectively.

If the customer decides not to pursue the oil consumption test then his choice of action will be determined by $\min\{1400, 0.6 \times 1200 + 0.4 \times 1600\} = 1360$, given by action a_2 (as we have already seen). If the customer decides to buy the information from an oil consumption test then he is entering the test with the likelihoods for a good and bad buy of 0.6 and 0.4, respectively. The original priors for θ_1 and θ_2 were of course equally likely, but after the road test of a particular car the likelihoods are revised in the light of the road test outcome. Thus, given a road test outcome of y_1 the process of updating to probabilities posterior to the oil consumption test takes as input (priors) to that test the probabilities resultant from the road test (i.e. the posteriors from that test). Thus, we have Table 5.15 where the priors are the posteriors from a good road test.

Table 5.15 The calculation of posterior probabilities from the oil consumption test when the 'priors' are the posteriors from a good road test

	z_1	z_2	z_3	Priors		z_1	z_2	z_3
θ_1	0.2	0.2	0.6	0.6		0.12	0.12	0.36
θ_2	0.4	0.3	0.3	0.4		0.16	0.12	0.12

	probability of z	0.28	0.24	0.48

Posteriors for		z_1	z_2	z_3
	θ_1	0.43	0.50	0.75
	θ_2	0.57	0.50	0.25

Note that the posteriors for θ_1 and θ_2 in the z_1 column take the same numerical value as those of the $z_1 y_1$ column of Table 5.14. In that table the outcomes z_1 and y_1 were amalgamated into a compound observation (i.e. we used $p(z_j \cap y_k | \theta_i)$ and the posteriors calculated in the normal (one-step) manner. This latest analysis has used the y_1 observation, calculated posteriors (using $p(y_k | \theta_i)$) from that outcome and taken these as input to a second updating. The second updating uses the original conditional information for the oil consumption test ($p(z_j | \theta_i)$) but the priors for this second stage are the posteriors for the states of nature from the first stage.

Similarly, the posterior entries of the z_2 and z_3 columns of Table 5.15 are in numerical agreement with the corresponding entries of the $z_2 y_1$ and $z_3 y_1$ columns of Table 5.14. The one-step updating using the compound observations and appropriate probabilities generates the same posteriors as the sequence of (two) updatings where the posteriors from the first updating become the priors to the second. The end result (i.e. posterior probability after the two tests) is the same regardless of how the outcome information is processed.

From Table 5.15 we can readily calculate the optimal response to each of the oil consumption test outcomes. Thus, following z_1 the better response is found by min $\{1400, 0.43 \times 1200 + 0.57 \times 1600\} = 1400$ for action a_1. On the other hand, following z_3 the optimal response has expected outcome giving min $\{1400, 0.75 \times 1200 + 0.25 \times 1600\} = 1300$ for action a_2. For result z_2 both actions have an expected outcome of 1400. Thus, given that we take the oil consumption test following a good performance on the road test the optimal strategy is to take action a_1 if z_1 results (for which the probability in Table 5.15 is seen to be 0.28) and obtain an expected outcome of 1400, take action a_1 (or a_2) in the case of z_2

(giving an outcome of 1400 with probability 0.24) and take action a_2 in the case of z_3 (giving an expected outcome of 1300 with probability 0.48). This optimal strategy has an expected outcome of $0.28 \times 1400 + 0.24 \times 1400 + 0.48 \times 1300 = \$1352$. To this must be added the cost of the test (\$10) giving a total of \$1362 as the expected loss given that the oil consumption test is taken after a good road test performance.

By comparison we earlier found that taking the best option on the basis of the road test alone, given that the car performed well on that test, had an expected loss of \$1360. Thus, if the option of taking up the oil consumption test can be pursued (or not) after the road test, the better decision is not to pursue it given that the car performed well on the road test.

If the car performs badly on the road test then from our opening analysis this gives (posterior) probabilities of good and bad buys of 0.4 and 0.6, respectively. Taking these as priors to the oil consumption test we obtain posteriors from that test as in Table 5.16. The posterior probability entries of the z_1, z_2 and z_3 columns here are numerically identical to the $z_1 y_2$, $z_2 y_2$ and $z_3 y_2$ entries, respectively, of Table 5.14. As before, the posterior probabilities are identical regardless of whether they have been found by a single update on the compound observation or two sequential updates with a single observation in each case.

Table 5.16 The calculation of posterior probabilities from the oil consumption test when the 'priors' are the posteriors from a bad road test

	z_1	z_2	z_3	Priors		z_1	z_2	z_3
θ_1	0.2	0.2	0.6	0.4		0.08	0.08	0.24
θ_2	0.4	0.3	0.3	0.6		0.24	0.18	0.18

probability of z	0.32	0.26	0.42

Posteriors for		z_1	z_2	z_3
	θ_1	0.25	0.31	0.57
	θ_2	0.75	0.69	0.43

From Table 5.16 we can readily calculate the optimal response to each oil consumption result, given that the test has been taken after a bad performance on the road test. Thus, for z_1 the optimal response is given by finding min $\{1400, 0.25 \times 1200 + 0.75 \times 1600\} = 1400$ for action a_1. For z_2 the optimal expected outcome is again 1400 (taking a_1), while for z_3 it is $0.57 \times 1200 + 0.43 \times 1600 = 1371.4$, by taking a_2. These three expected outcomes are achieved when z_1, z_2 and z_3 turn up, which they will in these circumstances with probabilities 0.32, 0.26 and 0.42, respectively. The optimum expected outcome from taking the test is then $0.32 \times 1400 + 0.26 \times 1400 + 0.42 \times 1371.4 = \$1388$. To this must be added the cost of the test, giving an optimum expected loss of \$1398.

If a decision is taken following a bad performance on the road test (with no oil consumption test) the best outcome has been seen to be an expected loss of $1400 (from taking action a_1). Thus, given a bad performance on the road test it is better to take the oil consumption test, following which an optimal response will give an expected loss of $1398 against the $1400 to be expected without the second test.

To summarize our analysis of the case where the decision on the oil test may be postponed until after the road test, we have found that in the case of a good performance on the road test it is better not to take the second test (giving an expected loss of $1360), while for a bad performance on the road test it is better to take the second test (where the optimal strategy will give an optimal expected loss of $1398). We see from our first analysis that the probability of a good performance on the road test is 0.5 (as is the probability of a bad performance). Thus, for the fifth option where the road test is taken, and after this a decision made on the second test, the expected outcome is $0.5 \times 1360 + 0.5 \times 1398$ = $1379. This, of course, is less than the optimal outcome where the commitment is to the two tests. Postponement of the commitment to the second test until the result of the first is known has given a superior expected outcome (for this cost structure). In Chapter 6 we offer a visual presentation of this last analysis. The actions and observations for this type of decision problem can be neatly displayed in a 'tree' format, and all the results of the previous pages summarized in this one diagram. In that same chapter we will state and solve another of these multiple observation problems, but this time entirely in the context of our new tree format. We conclude the present chapter with a few further remarks on the sequential versus single-stage updating, and a more formal statement of their equivalence.

So far we have seen the same posteriors emerge from a single-stage updating using the conditional probabilities of a compound observation $p\,(z_j \cap y_k | \theta_i)$ and a two-stage updating involving first the conditionals for the road test $p\,(y_k | \theta_i)$ and the original priors $g\,(\theta_i)$, and then a second update using the conditionals for the oil test result $p\,(z_j | \theta_i)$ and priors for this update which are the appropriate posteriors from the first update. In fact, if we reverse the order of the two-stage process, first updating the $g\,(\theta_i)$ using the conditionals of the oil consumption test, then use the posteriors from this as the priors to an updating with the conditionals of the road performance test, the same ultimate posterior probability values will emerge (see Exercise 5.5). The final value for the posterior probability is independent of the order in which we process the data relevant to that posterior. These remarks also apply to a problem with three (or more) experiments.

In conclusion, we demonstrate in a more formal manner the equivalence of the two updating processes for a problem where we have an observation for each of two experiments. Let these observations be $z \in Z$ and $y \in Y$, and let $p\,(z \cap y | \theta)$ be the conditional joint probability of z and y given θ. We do not assume any independence between z and y, but the reader is encouraged to attempt a proof of the equivalence under an independence assumption (see Exercise 5.22). Let $g\,(\theta_i)$ be the prior probabilities of θ_i for the finite set of such states of nature. If we treat the pair z, y as a compound observation then a straightforward application of

Bayes' Theorem to this observation gives us

$$g^*(\theta|z \cap y) = p(z \cap y|\theta)g(\theta)/p(z \cap y) = p(z \cap y|\theta)g(\theta)\bigg/\bigg(\sum_i p(z \cap y|\theta_i)g(\theta_i)\bigg),$$

where $g^*(\theta|z \cap y)$ is the posterior probability for θ given z and y.

Our alternative scheme first uses the z observation to derive $\hat{g}(\theta|z)$—the conditional probability of θ given z. Thus:

$$\hat{g}(\theta|z) = p(z|\theta)g(\theta)/p(z) = p(z|\theta)g(\theta)\bigg/\bigg(\sum_i p(z|\theta_i)g(\theta_i)\bigg)$$

where $p(z|\theta)$ is the conditional probability of z given θ.

Following this observation of z we obtain an observation of $y \in Y$ and we denote by $h(\theta|z \cap y)$ the posterior probability of θ given z followed by y. As the reader may verify, Bayes' Theorem gives us

$$h(\theta|z \cap y) = p(y|\theta \cap z)\hat{g}(\theta|z)\bigg/\bigg(\sum_i p(y|\theta_i \cap z)\hat{g}(\theta_i|z)\bigg),$$

where $p(y|\theta \cap z)$ is the conditional probability of y given θ and z. As in the numerical work we are using the conditionals of the second observation $(p(y|\theta \cap z))$ to update 'prior' probabilities which are the posteriors from the first observation $(g(\hat{\theta}|z))$. Now using rule (e) from the set of rules in Chapter 2, we can write

$$p(y|\theta \cap z)\hat{g}(\theta|z) = p(z \cap y|\theta)g(\theta)/p(z)$$

(A related problem is offered as Exercise 2.8 at the end of Chapter 2. The reader is urged to prove the result if he has not already done so.)

Thus:
$$h(\theta|z \cap y) = p(z \cap y|\theta)g(\theta)\bigg/\bigg(\sum_i p(z \cap y|\theta_i)g(\theta_i)\bigg) = g^*(\theta|z \cap y).$$

The posterior probability for θ given z and y is thus the same as the posterior probability given by an updating scheme which uses z followed by y. The two arithmetic schemes yield identical results.

5.7 Further Reading

With the work of this chapter we are firmly in the mainstream of decision analysis. The texts cited earlier, namely Aitchison (1970), Lindley (1971) and Raiffa (1968) all cover the issues of the proper use and value of information. More advanced is the work by LaValle (1978) which is recommended to readers with a more extensive mathematical background (mainly calculus).

Howard (1980) offers a general defense of the practice of decision analysis and in the same issue of that journal Krischer (1980) provides an annotated bibliography of the use of decision analysis in health care. In Kaufmann and Thomas (1977) are collected applications from both business and public areas while Moore, Thomas, Bunn and Hampton (1976) provide a collection of case studies.

Exercises for Chapter 5

The most important material in this chapter is that relating to the calculation of optimal strategies in the presence of information, and the value of information. The first few exercises allow the reader to formulate and solve some problems in probability processing, i.e. the use of Bayes' Theorem to proceed from prior to posterior probabilities. We strongly urge that these calculations be pursued using the format of Table 5.5, since it provides for some easy numerical checks. Most of the remaining exercises are concerned with questions of the purchase and use of information in decision analysis. Almost all examples avoid the use of utility, but only on the grounds of computational expediency. Non-linear utility functions are more unpleasant to handle in arithmetic work (as we have seen). Some attention is given to multiple observation problems, though these are covered more extensively in the exercises at the end of Chapter 6. In that chapter the arithmetic schemes we have explored are combined with a graphical device which allows of an easier progress through some multi-stage problems. In this chapter we have not made much use of diagrams of the form of Figures 5.2 or 4.15 (as opposed to those of the form of Figures 5.1 and 4.12). One of the exercises is designed to compensate for this and invites the reader to investigate the value of information via this alternative representation.

5.1 For the purposes of car insurance, drivers are graded as either good or bad risks. Valid driving licences carry either none, one or two endorsements and information is available on the proportion of these three possibilities for each of the two categories of driver. Thus, of good risks 70% have no endorsements, 20% have one and 10% have two, while of drivers who are bad risks 40% have no endorsements, 30% have one and 30% have two. Given that the driving population consists of 60% good risks and 40% bad risks, derive the posterior probabilities for good and bad risks, conditional on the number of endorsements held.

For drivers who hold one endorsement an insurance company demands that prospective customers take a written test. On this test good risks score well on 80% of occasions and bad risks score badly on 80% of occasions. Calculate the posterior probabilities for a driver who has one endorsement and scores badly on the written test.

5.2 In testing the quality of the output from a machine a preliminary visual inspection is made. The items under scrutiny are either fault-free or faulty, and at the preliminary inspection they can be failed or passed or referred to a second inspection.

At the preliminary inspection, of ten items which are fault-free eight will be passed, one will be failed and one will be referred to the second inspection. Out of ten faulty items the preliminary inspection will fail six, pass one and refer three for a second inspection. Given that the output is 80% fault-free, calculate the probability that an item is referred to a second inspection, and the probability that such an item is fault-free.

At the second inspection items are either passed or failed. Of items which are fault-free 90 % are passed and of items which are faulty 90 % are failed. Calculate, the probability that an item having been referred to the second inspection and passed is actually faulty.

5.3   Second-hand cars can be classed as either good buys or bad buys, and the latter account for 60% of the total. Among the good buys 20% have high oil consumption, compared to 60% among the bad buys. If a test was performed on a second-hand car and the result showed a low oil consumption, what is the probability that this car is a good buy? As an alternative to the test of oil consumption you could road test the car and try to assess its condition. On the assumption that you will recognize the true condition of the car 70% of the time, calculate the probability that a car which you assess as a good buy is in fact a bad buy.

Do you feel that one of the two tests (oil consumption or road test) is superior to the other, and if so, why?

If you were assessing a car which gave a low oil consumption and performed well on a road test, how confident do you feel about it being a good buy? (For this last part you should calculate the relevant probability by two methods—in one case taking the observations one at a time, and in the second case combining the observations so as to use Bayes' Theorem only once.)

5.4   A statistician demonstrating to his class declares that he is using one of three boxes A, B or C. Each box is divided into four compartments and each compartment has ten marbles, coloured either green or red. For each box and compartment the number of green marbles is given in the table.

		Compartment			
		1	2	3	4
Box	A	8	5	4	7
	B	4	5	6	3
	C	6	6	2	4

If a sequence of draws (one from each compartment) gives the result red, green, green, red calculate the posterior probabilities for A, B and C given that the statistician is as likely to use one box as another.

5.5   For the data given in Section 5.6 on the two observations for the car purchase example calculate the posterior probabilities for the condition of the potential exchange in the case where the oil consumption test is taken first, followed by the road test, i.e. use the posteriors from the application of the oil test to the equiprobable prior values (a calculation already performed in Section 5.4) as three sets of priors (one for each consumption) to be updated by the road test. Thus, confirm the values for the posteriors of Table 5.14.

5.6   Consider the two-state, two-action, three-observation decision problem where a decisionmaker has to choose between a_1 and a_2 in the face of an unknown state of nature θ_1 or θ_2. The following table gives the profit in dollars for each action–state pair:

	a_1	a_2
θ_1	0	60
θ_2	30	0

An observation X has three possible outcomes, x_1, x_2 or x_3, and the following table gives the probabilities of observation conditional on the state of nature:

	x_1	x_2	x_3	
θ_1	0.6	0.4	0	$p(x\vert\theta)$
θ_2	0.1	0.1	0.8	

Assuming an observation is made:

(a) List all possible strategies.

(b) Calculate (via action probabilities) the expected profit for each strategy and each state of nature.

(c) Given prior probabilities $g(\theta_1) = 0.6$ and $g(\theta_2) = 0.4$ find that strategy which maximizes expected profit, using the calculations of part (b).

(d) What is the expected value of the observation?

(e) Calculate the posterior probabilities for the states of nature (using the same priors as in part (c)), and hence find for each observation that action which maximizes expected posterior profit. Hence confirm the optimal strategy and associated expected profit found in (c).

(f) Calculate the expected value of perfect information for this problem, with the same priors as above.

5.7   A decisionmaker is faced with the prospect of choosing between two actions, a_1 or a_2, when the state of nature is unknown, but is either θ_1 or θ_2. The loss in dollars for each action–state pair is

	a_1	a_2
θ_1	0	5
θ_2	10	0

An experiment to help determine the unknown state of nature results in an observation z_1, z_2 or z_3. The conditional probabilities of observation given true state of nature are:

	z_1	z_2	z_3
θ_1	0.4	0.2	0.4
θ_2	0.3	0.2	0.5

(a) List all possible strategies and calculate their action probabilities.

(b) Calculate the expected loss for each strategy and state of nature.

(c) Given prior probabilities $g(\theta_1) = 0.6$ and $g(\theta_2) = 0.4$ find the strategy which minimizes expected loss using (b).

(d) Calculate the posterior probabilities for state of nature (using the same priors as in part (c)), and hence find for each observation that action which minimizes expected posterior loss. Hence, confirm the optimal strategy and associated expected loss found in (c).

(e) What is the maximum fee worth paying for this experiment?

(f) Calculate the expected value of perfect information for this problem, with the same priors as above.

5.8   The organizers of a theatrical event have three options open to them in deciding how to run the show. These options (a_1, a_2 and a_3) will give rise to different net profits depending on the size of the audience for the show. This audience will be either large (θ_1) or small (θ_2) and the following table gives the net profits in thousands of dollars for every possible outcome:

Option taken

		a_1	a_2	a_3
Audience	θ_1	25	30	15
size	θ_2	22	18	25

The audience can either buy tickets in advance or pay on the day of the show. As an aid to determining the audience size the organizers can investigate the rate at which advance tickets are being sold. This rate can be fast (z_1), medium (z_2) or slow (z_3) and the organizers' probabilities for these rates given the audience sizes are as follows:

Rate of sale

		z_1	z_2	z_3	
Audience	θ_1	0.6	0.3	0.1	$p(z\mid\theta)$
size	θ_2	0.1	0.1	0.8	

If the organizers' objective is to maximize the expected net profit from the event, and the audience sizes are initially regarded as equally likely, find the optimal policy given the information on advance sales. What is the expected value of this information? What is the expected value of perfect information for this problem?

5.9   Consider the problem of an investor who must take one of four options (a_1, a_2, a_3 or a_4) in the face of an unknown future rate of inflation. The profit from an investment depends on whether the inflation rate turns out to be high, medium or low (denoted by HR, MR and LR, respectively). The table below gives the profit (in thousands of dollars) for all combinations of investment option and inflation rate.

Option

		a_1	a_2	a_3	a_4
Inflation	LR	10	8	11	4
rate	MR	6	7	4	6
	HR	5	6	6	9

Prior probabilities for the inflation rate are $p(\text{LR}) = p(\text{MR}) = 0.25$ and $p(\text{HR}) = 0.5$. For a fee of \$500 it is possible to purchase a forecast of the forthcoming inflation rate from an institution. These forecasts are subject to error, and the performance of the forecasting service is summarized in the following table, which gives values to the conditional probability of forecasts being made, given the forthcoming inflation rate. Here LF, MF and HF denote forecasts of low, medium and high rates, respectively.

Forecast

		LF	MF	HF
Inflation	LR	0.6	0.2	0.2
rate	MR	0.1	0.6	0.3
	HR	0.1	0.3	0.6

Given that actions are evaluated in expected money terms, should this forecasting service be used, and if so which actions should be taken based on the forecast outcomes?

What is the expected value of perfect information for this problem? If the problem were tackled by enumerating and evaluating all strategies (as in our method of Section 5.2) how many strategies would there be?

5.10   A caterer is faced with the problem of deciding on the quantities of food he should prepare to sell at a forthcoming sports event. He normally sells toasted sandwiches and ice-cream and he knows that the demand for these items will depend on the weather at the time of the event. The three options he wishes to consider are:

a_1—prepare equal quantities of toasted sandwiches and ice-cream;

a_2—prepare mostly ice-cream and a few toasted sandwiches; and

a_3—prepare mostly toasted sandwiches and a little ice-cream.

The weather will be either hot and dry (θ_1) or cold and wet (θ_2) and the caterer has calculated the following net profits in hundreds of dollars for each action–state pair:

	a_1	a_2	a_3
θ_1	25	30	22
θ_2	25	20	27

If 60% of days are hot and dry at the time of the event what decision should the caterer take to maximize his expected profit?

As an aid to his decisionmaking the caterer can telephone his local Weather Centre which will give one of three forecasts:

z_1—cold and wet,

z_2—unsettled, or

z_3—hot and dry.

The caterer reckons that for days which turn out to be cold and wet the Weather Centre gives the appropriate forecast 80% of the time and the wrong (i.e. hot and dry) forecast 10% of the time. For days which turn out to be hot and dry the Centre gives the correct forecast 70% of the time and the incorrect (cold and wet) forecast 10% of the time. Find the caterer's optimal policy given that he uses the forecast, and the maximum fee he should pay for the forecast. How much is a perfect forecasting system worth to him?

5.11   The profits which a manufacturing company will make in the coming year are a function of the state of the market and the production policy which the company uses. The market may be either quiet (Q) or active (A), and the company has three possible production policies, a_1, a_2 and a_3. The table below gives the profits (in thousands of dollars) for all combinations of market state and production policy:

	a_1	a_2	a_3
Q	1000	600	300
A	400	800	1000

For a fee of \$5000 the company can commission a survey from Crystal Ball Inc., who will offer a prediction about the state of the market. Given that the market will be quiet, this will be correctly predicted 60% of the time, while an active market will be correctly predicted 70% of the time. The company has a prior probability for a quiet market of 0.6. If alternatives are evaluated in expected money terms, should the company commission the survey, and if it does how should it respond to the predictions made?

Consider the extended problem where another survey can be commissioned from a different organization, Future States Ltd. Predictions from this organization will be correct 60% of the time for a quiet market and 80% of the time for an active market. The manufacturing company can only commission this second survey after the result of the first survey is known. If the fee charged by Future States Ltd is \$10 000 show that the optimal policy for the manufacturing company is to commission the second survey only if the result of the first survey is a prediction of an active market.

5.12   Consider the oil company development problem which was posed in Exercise 4.8 (to be solved on the basis of prior information alone). At a cost of $200 000 some extra geological tests can be undertaken and will give a result of t_1, t_2 or t_3. The following table expresses the probability of test result conditional on field size:

		Test result		
		t_1	t_2	t_3
Field	small	1/3	1/3	1/3
size	medium	1/2	0	1/2
	large	1/4	1/4	1/2

Is it worth taking the test if the criterion used is that of maximizing expected money? What is the expected value of perfect information for this problem?

5.13   Consider the problem of a fisherman who trawls for fish which may be found in either large or small shoals. He has evolved two fishing techniques whose efficiency depends on whether the shoal being fished is large or small. Taking into account the time spent, fuel used, fish caught and sold, etc. he reckons that using his first technique will give a net profit of $10 000 if used on a small shoal and $12 000 a large shoal. The second technique will give corresponding net profits of $8000 used on a small shoal and $15 000 used on a large one. His real problem is to know whether any fish he discovers constitute a small or large shoal, and his experience shows that the two events are equally likely.

As an aid to discovering the whereabouts of fish and determining the shoal size the fisherman uses a sonar device which can give one of three different signals, z_1, z_2 or z_3. The probabilities of each type of signal given that the shoal is small are 0.6, 0.2 and 0.2, respectively, and the corresponding probabilities given that the shoal is large are 0.3, 0.4 and 0.3.

If the fisherman wishes to maximize his expected profit per catch, find his best strategy using the information from the sonar. If in the course of one season the fisherman reckons on discovering and catching fish from 100 shoals what is the upper limit on the net annual cost of the sonar device which would make it worthwhile using?

An alternative type of sonar is available, and this actually signals directly that a small or large shoal is present. The device is, however, not perfect. A small shoal will give rise to the incorrect signal 20% of the time and a large shoal will give rise to the incorrect signal 40% of the time. If this alternative device has the same annual cost as the one previously described, which one should the fisherman use?

What is the maximum annual cost the fisherman would pay for any device which gave information on shoal size?

5.14   In Section 5.5 we gave a formal definition for the expected value of perfect information (*EVPI*) for a problem where the outcomes were assessed in utility terms. Define the *EVPI* for a problem where the criterion is

(a) maximization of expected reward, or

(b) minimization of expected loss.

5.15   In Section 5.5 we found the expected money value of information (for the forecasts of Table 5.1) and the expected money value of perfect information, given that outcomes were evaluated in expected utility terms. For the same problem (where the priors are $g(\theta_1) = g(\theta_2) = 0.5$) find the expected value of the forecast and the expected value of perfect information when the criterion is now expected money.

5.16   Consider the two-state, two-action decision problem with dollar losses given by

	a_1	a_2
θ_1	10	0
θ_2	0	10

and prior probabilities $g(\theta_1) = g(\theta_2) = 0.5$.

It is possible to perform an informative experiment to observe X where the conditional probabilities of observation are:

	x_1	x_2	
θ_1	1/2	1/2	$p(x\|\theta)$
θ_2	1	0	

You may choose to act without taking any observations or observe X either once or twice before choosing an action. If you make any observations you may either

(a) pay \$2 for two independent observations on X in which case you will be told the observations simultaneously, or

(b) pay \$1 for a single observation on X with the option of paying \$1.25 for a further independent observation on X. In this case you are told the first observation before you have to decide whether to take the second.

Given an expected money criterion, what is your optimal policy?

5.17   From Exercise 5.11 consider the subproblem defined by the table of outcomes for that problem and the forecasts given by Crystal Ball Inc. If we have prior probabilities for quiet and active markets of p and $(1 - p)$, respectively, find

(i) the action which maximizes expected profit (as a function of p) in the absence of the forecast;

(ii) the optimal strategy (as a function of p) which uses the forecast provided; and

(iii) the expected value of the forecast information as a function of p.

Your solution should include a graphical illustration for all three parts of the question.

5.18   In a decision problem with two states of nature and two actions the payoffs in dollars are

$$
\begin{array}{c|cc}
 & a_1 & a_2 \\
\hline
\theta_1 & 10 & 5 \\
\theta_2 & 0 & 10
\end{array}
$$

For the prior probabilities $g(\theta_1) = p$, $g(\theta_2) = 1 - p$, find the expected value of perfect information as a function of p.

For an experiment with outcomes x_1 or x_2 the conditional probabilities $p(x|\theta)$ are given by

$$
\begin{array}{c|cc}
 & x_1 & x_2 \\
\hline
\theta_1 & 1/3 & 2/3 \\
\theta_2 & 2/3 & 1/3
\end{array}
$$

How much as a function of p would you pay for this experiment? If $p = 1/2$ in the above, and the outcome of the experiment is x_2, how much would you pay to perform the experiment a second time (to obtain another independent observation)?

5.19   Consider the problem where we have losses for each action–state pair given by

$$
\begin{array}{c|cc}
 & a_1 & a_2 \\
\hline
\theta_1 & 0 & 2 \\
\theta_2 & 1 & 0
\end{array}
$$

and prior probabilities $g(\theta_1) = p$, $g(\theta_2) = 1 - p$.

Plot the expected value of perfect information as a function of p for this problem.

If we have an observation with possible outcome x_1 or x_2, where the conditional probabilities of observation, given state of nature, are as in

$$
\begin{array}{c|cc}
 & x_1 & x_2 \\
\hline
\theta_1 & 3/4 & 1/4 \\
\theta_1 & 1/3 & 2/3
\end{array}
\qquad p(x|\theta)
$$

find as a function of p (and plot) the expected value of such an observation.

5.20   In our investigation of the value of information in the investor's problem, where outcomes are expressed in utility terms, we claimed that the introduction of the (then unknown) fee f into the money outcome, and its subsequent inclusion in the utility assessment, left the optimal strategy unchanged. Recall that this strategy is $d(z_1) = a_3, d(z_2) = a_1$. By finding the values for f which would induce a change from this strategy (by generating a better expected posterior outcome) verify our claim.

5.21   From Exercise 5.11 consider the subproblem defined by the table of outcomes for that problem and the forecasts given by Crystal Ball Inc. There are prior probabilities of 0.6 and 0.4 for quiet and active markets, respectively. Instead of expected money outcomes, let us use expected utility where the utility function is $u(x) = \sqrt{x}$ (given that x is in thousands of dollars). Calculate the maximum fee which the company should pay Crystal Ball Inc., and the maximum fee the company would pay for a perfect forecasting system.

5.22   At the end of Section 5.6 we gave a formal proof of the numerical equivalence of the two updating schemes which

(i) treat the sequence (here two) of observations as one 'super' observation and hence use Bayes' Theorem once, and

(ii) take each observation singly and use Bayes' Theorem to update the appropriate priors (i.e. the posteriors from the previous observation, or the original priors in the case of the first observation).

In fact our numerical work has concentrated on a sequence of independent observations, though the formal proof is more general. Under the assumption of independence re-work this proof.

5.23   In Chapter 5 we have explored the use and value of information via diagrams such as Figure 5.3 which was obtained from Figures 5.1 and 4.12. The reader is invited to develop an analysis of the value of information via the alternative graphical method, i.e. using Figures 5.2 and 4.4.

Chapter 6
Decision Trees

6.1 Introduction

In the final example of Chapter 5 where we analysed the car exchange problem when a sequence of tests (in this case two) could be undertaken, and decisions on further testing taken in the light of current results, the presentation of the analysis was fairly lengthy and the relative status of alternative options buried in the presentation. The complexity is not inherent in the problem itself, only in the communication of the results, and in this chapter we present a pictorial mechanism which provides an easily assimilated summary of the problem and the attendant calculations. This is not a different solution process, only a succinct device for presentation. It is particularly useful in those decision problems which involve a (small) number of sequential decisions.

After introducing a few necessary terms with illustrations we present in this pictorial context an analysis of the most complex version of the car exchange problem. This is followed by the analysis and solution of another sequential problem, which contains the germ of some ideas not explored in depth, but also reinforces some of the ideas of this and the previous chapter.

The device which we use to present our analysis is a *tree*, which is a collection of *nodes* and *arcs*, where this collection has certain properties. The nodes of the tree are joined by the arcs and these arcs have a *direction*. A *branch* in the tree consists of an arc and all elements which follow it (as implied by the direction of the first arc). Between any two nodes there is at most one arc, and no two branches from the same initial node can have elements in common. Thus, Figure 6.1 represents a legitimate tree where $a, b, c, d, e, f, g, h, i, j$ and k are the nodes and $A, B, C, D, E, F, G, H, I$ and J are the arcs, all of which are directed from left to right. The tree is drawn to have a unique initial node (a), but may have several terminal nodes (here c, e, g, j and k). Out of node a we have three branches (starting along arcs A, E and G) while at b and i there are two branches. There is no significance in the length of arcs, and the orientation of branches is only determined by the need for clarity of presentation.

In Figure 6.2 we have a diagram which is not a tree. Again all arcs are directed from left to right. The branch starting along arc C and that along arc E have node e in common, and this was proscribed in our 'definition' of a tree.

We will find it useful to distinguish between different types of nodes. Corresponding to a node which is a *decision point* we will draw the element as a square note □, while for nodes which correspond to *chance* or *uncontrollable*

140

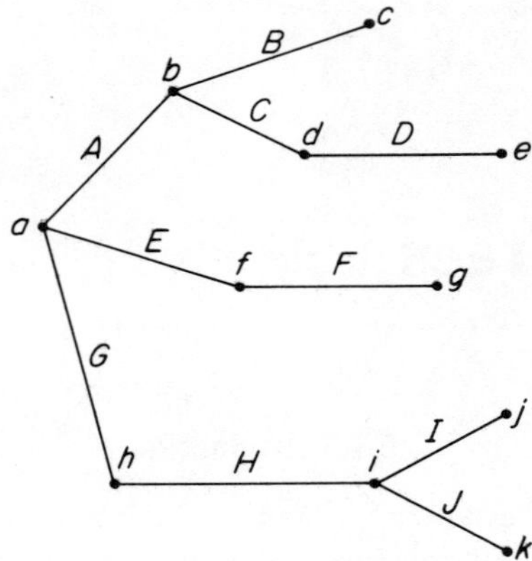

Figure 6.1 An example of a tree

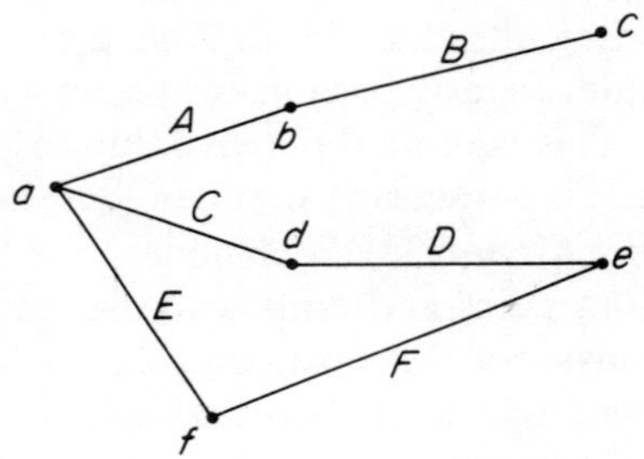

Figure 6.2 This is not a tree

events we will draw the element as a round node $\bigcirc$. Nodes at the *terminus* of any branch are also round but black, thus $\bullet$. For the car exchange problem without information we have a tree as shown in Figure 6.3.

At the first node the decision is taken to keep or exchange. After either decision

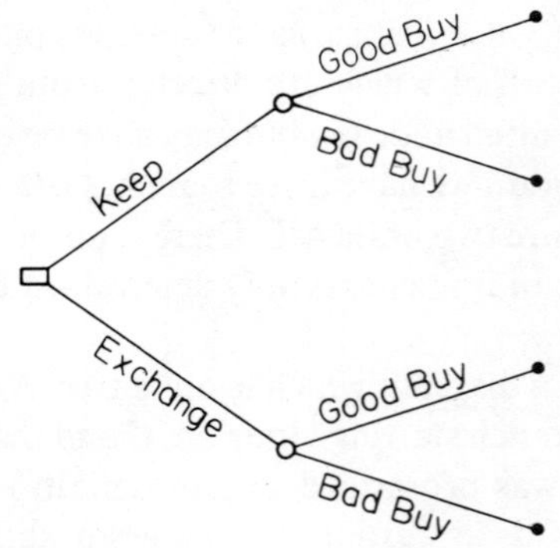

Figure 6.3 The tree for the car exchange
problem

(along each branch) at the next chance node the true state of nature reveals itself. Associated with each terminal node is some cost, given by the appropriate entry of Table 1.1. The likelihoods for each state of nature are given in the prior probability distribution, and thus with the arcs emanating from a chance node we can associate a probability. These probabilities and terminal costs have been added to Figure 6.3 to produce Figure 6.4, where we take $g(\theta_1) = 0.6$ and $g(\theta_2) = 0.4$, say.

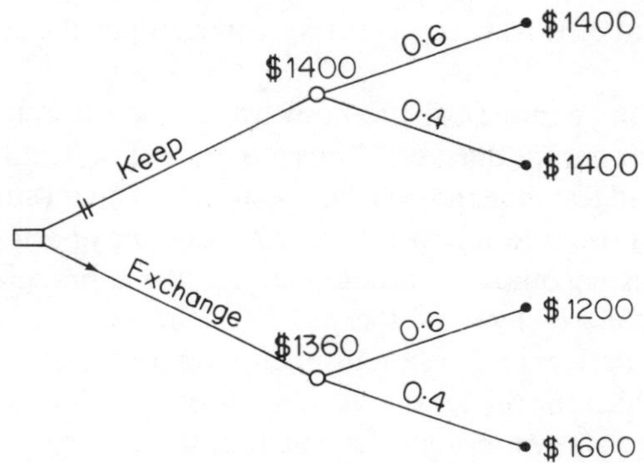

Figure 6.4 The tree for the car exchange problem
with data and results

At each chance node we can form the expected outcome giving $1400 for the node along the 'keep' branch and $1360 for the node along the 'exchange' branch. These have been incorporated in Figure 6.4 at the appropriate nodes. For the decisionmaker at the initial (decision) node the 'keep' branch shows an expected cost of $1400, while the 'exchange' branch is superior with an expected cost of $1360. This choice of action at the decision node is denoted by an arrow ($\rightarrow$) along the branch chosen and a double bar ($\|$) on the branch not chosen.

This small example displays all the features which are necessary for our larger scale work, and we now turn to the solution of the car exchange problem where the tests may be taken sequentially (i.e. oil test after road test, if desired).

6.2 A Sequential Test Problem

Consider again the five options for the car exchange problem explored in Section 5.6 of Chapter 5. These are:

(i) to decide without extra information (on the basis of the priors);

(ii) to decide on the basis of a free road test;

(iii) to decide after the result of an oil consumption test which costs $25;

(iv) to take a combined road and oil consumption test (at a cost of $10) and decide on the basis of this test;

(v) to take a road test and, after the result of that test is clear, either to take a decision on purchase or decide to take the oil consumption test (for a fee of $10) and postpone the purchase decision until the result is known.

The reader is invited to construct the decision tree incorporating these five options. These are five branches, corresponding to the five options above. Where appropriate in the tree he should use the symbols from Chapter 5 denoting the alternative actions, states of nature and outcomes for the road and oil consumption tests. Numbers associated with the nodes are losses (or expected losses) and are measured in dollars. Numbers on arcs emanating from a chance node are probabilities associated with these arcs. These may be conditional and should reflect the fact that the uncertain event is along the branch from (and therefore dependent on) an arc representing, for example, the occurrence of a test outcome.

Since a tree in the confines of the book would be severely cramped by the inclusion of all the relevant data, we choose to explore in detail only that branch which takes the road test first and has the possibility of an oil consumption test in addition. The other four branches of the tree have already been solved in Chapter 5 and the reader is encouraged to complete for these branches the numerical analysis akin to that which we now explore for the 'sequential test' branch. In Figure 6.6 we summarize the decision problem over all five options in a truncated form of the tree which the reader is invited to construct (that is, only solutions to the five options are shown, not all the calculations).

Figure 6.5 displays the sequential decision problem of road test followed by optional oil consumption test. Note that we build the tree from left to right, essentially in the direction in which it evolves. Thus, given that the road test is taken the outcome is either y_1 or y_2. For each outcome the purchaser has to decide between making a decision on the basis of the road test alone or proceeding with an oil consumption test. If the decision is to be made on the basis of the road test outcome, then either a_1 or a_2 is taken and finally the state of nature 'reveals' itself. If the oil consumption test is taken, then one of z_1, z_2 or z_3 is the result and following each of these the decision between a_1 and a_2 must be made. Only after this final decision does the true state of nature become known.

We are assuming, as in Chapter 5, that the prior probabilities for a good and bad buy are equally likely. Given that, we already have calculated the (unconditional) probabilities for y_1 and y_2, and these values (also 0.5 each) are associated with the branches which emanate from the first chance node. Suppose the road test result is y_1. The purchaser has to decide whether to opt for a_1 or a_2 on the evidence of the road test result, or take the oil consumption test. These two options give the two branches from the decision node following the y_1 arc. All numbers, other than the probabilities on the arcs, and all marks on the decision arcs should be ignored for the present. Exploring first the 'no test' decision, the purchaser must choose between a_1 and a_2, after which θ_1 or θ_2 reveals itself. In this part of the tree we are examining events posterior to a good road test result (y_1) and therefore the likelihood for the states of nature should be modified accordingly. Thus, the appropriate probability for θ_1 is the posterior for θ_1 given y_1 $(= 0.6)$, and similarly the probability for θ_2 is that conditional on y_1 $(= 0.4)$. These probabilities are shown on the arcs corresponding to θ_1 and θ_2 in the part of the tree under study. Action a_1 (keep the present car) gives an outcome of \$1400

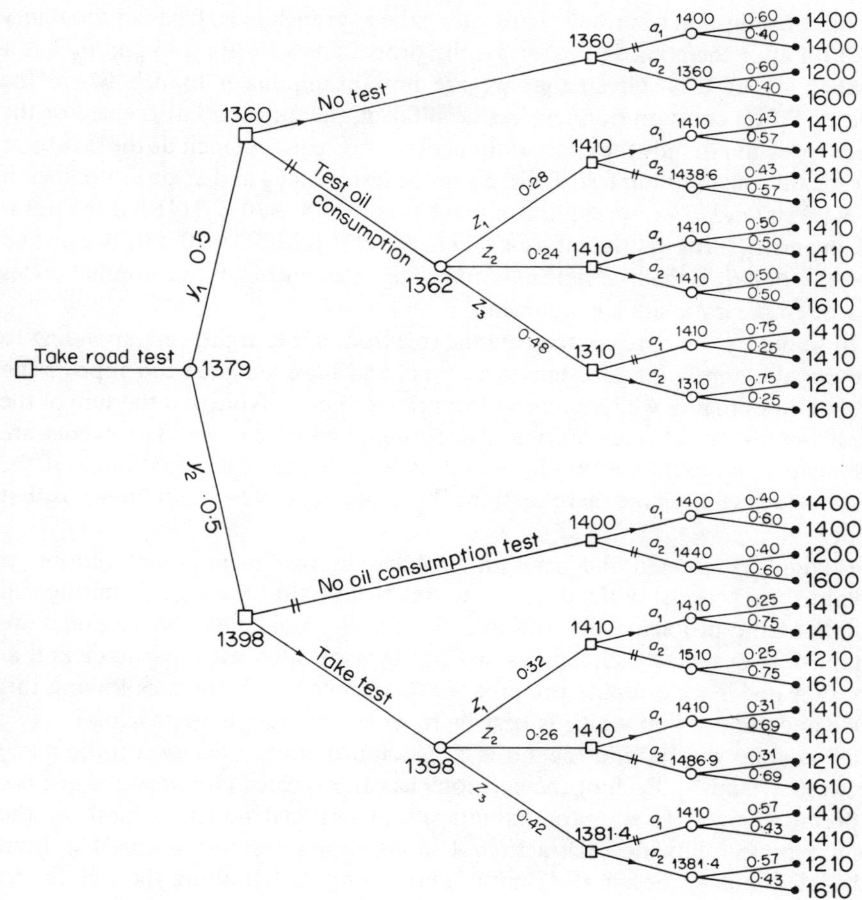

Figure 6.5 The tree for the car exchange problem starting with a decision to take the road test

irrespective of the true state of nature and hence associated with the terminal nodes following a_1 we have a cost of \$1400. Given a choice of a_2 the loss is \$1200 or \$1600 dependent on θ_1 or θ_2 being the true state, and these figures are to be found at the end of the θ_1 and θ_2 branches from the chance node after a_2.

Following the oil test decision (the other arc from the decision node after y_1) there is a chance node with three branches emanating from it, corresponding to high, medium and low oil consumption in the test result. The probabilities for these have been calculated in Section 5.6 of Chapter 5 using the conditionals of the oil consumption test and the priors for the states of nature appropriate to a previous result of y_1 on the road test. After the oil test result there is an option of a_1 or a_2 and, following each of these, the true state of nature manifests itself. The probabilities for these events have been calculated in Section 5.6 of Chapter 5 (in fact twice over) and are the likelihoods for θ_1 and θ_2 posterior to a road test and an oil consumption test result. Thus, along the z_1 branch (which has a probability of 0.28) after the choice of a_1 or a_2, the probability of θ_1 is 0.43 and θ_2 has a probability of 0.57. Given that we are now examining a branch where the additional oil consumption test has been taken, the outcomes at the end of the tree represent not only the effect of the action–state pair, but include the ($10) cost for the oil consumption test. Thus, given the test is taken and z_1 turns up, then if a_1 is taken (and θ_1 or θ_2 reveals itself) the cost is $1400 + 10 = \$1410$. If the test is taken and z_1 turns up, then if a_2 is taken, the cost is $\$1200 + 10$ if θ_1 is true and $\$1600 + 10$ if θ_2 is the true state of nature. The other entries at the terminal nodes can be found by a similar argument.

In summary, we have constructed the tree from left to right, corresponding to the possible unfolding of events over time, and have assigned the appropriate probabilities to arcs which emanate from chance nodes. Note that the sum of the probabilities on the arcs leaving chance nodes must be one. The events are exhaustive and exclusive. We have also assigned to each terminal node of the process the net outcome (here cost) for the unique path which terminates at that node.

Having represented the decision problem in this manner its solution is obtained by processing the data of the tree from right to left, i.e. from the end points of the problem back towards the starting point. At chance nodes we establish the expected outcome which can be associated with that node and at decision nodes we examine the prospects associated with the arcs leaving this node and choose that which is best (here with minimum expected cost).

Thus, following y_1 and the 'no test' decision there is a decision to be made between a_1 and a_2. Each of these actions has an expected cost which is just the expectation over the arcs (probabilities) and terminal nodes (values) for the chance node following each action. The appropriate expected cost has been calculated and set beside the chance node. Stepping left along the tree to the decision node (following the 'no test' decision) and looking to the prospective outcomes, the a_1 branch leads to an expected outcome of $1400 while the a_2 branch gives an expected cost of $1360. The superior expected outcome follows from the choice of a_2. As before this is denoted by an arrow along the preferred arc and a double bar across the inferior one. Should the purchaser ever find himself at this decision node, the best expected outcome thereafter is $1360, obtained by a choice of a_2. With this decision node we therefore associate the $1360 expected outcome, representing the best expected outcome to be had from this node. Stepping left yet again to the decision node with the 'no test' and 'test' branches from it, we can see that in looking forward from that node the decisionmaker has an appraisal of the best expected outcome along the 'no test' branch, and to make a choice at the current decision node he must evaluate the best outcome to be obtained from the 'test' decision. This is accomplished by again working from the terminal nodes of the 'test' branch, taking expectations at chance nodes and best options at decision nodes.

Thus, following the z_1 result of the test (which gives probabilities of 0.43 and 0.57 to θ_1 and θ_2, respectively) the expected outcomes associated with the chance nodes following a_1 and a_2 are found to be 1410 and 1438.6, respectively. At the decision node following z_1 the better option is therefore a_1. This branch is marked with an arrow, the a_2 branch 'barred' and the optimal value of 1410 associated with the decision node following z_1. Similarly, the values of 1410 (given by a_1 or a_2 following z_2) and 1310 (given by a_2 following z_3) are associated with the appropriate decision nodes. At the chance node following the 'test' arc we thus have three possible branches and we know the probability of each branch and its best expected outcome. The expectation (1362) is associated with that chance node.

Thus, at the 'no test' versus 'test' decision node the branches are seen to have expected values of 1360 and 1362, respectively. The 'no test' branch is marked as preferred and the value of 1360 associated with the decision node. This process can be repeated for that part of the tree following the y_2 outcome from the road test. In that case the better decision is to test, taking actions a_1, a_1 and a_2 for z_1, z_2 and z_3, respectively. As a consequence of this analysis we now see that following the decision to take the road test the expected outcome is $0.5 \times 1360 + 0.5 \times 1398$ = \$1379, and this is the value associated with the chance node following the 'road test' arc.

We have calculated an optimal response to all the contingencies which can arise in the case where we take the road test and have the option of following it with an oil consumption test. The results are identical to those of Section 5.6 of Chapter 5, but they are more easily seen in the context of Figure 6.5, which also displays some properties of the computational mechanism. Highlighted by this layout is the fact that since actions are calculated in terms of their expected outcomes, the early choices in a sequence of decisions cannot be explored until the consequences of any later actions have been evaluated. For example, in the 'no test' versus 'test' decision, the better option can only be chosen given that the optimal continuation of each option has been evaluated. In this case it means an analysis of the best expected outcome for the exclusive options of 'test' and 'no test'. By virtue of this fact we are also engaged in some redundant computation, finding responses for circumstances which the decisionmaker will not allow to happen. For example, given y_1, the better option is not to take the oil consumption test, so that all our optimal responses in the case of the three outcomes for that test are never needed. It is of course not possible to foretell which calculations are going to be redundant as far as the optimal policy is concerned. We must complete the calculation, compare results and discard inferior options. This redundancy is only inherent at the decision nodes where the decisionmaker is exercising his control over the evolution of the process. At the chance nodes (e.g. the first one where y_1 or y_2 can turn up) the choice of branch is not within the decisionmaker's control and he must have responses for all possible continuations.

In Figure 6.6 we summarize the five options of the car exchange problem. Essentially this is the relevant material taken from the full tree for that problem, i.e. we only include decisions which could be taken (dependent on outcomes) rather than the entire tree. We give optimal response and associated expected outcome. As before the best option from the five available is the road test followed

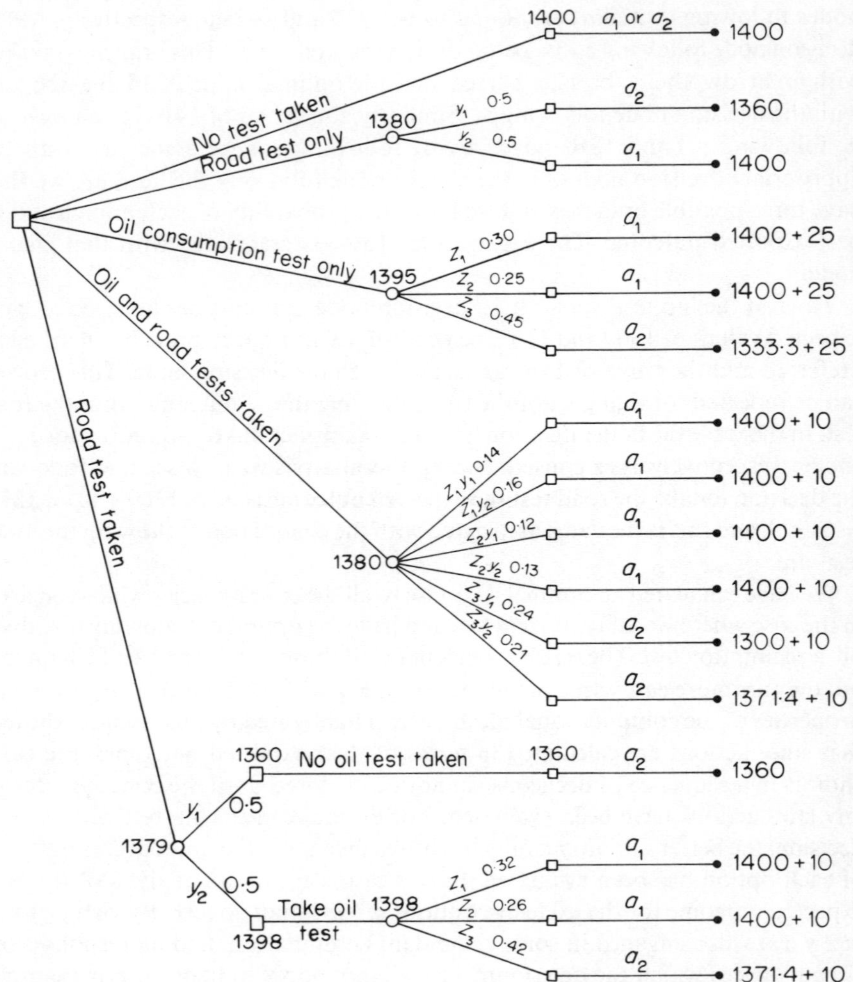

Figure 6.6 A summary of all options available in the car exchange problem, together with the optimal outcome and associated responses in all cases

by the oil consumption test taken only if the outcome of the road test is y_2 (poor performance).

6.3 Another Example of Sequential Decisionmaking

In this section we pose and solve a 'multi-test' problem which illustrates again the usefulness of the decision format. We make some comments on a possible amendment to the details of the calculation and demonstrate one feature of the analysis which is of some general use.

This example is placed in its simplest possible abstract context. It could be re-expressed in a more applied or realistic setting, but since our interest here is in the solution mechanism and not the problem, we have chosen the more economical problem statement format.

A gambler is faced with the problem of deciding with which of two boxes he is being confronted. The boxes, externally identical and both containing ten coloured balls, differ in the proportion of black and white balls present. Thus, box 1 contains six black and four white balls, while box 2 contains eight black and two white balls. If the gambler correctly guesses which box is before him he receives a prize of $100, otherwise he receives nothing. He has no reason to believe that box 1 is any more (or less) likely to be used than box 2, and his prior probability for the use of box 1 (or box 2) is thus 0.5. As an aid to the identification of the box, he is allowed to make samples from the box, at a cost of $3 per sample. The colour of the ball drawn from the box is noted and the ball returned to the box before any further draws are made. He is allowed to postpone the decision on any further sample until after the result of any current sample is known. If he is allowed up to two samples what is his optimal plan?

We use θ_1 and θ_2 to denote the use of box 1 and box 2, respectively. The gambler's actions are to nominate box 1 as the box in use (denote this by a_1) or to nominate box 2 as the box in use (denote this by a_2). The outcome from any sample is either a black ball (B) or a white ball (W). The reward table and conditional probabilities of observation (sample) dependent on the underlying state (box being used) are given in Table 6.1.

Table 6.1 Data for the sampling problem

	a_1	a_2			B	W
θ_1	100	0		θ_1	0.6	0.4
θ_2	0	100		θ_2	0.8	0.2

Rewards   Conditional probability
of observation

Figure 6.7 is the decision tree for this problem. Again decision and chance nodes are distinguished by square and round nodes, respectively. Terminal nodes are round and black. As before, the tree is constructed from left to right corresponding to a sequence of decisions. At the start of the problem and after every sample the gambler is free to choose a_1 or a_2, or take another sample (up to his limit of two).

We have omitted the a_1 and a_2 branches with the terminations in θ_1 and θ_2 for the sake of an uncluttered diagram. Instead, we insert the optimal expected outcome at the terminal node (together with a note of the action generating the optimal value). The details of this will become clear in the analysis. Given the equally likely priors the first sample gives the calculations of Table 6.2.

Hence, the probability of 0.7 on the B arc from the first chance node and the 0.3 on the W arc from that node. After a sample which gives B (and hence posteriors for θ_1 and θ_2 of 0.43 and 0.57, respectively) the actions a_1 and a_2 have expected outcomes $100 \times 0.43 + 0 \times 0.57$ $(= 42.86)$ and $0 \times 0.43 + 100 \times 0.57$ $(= 57.14)$,

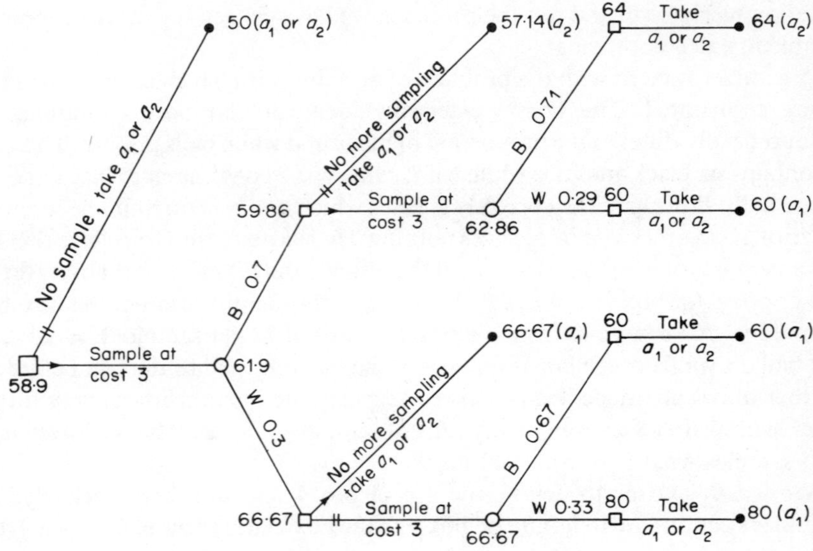

Figure 6.7 The tree for the sampling problem

Table 6.2 Posteriors from one sample

	B	W	Priors	B	W
θ_1	0.6	0.4	0.5	0.3	0.2
θ_2	0.8	0.2	0.5	0.4	0.1
Probabilities of colour				0.7	0.3

Posteriors for		B	W
	θ_1	0.43	0.67
	θ_2	0.57	0.33

respectively. The better action is a_2 giving the 57.14 value (which appears at the terminal node of that branch). Note that we have not yet included the cost of the test which has just been used. A similar calculation will show that a_1 is the better decision following a sample of white.

If after the B on the first sample another sample is taken then the priors for θ_1 and θ_2 for this sample are now the posteriors (given B) from the first sample. The standard update thus gives Table 6.3. This shows that at the chance node following the second sample after a first sample result of B, the probabilities for B and W are 0.71 and 0.29, respectively (as shown on Figure 6.7). The appropriate posterior for the second sample result enables us to calculate the better response to all (both) test outcomes. Thus, if the second sample gives B, the better action is that which gives max $\{0.36 \times 100 + 0.64 \times 0, 0.36 \times 0 + 0.64 \times 100\} = 64$, given by a_2. Similarly, the better response to W on this sample is to use a_1, which generates

Table 6.3 Posteriors from a second sample, given a black on the
first sample

	B	W	Priors	B	W
θ_1	0.6	0.4	0.43	0.26	0.17
θ_2	0.8	0.2	0.57	0.46	0.11

Probabilities 0.71 0.29
of colour

Posteriors for	θ_1	0.36	0.60
	θ_2	0.64	0.40

an expected outcome of 60. Thus, given that the second sample is taken after the **B** on the first the expected outcome is $0.71 \times 64 + 0.29 \times 60 = 62.86$ (again ignoring the cost of the sample).

A similar analysis on the second sample following a **W** on the first gives the optimal response shown in Figure 6.7 and an expected outcome using the second sample of 66.67 before counting the cost of sampling.

If we now examine the tree, bearing in mind the sampling costs, we can derive the gambler's optimal policy. At the decision node following the **B** on the first sample the options are either to decide now for the better of a_1 or a_2, or sample again (at a cost of \$3) and then make optimal use of that extra information. Thus, looking down the branches from that decision node, the gambler can see that the better decision of a_1 or a_2 is a_2 (which gives an expected outcome of \$57.14), and against this is the $\$(62.86 - 3)$ to be expected from an optimal response to the second sample. The better of these is the sampling decision, making optimal use of the second sample outcome. With this decision node we therefore associate the expected reward which the optimal policy will generate (from that node onwards). The arcs are marked accordingly.

Consideration of the decision node following **W** on the first sample indicates a comparison between sampling and best response (with net expected reward $(66.67 - 3)$) and decision a_1 (with expected reward of 66.67). The better of these is decision a_1 and the expected reward from that is associated with the decision node following **W** on the first sample. Again the arcs out of the decision node are marked accordingly.

If we step back to the chance node which gives the branches following the first sample decision, we can calculate the expected reward for that chance node. We have a probability of 0.7 for **B** and here an expected outcome of 59.86, while for **W** the probability is 0.3 and the expected outcome 66.67. Thus, the expected outcome is $0.7 \times 59.86 + 0.3 \times 66.67 = 61.9$. If we skip back yet again to the first decision node, the gambler has two options. One is to opt for the better of a_1 or a_2 with no further information and obtain an expected reward of \$50 (for either decision). Alternatively, a sample can be taken which will give a net expected reward of $(61.9 - 3) = \$58.9$, provided the information from that sample (and any subsequent sample) is properly used.

His optimal response is thus to take the first sample. If this turns out to give a black ball he should sample again and take a_2 if the second sample is black and a_1 if the second sample is white. If the first sample is white he should take no further samples, but take action a_1.

One major difference in our computational scheme has been to introduce costs (in this case sample costs) as they occur in the tree, rather than, as in the previous example, accumulate all costs and rewards for a particular path and associate this with the terminal node for that path. For problems where we have, for example, expected money outcomes, the two processes will yield identical results. If we are analysing a problem where the criterion involves the use of utility functions then only the second process should be used. Corresponding to a given action (or sequence of actions) it is the net outcome whose utility is used in any comparison. Except for simple expectations the net outcome cannot be evaluated by combining evaluations for its components.

To demonstrate this consider Figure 6.8 (which may be thought of as part of a larger decision problem). After taking a sample at cost c dollars the decisionmaker is faced with the option of a_1 or a_2. Given a choice of a_i if state of nature θ_j holds, the reward is r_{ij} dollars $(i, j = 1, 2)$ and this is shown at the terminal nodes of Figure 6.8. If we denote the probability of θ_1 by p (and thus the probability of θ_2 by $1 - p$) then in expected money terms the decisionmaker would opt for that action giving $\max \{pr_{11} + (1 - p)r_{12}, pr_{21} + (1 - p)r_{22}\} = R$ dollars, say. Thus, at the decision node where sampling is an option the sample branch has expected outcome $R - c$.

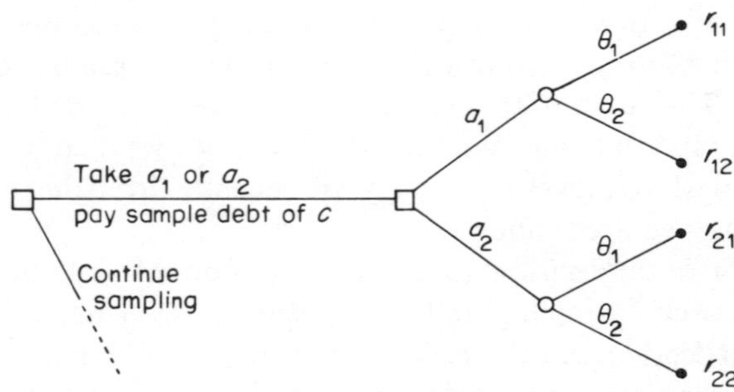

Figure 6.8 The tree with sample cost 'placed' on an arc

If the sample cost is deducted from the rewards, as in Figure 6.9, then the better action of a_1 and a_2 gives

$$\max \{p(r_{11} - c) + (1 - p)(r_{12} - c), p(r_{21} - c) + (1 - p)(r_{22} - c)\}$$
$$= \max \{pr_{11} + (1 - p)r_{12} - c, pr_{21} + (1 - p)r_{22} - c\} = R - c$$

as before. At the sample/no sample decision node the evaluation of the sample option is the same for the two calculations.

If it is appropriate for a utility function, say u, to be used in the analysis, then from Figure 6.9 the better action is found from

$$\max \{pu(r_{11} - c) + (1 - p)u(r_{12} - c), pu(r_{21} - c) + (1 - p)u(r_{22} - c)\}.$$

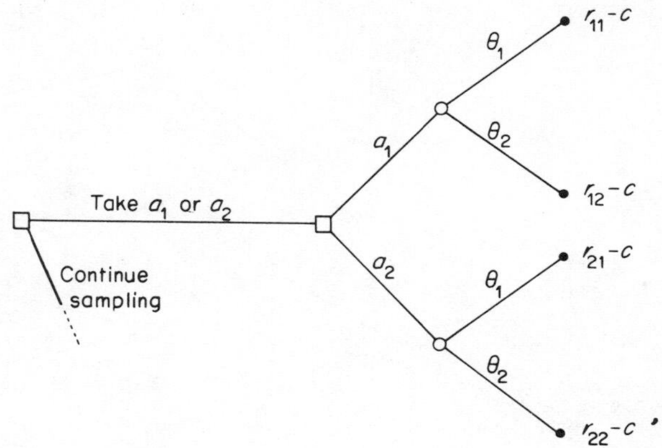

Figure 6.9 The tree with sample cost included in the pay-off at the terminal node

For a general utility function this will not be the same as

$$\max\{pu(r_{11})+(1-p)u(r_{12}),\ pu(r_{21})+(1-p)u(r_{22})\}-u(c).$$

This analysis is incorrectly constructed. Our analysis is properly applied to problems where the outcomes are inclusive of all cost and rewards leading up to the terminal node. Only for expected money outcome is the first process correct.

For the gambler's problem it is again true that proper use of the option to postpone further sampling until the result of the current sample is known enhances the expected outcome. Figure 6.10 gives an analysis of the problem where exactly none, one, two or three samples may be taken and paid for (at a cost of \$3 per sample), and then an optimal response taken to the entire sample output. On the sample result arcs we summarize the sample content in an obvious way, e.g. BW for one black and one white when the sample is taken twice. Note that the order is not significant and BW can refer to the case of a black followed by a white and the other possibility of a white followed by a black. After each action one or other of the states of nature will reveal themselves, and the tree displays the posterior probabilities for all the cases. The expected outcome for each action is calculated and the optimal responses marked in the usual way. The outcomes are all exclusive of sampling cost, which is given on the different sample size decision arcs.

To illustrate one set of prior to posterior calculations we present those relevant to the two-sample case. The values for the conditional probabilities for a two-sample test are calculated directly from those of the one-sample test. Thus,

$$p(\mathrm{BB}|\theta_1)=p(\mathrm{B}|\theta_1)p(\mathrm{B}|\theta_1)=0.6\times0.6=0.36.$$

The probability of a black and a white is

$$p(\mathrm{B}|\theta_1)p(\mathrm{W}|\theta_1)+p(\mathrm{W}|\theta_1)p(\mathrm{B}|\theta_1)=0.6\times0.4+0.4\times0.6=0.48,$$

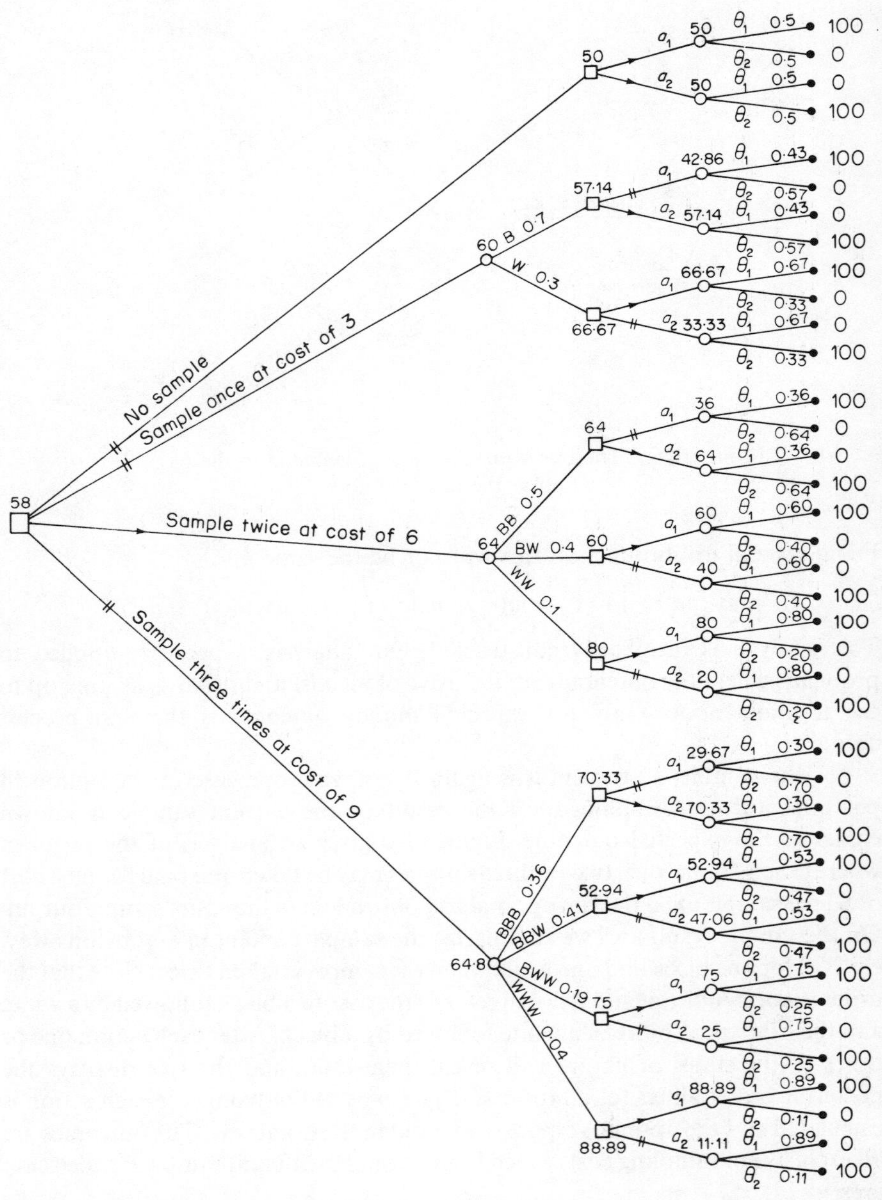

Figure 6.10 A summary of all options available in the sampling problem, together with the optimal outcome and associated responses in all cases

since we must consider the two exclusive and exhaustive mechanisms by which the pair can arise (i.e. black followed by white, and white followed by black). The other entries of the conditional table are argued in a similar manner (see Table 6.4).

Table 6.4 Posteriors from a sample of two balls drawn simultaneously

	BB	BW	WW	Priors	BB	BW	WW
θ_1	0.36	0.48	0.16	0.5	0.18	0.24	0.08
θ_2	0.64	0.32	0.04	0.5	0.32	0.16	0.02

Probabilities of sample: 0.50 0.40 0.10

Posteriors for	BB	BW	WW
θ_1	0.36	0.60	0.80
θ_2	0.64	0.40	0.20

From Figure 6.10 we see that the options and net outcomes are to take no sample (expected outcome $\$50$), to take one sample (expected outcome $60 - 3 = \$57$), to take two samples (expected outcome $64 - 6 = \$58$), and to take three samples (expected outcome $64.8 - 9 = \$55.8$). The best option is to take two samples where with optimal responses there is an expected reward of $\$58$. Compare this with the two-stage sampling where the expected outcome from the optimal policy is $\$58.9$.

The net reward for the three-sample option in Figure 6.10 is less than the two-sample option of that same figure, and this of course is less than the expected reward given that the gambler is allowed up to two (rather than exactly two) samples. By an extension of Figure 6.7, introducing the option of a third sample we could construct the optimal strategy for that problem. We would find that in no circumstances is this third sample ever taken. For example, after the black on the second sample the action a_2 yields an expected reward of 64 (before deduction of sample costs). If instead of taking a_2 a further sample was taken, the expected outcome using the third sample result in an optimal manner is 65.6. To compare with the alternative option we must deduct the third sample cost of three from this, leaving us with action a_2 (giving $\$64$) versus the third sample (giving $\$62.6$).

In fact we could apply a more general argument to the problem of taking a decision on the basis of current knowledge as against the option of taking another sample and responding optimally to the outcome of that sample. We look at the current versus sample decision by a process which has already been seen in the study of the expected value of information. If we have probabilities for states θ_1 and θ_2 of p and $(1 - p)$, respectively, then the standard procedure for calculating posteriors gives us the data of Table 6.5. The better response to B is given by $\max \{300p/(4 - p), 400(1 - p)/(4 - p)\}$, and to W is given by $\max \{200p/(1 + p), 100(1 - p)/(1 + p)\}$. The expected outcome given that the sample is taken (and neglecting for the moment the cost of such a sample) is given by

$$(4 - p)/5 \max \{300p/(4 - p), 400(1 - p)/(4 - p)\} + (1 + p)/5$$
$$\max \{200p/(1 + p), 100(1 - p)/(1 + p)\}$$
$$= \max \{60p, 80(1 - p)\} + \max \{40p, 20(1 - p)\} = F(p) \text{ say.}$$

154

Table 6.5 Posteriors from one sample using arbitrary priors

	B	W	Priors		B	W
θ_1	0.6	0.4	p		$0.6p$	$0.4p$
θ_2	0.8	0.2	$1-p$		$0.8(1-p)$	$0.2(1-p)$

Probabilities of colours $0.8-0.2p$ $0.2+0.2p$

Posteriors for		B	W
	θ_1	$3p/(4-p)$	$2p/(1+p)$
	θ_2	$4(1-p)/(4-p)$	$(1-p)/(1+p)$

Examination of the two component expressions shows that the 'break-points' in them are at $p = 1/3$ for the second and $p = 4/7$ for the first. Thus, for $0 \leqslant p \leqslant 1/3$, $F(p) = 80(1-p) + 20(1-p) = 100(1-p)$. For $1/3 \leqslant p \leqslant 4/7$, $F(p) = 80(1-p) + 40p = 80 - 40p$, while for $4/7 \leqslant p \leqslant 1$, $F(p) = 60p + 40p = 100p$. In Figure 6.11 the dotted line gives the function $F(p)$ over the range $0 \leqslant p \leqslant 1$. With only the probabilities of p and $(1-p)$ for the states of nature the best expected outcome is given by $\max\{100p, 100(1-p)\}$. The sample produces an improvement in expected outcome for p values in the range $1/3 < p < 4/7$ (and again this is before consideration of the cost of the sample). In Figure 6.12 we graph $[F(p) - \max\{100p, 100(1-p)\}]$ giving the expected value of sample information as a function of p.

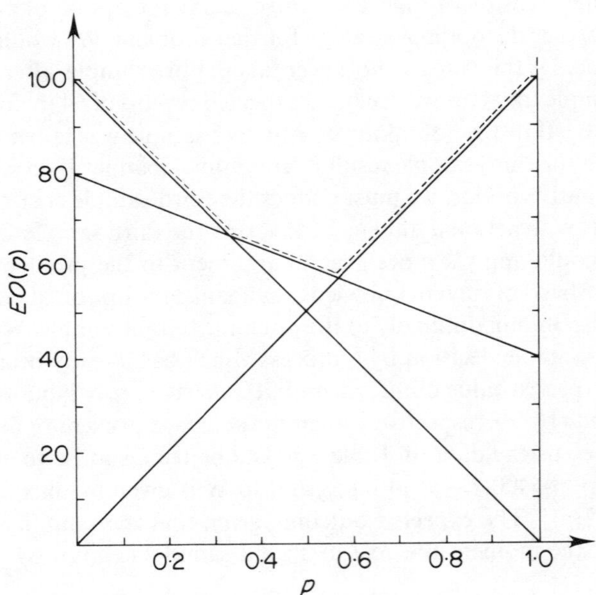

Figure 6.11 Expected outcome when one extra sample is allowed, for an arbitrary prior p in the range $0 \leqslant p \leqslant 1$

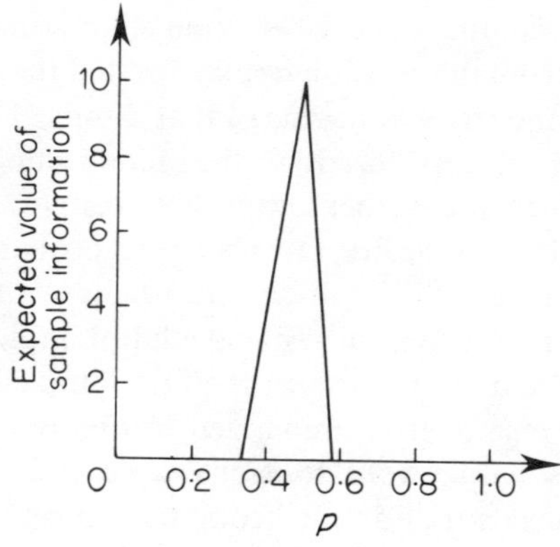

Figure 6.12 Expected value of sample information as a function of the prior p when one extra sample is allowed

We can easily see that the expected value of sample information is zero for $0 \leqslant p \leqslant 1/3$ and for $4/7 \leqslant p \leqslant 1$. For $1/3 \leqslant p \leqslant 1/2$ we have the difference as $(80 - 40p) - 100(1 - p) = 60p - 20$, while for $1/2 \leqslant p \leqslant 4/7$ it is $(80 - 40p) - 100p = 80 - 140p$.

From Figure 6.12 we easily see that no sample should cost more than \$10 if it is to be worthwhile (and that only for the case $p = 0.5$). If the cost of an extra sample is, say, \$3, we can easily find those p values for which this sample is cost effective. Solving $(60p - 20) = 3$ and $(80 - 140p) = 3$ gives p values of 0.383 and 0.550, respectively. For any p within this range proper use of one extra sample will give an expected outcome superior to that obtainable without the extra sample. This calculation does take into account the cost of the extra sample, since it is using (e.g. in Figure 6.12) a net expected outcome.

As an example of the use of this information, consider again the optional third sample discussed above (where the sample decision can be postponed until current sample results, if any, are known). We saw that after two successive blacks in the samples the optimal action is a_2, giving an expected outcome of \$64 (without taking into account sampling costs). If there is an option of a third sample here, then it is entered with a prior value for box 1 (the p value above) of 0.360. Since this is less than the smallest p value for which the expected value of (subsequent) sample information is non-negative ($p = 0.383$) the sample ought not to be taken. This agrees with our earlier assertion. Similarly, after a black and a white in the first two samples (in any order) the appropriate p value is 0.6, which is greater than the maximum p value for which the expected value of (subsequent) sample information is non-negative ($p = 0.583$). Again after two whites on the first two samples the p value ($= 0.80$) is outside the range for which one further sample is worthwhile.

We can in fact cast in this mould some of the decisions displayed in Figure 6.7, where we were investigating the gambler's problem with up to two samples.

Consider the problem at the stage where one sample has been taken. If the outcome is black then from the decision tree we see that the optimal response is to sample again and respond to the outcome of that sample. For a black on the first sample the prior for box 1 appropriate to the second sample is 0.43, and this is within the range for which one further sample has positive expected sample value. On the other hand, a white on the first sample gives a probability for box 1 of 0.66, and this is outside the range for which one further sample is known to be worthwhile. As in Figure 6.7, our current calculation indicates that the optimal policy is to sample again after a black on the first sample but not after a white.

The analysis whose results are summarized in Figure 6.12 is 'myopic' in the sense that the comparison is between decisions based on current information and decisions based on one extra sample from the current position. If we are interested in the problem of taking two extra samples as against a decision based on current information, then a parallel analysis will provide the expected value of sample information as a function of p, the current probability for box 1 being used. This is left as an exercise (see Exercise 6.6). More generally we might be interested in the problem of how many (if any) samples to take or, equivalently, when to stop sampling. For the case of one extra sample (and, in the exercise, two extra samples) the optimal decision is dependent upon the current state of knowledge of the system under study, namely the value for p. For the more general problem of optimal stopping (of the sampling process) this will again be the case. We note that with perfect information the expected reward the gambler can obtain is $0.5 \times 100 + 0.5 \times 100 = \$100$. With no information beyond the prior probabilities of 0.5 for box 1 (and box 2) the expected outcome is $0.5 \times 100 + 0.5 \times 0 = \$50$ (obtained from either a_1 or a_2). For these priors the expected value of perfect information is $100 - 50 = \$50$. If the cost per sample is \$3 then obviously no more than 50/3, i.e. 16, tests should ever be taken. This upper bound on the number of tests can be used in a scheme which determines the optimal sampling policy. A detailed analysis of multi-stage decision problems is pursued in subsequent chapters, where the standard format of the problems is somewhat different from that already used. We have, however, already seen the application of the principle which structures the decision process, although it has not been enunciated in a formal manner.

6.4 Further Reading

Decision trees are a major feature of the development by Raiffa (1968) and will be found in some form in most books on decision analysis. Many of the applications in Kaufmann and Thomas (1977) and Moore, Thomas, Bunn and Hampton (1976) make use of this format. The reader interested in applications is best directed to the operational research/management science journals such as *Operations Research, Journal of the Operational Research Society, Management Science, European Journal of Operational Research* and *Omega*, or to general business journals such as the *Harvard Business Review* and *Sloan Management Review*. Specialist journals (e.g. in medicine, engineering, planning) also carry applications of decision analytic techniques to problems in their own fields.

Exercises for Chapter 6

In addition to these exercises the reader is invited to re-attempt from the Chapter 5 set those which will yield to a decision tree format.

6.1   Your new job requires you to have the use of a car for the next two years, and the possibilities open to you are to opt for a new car costing $9000 or a second-hand car costing $6000. The guarantee on the new car covers all the repair charges for the period in question, but a second-hand car does not carry these guarantees and all costs have to be met by yourself.

In the second-hand market cars are distinguished as either good buys or bad buys. Over the two years in question a good buy will involve a total expenditure of $1500 on repairs, whilst a bad buy will accumulate bills of $4500 for repair.

For a fee of $150 a motoring organization will examine and road test the car, giving you a verdict as to whether the car is a good or a bad buy. This prediction can of course be in error, and the table below gives the probability of the predictions conditional on the true nature of the car.

		Prediction	
		Good buy	Bad buy
State	Good buy	0.7	0.3
	Bad buy	0.1	0.9

If the proportion of good buys in the second-hand market is 0.5, use a decision tree format to find your optimal policy. What is the maximum fee you would pay for a perfect prediction system?

Suppose the organization is slow to arrange the necessary tests, and the second-hand car which is your potential purchase may thus be lost to you before the test can be arranged. In this circumstance you are then obliged to purchase a new car. If the probability of the car being sold before your test can be arranged is 1/3, what is your optimal policy and how much would you now be willing to pay for a perfect prediction system?

6.2   A company sees a potential market for a new product. It will take a year to set up the manufacture of its product at a cost of one million dollars, and if the product proves successful it should make a net profit thereafter of $250 000 per year, for nine years. If unsuccessful, sales will just cover the cost of manufacture for each subsequent year. The company feels that, after ten years, new technology will make the proposed product obsolete, and that the chance of a successful product is 0.5.

The company has three options. It can go ahead with production, or decide not to produce at all. The third option is to test the market by interviewing prospective customers before any commitment to production. This will cost $250 000 and delay production by a year. The likelihoods for customer's opinions given the product's prospects are given in the table below.

| | *Customers are* | | |
	Enthusiastic	Indifferent	Hostile
Product successful	0.75	0.25	0
Product unsuccessful	0.25	0.25	0.5

At the end of the year's interviewing the company has to decide whether or not to produce. In a decision tree format find the strategy which maximizes the expected money outcome for the company.

6.3   You have \$1000 to use and you may either (a) deposit it in a bank and earn 10% per annum or (b) invest it in shares. Your objective is to maximize your expected money holding in two years' time. Regardless of your first decision it can be revised one year from now. While there is no reason to expect the interest rate at the bank to change, over each of the two years the stock market may rise, stay level or fall.

If it rises you gain \$200 per \$1000 invested at the beginning of the year, while if it falls you lose at a rate of \$100 per \$1000 invested. If it stays level your investment is unchanged. For the first year the probabilities of the market rising, staying level or falling are equal, but for the second year the probabilities are conditional on the first year's change, thus:

| | | *Change in second year* | | |
		Rise	Level	Fall
Change in first year	Rise	0.75	0.25	0
	Level	0.25	0.50	0.25
	Fall	0.50	0	0.50

Find your optimal strategy using a decision tree format.
What values of bank interest would make it
  (a) never worth investing in shares?
  (b) never worth putting money in the bank?

6.4   Consider the two-state, two-action, three-observation problem where a decisionmaker has to choose between two outcomes a_1 and a_2 in the face of an unknown state of nature θ_1 or θ_2. The table of losses is

	a_1	a_2
θ_1	10	60
θ_2	40	0

The observation can take one of three values, x_1, x_2 or x_3, and the table of conditional probabilities is

$$\begin{array}{c|ccc} & x_1 & x_2 & x_3 \\ \hline \theta_1 & 0.5 & 0.25 & 0.25 \\ \theta_2 & 0.20 & 0.20 & 0.60 \end{array} \quad p(x|\theta)$$

The states of nature have prior probabilities $g(\theta_1) = g(\theta_2) = 1/2$. Suppose the cost of observation depends on what is observed, i.e., no cost is incurred before the observation is made, but if x is observed a cost of $c(x)$ is incurred. If we have $c(x_1) = 3$, $c(x_2) = 9$ and $c(x_3) = 4$, use decision trees to find the strategy which minimizes expected losses.

6.5   From the data given in Exercise 5.11 where a company may use up to two forecasts before deciding on its production policy, use a decision tree format to find the strategy which maximizes expected utility given that the utility function is $u(x) = \sqrt{x}$, where x is in thousands of dollars. You may assume, as before, that the forecast from Future States Ltd can only be taken after the result from Crystal Ball Inc. has been announced.

6.6   Consider the example of Section 6.3 where an observation now consists of the draw of two balls from the box (with replacement of the ball from the first sample before the second is taken). The conditional probabilities of sample outcome given box used are thus those of the first part of Table 6.4. Using prior probabilities for θ_1 and θ_2 of p and $(1-p)$ respectively, calculate the expected value of sample information as a function of p. Produce illustrations for this problem corresponding to those of Figures 6.11 and 6.12.

6.7   For the example of Section 6.3, where up to two samples may be taken, find the optimal strategy given that any second sample is taken without replacement of the ball from the first sample.

Chapter 7

Sequential Decision Problems

7.1 Introduction and a First Example

The decision problems studied so far have involved the optimal selection from a set of allowable decisions A, and in so far as additional information could be obtained there was a sequential aspect to the problem. Decisions about information purchase are followed by the (one-off) selection of an action from the set A in the light of the information obtained. To solve the problem of information value (as part of the problem of information purchase) it is of course necessary to calculate the optimal response to many outcomes for the decision(s) to purchase extra information, but eventually one action $a \in A$ will be selected as the optimal response to the information obtained. Our concern is this chapter and those that follow is to study and solve a rather different type of sequential problem.

Instead of one action as the reaction to information, and the problem terminating with the outcome from this choice, we consider the problem where the choice of action has to be repeatedly made. Our interest is mainly in problems where the sequence of actions chosen does not determine exactly the evolution of the system which we are attempting to control. In Sections 7.4, 7.5 and 7.6 we offer some examples of the use of our insights to deterministic problems, but our main effort is concentrated on (sequential) decision making under uncertainty, and Sections 7.4, 7.5 and 7.6 could be skipped without prejudice.

As an example of the problem type we will formulate and solve, consider the following description which is a numerical instance of Example 1.5. Demand for an item in any period (say a week) can be either high (H) or low (L) and it has been observed that demand in a given period does presage (but does not determine) demand in the succeeding week. Thus, a week of high demand is as likely to be followed by another week of high demand as it is by a week of low demand. On the other hand, a week of low demand will in 75 % of cases be followed by another week of low demand, the remaining 25 % being weeks of high demand. This information can be summarized in the matrix below which we will call P^I. Thus,

$$P^I = \begin{array}{cc} & \begin{array}{cc} \text{H} & \text{L} \end{array} \\ \begin{array}{c} \text{H} \\ \text{L} \end{array} & \begin{bmatrix} 0.5 & 0.5 \\ 0.25 & 0.75 \end{bmatrix} \end{array}.$$

There are economic consequences allied to this process, and the net profits associated with these same pairs of demands in successive weeks is summarized in R^{I} below, where the units are thousands of dollars:

$$R^{\mathrm{I}} = \begin{array}{c} \\ \mathrm{H} \\ \mathrm{L} \end{array} \begin{array}{cc} \mathrm{H} & \mathrm{L} \\ \begin{bmatrix} 20 & 10 \\ 15 & 8 \end{bmatrix} \end{array}.$$

Thus, a week of high demand following on from a week of high demand generates a profit of \$20 000, but a week of high demand following on from a week of low demand generates only \$15 000 profit. It is possible for the vendor of the article to influence demand by advertising. For a fee of \$2000 he can influence successive demand levels as described by P^{II} below:

$$P^{\mathrm{II}} = \begin{array}{c} \\ \mathrm{H} \\ \mathrm{L} \end{array} \begin{array}{cc} \mathrm{H} & \mathrm{L} \\ \begin{bmatrix} 0.8 & 0.2 \\ 0.5 & 0.5 \end{bmatrix} \end{array}.$$

Thus, demand at a high level is more likely to stay high while demand at a low level is more likely to be enhanced to the higher level in the following week than if no advertising takes place. The net rewards given by R^{II} below reflect the cost of advertising:

$$R^{\mathrm{II}} = \begin{array}{c} \\ \mathrm{H} \\ \mathrm{L} \end{array} \begin{array}{cc} \mathrm{H} & \mathrm{L} \\ \begin{bmatrix} 18 & 8 \\ 13 & 6 \end{bmatrix} \end{array}.$$

The advertising is assumed to have an influence for one time period only, and if its effects are to be continued the fee must be paid for every occasion on which its influence is desired. Note that the decision to advertise or not does not determine the demand level following some current level, it merely influences the probabilities of successive demand levels. Given that there has just been a week of high demand, what is the optimal policy if the system is to be controlled for, say, two periods?

Before attempting a solution there are two features of the problem which need to be examined. In the first instance we have talked of an optimal solution without reference to a criterion. The obvious one, and that which we use, is to seek the maximum total profit, and since profit levels are not determined by a given policy, we use the expectation of profit as our guide. It has been established that the problem starts in a week following a week of high demand. Obviously as the demand manifests itself over time the sequence of demands could end with either a low or high demand. We assume (in this version of the problem) that there is no distinction between these demand levels as terminal manifestations of demand, though they do of course give rise to different contributions to the total expected reward. The rationale for this assumption (which only simplifies the calculations and does not invalidate the method if it is not true) will become clear as we construct the decision tree for the problem given in Figure 7.1. Building from left to right as usual the first arc records the occurrence of a week of high demand just

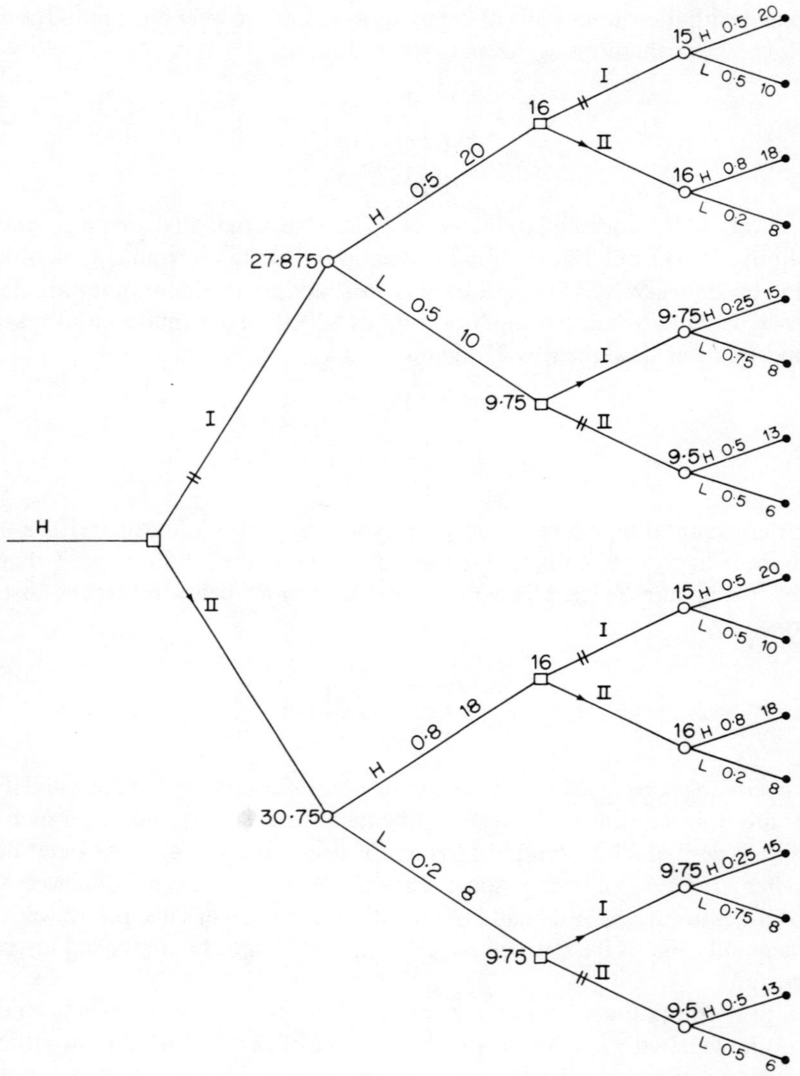

Figure 7.1 The tree for the demand level problem where demand is initially high and the system is to be controlled over two weeks

finishing. There is no contribution from this to total expected profit, it merely distinguishes the elements of the P and R matrices which are relevant to this part of the tree.

At the first decision node the choice is between using the advertising option (II) or continuing without advertising (I). Concentrating initially on the branch starting with the 'no advertising' option demand will manifest itself as high (H) or low (L) with probabilities 0.5 each (i.e. those given by the H row of P^I) and the appropriate rewards for these occasions are given by the H row of R^1. The probabilities and rewards are included on the appropriate arcs of the tree.

Continuing down the same branch after the initial choice of I and, say, the H demand turning up, there is a second decision to be taken (corresponding to the second and last of the two weeks over which the problem is being analysed). Again at the decision node the branches are marked I and II, and following each of these the demand manifests itself. The relevant probabilities and profits are those corresponding to a previous demand (in week 1) which was high. Thus, following I and II in week 2 the arcs are marked with demand levels and probabilities and rewards for those levels.

Similarly, if the demand had been L after the initial choice of I the demands in the second week following choices of I or II are those from the second (bottom) row of the P and R matrices. Again all demand level arcs are marked with the corresponding probability and reward. The branch with initial choice of II following the starting condition of a previous week of high demand is constructed and annotated in a similar manner. The problem terminates after two weeks (in this version) only to maintain a decision tree of manageable proportions. We have assumed that there is no difference between the system after it has finished with a low or a high demand.

To evaluate options we again work back from right to left, taking expectations at chance nodes and choosing the better actions at decision nodes. Thus, along the branch with I followed by H followed by I, at the last chance node we have a high demand with probability 0.5 and profit 20 and a low demand with probability of 0.5 and profit of 10. There is no value associated with the terminal nodes (unlike our earlier decision trees) since we do not discriminate between the terminal conditions of the system. The action associated with I therefore has an expected outcome of $0.5 \times 20 + 0.5 \times 10 = 15$, and similarly the action associated with II gives an expected outcome of $0.8 \times 18 + 0.2 \times 8 = 16$. Thus, stepping back to the earlier decision node the optimal choice is along the II branch (so marked) and the expected outcome of 16 is associated with that decision node. The actions corresponding to I and II following the L branch (along the first I branch) have expected outcomes of $0.25 \times 15 + 0.75 \times 8$ and $0.5 \times 13 + 0.5 \times 6$, respectively. The better of these is the first and the I branch is marked preferred at the decision node and the value of 9.75 associated with that node.

Stepping back along the tree to the first chance node following the initial I branch the two arcs of H and L are marked with their probabilities and rewards. Recall that these are given by the numbers from the H rows of P^1 and R^1 (since this node is after an initial occurrence of H). Given the option I is taken, then with probability 0.5 there is high demand giving a profit of 20 and a best profit from continuation along that branch of 16, while with probability 0.5 there is low demand giving a profit of 10 and a best profit from continuation along that branch of 9.75. The expected profit from this initial decision of I and optimal continuation (i.e. response to manifest demand) is $0.5(20 + 16) + 0.5(10 + 9.75) = 27.875$.

The lower half of the tree can be analysed similarly. Along the II branch, examining the options after the occurrence of H, option I gives H and L with probabilities 0.5 each and profits of 20 and 10, respectively. Option II gives H and L with probabilities of 0.8 and 0.2 and profits of 18 and 8 respectively. Note that this part of the tree is identical to that in the upper half where I and II are examined after H following the I option. The initial option of I or II is irrelevant to the determination of the profit levels and probabilities. All that matters is the demand in the previous period (here H) and the option being pursued (I or II). The expectations and optimal actions are calculated and marked as before. Similarly for the action evaluation following L. The fact that the low demand is preceded by II (or I) is irrelevant. It is the combination of L and then the choice of I (or II) which settles the demand probabilities and profits. The penultimate decision nodes along this lower half thus have the same values associated with them (and actions generating these values) as corresponding nodes of the upper half. This permits a more compact representation which we shortly investigate.

If we step left again to the chance node following the initial choice of II, the H and L arcs following from a choice of II are the demands when the previous demand was H. The probabilities are therefore 0.8 for H (with profit 18) and 0.2 for L (with profit 8). The expectation at the chance node combining immediate profit and optimal continuation gives an expected value of $0.8(18 + 16) + 0.2(8 + 9.75) = 30.75$ and this is the value associated with that chance node.

Stepping back to the initial decision node the initial option I can be seen to offer an expected profit of 27.875 which is inferior to the expected profit from II of 30.75. The optimal solution to the two-period problem is therefore to advertise (option II) in the first period. If demand turns out to be high then advertise again in the last period, but if demand turns out to be low then do not advertise in the last period.

From our observation that parts of the tree are essentially identical we can generate a rather more compact representation of the problem than Figure 7.1. In that figure we saw that when evaluating the options I or II in the second period after a high demand in the first period it did not matter if this high demand took place as a consequence of the choice of I or II in the first period. The only influence on the probability of demand in any period is the demand level of the previous period (and of course the decision being taken). It is the current *state* of the system (here demand level) which influences behaviour, not the history of the system up to the present state.

Thus, to display the problem we need only represent each state once in any period, as in Figure 7.2. Here the number of periods to go is enumerated along the 'axis' and at each of these *stages* the two possible states are shown. With two weeks to go where we have just had a period of high demand we are in state H at the leftmost stage. A decision here of I or II will influence, but not determine, the *transition* we make to H or L at the next stage (where we have one week to go). The probabilities of transition and corresponding rewards under decision k are marked on the links from H to H and H to L. With one period to go we could be in either state. If in H then transition (and reward) to H and L at the last stage is possible,

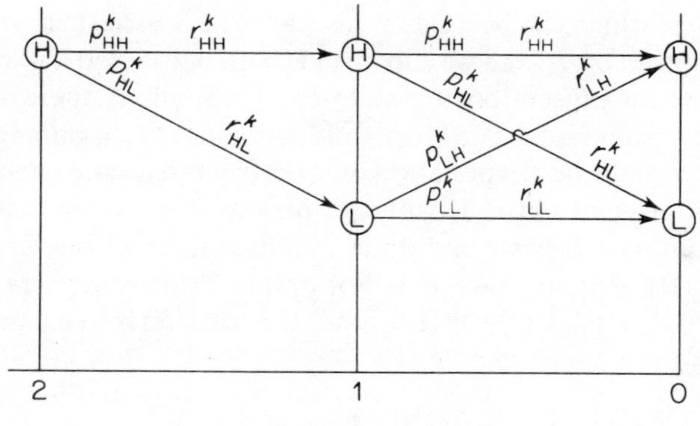

Figure 7.2 An alternative rendering of the structure of the tree
in Figure 7.1

and similarly from L at the penultimate stage, transition is possible to H and L at the last stage. The probabilities and profits are marked on the appropriate links.

It is a feature of the problem that there is no discrimination between the terminal states. Note that probabilities and profits apply in this description to the links joining states. Thus, the H to H link generates profit of 20 (under I) and 18 (under II). The fact that the transition ends up in H is only relevant from that stage on in determining the appropriate transition probabilities (i.e. those starting in this state). Let us define $v_n(i)$ to be the *expected profit to be made using an optimal policy when the state of the system is i and there are n weeks to go before the problem terminates.* Thus, here the state of the system is the demand level which has just taken place (i.e. H or L) and we are interested in the problem where n is two.

From the indifference between the terminal stages we have $v_0(H) = v_0(L)$ and for simplicity we take both of these as zero, though any finite number would do. If we step left to the stage where there is one week to go, then when in state H the options are I giving expected profit

$$p^I_{HH}(r^I_{HH} + v_0(H)) + p^I_{HL}(r^I_{HL} + v_0(L)) = 0.5 \times 20 + 0.5 \times 10 = 15,$$

and II giving expected profit

$$p^{II}_{HH}(r^{II}_{HH} + v_0(H)) + p^{II}_{HL}(r^{II}_{HL} + v_0(L)) = 0.8 \times 18 + 0.2 \times 6 = 16.$$

The better of these is given by II, and thus $v_1(H) = 16$. If we denote by $d_n(i)$ the *optimal response when in state i with n periods to go*, then $d_1(H) = II$. Similarly,

$$v_1(L) = \max_k \{p^k_{LH}(r^k_{LH} + v_0(H)) + p^k_{LL}(r^k_{LL} + v_0(L))\}$$
$$= \max\,(0.25 \times 15 + 0.75 \times 8,\ 0.5 \times 13 + 0.5 \times 6) = 9.75$$

and $d_1(L) = I$. Thus, in all (both) states with one stage to go we have found the best profit which can be expected if these states are entered, and the decisions which generate these best expected profits.

If we step left yet again to the state H with two periods to go, then again there are two options which can be used in this state. If I is used then with probablity p_{HH}^{I} there is a profit of r_{HH}^{I} and we end up in H with one period left to go, knowing that the best we can expect from that state is $v_1(H)$. Similarly, there is a probability p_{HL}^{I} that the transition is to state L with one period left to go, gaining profit r_{HL}^{I} on the way, and with the best expectation of $v_1(L)$ from that state onward. Thus, the expected profit using I out of H with two periods to go, given that we continue optimally from wherever we end up as a consequence of our first decision, is $p_{HH}^{I}(r_{HH}^{I} + v_1(H)) + p_{HL}^{I}(r_{HL}^{I} + v_1(L))$. For option II the equivalent expression is $p_{HH}^{II}(r_{HH}^{II} + v_1(H)) + p_{HL}^{II}(r_{HL}^{II} + v_1(L))$. Since the criterion is to maximize expected profit we have

$$
\begin{aligned}
v_2(H) &= \max_{k} \{p_{HH}^{k}(r_{HH}^{k} + v_1(H)) + p_{HL}^{k}(r_{HL}^{k} + v_1(L))\} \\
&= \max \{0.5(20+16)+0.5(10+9.75),\ 0.8(18+16)+0.2(8+9.75)\} \quad (1) \\
&= \max \{29.875,\ 30.75\} = 30.75 \text{ and } d_2(H) = II.
\end{aligned}
$$

Before continuation of the solution to other states and stages, consider the relative content of Figures 7.1 and 7.2. In Figure 7.1 we have 31 nodes (and 31 arcs) while in Figure 7.2 we have 5 'nodes' and 6 'arcs'. Figure 7.2 is not a tree hence our hesitation to use without qualification the terminology from the trees.

If we wish to find the optimal policy given that the problem starts from a state where the demand has just been low, then the solution in the format of Figure 7.1 would require a new tree to be drawn since the initial H and L probabilities following the options of I or II different from those of Figure 7.1. Using the format of Figure 7.2 we need only add the arcs from L (with two periods to go) to H and L (with one period to go) and use the formula (analogous to (1) above):

$$
\begin{aligned}
v_2(L) &= \max_{k} \{p_{LH}^{k}(r_{LH}^{k} + v_1(H)) + p_{LL}^{k}(r_{LL}^{k} + v_1(L))\} \\
&= \max \{0.25(15+16)+0.75(8+9.75),\ 0.5(13+16)+0.5(6+9.75)\} \\
&= \max \{21.0625,\ 22.375\} = 22.375 \text{ with } d_2(L) = II.
\end{aligned}
$$

If we write

$$
D_n = \begin{pmatrix} d_n(H) \\ d_n(L) \end{pmatrix}
$$

to summarize the optimal decisions for every state with n periods to go we have found

$$
D_1 = \begin{pmatrix} II \\ I \end{pmatrix} \quad \text{and} \quad D_2 = \begin{pmatrix} II \\ II \end{pmatrix}.
$$

If the problem is extended to say three weeks rather than two then the figure analogous to Figure 7.1 for the tree following a week of high demand would have 127 nodes and the same number of arcs, while the corresponding figure in our new format would have 7 nodes and 10 arcs. Given our new notation the diagram is now rather redundant and these sequential problems can be readily solved and understood from the equations alone. Thus, for the three week problem we have

$$v_3(\text{H}) = \max_k \{p_{\text{HH}}^k (r_{\text{HH}}^k + v_2(\text{H})) + p_{\text{HL}}^k (r_{\text{HL}}^k + v_2(\text{L}))\}$$

$$= \max \{0.5(20 + 30.75) + 0.5(10 + 22.375),$$
$$0.8(18 + 30.75) + 0.2(8 + 22.375)\}$$
$$= \max \{41.5625,\ 45.075\} = 45.075 \text{ with } d_3(\text{H}) = \text{II},$$

and

$$v_3(\text{L}) = \max_k \{p_{\text{LH}}^k (r_{\text{LH}}^k + v_2(\text{H})) + p_{\text{LL}}^k (r_{\text{LL}}^k + v_2(\text{L}))\}$$

$$= \max \{0.25(15 + 30.75) + 0.75(8 + 22.375),$$
$$0.5(13 + 30.75) + 0.5(6 + 22.375)\}$$
$$= \max \{34.22,\ 36.06\} = 36.06 \text{ with } d_3(\text{L}) = \text{II}.$$

Thus,

$$D_3 = \begin{pmatrix} \text{II} \\ \text{II} \end{pmatrix},$$

which is of course the value found for D_2. In fact if the problem is extended to four, five or n weeks we would find

$$D_4 = D_5 = \ldots = D_n = \begin{pmatrix} \text{II} \\ \text{II} \end{pmatrix}.$$

Apart from D_1 (where the decisions are taken on the basis that there is one period left to go) the *optimal decision vectors* are identical. We return to this property in Chapter 9.

We conclude this section with a formal restatement of the numerical process which we have used in both the methods above. The earliest appearance of the underlying principle can be found in the decision tree work of Chapter 6. The basic data for our typical sequential decision problem will often (but not invariably) be found given in the form of a collection of probabilities $P^k = [p_{ij}^k]$ and rewards $R^k = [r_{ij}^k]$. Here k indexes the set of matrices ($k = \text{I}$ or II in our example above). The probability p_{ij}^k and reward r_{ij}^k are those associated with the transition from state i (at one stage) to state j (at the succeeding stage) under option k. Thus, in the above example we have i (and j) as H or L. Using our earlier definition of $v_n(i)$ as the optimal expected outcome (here profit) when starting in state i with n periods (transitions) to go we have made repeated use of particularizations of

$$v_n(i) = \max_k \left\{ \sum_j p_{ij}^k (r_{ij}^k + v_{n-1}(j)) \right\}, \qquad n \geqslant 1. \tag{2}$$

In our example with only two values for k and two values for j the choice of maximum is between two summations, each of which has only to components.

What this equation is describing is the relationship between an n-stage problem and an $(n-1)$-stage problem. If in state i with n periods to go we take option k

168

then with probability p_{ij}^k there is a transition to state j at the next stage (where we have $(n-1)$ periods to go). Such a transition has associated profit r_{ij}^k and on transition the system is now in state j with $(n-1)$ periods to go. The expected outcome given k is thus $\sum_j p_{ij}^k (r_{ij}^k + v_{n-1}(j))$ on the assumption that the best continuation is taken from whatever state the system makes a transition into, and since k is at the discretion of the decisionmaker then this expectation will be maximized over all k.

For a numerical solution we must have v_{n-1} values before v_n values can be found. If the problem therefore starts with some easily calculated values, for example $v_0(i) = 0$ for all states i as above, then we can find v_1, v_2, etc. We can write (2) as

$$v_n(i) = \max_k \left\{ \sum_j p_{ij}^k r_{ij}^k + \sum_j p_{ij}^k v_{n-1}(j) \right\}$$

$$= \max_k \left\{ q^k(i) + \sum_j p_{ij}^k v_{n-1}(j) \right\}, \qquad n \geqslant 1, \quad \ldots \ldots \ldots \ldots \ldots \quad (3)$$

where $q^k(i) = \sum_j p_{ij}^k r_{ij}^k$ is the *immediate expected profit on taking option k when in state i*. Note that the stage (subscript) does not enter into this quantity. Thus, $q^{\mathrm{I}}(\mathrm{H}) = 0.5 \times 20 + 0.5 \times 10 = 15$ and similarly $q^{\mathrm{I}}(\mathrm{L}) = 9.75$, $q^{\mathrm{II}}(\mathrm{H}) = 16$ and $q^{\mathrm{II}}(\mathrm{L}) = 9.5$.

With one stage to go (since $v_0(\mathrm{H}) = v_0(\mathrm{L}) = 0$) then $v_1(i) = \max_k \{q^k(i)\}$, i.e. the decision is taken on the basis of immediate expected reward. No further rewards are forthcoming to influence the decision. For stages farther away from the termination of the problem the optimal decisions are given by $\binom{\mathrm{II}}{\mathrm{II}}$.

Although option II for state H is that which maximizes immediate expected reward, in state L the optimal decision (II) is not that which maximizes immediate expected reward (I) and this demonstrates that the solution method is not myopic. Considerations other than immediate outcome influence the decision rule for stages sufficiently distant (in this case two periods) from the termination of the problem.

In solving the problem over several stages there is no redundancy in the calculations. It is necessary to have a response for every state at every stage since for any particular 'run' of the problem any of the states can be entered, though of course only some will be entered. Such a sequence of *decision rules*, one per stage, is a *policy*.

An equation of the type (2) above is known as a *functional equation*. It embodies the *Principle of Optimality* for sequential decision problems which may be stated (in the words of Bellman) thus:

> *An optimal policy has the property that whatever the initial state and initial decision are, the remaining decisions must constitute an optimal policy with regard to the state resulting from the first decision.*

Principles of Optimality occur in other areas of mathematics, e.g. in the differential calculus, where the extrema of a function $f(x)$ can be explored by examining $df/dx = 0$. Solving the equation where the first derivative is set equal to zero gives values for x which may maximize or minimize the function. Although not sufficient the condition is necessary.

7.2 Another Example

To reinforce the solution mechanism used in the first section we state and solve another (finite stage) sequential decision problem. The transitions for this problem can be described in the same way as for our earlier example but the reward structure is different.

Suppose we have in our possession an asset whose worth is high (\$1000), medium (\$800) or low (\$600). The value of the asset changes from time period to time period according to the matrix P^{I} where

$$
\begin{array}{c}
\phantom{P^{\mathrm{I}} = \begin{array}{c} L \\ M \\ H \end{array}} \quad L \quad\; M \quad\; H \\
P^{\mathrm{I}} = \begin{array}{c} L \\ M \\ H \end{array} \begin{bmatrix} 0.6 & 0.4 & 0 \\ 0.3 & 0.4 & 0.3 \\ 03 & 0.3 & 0.4 \end{bmatrix},
\end{array}
$$

and L, M and H are the states of low, medium and high worth, respectively. For a premium of \$55 the asset can be advertised for one time period, and the effect of this advertising will be to enhance the likelihood of transition to more favourable states. The probabilities of transition for any period in which advertising is bought are given by P^{II} where

$$
\begin{array}{c}
\phantom{P^{\mathrm{II}} = \begin{array}{c} L \\ M \\ H \end{array}} \quad L \quad\; M \quad\; H \\
P^{\mathrm{II}} = \begin{array}{c} L \\ M \\ H \end{array} \begin{bmatrix} 0.4 & 0.5 & 0.1 \\ 0.2 & 0.4 & 04 \\ 0.1 & 0.4 & 0.5 \end{bmatrix}.
\end{array}
$$

We have the asset in our possession but must dispose of it at latest two time periods from now. Thus, we can allow at most two transitions in price before having to sell for the price then current. If we sell before the deadline the money can be invested to give a rate of return of 5 % per period. What is the policy which maximizes the expected cash outcome at the deadline from disposal of the asset?

The solution procedure is similar to that of the previous example, i.e. we work backwards from the problem deadline, building up our optimal decision rules at each stage to give an optimal policy. There are up to three options which can be taken in any state. If there is still time available before the deadline we can hold onto the asset without advertising (option I), keep the asset but advertise for that period at a cost of \$55 (option II), or sell the asset and invest the money until the deadline (option III). At the deadline there is only one option and that is to sell the asset for the price then current. Denote this again by option III. As before we use $v_n(i)$ to denote the best expected outcome over n stages starting in state i, $d_n(i)$ for the optimal response in state i with n stages to go and

$$D_n = \begin{pmatrix} d_n(\text{L}) \\ d_n(\text{M}) \\ d_n(\text{H}) \end{pmatrix}$$

for the optimal decision rule with n stages to go. At the deadline the only (and therefore the optimal) option is to sell for the price then current. Thus, $v_0(\text{L}) = 600$, $v_0(\text{M}) = 800$ and $v_0(\text{H}) = 1000$, with

$$D_0 = \begin{pmatrix} \text{III} \\ \text{III} \\ \text{III} \end{pmatrix}$$

To find the optimal decision with one transition to go when in state L we have

$$v_1(\text{L}) = \max \left\{ \begin{array}{lr} \text{I: } 0.6v_0(\text{L}) + 0.4v_0(\text{M}) & = 680 \\ \text{II: } 0.4v_0(\text{L}) + 0.5v_0(\text{M}) + 0.1v_0(\text{H}) - 55 = 685 \\ \text{III: } 600 \times 1.05 & = 630 \end{array} \right\}$$
$$= 685 \text{ using } d_1(\text{L}) = \text{II}.$$

Similarly,

$$v_1(\text{M}) = \max \left\{ \begin{array}{lr} \text{I: } 0.3v_0(\text{L}) + 0.4v_0(\text{M}) + 0.3v_0(\text{H}) & = 800 \\ \text{II: } 0.2v_0(\text{L}) + 0.4v_0(\text{M}) + 0.4v_0(\text{H}) - 55 = 785 \\ \text{III: } 800 \times 1.05 & = 840 \end{array} \right\}$$
$$= 840 \text{ using } d_1(\text{M}) = \text{III}.$$

It is obvious that the asset should be sold if the price is high (with the money invested) and a calculation like those above will confirm this. Thus, $v_1(\text{H}) = 1050$ with $d_1(\text{H}) = \text{III}$, giving

$$D_1 = \begin{pmatrix} \text{II} \\ \text{III} \\ \text{III} \end{pmatrix}.$$

To find the optimal decision when in state L with two stages left to go we have

$$v_2(\text{L}) = \max \left\{ \begin{array}{lr} \text{I: } 0.6v_1(\text{L}) + 0.4v_1(\text{M}) & = 747 \\ \text{II: } 0.4v_1(\text{L}) + 0.5v_1(\text{M}) + 0.1v_1(\text{H}) - 55 = 744 \\ \text{III: } 600 \times (1.05)^2 & = 661.5 \end{array} \right\}$$

$$= 747 \text{ with } d_2(\text{L}) = \text{I}.$$

Similarly, $v_2(\text{M}) = 882$ with $d_2(\text{M}) = \text{III}$ and $v_2(\text{H}) = 1102.5$ with $d_2(\text{H}) = \text{III}$, giving

$$D_2 = \begin{pmatrix} \text{II} \\ \text{III} \\ \text{III} \end{pmatrix}.$$

The optimal policy is thus to sell the asset and invest the money if the price is ever medium or high. If the price is low with two periods to go then keep the asset but do not advertise. Should the price increase then sell but if it remains low then advertise in the last period before the deadline (and inevitable sale).

This example differs from the first in that the terminal states do have distinct values associated with them and there is not the same reward structure as for our first example, i.e. we are missing the R matrices of that problem. In the example of the next section we solve a system where there are economic consequences associated with transitions and terminal states.

7.3 A Third Example

A machine can be characterized as being in one of three conditions:
   (i)   fully operational (FO),
   (ii) partially operational (PO), or
   (iii) broken down (BD).
In any condition there are two options which we can take in seeking to control the expected economic returns from operating the machine. For option I the probabilities of transition from state to state in one period are given by

$$P^{\mathrm{I}} = \begin{array}{c} \\ \mathrm{FO} \\ \mathrm{PO} \\ \mathrm{BD} \end{array} \begin{array}{ccc} \mathrm{FO} & \mathrm{PO} & \mathrm{BD} \\ \left[\begin{array}{ccc} 0.6 & 0.2 & 0.2 \\ 0 & 0.6 & 0.4 \\ 0.5 & 0.5 & 0 \end{array}\right] \end{array}.$$

In the event of machine breakdown repair takes one period and note from the matrix above that such a repair does not necessarily return the machine to a fully operational condition. With this option we have associated reward matrix R^{I} (giving the income in thousands of dollars)

$$R^{\mathrm{I}} = \begin{array}{c} \\ \mathrm{FO} \\ \mathrm{PO} \\ \mathrm{BD} \end{array} \begin{array}{ccc} \mathrm{FO} & \mathrm{PO} & \mathrm{BD} \\ \left[\begin{array}{ccc} 20 & 10 & 0 \\ 0 & 10 & 0 \\ -3 & -3 & 0 \end{array}\right] \end{array}.$$

The interpretation of this is straightforward. A period which begins and ends with a fully operational machine generates an income of $20 000. A period which begins with a fully operational machine and finishes with a partially operational one generates an income of $10 000. To be precise, the state description (machine condition) refers to the machine at the beginning of a period, and the elements of P^{I} and R^{I} are the probabilities and rewards, respectively, for transitions from conditions at the beginning of one period to conditions at the beginning of the next period. Since the periods succeed each other without interruption we assume for ease of exposition that the condition of the machine at the end of a given period is the same as its initial condition in the next period.

For the second option transition to less favourable machine conditions is less likely, and the likelihood of repair resulting in a fully operational machine is greater, but these desirable qualities can only be achieved by, for example, spending more on breakdown repairs or running the machine at a slower production rate, and therefore generating less profit in a period. The transition probability matrix for this second option is

$$
P^{II} = \begin{array}{c} \\ FO \\ PO \\ BD \end{array} \begin{array}{ccc} FO & PO & BD \\ \begin{bmatrix} 0.8 & 0.2 & 0 \\ 0 & 0.8 & 0.2 \\ 0.7 & 0.3 & 0 \end{bmatrix} \end{array},
$$

and the matrix of profits is

$$
R^{II} = \begin{array}{c} \\ FO \\ PO \\ BD \end{array} \begin{array}{ccc} FO & PO & BD \\ \begin{bmatrix} 15 & 8 & 0 \\ 0 & 8 & 0 \\ -4 & -4 & 0 \end{bmatrix} \end{array}.
$$

At the end of our finite stage problem the machine is to be sold and while a fully operational machine will fetch \$5000, one which is partially operational or broken down is worth only \$4000. Given that we are to operate the machine for three periods before selling it, what is the policy which maximizes our net expected profit?

As before we define $v_n(i)$ to be the expected profit with n periods to go, starting in state i and using an optimal policy. The optimal response for that state and stage is $d_n(i)$ and the optimal decision rule is given by

$$
D_n = \begin{pmatrix} d_n(FO) \\ d_n(PO) \\ d_n(BD) \end{pmatrix}.
$$

For this problem we have the data in a form which matches that of our first example, i.e. we have matrices P^k ($k = $ I or II) and R^k ($k = $ I or II). The functional equation which we solve is thus that of (2) above, or rather we solve it in its processed (but equivalent) form (3), where the one-off calculation of the immediate expected rewards $q^k(i)$ slightly reduces the numerical effort. Here i is FO, PO or BD and k is I or II. Thus, $q^I(FO) = 0.6 \times 20 + 0.2 \times 10 + 0.2 \times 0 = 14$, and similarly $q^I(PO) = 6$, $q^I(BD) = -3$, $q^{II}(FO) = 13.6$, $q^{II}(PO) = 6.4$ and $q^{II}(BD) = -4$. Given that the machine condition dictates its worth at the end of the sequence of production periods we have $v_0(FO) = 5$, $v_0(PO) = v_0(BD) = 4$. To find $v_1(FO)$ we then apply equation (3) with $n = 1$, $i = $ FO and $k = $ I or II, giving

$$
v_1(FO) = \max \begin{cases} \text{I: } & q^I(FO) + 0.6v_0(FO) + 0.2v_0(PO) + 0.2v_0(BD) & = 18.6 \\ \text{II: } & q^{II}(FO) + 0.8v_0(FO) + 0.2v_0(PO) & = 18.4 \end{cases}
$$

$$
= 18.6 \text{ with } d_1(FO) = \text{I}.
$$

Similarly, we obtain $v_1(\text{PO}) = 10.4$ (with $d_1(\text{PO}) = \text{II}$) and $v_1(\text{BD}) = 1.5$ (with $d_1(\text{BD}) = \text{I}$). The optimal decision rule at this stage is

$$D_1 = \begin{pmatrix} \text{I} \\ \text{II} \\ \text{I} \end{pmatrix}.$$

To find $v_2(\text{FO})$ we apply equation (3) with $n = 2$ and $i = \text{FO}$ giving

$$v_2(\text{FO}) = \max \begin{cases} \text{I:} & q^{\text{I}}(\text{FO}) + 0.6v_1(\text{FO}) + 0.2v_1(\text{PO}) + 0.2v_1(\text{BD}) & = 27.54 \\ \text{II:} & q^{\text{II}}(\text{FO}) + 0.8v_1(\text{FO}) + 0.2v_1(\text{PO}) & = 30.56 \end{cases}$$

$$= 30.56 \text{ with } d_2(\text{FO}) = \text{II}.$$

The reader may confirm that $v_2(\text{PO}) = 15.02$ (using $d_2(\text{PO}) = \text{II}$) and $v_2(\text{BD}) = 12.14$ (using $d_2(\text{BD}) = \text{II}$). The optimal decision rule with two stages to go is thus

$$D_2 = \begin{pmatrix} \text{II} \\ \text{II} \\ \text{II} \end{pmatrix}.$$

To find the decision rule with three stages to go apply (3) with $n = 3$ and we will find

$$D_3 = \begin{pmatrix} \text{II} \\ \text{II} \\ \text{II} \end{pmatrix}$$

and the corresponding state values are $v_3(\text{FO}) = 41.05$, $v_3(\text{PO}) = 20.84$ and $v_3(\text{BD}) = 21.90$.

In summary the second option should be taken in any machine condition with three or two time perods to go. At the beginning of the last period option I should be taken if the machine is fully operational or broken down, while option II is optimal if the machine is partially operational.

If the problem is extended to four periods the optimal decision rule will be found to be to take option II for all three states. Note that for two of the three states (FO and BD) this decision rule is actually yielding an immediate expected reward which is inferior to that found by using option I. A myopic solution to the problem would seek maximal immediate expected reward, while our genuinely sequential approach, considering as it does the future as well as the immediate expected consequences, takes actions which are inferior in the short (one-period) term—away from the end of the problem. We will return to these and related considerations in Chapter 9. In the next chapter we examine some properties of the probability structure underlying the problems we have just studied, before returning in Chapter 9 to our decision-oriented development.

7.4 A First Deterministic Example

Although our interest in the sequential decisionmaking area centres on problems where uncertainty is a dominant feature, modelled by the use of appropriate probabilities, there is an extensive area of application in deterministic problems. In this section and the two which follow we offer a compact presentation of the formulation and solution of one classic problem. In this section a particular variant of the problem is studied while Sections 7.5 and 7.6 include material on the more general problem and two methods of solution. These methods appear again in Chapter 9 (though only one of them in any detail). In that chapter they are developed independent of the material of this section or those following, though obviously an understanding of the processes in a deterministic problem will not hinder the reader's understanding of their development in the non-deterministic setting.

Consider the problem of finding the shortest paths from town to town, where links between towns are as in Figure 7.3. In particular we are interested in the shortest path from town A to town T (the designated target town) where the links of Figure 7.3 are directed from left to right and the single link distances are as given on the arcs of that figure.

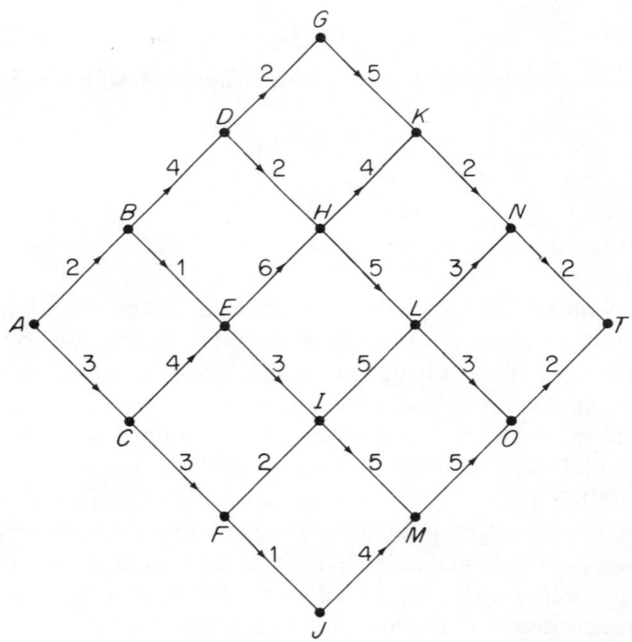

Figure 7.3 The nature and length of links between towns for the shortest path problem

Any path from A to T must pass through either B or C and if the shortest paths from B and C (to T) are known then this can be used to find the shortest path from A to T. With regard to the shortest path from B to T, this can be computed once the shortest paths from D to T and E to T are known, and similar remarks hold on the calculation of the shortest path out of C.

Because of the directed nature of the grid, shortest paths from any town (to the target town T) can be calculated once the shortest paths of 'successor' towns are known. Again the directed nature of the grid determines the length of paths from any town to T. All paths from A to T involve 6 links, while all paths from B or C involve 5 links, etc. Let us denote the (single link) distance from town i to town j by d_{ij} and let $v_n(i)$ be the length of the shortest path from town i to the target town T, involving the appropriate (fixed) number of links n. We thus seek $v_6(A)$. Since any path from A must pass through B or C, the shortest path from A must consist of the link AB followed by the optimal continuation (shortest path) from B to T, or the link AC followed by the optimal continuation (shortest path) from C to T. Thus,

$$v_6(A) = \min \{d_{AB} + v_5(B), d_{AC} + v_5(C)\},$$

and similarly

$$v_5(B) = \min \{d_{BD} + v_4(D), d_{BE} + v_4(E)\}.$$

For any town i let $S(i)$ denote the set of 'successor' towns to i, that is the towns reachable in one link from town i. Then, for example, $S(A) = \{B, C\}$ and $S(G) = K$.

A general statement of the functional equation is thus

$$v_n(i) = \min_{j \in S(i)} \{d_{ij} + v_{n-1}(j)\}, \qquad n \geqslant 1. \ldots \ldots \ldots \ldots (4)$$

Since town T is the target we take $v_0(T) = 0$.

The results from the calculations which follow are displayed in Figure 7.4, where the shortest distance from each town to town T is displayed at the town and the first link out of each town on the shortest path to T is marked $\rightarrow$. Sub-optimal initial links are marked with a bar ($||$).

Calculating backwards from the target we obtain

$$v_1(N) = 2; v_1(O) = 2; v_2(K) = d_{KN} + v_1(N) = 4; v_2(M) = d_{MO} + v_1(O) = 7,$$
$$v_2(L) = \min\{d_{LN} + v_1(N), d_{LO} + v_1(O)\} = \min\{5, 5\} = 5,$$
$$v_3(G) = d_{GK} + v_2(K) = 9; \qquad v_3(J) = d_{JM} + v_2(M) = 11,$$
$$v_3(H) = \min\{d_{HK} + v_2(K), d_{HL} + v_2(L)\} = \min\{8, 10\} = 8,$$
$$v_3(I) = \min\{d_{IL} + v_2(L), d_{IM} + v_2(M)\} = \min\{10, 12\} = 10,$$
$$v_4(D) = \min\{d_{DG} + v_3(G), d_{DH} + v_3(H)\} = \min\{11, 10\} = 10,$$
$$v_4(E) = \min\{d_{EH} + v_3(H), d_{EI} + v_3(I)\} = \min\{14, 13\} = 13,$$
$$v_4(F) = \min\{d_{FI} + v_3(I), d_{FJ} + v_3(J)\} = \min\{12, 12\} = 12,$$
$$v_5(B) = \min\{d_{BD} + v_4(D), d_{BE} + v_4(E)\} = \min\{14, 14\} = 14,$$
$$v_5(C) = \min\{d_{CE} + v_4(E), d_{CF} + v_4(F)\} = \min\{17, 15\} = 15,$$
$$v_6(A) = \min\{d_{AB} + v_5(B), d_{AC} + v_5(C)\} = \min\{16, 18\} = 16.$$

The shortest distance from A to T is thus 16, and to find the path(s) of that distance we use the information stored in Figure 7.4. Out of A we are first directed

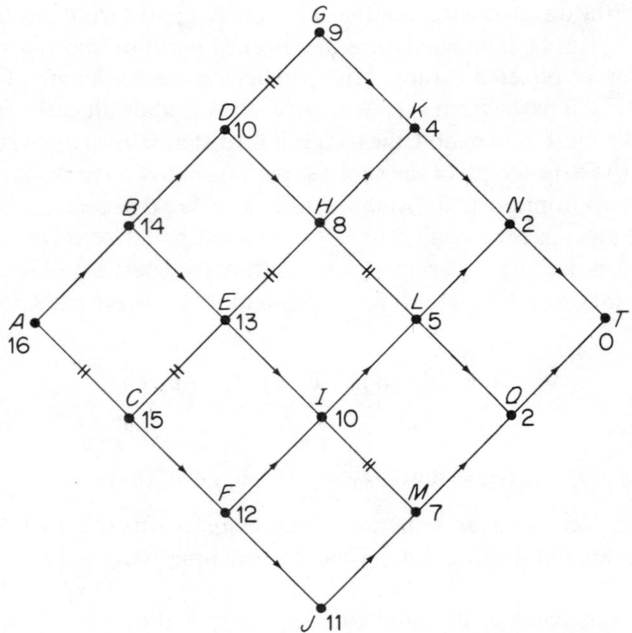

Figure 7.4 A summary of the calculations of minimum length
and optimal successor

to B, from which there are two optimal continuations. We will follow these in turn. If we proceed from B to D then the path marked by the arrows is D to H to K to N and finally to T. Alternatively, from B we can proceed to E, I, L, O and T, or to E, I, L, N and T (since there are two paths of equal length from L to T).

The three optimal paths are thus $A—B—D—H—K—N—T$, $A—B—E—I—L—O—T$ and $A—B—E—I—L—N—T$. The reader can easily check that these paths are indeed of total length 16.

The structure of the grid for this problem allows us to make some computational comparisons between the method we have just applied and an alternative scheme of enumeration and evaluation. We note first that the scheme used above has performed a number of calculations which prove to be redundant. For example we have calculated and can readily construct from Figure 7.4 a shortest path from C to T (e.g. $C—F—I—L—O—T$ or $C—F—J—M—O—T$), but this is never used in the optimal solution to the overall problem. From A we go to B and hence make use of the shortest path from B to T, but we never visit C on the shortest path from A to T. This redundancy cannot of course be readily foreseen. It is only after consideration of the path from A to T through C (as part of the final $v_6(A)$ calculation) that this option can be rejected.

This redundancy is unavoidable in deterministic problems, though schemes exist which attempt to minimize its impact. For non-deterministic problems the redundancy in sub-problem calculation is generally absent. For the example in the first section of this chapter, there is no redundancy in the calculation of the optimal response at any stage. In that problem the states visited over time (the demand levels) are not determined by the decisionmaker, although he does choose the transition probabilities, and it is therefore necessary to have an optimal response to all possible states. In the shortest path problem the state of the system (i.e. the town to be visited) at each stage is determined by the decisionmaker. Given that he can control the transition exactly then only a subset of the towns will be visited (those on the optimal path from A to T) and for the other towns the calculations have been strictly unnecessary—but only in hindsight.

Even with this redundancy the computational scheme used above is superior to an obvious alternative which considers all possible paths and evaluates them to find the shortest. In the grid of Figure 7.3 there are 20 distinct paths from A to T. Each of these involves 6 links so that the evaluation of one path involves 5 additions. To find the shortest path from the 20 evaluated involves 19 comparisons. As a measure of the work involved in the enumeration and evaluation scheme we thus have that it involves 100 additions and 19 comparisons.

From the calculations above (and also from Figure 7.3) we see that there are six towns where only one addition is performed (and no comparison). These are G, K, N, J, M and O. At nine towns (A, B, C, D, E, F, H, I and L) there are 2 additions and 1 comparison. In total we thus have 24 additions and 9 comparisons, considerably less than the crude enumeration and evaluation scheme.

The difference in computational effort becomes rather more startling as the size of the problem increases. For a 10-link grid the sequential scheme involves 60 additions and 25 comparisons against 2268 additions and 251 comparisons under enumeration and evaluation. In the case of a 20-link grid the sequential scheme involves 220 additions and 100 comparisons against approximately 3.5 million additions and 184 755 comparisons in the enumerative scheme.

7.5 A Second Deterministic Example and First Solution Technique

As a more general deterministic example we again use a shortest path problem, but this time the grid pattern of links (as in Figure 7.3) is absent. For this problem we derive a formulation which is representative of many in sequential decisionmaking. Two solution mechanisms are developed, the second of which re-emerges in Chapter 9 as a major solution tool while the other is only given passing attention at that stage.

The structure of and data for the shortest path problem is given in Figure 7.5, while the data is repeated in Table 7.1. In that table the single-link distances between pairs of towns are given. The table is symmetric, and ∞ denotes the absence of a single link between pairs, for example A and D. The problem is to find the shortest path from each town to the target town E. Note that the links of Figure 7.5 are not directed, i.e. we can travel from B to C or C to B along the link between these two towns.

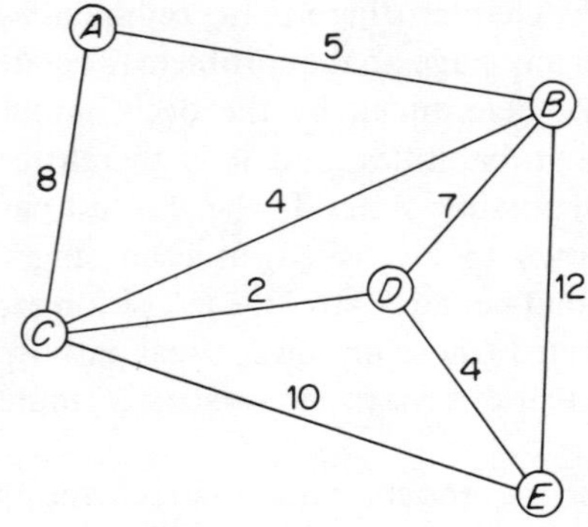

Figure 7.5 The nature and length of links
for a general shortest path problem

	A	B	C	D	E
A	0	5	8	∞	∞
B	5	0	4	7	12
C	8	4	0	2	10
D	∞	7	2	0	4

Table 7.1 The (single-link) distances between pairs
of towns

In problems of this type a useful rule for formulation is to define a function which is exactly the problem we seek to solve, and construct the functional equation accordingly. Thus, we define $v(i)$ to be the minimum distance from town i to the target town E. For one value of i, namely E, we have an easy assessment of the function since $v(E) = 0$. As before let us use d_{ij} to denote the single link distance from town i to town j. If the decision in town i is to go next to town j then this involves a single link distance of d_{ij} and leaves us with the residual problem of proceeding from town j to the target town E in minimum distance. Thus, given that the first step is to town j and an optimal policy is followed thereafter the total distance is $\{d_{ij} + v(j)\}$. Since we are free to choose the next town to go to we have

$$v(i) = \min_{j} \{d_{ij} + v(j)\}. \dots\dots\dots\dots\dots\dots (5)$$

If we attempt to use equation (5) on the problem of this section then, taking $i = A$ we have

$$v(A) = \min \{d_{AB} + v(B), d_{AC} + v(C)\},$$

and taking $i = B$ we have

$$v(B) = \min \{d_{BA} + v(A), d_{BC} + v(C), d_{BD} + v(D), d_{BE}\}.$$

To find $v(A)$ we need $v(B)$ and to find $v(B)$ we need $v(A)$. A direct solution of equation (5) is therefore ruled out.

Comparison of (5) with the functional equation (4) of the previous section gives an insight to the source of the difficulty, and a clue to the construction of a suitable solution method. Equation (5) lacks the explicit stage variable n of equation (4). A shortest path from a given town to the target town E does not consist of a number of links known in advance, unlike the problem of Figure 7.3.

It is obvious that the shortest distance from any town to the target E in Figure 7.5 can involve at most four links. A path with more than four links in this problem would necessarily visit some town(s) at least twice. The path would contain a loop, which is obviously a sub-optimal procedure.

To solve (5) we thus solve a succession of problems where the shortest path from i to E is found first with the restriction that at most one link is used, then at most two, etc. We define $v_n(i)$ to be the shortest distance from town i to town E using *at most* n links. The usefulness of using 'at most' rather than, for example, 'exactly' will shortly be revealed. The argument which led us to (5) gives us

$$v_n(i) = \min_j \{d_{ij} + v_{n-1}(j)\}, \qquad n \geqslant 2, \ldots \ldots \ldots \ldots (6)$$

and

$$v_1(i) = d_{iE},$$

where we use ∞ to denote the absence of a direct line from i to E. In keeping with the notation of this chapter we use $s_n(i)$ to be the optimal successor to town i given that there are at most n links to use, i.e. $s_n(i)$ is the optimizing value of j in equation (6).

Thus, we have $v_1(A) = \infty$ (taking $s_1(A) = E$ for convention), $v_1(B) = 12$, $v_1(C) = 10$, $v_1(D) = 4$, $v_1(E) = 0$ and $s_1(B) = s_1(C) = s_1(D) = s_1(E) = E$. We could exclude calculations involving E from this development but choose to retain them. These results and those we are about to derive are summarized in Table 7.2.

	(i)				
	A	B	C	D	E
$v_1(i)$	∞	12	10	4	0
$s_1(i)$	E	E	E	E	E
$v_2(i)$	17	11	6	4	0
$s_2(i)$	B	D	D	E	E
$v_3(i)$	14	10	6	4	0
$s_3(i)$	C	C	D	E	E
$v_4(i)$	14	10	6	4	0
$s_4(i)$	C	C	D	E	E

Table 7.2 A summary of the calculations where shortest paths involving one, two, three, etc. links are calculated successively

Now that we have values for $v_1(i)$ an application of (6) with $n = 2$ will yield $v_2(i)$. Thus,

$$v_2(A) = \min\{d_{AB} + v_1(B), d_{AC} + v_1(C)\} = \min\{17, 18\} = 17, \text{ with } s_2(A) = B.$$

180

Similarly,

$v_2(B) = \min\{5 + \infty,\ 0 + 12,\ 4 + 10,\ 7 + 4,\ 12 + 0\} = 11$, with $s_2(B) = D$, and $v_2(C) = 6$, with $s_2(C) = D$.

When we come to $i = D$ we have

$$v_2(D) = \min\{\infty + \infty,\ 7 + 12,\ 2 + 10,\ 0 + 4,\ 4 + 0\} = 4,$$

and the minimum is given by $s_2(D) = D$ or E. We have $v_1(D) = v_2(D)$ so that the freedom of an extra link has not reduced the minimum distance from town D (compared with, for example, $v_2(B)$ which is strictly less than $v_1(B)$). For this town we have a link 'to spare'.

If we again apply equation (6) with $n = 3$ we obtain, for example,

$$v_3(A) = \min\{d_{AB} + v_2(B),\ d_{AC} + v_2(C)\} = \min\{16, 14\} = 14, \text{ with } s_3(A) = C.$$

The other values of v_3 and s_3 are readily found. Again we have improvement in the values for shortest paths from A and from B, but not from C. Allowing up to three links from A to E (and B to E) gives a shorter path length than operating with at most two links. From town C the extra link is not useful since the shortest path to E involves two links.

If we apply equation (6) with $n = 4$ we find that $v_4(i) = v_3(i)$ and $s_4(i) = s_3(i)$ for $i = A, B, C, D$ and E. Thus, for none of the towns is there any improvement by allowing up to four links rather than three, and in fact we have $v(i) = v_4(i)$ for all i. We have found the shortest path from each town i to to E (regardless of the number of links), and we write $s(i) = s_4(i)$ for all i as the optimal successor to town i. Thus, the shortest paths from each town to town E are $A \to C \to D \to E, B \to C \to D \to E, C \to D \to E$ and $D \to E$ for A, B, C and D, respectively. From this we see that the shortest paths from A and B require three links, that from C requires two links, and from D a single link is sufficient.

The reader is urged to confirm that the values found for the v and s functions do satisfy equation (5) for all towns i. The *successive approximations* of equation (6) have converged to a solution of the original equation (5). When none of the values for path length improve in an iteration then it is an indication that the optimal solution has been reached—a property we do not prove.

7.6 A Second Solution Technique

In finding the length of the shortest path to the target town the technique of the previous section also provides a policy which generates that length. A policy is found (i.e. a successor to each town in the grid) such that application of that policy gives paths of appropriate lengths. Our second solution technique involves the creation of a policy, its evaluation in terms of the path lengths it implies and its improvement (if possible) to a policy which is in turn evaluated and then improved, etc.

To start the process we need some policy which will not generate loops when applied to the problem. In this initial policy let us denote the successor of i by $s_0(i)$, and for this example we will take $s_0(A) = B$, $s_0(B) = E$, $s_0(C) = D$, $s_0(D) = E$, $s_0(E) = E$. Using this policy we then solve for the path lengths from each town to E (which this policy implies). Denote by $v_0(i)$ the length of the path from i to E given that policy s_0 is used. Then

$$v_0(A) = d_{AB} + v_0(B),$$
$$v_0(B) = d_{BE} + v_0(E),$$
$$v_0(C) = d_{CD} + v_0(D),$$
$$v_0(D) = d_{DE} + v_0(E),$$
$$v_0(E) = 0.$$

A sketch of the links used will make this clear.

In each case the successor town is that given by the policy. Since the policy has no loops this system of equations can be solved to give

$$v_0(E) = 0; \qquad v_0(D) = 4; \qquad v_0(C) = 6; \qquad v_0(B) = 12; \qquad v_0(A) = 17.$$

Using these values we now attempt to improve the policy, i.e. for town i we calculate $\min_j \{d_{ij} + v_0(j)\}$ and denote the minimizing j by $s_1(i)$. Thus, for town A we calculate:

$$\min \{d_{AB} + v_0(B), d_{AC} + v_0(C)\} = \min \{17, 14\} = 14 \text{ and take } s_1(A) = C.$$

Similarly, for town B we find $\min \{5 + 17, 4 + 6, 7 + 4, 12 + 0\} = 10$, with $s_1(B) = C$. The reader can easily confirm that $s_1(C) = D$, $s_1(D) = E$ and $s_1(E) = E$.

With this policy we now calculate the implied path lengths by solving

$$v_1(A) = d_{AC} + v_1(C),$$
$$v_1(B) = d_{BC} + v_1(C),$$
$$v_1(C) = d_{CD} + v_1(D),$$
$$v_1(D) = d_{DE} + v_1(E),$$
$$v_1(E) = 0.$$

Again a sketch will clarify this.

This gives $v_1(E) = 0$, $v_1(D) = 4$, $v_1(C) = 6$, $v_1(B) = 10$ and $v_1(A) = 14$. If we now attempt to improve on this policy, then for town i we seek $\min_j \{d_{ij} + v_1(j)\}$ and denote the optimizing j by $s_2(i)$.

Thus for town A we have $\min \{d_{AB} + v_1(B), d_{AC} + v_1(C)\} = \min \{15, 14\} = 14$ and $s_2(A) = C$. In fact for all of the towns we would find $s_2(i) = s_1(i)$, so that no improvement is possible. This is the optimal policy.

An alternative choice of initial policy could lead to a different number of iterations before the policy repeats—the sign of optimality.

This *policy iteration* technique is used again in Chapter 9 where we tackle non-deterministic problems of unbounded duration.

7.7 Further Reading

The subject-matter of this chapter, and much of what follows, is most generally known as *dynamic programming*, a name coined by Bellman (1957) for the 'mathematical theory of multi-stage decision processes'. The term 'dynamic' is intended to suggest the sequential structure of the problems studied (often time-based but not inevitably so), and 'programming' refers to 'optimization methods'. The name was coined before the term 'programming' became synonymous with computer programming. The book already cited and another by Bellman and Dreyfus (1962) are the earliest texts and convey much of the fresh enthusiasm of the authors. However, these are not elementary texts, and the reader seeking a more structured approach to the subject is better served by Nemhauser (1966). A wide range of applications is covered in White (1969), though at a technically demanding pace.

Elementary textbooks in Operations Research and optimization often contain sections on dynamic programming. The approach of the Principle of Optimality is used by other workers who refer to the problem/sub-problem relationship in distinctive ways. Statisticians are prone to describe the process as 'backward induction' while computer scientists tend to refer to a strategy of 'divide and conquer' (though this has additional meanings).

Exercises for Chapter 7

These exercises provide an opportunity for the reader to test his understanding of the formulation and solution mechanisms for finite stage sequential decision problems, i.e. dynamic programming problems. Following the order of development in the chapter the non-deterministic work precedes the deterministic problems. In succeeding chapters no knowledge of deterministic processes is needed.

7.1   The general health of a car can be described by one of two states either 'on tune' or 'off tune'. The motorist can, in either of these states, choose to ignore the condition of the car and keep on driving (option I), give the car a minor service (option II) or give the car a major service (option III). The cost in one period of the car beginning in one of the states and ending in one of the states is given by

$$
\begin{array}{cc}
 & \text{On} \quad \text{Off} \\
\begin{array}{c} \text{On} \\ \text{Off} \end{array} &
\begin{bmatrix} 10 & 16 \\ 12 & 20 \end{bmatrix}
\end{array} .
$$

If the motorist chooses to do nothing then the probabilities of one state following another after one period are given by

$$
P^1 = \begin{array}{cc}
 & \text{On} \quad \text{Off} \\
\begin{array}{c} \text{On} \\ \text{Off} \end{array} &
\begin{bmatrix} 1/4 & 3/4 \\ 1/6 & 5/6 \end{bmatrix}
\end{array} .
$$

If the motorist wishes to give the car a minor service then this will cost him 3 units in addition to the running cost given above and the resultant transition probabilities are given by

$$P^{II} = \begin{array}{c} \text{On} \\ \text{Off} \end{array} \begin{bmatrix} \text{On} & \text{Off} \\ 1/2 & 1/2 \\ 1/2 & 1/2 \end{bmatrix}.$$

A major service will cost 8 units on top of the normal running costs and the resultant transition probabilities are given by

$$P^{III} = \begin{array}{c} \text{On} \\ \text{Off} \end{array} \begin{bmatrix} \text{On} & \text{Off} \\ 3/4 & 1/4 \\ 1 & 0 \end{bmatrix}.$$

Find the policy which minimizes total expected cost for the case where we regard the car to have a lifetime of only three periods, and we are indifferent to the final state of the car.

7.2   A production process can use up to two identical machines, each of which generates a profit of \$100 per day when in operation. Given that the process starts the day with a number i of operable machines, the number j of machines available for use the following day depends on the maintenance policy adopted by the company. The company has to make a daily choice on maintenance, and the effect of each option $k\,(= 1, 2, 3)$ is summarized in the three transition probability matrices given below. The entries of $P^{(k)}$ are p_{ij}^k (for $i,j = 0, 1, 2$ and $k = 1, 2, 3$) where p_{ij}^k is the probability of going from i to j under k:

$$P^{(1)} = \begin{bmatrix} 1 & 0 & 0 \\ 1/2 & 1/2 & 0 \\ 1/4 & 1/2 & 1/4 \end{bmatrix},$$

$$P^{(2)} = \begin{bmatrix} 1/4 & 1/2 & 1/4 \\ 1/4 & 1/4 & 1/2 \\ 1/4 & 1/4 & 1/2 \end{bmatrix},$$

$$P^{(3)} = \begin{bmatrix} 0 & 1/2 & 1/2 \\ 1/4 & 1/4 & 1/2 \\ 0 & 1/2 & 1/2 \end{bmatrix}.$$

The daily cost of option 1 is zero. Option 2 costs \$30 per day and option 3 \$50 per day. The scrap value of operable machines is \$50 each, and the company starts a 3-day operation with two operable machines. Use dynamic programming to calculate a policy which maximizes the total expected profit for the 3-day operation.

7.3   Consider the problem where we have in our possession an asset whose selling price can be low (\$200), medium (\$250) or high (\$300). We estimate that the value of the asset changes from month to month according to the matrix of probabilities:

$$P^{\mathrm{I}} = \begin{array}{c} \\ \mathrm{L} \\ \mathrm{M} \\ \mathrm{H} \end{array} \begin{array}{ccc} \mathrm{L} & \mathrm{M} & \mathrm{H} \\ \begin{bmatrix} 1/2 & 1/4 & 1/4 \\ 1/4 & 1/2 & 1/4 \\ 1/4 & 1/2 & 1/4 \end{bmatrix} \end{array},$$

where L = low, M = medium and H = high.

For a premium of \$10 we can advertise the asset for one month and consequently change the transition probability matrix for that month to

$$P^{\mathrm{II}} = \begin{array}{c} \\ \mathrm{L} \\ \mathrm{M} \\ \mathrm{H} \end{array} \begin{array}{ccc} \mathrm{L} & \mathrm{M} & \mathrm{H} \\ \begin{bmatrix} 1/3 & 1/3 & 1/3 \\ 0 & 4/5 & 1/5 \\ 1/4 & 1/2 & 1/4 \end{bmatrix} \end{array}.$$

Alternatively, for a premium of \$15 we can advertise the asset for one month and consequently change the matrix of transition probabilities for that month to

$$P^{\mathrm{III}} = \begin{array}{c} \\ \mathrm{L} \\ \mathrm{M} \\ \mathrm{H} \end{array} \begin{array}{ccc} \mathrm{L} & \mathrm{M} & \mathrm{H} \\ \begin{bmatrix} 1/5 & 3/5 & 1/5 \\ 1/5 & 1/5 & 3/5 \\ 0 & 1/2 & 1/2 \end{bmatrix} \end{array}.$$

On the assumption that we can allow at most two transitions in price before being compelled to sell the asset for the price then current, derive the decision rules which will maximize our expected income from disposal of the asset.

If the asset could be sold before the deadline and the income were able to be invested to give a return of 5% per month, find the optimal policy, given that the asset has a low value now and that two months may elapse before the compulsory sale.

7.4 Consider a queueing system in which a customer has to be processed at two stations in succession and must complete his service at the first station before entering the second.

In unit time the probability of one arrival at the system is α, while if only one station is occupied the probability of a departure from the occupied station is β. If both stations are occupied at the beginning of any unit time interval the customer in the first station has zero probability of departing from his station in the interval while the customer at the second station has probability β of departing from his station. Neither station can accept an arrival and complete a service in the same time period, and there is no more than one arrival per period.

Given a limit of 1 on queue size at each station, queue size being defined to include any customer being served, show that the transition probability matrix for this system is

$$P^{\mathrm{I}} = \begin{array}{c} (0\,0) \\ (0\,1) \\ (1\,0) \\ (1\,1) \end{array} \begin{bmatrix} (1-\alpha) & 0 & \alpha & 0 \\ \beta(1-\alpha) & (1-\alpha)(1-\beta) & \alpha\beta & \alpha(1-\beta) \\ 0 & \beta & (1-\beta) & 0 \\ 0 & 0 & \beta & (1-\beta) \end{bmatrix},$$

where the state (IJ) $(I, J = 0, 1)$ denotes the number I in the queue at the first service station and the number J in the queue at the second service station.

As a service option it is possible to double the service effort at either station by a transfer of personnel. This increases the service probability for that station to 2β, but means that no service is available at the other station. Given that we take this option only when a customer is at a service station, and in the case of a customer at each station we transfer personnel to the second station, construct the corresponding transition probability matrix (with the same limit on queue size).

If we are to operate this system for two time periods, and each customer left in the system at the end means a penalty of 10 units, find the optimal policy, given that $\beta = 1/2$ and the second operating option is taken at a cost of 4 units. (N.B. We seek the policy with minimum expected cost.)

7.5   In a queueing problem with a limit of 1 on queue size and an arrival probability in any period of $1/2$ we can operate either of two options. Option I has a service probability in any period of $3/4$ and the transition probability matrix for the process is consequently

$$P^{\mathrm{I}} = \begin{array}{c} 0 \\ 1 \end{array} \begin{bmatrix} 1/2 & 1/2 \\ 3/4 & 1/4 \end{bmatrix}.$$

The corresponding reward matrix is R^{I} and is given by

$$R^{\mathrm{I}} = \begin{array}{c} 0 \\ 1 \end{array} \begin{bmatrix} 0 & -1 \\ r & -2 \end{bmatrix}.$$

The negative entries correspond to some waiting costs and the r is the reward received when a customer is processed by the system. We associate zero costs to the idle time of the system (in the interests of simplicity, not reality).

Our alternative option has the transition probability matrix P^{II} and reward matrix R^{II} given by

$$P^{\mathrm{II}} = \begin{array}{c} 0 \\ 1 \end{array} \begin{bmatrix} 1/2 & 1/2 \\ 1 & 0 \end{bmatrix} \quad \text{and} \quad R^{\mathrm{II}} = \begin{array}{c} 0 \\ 1 \end{array} \begin{bmatrix} 0 & -4 \\ r & -2 \end{bmatrix}.$$

We are seeking to control the system over 4 time periods in such a manner as to maximize our expected income over these four periods. On the assumption that any customer left in the system at the end of these 4 periods means a penalty to us of 5 units (by way of compensation for not being served) derive the optimal policy.

7.6   Consider the problem of controlling a manufacturing process which is defective in that the number of items put into production per period will not be the same as the number of 'good' items produced at the end of the period. We have an upper limit of three on the number of items put into production in any period, and the characterisitics of the process can be described by a matrix P where the entry p_{ij} is the probability of producing j good items in one period given that i are put into production in that period. We have

$$
P = \begin{array}{c c} & \begin{array}{c c c c} 0 & 1 & 2 & 3 \end{array} \\ \begin{array}{c} 0 \\ 1 \\ 2 \\ 3 \end{array} & \left[\begin{array}{c c c c} 1 & 0 & 0 & 0 \\ 0.3 & 0.7 & 0 & 0 \\ 0.1 & 0.2 & 0.7 & 0 \\ 0.1 & 0.1 & 0.1 & 0.7 \end{array} \right] \end{array}.
$$

In one period if n items are put into production then the cost of production is $(15 + 5n)$ units, where $n \geqslant 1$. The cost of producing no items is assumed to be zero.

   Suppose we have to produce a total of 4 items in 2 periods, with a penalty cost of 30 units per item not produced by the deadline. Given that overproduction has no value find that policy which minimizes total expected cost.

7.7   The price of a commodity may be high (H), medium (M) or low (L) in each time period, and changes of price level from one time period to the next are described by the transition probability matrix P where

$$
P = \begin{array}{c c} & \begin{array}{c c c} H & M & L \end{array} \\ \begin{array}{c} H \\ M \\ L \end{array} & \left[\begin{array}{c c c} 0.6 & 0.2 & 0.2 \\ 0.3 & 0.4 & 0.3 \\ 0.2 & 0.4 & 0.4 \end{array} \right] \end{array}.
$$

Prices per unit of the commodity are H = \$100, M = \$90 and L = \$80 and there is a holding cost of \$5 per unit per time period (not incurred in the period in which purchase takes place). There is a target level of t units which must be purchased by a deadline. If there are 3 time periods until the deadline (i.e. three purchasing opportunities) use dynamic programming to derive the purchasing strategy which minimizes the expected cost of meeting the target level, given that the price initially is low.

   If the holding cost is \$3 per unit per time period what is the optimal strategy?

   For the case where at least half of the target level has to be purchased before the last period, formulate as a dynamic programme (but do *not* solve!).

7.8   A machine can be in one of three conditions, i.e. fully operative (F), partially operative (P) or broken down (B). There are two possible maintenance options.

The first has transition probability matrix and reward matrix (in dollars) given by

$$
\begin{array}{c}
\begin{array}{ccc} \text{F} & \text{P} & \text{B} \end{array} \\
\begin{array}{c} \text{F} \\ \text{P} \\ \text{B} \end{array}
\begin{bmatrix}
0.5 & 0.5 & 0 \\
0 & 0.3 & 0.7 \\
0.5 & 0.5 & 0
\end{bmatrix}
\end{array}
\quad \text{and} \quad
\begin{array}{c}
\begin{array}{ccc} \text{F} & \text{P} & \text{B} \end{array} \\
\begin{array}{c} \text{F} \\ \text{P} \\ \text{B} \end{array}
\begin{bmatrix}
100 & 50 & 0 \\
0 & 50 & 0 \\
-20 & -20 & 0
\end{bmatrix},
\end{array}
$$

respectively. The second option has transition probability matrix and reward matrix (in dollars) given by

$$
\begin{array}{c}
\begin{array}{ccc} \text{F} & \text{P} & \text{B} \end{array} \\
\begin{array}{c} \text{F} \\ \text{P} \\ \text{B} \end{array}
\begin{bmatrix}
0.8 & 0.1 & 0.1 \\
0 & 0.6 & 0.4 \\
0.8 & 0.1 & 0.1
\end{bmatrix}
\end{array}
\quad \text{and} \quad
\begin{array}{c}
\begin{array}{ccc} \text{F} & \text{P} & \text{B} \end{array} \\
\begin{array}{c} \text{F} \\ \text{P} \\ \text{B} \end{array}
\begin{bmatrix}
80 & 30 & -20 \\
0 & 30 & -20 \\
-30 & -30 & -30
\end{bmatrix},
\end{array}
$$

respectively.

You have to run the machines for three transitions. If after the third transition the machine is fully operative you receive an extra reward of \$50. Given that you start with a fully operative machine what is your optimal strategy?

7.9   For a set of eight towns we have the following table of distances $d(I, J)$ from town I to town $J(I, J = A, B, \ldots, H)$. A blank entry in the table denotes the absence of a direct route for the appropriate pair of towns.

	A	B	C	D	E	F	G	H
A	0	2	3	1				
B		0	2			4		
C		2	0	1	1	1		
D			1	0	4			
E					0	2	2	
F					2	0	3	2
G						3	0	1
H								0

Find the shortest route from town A to town H. (Use the methods of both Sections 7.5 and 7.6.) What is the shortest route from A to H passing through at most two other towns?

7.10 The following table gives the direct distance between pairs of towns, where an X denotes that there is no direct link. Using a dynamic programming formulation find the shortest route from each town to town F by (a) the successive approximation method, and (b) the method of policy improvement.

	A	B	C	D	E	F
A	0	1	1	2	6	20
B	1	0	6	1	7	13
C	1	6	0	8	X	20
D	2	1	1	0	3	10
E	6	7	X	3	0	6

7.11 Bus services between six cities A, B, C, D, E and F have travel times (in hours) for the direct links as given in the table below. A blank indicates that no direct service exists between the cities. Changing buses in any city takes 30 minutes, so that a journey from A to D via B takes $(2.5 + 0.5 + 2.25)$ hours:

From \ To	A	B	C	D	E	F
A		2.5	7.0	3.75	3.25	8.5
B	2.5			2.25	2.0	6.5
C	7.0			1.5		2.0
D	3.75	2.25	1.5		2.75	4.25
E	3.25	2.0		2.75		7.5

Using an appropriate dynamic programming method find the quickest way from each town to F.

For a traveller who finds intolerable bus journeys of three hours or more without a break, what is the quickest way from A to F?

7.12 Consider the problem facing a gas supply company where the capacity of the distribution network has to be expanded from time to time to ensure that all demand can be satisfied. The company is interested in planning its capacity expansion programme over a time period from the present (where capacity equals demand) to a time horizon N periods from now. Demand in period n is given by an increasing function $d(n)$, and the cost of installing extra capacity k is $a + bk$, for $k > 0$, where a and b are positive numbers. Assume that the time to make an installation is negligible and all costs are incurred at the beginning of the period in which installation is made. The company's objective is to minimize the total discounted cost of meeting demand over the time horizon given, with the discount factor α used to reduce costs to the present day.

Defining $F(n)$ to be the minimum discounted cost of meeting demand from the present until the end of period $n (\leqslant N)$, where again capacity and demand are equal, show that

$$F(n) = \min_{0 \leqslant r < n} \{ F(r) + \alpha^r (a + b(d(n) - d(r))) \}, \quad \text{for } 0 < n \leqslant N,$$

and $F(0) = 0$, where time zero is the present.

Solve the problem when $d(n) = 2n$, $a = 2$, $b = 1$, $\alpha = 0.8$ and $N = 4$.

Chapter 8
Markov Chains

8.1 Introduction

We have already used in the previous chapter many of the terms for which we now offer a more general setting. Our interest is in the study of sequential decisionmaking under uncertainty, where the sequence is commonly, but not invariably, over time. Intervals of time separate the stages at which decisions must be made, and the effect of a decision at any stage is to influence the transition from current to succeeding state. The state is a 'sufficient description' of the system, and should contain enough information to characterize the system for the purposes of the investigation. Examples of possible state descriptions are:

(i)   the level of demand for a product (as in the first example of Chapter 7);

(ii)   the market price for a good (as in the second example of Chapter 7);

(iii)   the operational condition of a machine (as in the third example of Chapter 7);

(iv)   the number in a queue (in a waiting line problem);

(v)   the stock level of an item (in an inventory control problem);

(vi)   the delinquency of an account (in a model for credit control in a department store);

(vii)   the class (for example manual, skilled, professional) in a model of social mobility;

(viii)   the level (or grade) of a student at university (in a model which describes his progress or otherwise through university);

(ix)   a gambler's capital (in a model of his fate at a casino).

The state of a system is specified when the values of all state variables are known. In example (i) this is just 'high demand' or 'low demand', while a more refined version of this could have 100 levels for demand going from say 10 per week, through 20 per week up to 1000 per week. In any given week one and only one demand level can turn up. The state need not have only one dimension, e.g. in example (ii) the stock level for an item could be say zero up to 1000 in increments of five, while if we have two distinct item types in stock our state variable is the number in stock of each item type. For the more general case of n item types the state is represented by an n-vector. In principle our analysis is valid for both single and multidimensional state descriptions but the latter are more burdensome to solve numerically. Even on a computer the efficient solution of a problem of relatively small dimension involves more than the simple techniques which are within the scope of our study. This is a very active area of research and reference to more advanced work will be found in the appropriate section of Chapter 9. Our study will be confined to problems where there are only a finite number of one-dimensional state values. For instance, in example (v) above where the state variable is the number of items in stock, we will have upper and lower limits on the number of items held in stock (not a great restriction from the applicability of the model), while in example (iv) we would have an upper limit on queue size, any arrivals which take place when this limit has been reached being turned away and not entering the queue.

A system when observed over time will be seen to be in different *states* at different times, and we call the changes state transitions, or just *transitions*. Suppose our system has N states labelled $1, 2, \ldots, N$. The behaviour of the system over time is specified by the state the system is in at each *stage* in time. Our stage structure for these sequential problems (whether time based or not) will always be discrete. Models with a continuous time structure can be built and analysed, but only with the use of mathematics more advanced than we currently assume. The system runs over a sequence of stages, e.g. for a set of time periods indexed by $t = 0, 1, 2, \ldots$. If we denote the state of the system in time period t by $s(t)$ then the sequence $s(0), s(1), s(2), \ldots$ is a description of system behaviour. We have already declared that our system is not deterministic, and hence any exact future (i.e. succession of states over time) can be neither prophecied nor achieved. We could deduce some statistical description of the behaviour of the process if we knew the probabilities $p\{s(n) = j \mid s(n-1) = i, \; s(n-2) = k, \ldots, \; s(0) = m\}$ for all values of $j, i, k, \ldots, m$ such that $1 \leqslant j, i, k, \ldots, m \leqslant N$ and for $n = 1, 2, \ldots$. When the state transition is such that the above probability is of the form $p\{s(n) = j \mid s(n-1) = i\} = p_{ij}(n)$, say, for $1 \leqslant i, j \leqslant N$ and $n = 1, 2, \ldots$, then the system is described as a *finite Markov chain*, in eponymous tribute to the Russian mathematician who made an early study of this area. The $p_{ij}(n)$ is the transition probability from i to j if the transition takes place as the nth step. The Markovian assumption is that only the present stage (n) and state (i) are relevant to the determination of the future behaviour of the system. This system is sometimes described as being memoryless. Although a strong assumption, it will become clear that the Markov chain is an attractive and useful model for a large class of systems.

8.2 Markov Chains

A finite Markov chain is *time-homogeneous* if for every pair of states i and j we have $p_{ij}(n) = p_{ij}$ for $n = 1, 2, \ldots$. The chain is also described as having *stationary transition probabilities*. A common distinction is to describe continuous time (stage) structures as Markov processes and those with a discrete stage structure as Markov chains. Our study is confined to time-homogeneous finite Markov chains, but recall that finite refers to the state and not the stage description.

The *transition matrix* for a Markov chain is the $N \times N$ matrix $P = [p_{ij}]$, where the N is the number of states. Since each p_{ij} is a probability we must have $0 \leqslant p_{ij} \leqslant 1$, for $1 \leqslant i, j \leqslant N$. The system must be in one of the N states after the transition from any state i and thus $\sum_{j=1}^{N} p_{ij} = 1$ for $i = 1, 2, \ldots, N$. A matrix whose elements all lie in the range from zero up to one and whose rows sum to one is a *stochastic matrix*. The transition probability matrix for a Markov chain is thus a stochastic matrix.

We shall offer below a (partial) classification of Markov chains but first give an indication of the scope of applicability of the Markov chain idea.

Example 8.1

We have already seen in Chapter 7 a demand level model for a product where demand in any given period influences the level of demand in the subsequent period. The transition probability matrix used (for the case where no advertising takes place) is

$$
P = \begin{array}{cc}
 & \begin{array}{cc} \text{H} & \text{L} \end{array} \\
\begin{array}{c} \text{H} \\ \text{L} \end{array} & \begin{bmatrix} 0.5 & 0.5 \\ 0.25 & 0.75 \end{bmatrix}
\end{array}
$$

Prior to any notion of exercising control over the system for economic reward there are a number of questions which can be posed. For example, how does the probability of high demand in a given period depend on the initial demand and on the number of periods which have elapsed since then? Can we say anything about the long-term behaviour of the system, i.e. proportion of periods of high and low demand when the system is allowed to operate over very many periods? Where we have rewards and losses associated with the transitions and can exercise some degree of control, we have seen how the optimal policy can be calculated, where the system has a finite specified life, e.g. three periods. If we do not wish to put such a time horizon to the problem, but envisage the system as running effectively indefinitely, how do we formulate and solve such a problem?

Example 8.2

Consider the problem where we have a queue catered for by a single server with a limit on queueing capacity of m say. Let the probability of an arrival in one period be a and let the probability of a service, that is a customer leaving the system, in one period be b. Assume that the period is of small enough duration to allow us to 'exclude' the possibility of more than one arrival or more than one service in a period. We can have an arrival and a service in the same period as long as the arrival and the service do not involve the same customer. To model this as a finite Markov chain we define the state i to be the number in the system at the beginning of each period (including any customer being served). This gives an

$(m+1) \times (m+1)$ transition probability matrix P where

$$P = \begin{array}{c} \\ 0 \\ 1 \\ 2 \\ . \\ . \\ . \\ m-1 \\ m \end{array} \begin{array}{cccccc} 0 & 1 & 2 & & m-1 & m \\ \left[\begin{array}{cccccc} (1-a) & a & 0 & & & \\ b(1-a) & (1-a)(1-b)+ab & a(1-b) & & & \\ 0 & b(1-a) & & & & \\ . & . & . & . & & \\ . & . & . & . & . & . \\ . & . & . & . & . & . \\ 0 & & & & (1-a)(1-b)+ab & a(1-b) \\ 0 & 0 & & & b & (1-b) \end{array}\right] \end{array}$$

In general

$$p_{ij} = \begin{cases} b(1-a), & j = i-1 \\ (1-a)(1-b)+ab, & j = i \\ a(1-b), & j = i+1 \\ 0, & \text{for all other } j \end{cases}, \quad \text{for } 1 \leqslant i \leqslant m-1.$$

$p_{00} = (1-a)$, $p_{01} = a$, $p_{0j} = 0$ (for $2 \leqslant j \leqslant m$), $p_{m,m-1} = b$, $p_{mm} = 1-b$, $p_{mj} = 0$ (for $0 \leqslant j \leqslant m-2$). If we have none in the queue the only possible transition is to none in the queue (if there is no arrival) or to one in the queue (if there is an arrival). The probabilities of these events are $(1-a)$ and a, respectively, and hence the 'zeroth' row of P. If the system is full (number in the system is m) then the only possible transition is to m in the system (if there is no service) or to $(m-1)$ in the system (if there is a service). The probabilities of these events are $(1-b)$ and b, respectively, and hence the mth row of P. For any other state where we have i in the system namely $i \neq 0, m$) there will be one less in the system after one period if there is a service (probability b) and no arrival (probability $1-a$). For the same range of i in the system, there will be one extra after a period's elapse if there is an arrival and no service in that period. The probability of this event is $a(1-b)$. Finally, the number in the system can remain the same in two successive periods by virtue of two exclusive mechanisms. If there is neither arrival nor service in the period, or an arrival and a service (but not to the same customer), then the number in the queue remains the same. The first mechanism has probability $(1-a)(1-b)$ and the second ab. Their sum gives the probability of transition leaving the queue length unchanged. Note the significance of the state description here—the persons in the queue could have changed but the number has not, and it is this which is deemed to be of interest.

One of the variables of the system, say the service rate, may be controllable and a question which arises naturally in queueing problems is: How do we balance the waiting costs associated with a given service rate and the costs of providing the service? The proportion of customers arriving to find a full queue and thus being rejected by the system may be important, as may be the 'idle time' of the server, i.e. the proportion of time when the server has no customer to keep him engaged.

Example 8.3

Consider the problem of controlling a system in which a demand is made on stock in each week, the probabilities of demand levels being known. When we decide to increase stock level (by producing or procuring the items) assume that such replenishment is instantaneous and can thus be used to satisfy demand in the week where replenishment is taking place. Only one replenishment per week is allowed. Alternative assumptions can be accommodated within similar models. We can use one of several operating doctrines (described below) in seeking to control the system, and the objective is to optimize some relevant measure of system performance. Our concern here is to deduce the appropriate Markov chain for each operating doctrine. Solution of the problem taking cognizance of the economic consequences of options is postponed until the following chapter.

Suppose demand can be zero, one or two items per week, with probabilities 0.2, 0.4 and 0.4, respectively, and consider the following operating doctrines:

I. We have maximal stock level of three and every time stock falls to one or below we bring the stock level up to three again. This critical level (here one) is called the *re-order level*. Note that no shortages are ever incurred in operating the system i.e. demand can always be met.

II. We again have a maximal stock level of three, but this time our re-order level is taken to be zero. Under this doctrine shortages can occur (for the case where stock level is one and a demand of two arises) and we will assume that any demand which cannot be met results in a *lost sale* (for which there will be a penalty cost).

III. Here we operate with a maximal stock level of two and re-order level of zero but we allow demand which cannot be met immediately to be *back-ordered*, namely in the situation described under II the unsatisfied demand will be met in the next period but at some penalty.

For each of these operating doctrines we derive a corresponding transition probability matrix. In each case we take the state to be the number of items in stock at the end of each period (week) i.e. after demand has been met or lost or back-ordered. For the first doctrine we have the transition probability matrix given by P^{I} where

$$
P^{\text{I}} = \begin{array}{c} 0 \\ 1 \\ 2 \\ 3 \end{array}
\begin{array}{cccc} 0 & 1 & 2 & 3 \end{array}
\left[\begin{array}{cccc}
0 & 0.4 & 0.4 & 0.2 \\
0 & 0.4 & 0.4 & 0.2 \\
0.4 & 0.4 & 0.2 & 0 \\
0 & 0.4 & 0.4 & 0.2
\end{array}\right].
$$

Recall that we have re-order level of one with this option. Thus, if stock level is zero or one at the end of any period it is (instantaneously) raised to three in time to meet the demand in the next period. That demand is zero with probability 0.2 (leaving a stock level of three), one with probability 0.4 (leaving a stock level of two), and two with probability of 0.4 (leaving a stock level of one), and this gives

The first two rows of P^I. If stock level is two at the end of a period no re-stocking takes place before the next demand. The stock is then reduced to zero, one or two with the probability of demand two, one or zero, respectively. If stock level is three again no re-stocking takes place and the stock is reduced in one period to a level of one, two or three with the probability of demand two, one and zero, respectively.

Under the second doctrine the transition probability matrix is

$$P^{II} = \begin{array}{c} 0 \\ 1 \\ 2 \\ 3 \end{array} \begin{array}{cccc} 0 & 1 & 2 & 3 \\ \left[\begin{array}{cccc} 0 & 0.4 & 0.4 & 0.2 \\ 0.8 & 0.2 & 0 & 0 \\ 0.4 & 0.4 & 0.2 & 0 \\ 0 & 0.4 & 0.4 & 0.2 \end{array}\right] \end{array}.$$

The re-order level is now zero—hence the derivation of the zero row of P^{II}. If the stock level is one then it will be reduced to zero if demand is one or two, which will happen with probability $(0.4 + 0.4)$. Only if demand is zero (with probability 0.2) does the stock level stay at one. The other rows of P^{II} are identical to those of P^I.

For the third option we have an upper limit on stock of two, a re-order level of zero and the possibility of allowing any demand in excess of stock to be satisfied in the following period. With a maximum demand in any period of two and a re-order level of zero the maximum unsatisfied demand can be one (if there is demand of two when the stock level is one) and the maximum number of back-orders is therefore one. We use 0, 1, and 2 for stock levels and -1 for a back-order at the end of a period. The transition probability matrix is easily seen to be given by

$$P^{III} = \begin{array}{c} -1 \\ 0 \\ 1 \\ 2 \end{array} \begin{array}{cccc} -1 & 0 & 1 & 2 \\ \left[\begin{array}{cccc} 0 & 0.4 & 0.4 & 0.2 \\ 0 & 0.4 & 0.4 & 0.2 \\ 0.4 & 0.4 & 0.2 & 0 \\ 0 & 0.4 & 0.4 & 0.2 \end{array}\right] \end{array}.$$

In this chapter we analyse some statistical properties of these doctrines and later construct the solution which takes account of the economic consequences such as stock-holding costs, shortage costs and finally costs for back-ordering.

Example 8.4

Consider a model which illustrates student progress through university. Students have a three-year course to endure and in each of the three years there is a probability p of passing that year (either onto the next year, or from the final year to the state of graduate), a probability r of repeating the year and a probability f of failing irretrievably and leaving the system. In our Markov model there are five states—three corresponding to years one, two and three at university (denoted by

YR1, YR2 and YR3, respectively), one corresponding to the state of graduate (denoted by GRAD) and one corresponding to the state of permanent failure (denoted by FAIL). The transition probability matrix is easily seen to be

$$
\begin{array}{c@{\qquad}ccccc}
 & \text{GRAD} & \text{FAIL} & \text{YR1} & \text{YR2} & \text{YR3} \\
\begin{array}{c}\text{GRAD}\\ \text{FAIL}\\ \text{YR1}\\ \text{YR2}\\ \text{YR3}\end{array} &
\left[\begin{array}{ccccc}
1 & 0 & 0 & 0 & 0 \\
0 & 1 & 0 & 0 & 0 \\
0 & f & r & p & 0 \\
0 & f & 0 & r & p \\
p & f & 0 & 0 & r
\end{array}\right]
\end{array}
$$

Note that we assume no limit on the number of repetitions in any year, or a total across the years. It is possible to place such a sensible and realistic restriction on repetition by a more complicated state description, which we avoid. The states of graduate and failure have the property that once entered they are never left. Thus, a single student can end up in only one of these *absorbing states*. Questions we can ask are:

(i)   What are the probabilities of graduating and failing?

(ii)   How long would we expect a student to attend before either graduating or failing?

(iii) How many times would we expect a student to repeat a given year?

In more realistic problems we may have some control over the transition probabilities and rewards and penalties associated with absorption in different states. We are then faced with the problem of deciding how to exercise control in an optimal manner.

Example 8.5

A blood bank services two hospitals (X and Y) as well as functioning as a reception and testing centre. New blood (NB) enters the system and is either banked as fresh blood (FB), sent to hospital X or hospital Y as fresh blood (XF and YF, respectively) or wasted (W), i.e. rejected since it came from a donor with an inappropriate infection, or was in some other way spoiled. Blood can be stored at the bank or in the hospitals, but is never kept at the hospitals for more than two weeks, or at the blood bank for more than a week. Thus, at the hospitals we can have fresh blood (XF or YF), blood which is one week old (X1 or Y1) and blood which is two weeks old (X2 or Y2). Blood is either used (U), ages, or is wasted (W). Fresh blood can be sent to hospitals as can blood of age 1, but in both cases it is assumed to have aged one week before arrival (and hence the complete wastage of any blood older than one week at the bank, since it would be three weeks old on arrival at the hospitals and past its useful life). Figure 8.1 illustrates the possible transitions for the system (only possible along the arcs in the directions indicated) and in the matrix P of Figure 8.2 the non-zero elements are denoted by an asterisk. Numerical values are omitted. The only restriction is that the row sums should be one, and thus the U to U and W to W elements are both one.

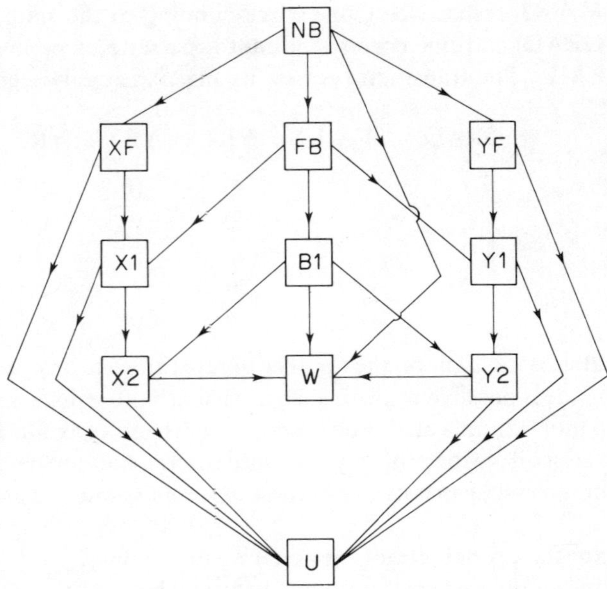

Figure 8.1 The 'flow' of blood in the blood-bank example

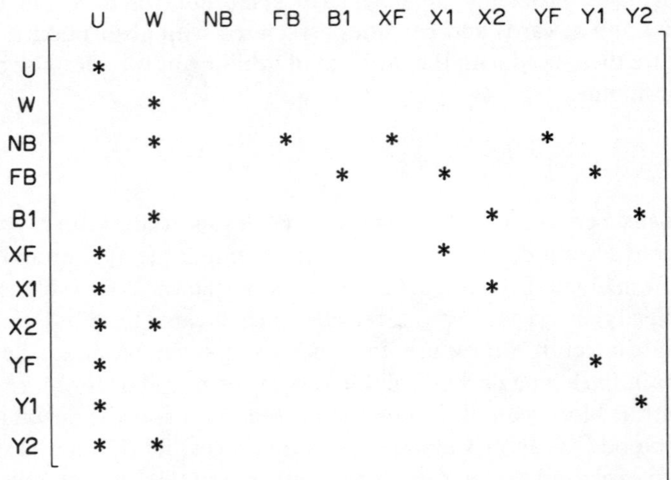

	U	W	NB	FB	B1	XF	X1	X2	YF	Y1	Y2
U	*										
W		*									
NB		*		*		*			*		
FB				*			*			*	
B1		*						*			*
XF	*						*				
X1	*							*			
X2	*	*									
YF	*									*	
Y1	*										*
Y2	*	*									

Figure 8.2 A transition probability matrix compatible with the
structure of Figure 8.1

8.3 Multi-step Transition Probabilities

Having demonstrated the potential applicability of Markov chains we now study
some of the properties which prove enlightening in our work on infinite stage
Markovian decision problems, as well as giving insight into the implications of

the Markovian assumption for modelling dynamic processes. Note that in the previous chapter we have been solving finite stage Markovian decision problems, but nowhere did we need any properties of the transition probability matrix.

The transition probability matrix P describes the likelihoods of transition in one step from state to state, and it is natural to pursue the question of *multi-step transition probability* values. For example, what is the probability that the system is in state j after n transitions given that it started in state i at time zero? If we define $\phi_{ij}(n) = p\{s(n) = j \mid s(0) = i\}$ for $1 \leqslant i, j \leqslant N$ and $n = 0, 1, 2 \ldots$ as the n-*step transition probabilities* for the Markov chain (defined by P), what can we say of the $\phi_{ij}(n)$?

If the system starts in state i at time zero and is in state j at time $(n+1)$ (after $n+1$ transitions) this must have been achieved by transition in n steps from state i to some state k (for which the probability is $\phi_{ik}(n)$) followed by transition from k to j is one step (for which the probability is p_{kj}). Thus, given that the state at the nth step is k, the probability of transition to j in $n+1$ steps is $\phi_{ik}(n)p_{kj}$. In fact the state at the nth step can be any $k = 1, 2, \ldots, N$ and since these N mechanisms for the transition from i to j in $n+1$ steps via a given state at the nth step are mutually exclusive and exhaustive we have

$$\phi_{ij}(n+1) = \sum_{k=1}^{N} \phi_{ik}(n)p_{kj}.$$

Many of our arguments in this chapter follow a similar line, and to substantiate and reinforce the above we offer a variant of the proof as follows:

$$\phi_{ij}(n+1) = p\{s(n+1) = j \mid s(0) = i\} = \sum_{k=1}^{N} p\{s(n+1) = j \text{ and } s(n) = k \mid s(0) = i\}$$

$$= \sum_{k=1}^{N} p\{s(n) = k \mid s(0) = i\} p\{s(n+1) = j \mid s(n) = k \text{ and } s(0) = i\}$$

from the definition of conditional probability

$$= \sum_{k=1}^{N} p\{s(n) = k \mid s(0) = i\} p\{s(n+1) = j \mid s(n) = k\}$$

by the Markovian assumption

$$= \sum_{k} \phi_{ik}(n)p_{kj}, \ldots \ldots \ldots \ldots \ldots \ldots \ldots \ldots \ldots (1)$$

as before.

Define $\phi_{ij}(0)$ as follows:

$$\phi_{ij}(0) = \delta_{ij} = \begin{cases} 1, & \text{if } i = j, \\ 0, & \text{if } i \neq j. \end{cases}$$

This useful shorthand is known as the *Kronecker delta function* and will be used on several occasions. Since we are dealing with probabilities the multi-step transition probabilities must satisfy the relationship $0 \leqslant \phi_{ij}(n) \leqslant 1$ for $1 \leqslant i$, $j \leqslant N$ and $n = 0, 1, \ldots$, and $\sum_{j=1}^{N} \phi_{ij}(n) = 1$ for $1 \leqslant i \leqslant N$ and $n = 0, 1, \ldots$.

198

The equation for the multi-step transition probabilities can be represented in matrix form. Define $\Phi(n) = [\phi_{ij}(n)]$ as the *n-step transition probability matrix* for $n = 0, 1, \ldots$. From the properties above we immediately see that $\Phi(n)$ is a stochastic matrix. The right-hand side of (1) above is the product of the ith row of $\Phi(n)$ and the jth column of P, and we can thus write that equation as

$$\Phi(n+1) = \Phi(n)P, \quad \text{for} \quad n = 0, 1, \ldots,$$
$$\Phi(0) \quad = I,$$

where I is the $N \times N$ identity matrix (i.e. diagonal elements of 1, all other numbers zero).

Thus, we have
$$\Phi(1) = \Phi(0)P = P,$$
$$\Phi(2) = \Phi(1)P = P^2,$$
$$\Phi(3) = \Phi(2)P = P^3$$

and in general $\Phi(n) = \Phi(n-1)P = P^{n-1}P = P^n$ for $n = 0, 1, \ldots$. (Note that $P^0 = I$.) From this result we can actually deduce a more general version of equation (1) above. We have

$$\Phi(n+1) = P^{n+1} = P^t P^{n+1-t} = \Phi(t)\,\Phi(n+1-t),$$

and thus

$$\phi_{ij}(n+1) = \sum_{k=1}^{N} \phi_{ik}(t)\,\phi_{kj}(n+1-t),$$

since the (i, j)th element of the product $\Phi(n+1)$ is the (inner) product of the ith row of $\Phi(t)$ and jth column of $\Phi(n+1-t)$. This is sometimes known as the *Chapman–Kolmogorov* equation. Equation (1) is the special case where $t = n$. Where we previously constructed the probability for transition over $(n+1)$ steps from an n-step transition followed by a single step, the Chapman–Kolmogorov equation expresses the $(n+1)$-step probability as a t-step followed by an $(n+1-t)$-step transition, for an arbitrary t.

Turning to Example 8.1, we generate the following multi-step transition probability matrices:

$$\Phi(0) = I = \begin{bmatrix} 1 & 0 \\ 0 & 1 \end{bmatrix}; \qquad \Phi(1) = P = \begin{bmatrix} 1/2 & 1/2 \\ 1/4 & 3/4. \end{bmatrix},$$

$$\Phi(2) = P^2 = \begin{bmatrix} 3/8 & 5/8 \\ 5/16 & 11/16 \end{bmatrix}; \qquad \Phi(3) = P^3 = \begin{bmatrix} 11/32 & 21/32 \\ 21/64 & 43/64 \end{bmatrix},$$

$$\Phi(4) = P^4 = \begin{bmatrix} 43/128 & 85/128 \\ 85/256 & 171/256 \end{bmatrix}, \quad \text{and so on.}$$

Thus, $\phi_{\text{HH}}(4) = 43/128$ means that the probability of high demand in period four, given that initial demand is high, is $43/128$. Note that with increasing n the 'difference' between the rows of $\Phi(n)$ is diminishing. For example, looking at the elements in the first column of each of the $\Phi(n)$ we have $\phi_{\text{HH}}(1) - \phi_{\text{LH}}(1) = 1/4$, $\phi_{\text{HH}}(2) - \phi_{\text{LH}}(2) = 1/16$, $\phi_{\text{HH}}(3) - \phi_{\text{LH}}(3) = 1/64$, and $\phi_{\text{HH}}(4) - \phi_{\text{LH}}(4) = 1/256$. A similar behaviour can be found in the second (L) column of the $\Phi(n)$. After each extra step the difference is one-quarter what it was before. Thus, we may ask: What is the limiting behaviour (if any) of the matrix $\Phi(n)$ as n becomes very large? If we carry out sufficient calculations we can show that the entries of $\Phi(n)$ approach those of Φ where

$$\Phi = \begin{bmatrix} 1/3 & 2/3 \\ 1/3 & 2/3 \end{bmatrix},$$

and here the rows are identical.

By the fifth step the difference between elements in a column of $\Phi(n)$ is less than 10^{-3} while by the tenth step it is less than 10^{-6}. We can in fact provide an inductive proof of the limiting behaviour.

Assume that $\Phi(n)$ can be written in the form

$$\Phi(n) = \begin{bmatrix} a_n & 1-a_n \\ a_n - \dfrac{1}{2^{2n}} & 1-a_n + \dfrac{1}{2^{2n}} \end{bmatrix},$$

where $\dfrac{1}{2^{2n}} \leqslant a_n \leqslant 1$. This is true for $n = 1$ with $a_1 = 1/2$. The reader may verify that $\Phi(1)$ above is identical to the original P of the problem. Assume then that the above form is correct up to step n. Now

$$\phi(n+1) = \Phi(n)P$$

$$= \begin{bmatrix} a_n & 1-a_n \\ a_n - \dfrac{1}{2^{2n}} & 1-a_n + \dfrac{1}{2^{2n}} \end{bmatrix} \begin{bmatrix} 1/2 & 1/2 \\ 1/4 & 3/4 \end{bmatrix}$$

$$= \begin{bmatrix} \tfrac{1}{4}(1+a_n) & 1-\tfrac{1}{4}(1+a_n) \\ \tfrac{1}{4}(1+a_n) - \dfrac{1}{2^{2(n+1)}} & 1-\tfrac{1}{4}(1+a_n) + \dfrac{1}{2^{2(n+1)}} \end{bmatrix}.$$

If we write $a_{n+1} = \tfrac{1}{4}(1+a_n)$ then $a_{n+1} \leqslant 1$ and $a_{n+1} \geqslant \tfrac{1}{4}\left(1+\dfrac{1}{2^{2n}}\right) = \tfrac{1}{4} + \dfrac{1}{2^{2(n+1)}}$

$\geqslant \dfrac{1}{2^{2(n+1)}}$. Thus, $\Phi(n+1)$ can be written in the form

$$\Phi(n+1) = \begin{bmatrix} a_{n+1} & 1-a_{n+1} \\ a_{n+1} - \dfrac{1}{2^{2(n+1)}} & 1-a_{n+1} + \dfrac{1}{2^{2(n+1)}} \end{bmatrix},$$

and our assumption about the form of $\Phi(n)$ is correct for $n = 0, 1, 2, \ldots$. The difference between two column elements in $\Phi(n)$ is $\dfrac{1}{2^{2n}}$ and thus as n increases the difference decreases and in the limit is zero, i.e. the rows are identical. Now we have $a_{n+1} = \tfrac{1}{4}(1+a_n)$, and assuming that $\lim_{n \to \infty} a_n = a$ exists we have $a = \tfrac{1}{4}(1+a)$, giving $a = 1/3$. Thus, the limiting form of $\Phi(n)$ is

$$\begin{bmatrix} 1/3 & 2/3 \\ 1/3 & 2/3 \end{bmatrix}$$

as before.

We define $\Phi = \lim_{n \to \infty} P^n$ (if it exists) and call Φ the *limiting multi-step transition probability matrix* for the chain. As the number of transitions increases so the influence of the original state diminishes dramatically. After five transitions the difference between a high demand given an originally high demand and a high demand given an originally low demand is less than 10^{-3}, and in the limit (after an unbounded number of transitions) the two probabilities are identical. Since the rows of Φ are identical we are led to the conclusion that, in the limit, the probabilities of high and low demand are independent of the initial demand. This is intuitively reasonable since the Markovian assumption attributes no memory to the system, and we would not expect the influence of the initial state to be significant beyond a few transitions.

It is important that the distinction between Φ and P be kept clear. At any stage of the problem the probabilities of transition from state to state are fully described by P. The matrix Φ is essentially summarizing information about the long-term behaviour of the system, a point we return to after a short exploration of a less 'well-behaved' example. In this section the form of the matrix was found from the trend of the P^n matrices or the inductive form for $\Phi(n)$. We shall see below how neither of these somewhat unsatisfactory techniques is necessary for some types of chains, and how the elements of Φ can be found by solving a set of equations involving the elements of P—a method both finite and not relying on guesswork.

For a problem where demand can be low (L), medium (M) or high (H) suppose we have the following transition probability matrix:

$$P = \begin{array}{c} \\ L \\ M \\ H \end{array} \begin{array}{ccc} L & M & H \\ \left[\begin{array}{ccc} 0 & 1 & 0 \\ 1/2 & 0 & 1/2 \\ 0 & 1 & 0 \end{array}\right] \end{array}.$$

Thus, a week of low high demand is followed by a week of medium demand, which in turn is followed by a week of high or low demand, etc. If the problem starts with medium demand in the first week, it will be medium in the third, fifth, seventh, etc. weeks, and either high or low in the second, fourth, sixth, etc. weeks. If we form $P^2, P^3 \ldots$ we obtain:

$$P^2 = \begin{bmatrix} 1/2 & 0 & 1/2 \\ 0 & 1 & 0 \\ 1/2 & 0 & 1/2 \end{bmatrix}; \quad P^3 = \begin{bmatrix} 0 & 1 & 0 \\ 1/2 & 0 & 1/2 \\ 0 & 1 & 0 \end{bmatrix} = P,$$

and thus $P^n = P$ if n is odd and

$$P^n = \begin{bmatrix} 1/2 & 0 & 1/2 \\ 0 & 1 & 0 \\ 1/2 & 0 & 1/2 \end{bmatrix}$$

if n is even. Since P^n alternates between two distinct forms there does not exist a unique limit to which the multi-step transition probability matrices tend.

The recurrence relationship which expresses multi-step transition probabilities as a power of the single-step transition probability matrix P was argued for an arbitrary stochastic matrix. No use was made of any special properties of the matrix, though we did see differences in the behaviour of the series $P^n (n = 0, 1, 2, \ldots)$ for different P.

Consider again Example 8.4 with probability assignments of $p = 0.8$, $r = 0.1$ and $f = 0.1$. Thus, in any year there is a one in ten chance that a student fails, the same chance that he repeats the year and a probability of 0.8 that he passes onto the next year (or graduates from the third year). The matrix of probabilities is then

$$
\begin{array}{c}
 \\
\text{GRAD} \\
\text{FAIL} \\
\text{YR1} \\
\text{YR2} \\
\text{YR3}
\end{array}
\begin{array}{ccccc}
\text{GRAD} & \text{FAIL} & \text{YR1} & \text{YR2} & \text{YR3} \\
\left[\begin{array}{ccccc}
1 & 0 & 0 & 0 & 0 \\
0 & 1 & 0 & 0 & 0 \\
0 & 0.1 & 0.1 & 0.8 & 0 \\
0 & 0.1 & 0 & 0.1 & 0.8 \\
0.8 & 0.1 & 0 & 0 & 0.1
\end{array}\right]
\end{array}.
$$

Over three transitions this gives

$$
P^3 = \begin{array}{c}
 \\
\text{GRAD} \\
\text{FAIL} \\
\text{YR1} \\
\text{YR2} \\
\text{YR3}
\end{array}
\begin{array}{ccccc}
\text{GRAD} & \text{FAIL} & \text{YR1} & \text{YR2} & \text{YR3} \\
\left[\begin{array}{ccccc}
1 & 0 & 0 & 0 & 0 \\
0 & 1 & 0 & 0 & 0 \\
0.512 & 0.271 & 0.001 & 0.024 & 0.192 \\
0.768 & 0.207 & 0 & 0.001 & 0.024 \\
0.888 & 0.111 & 0 & 0 & 0.001
\end{array}\right]
\end{array}.
$$

Examination of the YR1 row shows that the probability that a student having entered in first year graduates in exactly three years is 0.512. Note that the probability of three straight passes through the years (which is the only way in which he can graduate in three years) is $0.8^3 = 0.512$. There is a probability 0.271 that he has failed in those three years, and this includes all three possibilities of failure in first, second or third year. There are several mechanisms by which these failures could have come about. For example, failure in the first year could have been at the first attempt, at the second attempt (due to repeating first year) or at the third attempt (due to repeating first year twice). These exclusive events have a combined probability of $0.1 + 0.1^2 + 0.1^3 = 0.111$. Failure in the second year could have happened in the student's second or third year of attendance. In the first instance this means a pass in the first year followed by a failure in the second for which the probability is $0.8 \times 0.1 = 0.08$. Failure in the third year of attendance in the second year of the course can only be achieved by either repeating then passing the first year followed by failure in the second year, or by passing in the first year, repeating, then failing in the second year. The combined probability of these exclusive events is $0.8 \times 0.1 \times 0.1 + 0.1 \times 0.8 \times 0.1 = 0.016$.

Failure in the third year can only be achieved after three years' attendance by two consecutive passes in the first and second years, followed by failure in the third year at the first attempt. This has probability $0.8^2 \times 0.1 = 0.064$. Thus, the probability of failing sometime in the three years is $(0.111 + 0.08 + 0.016 + 0.064) = 0.271$, as in the matrix.

Of the other entries of the YR1 row, these express the probability of the student still being in the first, second or third year after three years' study, and can be verified by arguments similar to those above. If we allow two more transitions we obtain (with an accuracy of five decimal places):

$$
P^5 = \begin{array}{c} \\ \text{GRAD} \\ \text{FAIL} \\ \text{YR1} \\ \text{YR2} \\ \text{YR3} \end{array}
\begin{array}{ccccc}
\text{GRAD} & \text{FAIL} & \text{YR1} & \text{YR2} & \text{YR3} \\
\left[\begin{array}{ccccc}
1 & 0 & 0 & 0 & 0 \\
0 & 1 & 0 & 0 & 0 \\
0.69632 & 0.29687 & 0.00001 & 0.0004 & 0.0064 \\
0.78976 & 0.20983 & 0 & 0.00001 & 0.0004 \\
0.88888 & 0.11111 & 0 & 0 & 0.00001
\end{array}\right].
\end{array}
$$

Again examining the YR1 row we see that there is only a very small probability that the student has not either graduated or failed, i.e. made a transition into one of the states GRAD or FAIL.

If we allow a total of ten transitions we have the following matrix, where the accuracy of the numbers is to six decimal places:

$$
P^{10} = \begin{array}{c} \\ \text{GRAD} \\ \text{FAIL} \\ \text{YR1} \\ \text{YR2} \\ \text{YR3} \end{array}
\begin{array}{ccccc}
\text{GRAD} & \text{FAIL} & \text{YR1} & \text{YR2} & \text{YR3} \\
\left[\begin{array}{ccccc}
1 & 0 & 0 & 0 & 0 \\
0 & 1 & 0 & 0 & 0 \\
0.702332 & 0.297668 & 0 & 0 & 0 \\
0.790123 & 0.209877 & 0 & 0 & 0 \\
0.888889 & 0.111111 & 0 & 0 & 0
\end{array}\right].
\end{array}
$$

The probability that after ten transitions the student has not either graduated or failed is in fact less than 10^{-10}. The student's probability of (eventually) graduating is 0.702332, and this includes allowance for all possible mechanisms by which this can have been achieved in up to ten years.

With numerical values for the transition probabilities of Example 8.5 we could derive similar information about the eventual use and wastage of new blood. All of our analysis has so far relied on iterative numerical schemes to produce properties of the system, but later sections of this chapter provide alternative direct solution methods.

8.4 State Probabilities

The multi-step transition probability matrices for $n = 0, 1, \ldots$ give the probabilities of transition to states, conditional on some starting state. Our concern in this section is with unconditional state occupancy probabilities. We define $\pi_i(n) = p\{s(n) = i\}$ for $i = 1, \ldots, N$ and $n = 0, 1, \ldots$. The $\pi_i(n)$ is the probability that state i is occupied at time n, known as the *state probability*. We must have $\sum_{i=1}^{N} \pi_i(n) = 1$ for $n = 0, 1, \ldots$. The case of $n = 0$ gives a method of specifying a set of probabilities for the initial state, if appropriate. Note that

$$
p\{s(n) = j\} = \sum_{i=1}^{N} p\{s(0) = i\} \times p\{s(n) = j \,|\, s(0) = i\},
$$

that is

$$\pi_j(n) = \sum_{i=1}^{N} \pi_i(0)\phi_{ij}(n), \quad \ldots \ldots \ldots \ldots \ldots \ldots (2)$$

and this is true for $1 \leqslant j \leqslant N$ and $n = 0, 1, \ldots$. The system starts in i with probability $\pi_i(0)$ and the n-step transition probability from i to j is $\phi_{ij}(n)$. Hence, the probability that the system starts in i and makes the transition to j in n steps is $\pi_i(0)\phi_{ij}(n)$. The events of starting in the N different states are mutually exclusive and exhaustive, hence (2).

If we define the row vector $\pi(n)$ by $\pi(n) = [\pi_1(n), \pi_2(n), \ldots, \pi_N(n)]$ for $n = 0, 1, \ldots$, then from (2) we see that the jth element of $\pi(n)$ is found by the product of $\pi(0)$ and the jth column of $\Phi(n)$. Thus,

$$\pi(n) = \pi(0)\Phi(n), \qquad n = 0, 1, \ldots$$
$$= \pi(0)P^n, \qquad n = 0, 1, \ldots.$$

We call $\pi(n)$ the *state probability vector* at time n. Note that

$$\pi(n+1) = \pi(0)P^{n+1} = \pi(0)P^n P = \pi(n)P. \quad \ldots \ldots \ldots \ldots (3)$$

As an illustration of the use of the concept, suppose that in Example 8.1 instead of having a known initial demand (high or low) we have a probability of initial high demand of 0.4 and hence a probability of initial low demand 0.6. We thus have $\pi(0) = [0.4 \quad 0.6]$. To find the state probabilities after, say, two transitions, we calculate

$$\pi(2) = \pi(0)P^2$$
$$= [0.4 \quad 0.6] \begin{bmatrix} 3/8 & 5/8 \\ 5/16 & 11/16 \end{bmatrix} = [27/80 \quad 53/80].$$

The probability of high demand in the second period is thus 0.3375. This is less than the probability of high demand (on the same occasion) if we know that the initial demand is indeed high ($\phi_{HH}(2) = 0.375$), but greater than the probability of high demand if we know that the initial demand is indeed low ($\phi_{LH}(2) = 0.3125$).

Consider the general case where we have $\pi_H(0) = p$, $\pi_L(0) = (1-p)$, and use the inductive form for $\Phi(n)$ justified in Section 8.3. Then

$$\pi(n) = [p \quad 1-p] \begin{bmatrix} a_n & 1-a_n \\ a_n - \dfrac{1}{2^{2n}} & 1-a_n+\dfrac{1}{2^{2n}} \end{bmatrix}$$
$$= [a_n - (1-p)/2^{2n} \quad (1-a_n) + (1-p)/2^{2n}].$$

As n increases the first term deviates less and less from a_n, while the second is nearly $(1-a_n)$. If we denote the *limiting state probability vector* (where it exists) by π then $\pi = \lim_{n \to \infty} \pi(n)$ and in this case

$$\pi = \lim_{n \to \infty} [a_n - (1-p)/2^{2n} \quad (1-a_n) + (1-p)/2^{2n}]$$
$$= [a \quad 1-a],$$

where $a = \lim_{n \to \infty} a_n$. Thus, for this example the limiting state probability vector is just the same as the identical rows of Φ, and in fact since $a = 1/3$, $\pi = [1/3 \quad 2/3]$. There is no dependence in the limiting state probability vector on the initial probabilities of high and low demand. Given an unbounded number of transitions the probabilities of high and low demand are $1/3$ and $2/3$, respectively. Thus, given that the system has been running for a sufficient number of transitions, these fractions will give the approximate proportions of time spent in states of high and low demand, respectively. Again we remind the reader that any single transition is in obedience to the probabilities of P, and both the limiting state probability vector and limiting multi-step transition probability matrix are summary statistics. The elements of π are sometimes known as *steady state probabilities*.

For this chain, and those with similar limiting characteristics (which we later enunciate) this limiting state probability vector can be found directly from a set of linear equations derived from the transition matrix P. From (3) we have that $\pi(n+1) = \pi(n)P$ so that if $\pi = \lim_{n \to \infty} \pi(n)$ exists, then taking the limit on both sides of the equation we have

$$\pi = \pi P. \qquad \qquad (4)$$

or

$$\pi_j = \sum_{i=1}^{N} \pi_i p_{ij}, \qquad 1 \leqslant j \leqslant N. \qquad (5)$$

This is a set of N linear equations in N variables (π_i, $i = 1, \ldots, N$) but the equations are not independent. For Example 8.1 we have

$$[\pi_H \quad \pi_L] = [\pi_H \quad \pi_L] \begin{bmatrix} 0.5 & 0.5 \\ 0.25 & 0.75 \end{bmatrix},$$

i.e.

$$\pi_H = 0.5\pi_H + 0.25\pi_L,$$
$$\pi_L = 0.5\pi_H + 0.75\pi_L,$$

and both of these equations rationalize to $0.5\pi_H = 0.25\pi_L$. However, we have not so far used the fact that

$$\sum_{i=1}^{N} \pi_i = 1, \qquad \qquad (6)$$

since the π_i are probabilities over an exclusive and exhaustive set of events. Thus, we have $0.5\pi_H = 0.25\pi_L$ together with $\pi_H + \pi_L = 1$ gives $\pi_H = 1/3$, $\pi_L = 2/3$, as before. In the general case we would take $(N-1)$ of the equations of (5) together with (6) to give N independent linear equations in N unknowns.

Although (3) is a valid recurrence relationship regardless of the nature of the underlying chain, it is only when the limiting state probability vector exists that (4) is valid. Thus, our demand level example of Section 8.3 (where there are three states and the form of P^n alternated with odd and even values of n) will not lend itself to an analysis of the above form, though some statistics on state occupancy can still be generated (see Exercise 8.9).

8.5 Some Classes of Markov Chain

We have already seen in the examples and the discussion above some of the different types of Markov chains, but we have not made and will not make an exhaustive classification. Our taxonomy is essentially in terms of the communication which exists between states, or among members of a group of states. Chains are classified by the properties which their constituent states possess.

State i can *communicate* with state j (written $i \rightarrow j$) if for some integer n $\phi_{ij}(n)$ > 0. Thus, $i \rightarrow j$ if there is a possibility of transition from i to j in some number of steps n. We say that i and j communicate (written $i \leftrightarrow j$) if and only if $i \rightarrow j$ and $j \rightarrow i$. Thus, two states communicate if transition is possible in either direction in some finite number of steps. The number need not be the same for the two directions of communication. A most important property of the relationship of communication is its transitivity, i.e. if $i \leftrightarrow j$ and $j \leftrightarrow k$, then $i \leftrightarrow k$. This is readily demonstrated. Since $i \leftrightarrow j$ and $j \leftrightarrow k$, then there exist numbers n_1 and n_2 such that $\phi_{ij}(n_1)$ and $\phi_{jk}(n_2)$ are both positive. Thus, from the Chapman–Kolmogoromov equation

$$\phi_{ik}(n_1 + n_2) = \sum_{l=1}^{N} \phi_{il}(n_1)\phi_{lk}(n_2) \geqslant \phi_{ij}(n_1)\phi_{jk}(n_2) > 0.$$

Communication from k to i is similarly established.

In any Markov chain we can find sets of states (or rather at least one set of states) where all states which are members of the same set communicate with one another. Thus, in Example 8.1 the two demand levels can be reached from one another in a single transition and both states of the chain thus communicate. In this case the entire chain is the one 'communicating set'. For the queueing problem of Example 8.2, again all states communicate. It is possible to go from any queue length to any other queue size in a certain number of steps (at most m). The transition probability matrices for the doctrines described in the stock control model of Example 8.3 again show that all states communicate since at most two transitions are needed to go from any state to any other state (in all three doctrines). For Example 8.4 we have a different structure. The state of GRAD communicates with itself, as does the state of FAIL, but these are the only two sets of states where communication between constituent states is possible. The sets (both with one element) of GRAD and FAIL can be entered from the other states, but cannot be left. Among the states YR1, YR2 and YR3 we have, for instance, YR1 $\rightarrow$ YR2, YR1 $\rightarrow$ YR3 and YR2 $\rightarrow$ YR3, but there is no communication in the opposite directions. Finally, for Example 8.5 the state W communicates only with itself, as does the state U, and these are therefore both sets (albeit with only one element each) where communication between member states is feasible. These are no other sets in this chain consisting of states in communication. All other links are in one direction only.

As an example of a chain with a different structure consider that described by the transition probability matrix P^*, where

$$
\begin{array}{c}
\begin{array}{ccccc} A_1 & A_2 & T & B_1 & B_2 \end{array} \\
P^* = \begin{array}{c} A_1 \\ A_2 \\ T \\ B_1 \\ B_2 \end{array}
\left[\begin{array}{ccccc}
1/3 & 2/3 & 0 & 0 & 0 \\
1/2 & 1/2 & 0 & 0 & 0 \\
0 & 1/4 & 1/4 & 1/2 & 0 \\
0 & 0 & 0 & 1/4 & 3/4 \\
0 & 0 & 0 & 1/2 & 1/2
\end{array}\right].
\end{array}
$$

Here $A_1 \leftrightarrow A_2$ and $B_1 \leftrightarrow B_2$, and $T \to A_2, T \to B_1$, so that the sets $\{A_1, A_2\}$ and $\{B_1, B_2\}$ are examples of sets whose members communicate only between themselves. If this system started in say A_1, then all transitions would leave it in the communicating set $\{A_1, A_2\}$. Similarly, if the system started in either of B_1 or B_2 all transitions are such that these are the only states which can turn up thereafter. If the system starts in T, then (apart from transitions to T) it can make transitions into either $\{A_1, A_2\}$ or $\{B_1, B_2\}$ and having entered one of these sets it is trapped in it thereafter.

We define an *ergodic set of states* to be a set in which every state communicates with every other state of the set. Thus, $\{A_1, A_2\}$ and $\{B_1, B_2\}$ above are ergodic sets. In each of the Examples 8.1, 8.2 and 8.3 the entire set of states for the chain is an ergodic set. Consider again the doctrine I for the stock control Example 8.3. The states $\{0, 1, 2\}$ form an ergodic set, but so do the states $\{1, 2\}$ (for our definition). The latter set however is not *maximal*, i.e. we can add more states to the set without destroying the ergodicity. Without exception we mean maximal ergodic sets whenever we refer to ergodic sets. Thus, a (maximal) ergodic set of states is a set of states in which every state can be reached from every other state of the set, and once the set is entered there can be no transition out of the set. An *ergodic state* is an element of an ergodic set.

In Example 8.4 (and 8.5) the ergodic sets are $\{\text{GRAD}\}$ and $\{\text{FAIL}\}$ (and $\{\text{W}\}$ and $\{\text{U}\}$). States of this last type which once entered cannot be left, are *absorbing* (or *trapping*) *states*. State i is an absorbing state if and only if $p_{ii} = 1$ (and thus $p_{ij} = 0$ for all $j \neq i$).

Ergodic sets can thus be thought of as 'collective' trapping states. *Every Markov chain contains at least one (maximal) ergodic set*, a property which we do not prove. If a chain contains more than one ergodic set then these sets obviously have no states in common (or their ergodicity would be contradicted).

In any chain there may be states which do not belong to an ergodic set. These states constitute a *transient set* and are called *transient states*. Thus, in our last example with transition probability matrix P^* the transient set is the single state $\{T\}$. In Example 8.4 the ergodic sets are $\{\text{GRAD}\}$ and $\{\text{FAIL}\}$, while the transient set is $\{\text{YR1}, \text{YR2}, \text{YR3}\}$. In Examples 8.1, 8.2 and 8.3 there are no transient states and the entire chain is one ergodic set. A Markov chain whose states form a single ergodic set is an *ergodic chain*. For these same examples we can see that for a sufficiently large n the multi-step transition probability matrix

$\Phi(n) = P^n$ (for the appropriate P) has all entries greater than zero. For Example 8.1, $n = 1$ is sufficient, while for any of the doctrines of Example 8.3, $n = 2$ is enough. In Example 8.2, $n = m$ will give a matrix P^m with all entries positive. An ergodic set with this property is *regular*. Since $\Phi(n+1) = P\Phi(n)$, then P^{n+1} will have no zero entries if P^n does not have any. Thus, having reached a critical number of transitions at which all state to state transitions are possible, additional transitions never lead to any of the state to state transitions having zero probability again. An ergodic chain which is regular is a *regular chain*.

For the problem with transition probability matrix

$$P = \begin{matrix} & \begin{matrix} \text{L} & \text{M} & \text{H} \end{matrix} \\ \begin{matrix} \text{L} \\ \text{M} \\ \text{H} \end{matrix} & \begin{bmatrix} 0 & 1 & 0 \\ 1/2 & 0 & 1/2 \\ 0 & 1 & 0 \end{bmatrix} \end{matrix}$$

we saw that P^n alternates between the form above (when n is odd) and

$$\begin{matrix} & \begin{matrix} \text{L} & \text{M} & \text{H} \end{matrix} \\ \begin{matrix} \text{L} \\ \text{M} \\ \text{H} \end{matrix} & \begin{bmatrix} 1/2 & 0 & 1/2 \\ 0 & 1 & 0 \\ 1/2 & 0 & 1/2 \end{bmatrix} \end{matrix}$$

when n is even. Thus, there is no power of P for which the resultant matrix is free of zero entries. This ergodic chain—all states do communicate—is certainly not regular. If the problem starts in the state M say at time zero then it in state M again at time $2, 4, 6, \ldots$ and in one of the states $\{\text{L}, \text{H}\}$ at time $1, 3, 5, \ldots$. Ergodic sets which exhibit this type of periodicity are known as *cyclic*. In a cyclic chain a state may only be entered at periodic intervals (but of course need not be, since there may be other states which can be entered at the same time, e.g. L and H in the above problem).

Finally, we define an *absorbing chain* to be a Markov chain all of whose ergodic states are absorbing. Examples 8.4 and 8.5 are absorbing chains.

There is a distinction to be made between chains which have transient states and those which do not. In the second category we further distinguish between chains which have one ergodic set and those which have more than one. Examples 8.1, 8.2 and 8.3 all have ergodic sets and no transient states. If there are, for example, two ergodic sets and no transient states, then the transition probability matrix will have a form something akin to

$$\begin{matrix} & \begin{matrix} A_1 & A_2 & B_1 & B_2 \end{matrix} \\ \begin{matrix} A_1 \\ A_2 \\ B_1 \\ B_2 \end{matrix} & \begin{bmatrix} 1/2 & 1/2 & 0 & 0 \\ 1/4 & 3/4 & 0 & 0 \\ 0 & 0 & 1/3 & 2/3 \\ 0 & 0 & 1/2 & 1/2 \end{bmatrix} \end{matrix}.$$

There is no interaction between the ergodic sets $\{A_1, A_2\}$ and $\{B_1, B_2\}$ and properties of the chain can be derived from a study of the two chains whose states are $\{A_1, A_2\}$ with transition probability matrix $\begin{bmatrix} 1/2 & 1/2 \\ 1/4 & 3/4 \end{bmatrix}$, and $\{B_1, B_2\}$ with transition probability matrix

$$
\begin{array}{c c}
 & \begin{array}{cc} B_1 & B_2 \end{array} \\
\begin{array}{c} B_1 \\ B_2 \end{array} & \begin{bmatrix} 1/3 & 2/3 \\ 1/2 & 1/2 \end{bmatrix}
\end{array} .
$$

Thus, for chains with no transient states it is sufficient to study the component ergodic sets as ergodic chains. In Section 8.7 we examine some properties of ergodic chains.

As we shall later demonstrate, if a chain has ergodic and transient states then as the number of transitions increases the probability of the system still being in a transient state decreases and in the limit is zero. The system is moving towards the ergodic sets and (by definition) once it is in an ergodic set it cannot escape from it. We mention and illustrate two types of chains which fall into this category.

If all the ergodic states are absorbing then the chain is an absorbing chain, and in this case the system is eventually trapped in a single state. Examples 8.4 and 8.5 are of this type. Another type of chain has ergodic sets with more than one state (i.e. not absorbing states), for example that given by the transition probability matrix P^* above. If the system starts in T then it will eventually enter one of the ergodic sets $\{A_1, A_2\}$ or $\{B_1, B_2\}$.

Our classification does not exhaust all the possible structures which can occur. We have, for example, made no recent mention of ergodic sets which are cyclic, and it is perfectly possible to generate models with for instance a transient set and several ergodic sets, some of which may be cyclic and some regular. In our later chapters on decision problems we concentrate only on regular and absorbing chains, and thus make no further study of cyclic sets.

For chains with transient states two questions are:

(i) How does the system behave until the (inevitable) transition into one of the ergodic sets?

(ii) What can we say of system behaviour after capture by an ergodic set?

Partial answers to these have already been seen. For Example 8.4 we have some numerical evidence of the rate at which graduation and failure take place, though little direct measure of the (expected) time to these events. In answer to (ii) we know that if trapped by an absorbing state the system is forever in that state, whilst if captured by an ergodic set, which is in effect a regular chain our analysis from Sections 8.3 and 8.4 can be used to describe behaviour in that set.

In any finite Markov chain it is a fundamental property that the probability that the system is in an ergodic state after n transitions tends to one as n tends to infinity, regardless of the initial state of the system. For any transient state, i say, there is a number n_i such that it is possible to reach an ergodic state in not more than n_i transitions, i.e. if such a reachable of ergodic state is j we have $p_{ij}^{n_i} > 0$. Thus, considering all the (finite number of) transient states there is a number $n\,(= \max n_i$ say) such that it is possible to reach an ergodic state from any transient state in at most n transitions. Hence, there exists a positive p such that the probability of entering an ergodic state in at most n transitions is at least p. Starting from a transient state the probability of not reaching an ergodic state within n transitions is $(1 - p)$ or less, and thus the probability of not reaching an ergodic state within mn transitions is $(1 - p)^m$, or less. Since $(1 - p)$ is strictly less than one, then $(1 - p)^m$ tends to zero as m tends to infinity. Thus, in the limit the probability of transition from transient state to transient state is zero, and hence transition from transient to ergodic state has probability one. If the system starts in an ergodic state then the above limiting property is trivially true.

8.6 Absorbing Markov Chains

In an absorbing Markov chain all ergodic states are absorbing and hence we can arrange the transition probability matrix to be of the form

$$P = \begin{bmatrix} I & 0 \\ R & Q \end{bmatrix}.$$

We place the absorbing states at the beginning of the list, and if there are r of these we have an $r \times r$ identity matrix I for transitions between absorbing states (i.e. for absorbing state i we have $p_{ii} = 1$ and $p_{ij} = 0$ for $j \neq i$). The remaining $(N - r)$ states are transient and the 0 matrix of P is thus $r \times (N - r)$, corresponding to transition probabilities from absorbing to transient states. The $(N - r) \times (N - r)$ submatrix Q gives the single-step transition probabilities for transient to transient state moves, while the $(N - r) \times r$ matrix R gives transition probabilities from transient states to absorbing states. Thus, in Example 8.4 above $N = 5$, $r = 2$:

$$Q = \begin{array}{c} \\ \text{YR1} \\ \text{YR2} \\ \text{YR3} \end{array} \begin{array}{ccc} \text{YR1} & \text{YR2} & \text{YR3} \\ 0.1 & 0.8 & 0 \\ 0 & 0.1 & 0.8 \\ 0 & 0 & 0.1 \end{array} \quad \text{and} \quad R = \begin{array}{c} \\ \text{YR1} \\ \text{YR2} \\ \text{YR3} \end{array} \begin{array}{cc} \text{GRAD} & \text{FAIL} \\ 0 & 0.1 \\ 0 & 0.1 \\ 0.8 & 0.1 \end{array}.$$

This version of the transition probability matrix is our *canonical form*. Using the canonical form we can examine the multi-step transition probability matrices derived from P. Thus,

$$P^2 = \begin{bmatrix} I & 0 \\ R + QR & Q^2 \end{bmatrix}; \quad P^3 = \begin{bmatrix} I & 0 \\ R + QR + Q^2 R & Q^3 \end{bmatrix}$$

$$= \begin{bmatrix} I & 0 \\ (I + Q + Q^2)R & Q^3 \end{bmatrix},$$

and in general

$$P^n = \begin{bmatrix} I & 0 \\ \left(\sum_{k=0}^{n-1} Q^k \right) R & Q^n \end{bmatrix}, \quad \text{for } n = 1, 2, \dots.$$

The elements of Q^n are the n-step transition probabilities from transient state to transient state, and from the fundamental property of the last section we have that these are tending to zero with increasing n. Thus, Q^n is tending to the $(N-r) \times (N-r)$ zero matrix 0 as n tends to infinity. We now prove a property held by matrices of this type which is useful in our examination of the P^n.

If a matrix Q is such that Q^n tends to the zero matrix (of same dimension) as n tends to infinity then $(I-Q)$ has an inverse and

$$(I-Q)^{-1} = I + Q + Q^2 + \ldots = \sum_{k=0}^{\infty} Q^k.$$

Here I is dimensioned compatibly to Q. By multiplying out the left-hand side we can confirm that

$$(I-Q)(I + Q + Q^2 + \ldots + Q^{n-1}) = I - Q^n.$$

If Q^n tends to the zero matrix as n tends to infinity, then the right-hand side of this equality tends to the identity matrix. The determinant of I is 1 and thus for sufficiently large n the determinant of $I - Q^n$ is non-zero. Now for compatible matrices B and C we have determinant $(BC) =$ determinant $(B) \times$ determinant (C) and thus $(I - Q)$ has non-zero determinant (on applying the result to the equality above). Thus, $(I - Q)$ has an inverse and we obtain from the above

$$I + Q + Q^2 + \ldots + Q^{n-1} = (I-Q)^{-1}(I-Q^n).$$

Taking the limit we obtain

$$I + Q + Q^2 + \ldots = (I-Q)^{-1}.$$

For an absorbing Markov chain with the transition probability matrix in canonical form we define the *fundamental matrix* to be $N = (I-Q)^{-1}$. Referring to the multi-step transition probability matrix expressed as a power of the original transition probability matrix in its canonical form we have that

$$\lim_{n \to \infty} P^n = \begin{bmatrix} I & 0 \\ \left(\sum_{k=0}^{\infty} Q^k\right)R & \lim_{n \to \infty} Q^n \end{bmatrix} = \begin{bmatrix} I & 0 \\ NR & 0 \end{bmatrix}.$$

In the limit the system has zero probability of being in a transient state and the *absorption probabilities* (i.e. probabilities for transient state to absorbing state transition) are given by the matrix product NR. For Example 8.4 we have

$$N = \begin{bmatrix} 0.9 & -0.8 & 0 \\ 0 & 0.9 & -0.8 \\ 0 & 0 & 0.9 \end{bmatrix}^{-1} = \begin{array}{c} YR1 \\ YR2 \\ YR3 \end{array} \begin{array}{ccc} YR1 & YR2 & YR3 \\ \begin{bmatrix} 1.1111 & 0.98765 & 0.87791 \\ 0 & 1.11111 & 0.98765 \\ 0 & 0 & 0.11111 \end{bmatrix} \end{array}$$

and thus

$$NR = \begin{bmatrix} 1.1111 & 0.98765 & 0.87791 \\ 0 & 1.11111 & 0.98765 \\ 0 & 0 & 1.11111 \end{bmatrix} \begin{bmatrix} 0 & 0.1 \\ 0 & 0.1 \\ 0.8 & 0.1 \end{bmatrix}$$

$$= \begin{bmatrix} 0.702332 & 0.297668 \\ 0.790123 & 0.209877 \\ 0.88889 & 0.111111 \end{bmatrix},$$

which is in numerical agreement with the appropriate submatrix of, for example, P^{10}, and not too different from the appropriate submatrix of P^5 (see Section 8.3 of this chapter). Thus, our student, fresh in YR1, has a probability of graduating of approximately 0.702. From YR2 his chances are enhanced and from YR3 they are higher still. This is intuitively reasonable since as he progresses from year to year there are fewer opportunities for failure.

The probability of absorption in state j, given that the system starts in state i, can in fact be argued directly. We offer the argument which is typical of those used in our development.

Let b_{ij} be the probability of absorption in state j given that the system started in transient state i, and let $B = [b_{ij}]$ (i.e. the matrix with i, jth element b_{ij}).

Starting in transient state i there is a probability p_{ij} that the system is in state j after one transition. Should this not be the case then the system either moves to another absorbing state (and hence can never be captured by j) or it moves with probability p_{ik} to transient state k, and still has probability b_{kj} of being absorbed in j (from this state k). Since transition to j or another absorbing state or to a transient state are exclusive options we have

$$b_{ij} = p_{ij} + \sum_{k \in T} p_{ik} b_{kj}.$$

Where T is the index set of transient states

Recall that i to j is a transient to absorbing transition so that the p_{ij} is an element of R and the $p_{ik}(k \in T)$ are from the same row of Q. In matrix form the equation becomes

$$B = R + QB$$

and thus $(I - Q)B = R$ giving $B = (I - Q)^{-1} R = NR$, as before.

The fundamental matrix, in fact, also provides information about the expected number of transitions spent in the transient states. For $j \in T$ let $v(j)$ be the number of times that the system is in state j. Transitions are of course not deterministic in general and any information about the number $v(j)$ must be of an expected form. Thus, for $i, j \in T$ we let $E_i(v(j))$ be the expected number of times the system is in transient state j given that it starts in transient state i.

As before we find useful the shorthand of the Kronecker delta function (see Section 8.3 of this chapter). If the system starts in the state whose number of visits we are counting, then this contributes one to the total (of number of visits). Out of

212

state i the transition will be to either another transient state, say $k \in T$ with probability p_{ik}, and from that state we have a contribution of $E_k(v(j))$ as the expected number of times that the state of interest (here j) will be visited starting in the transient state k, or if the transition is to an absorbing state then there is no further contribution to the number of visits to a particular transient state. This argument is summarized thus:

$$E_i(v(j)) = \delta_{ij} + \sum_{k \in T} p_{ik} E_k(v(j)).$$

In matrix form this is

$$[E_i(v(j))] = I + Q[E_i(v(j))]$$

and thus

$$(I - Q)[E_i(v(j))] = I,$$
$$[E_i(v(j))] = (I - Q)^{-1} = N.$$

The fundamental matrix provides the information we seek.

Thus, for Example 8.4 a student starting in year one will spend on average 1.111 years in YR1, 0.98765 years in YR2 and 0.87791 years in YR3, before either graduation or failure. The average number of years in YR1 is greater than one, due to potential repetition of that year. The average length of stay in YR2 and YR3 a student can look forward to is less than one. This is due to the possibility of failure in YR1, which of course means zero time spent in YR2 (or YR3). Given that a student is in YR2 then we see that from N he can expect a length of stay of 1.1111 years in YR2 but 0.988 years in YR3, and these figures have the same rationale as those for the YR1 row. A new student can therefore expect to spend a total of $(1.111 + 0.98765 + 0.87791) = 2.98$ years in the system before absorption as a graduate or a failure. In general the expected time to absorption starting from a transient state i is $\sum_{j \in T} b_{ij}$.

8.7 Regular Markov Chains

In a regular Markov chain the multi-step transition probability matrix P^n will at some value of n have all entries positive, and we have already seen the regularity of Examples 8.1, 8.2 and 8.3 demonstrated in earlier sections. After a critical number of transitions (values for which were earlier found for our examples) the entries of higher-order multi-step transition probability matrices maintain this property. We have already seen an instance of the limiting multi-step transition probability matrix Φ for Example 8.1, where the rows of Φ are identical. Thus, after an unbounded number of transitions the probability of, for example, high demand is independent of the initial demand (since $\phi_{HH} = \phi_{LH}$). Given the Markovian assumption of no system memory this conclusion is unsurprising.

It is a property of regular Markov chains (which we do not prove) that the limiting multi-step transition probability matrix $\Phi = [\phi_{ij}]$ will have identical rows, i.e. $\phi_{ij} = \phi_j$, $1 \leqslant i \leqslant N$ for $j = 1, \ldots, N$. From $\pi(n) = \pi(0)\Phi(n)$ we have $\pi = \pi(0)\Phi$ by taking the limit of both sides as n tends to infinity. In terms of one of the N equations we have:

$$\pi_j = \sum_{i=1}^{N} \pi_i(0)\phi_{ij} = \sum_{i=1}^{N} \pi_i(0)\phi_j \quad \text{from the regularity of the chain}$$

$$= \phi_j \sum_{i=1}^{N} \pi_i(0) = \phi_j \qquad \begin{array}{l} \text{since the } \pi_i(0) \text{ are probabilities over} \\ \text{an exhaustive set of events.} \end{array}$$

For a regular Markov chain we thus have that the limiting state probability vector π is independent of the initial state probability vector $\pi(0)$, and is the same as the identical rows of the limiting multi-step transition probability matrix Φ.

We have already seen the independence from $\pi(0)$ implied by our ability to solve for π directly from $(N-1)$ of the equations of $\pi = \pi P$ together with $\sum_{i=1}^{N} \pi_i = 1$. As we have seen, the elements of the limiting state probability vector have an interpretation as the proportion of periods spent in these states if the system is allowed to run for an unbounded number of transitions. Given that there are rewards and losses for transitions we show in Chapter 9 how to aggregate the statistical and economic aspects into a criterion and offer a solution process for optimal control of the infinite stage problem.

We complete the current chapter with an investigation of one more statistic of interest to us. For the queueing problem of Example 8.2 it is possible to find the limiting state probability vector by the solution of a set of $(m+1)$ linear equations (if m is the limit on queue size) and we can therefore find the proportion of time spent with the server idle (no people in the system) or the system full (and arrivals being turned away), or the proportion of time spent with any queue size in between. It may also be of interest to know something about the expected time for particular events to happen. For example, if we start with no people in the system what is the expected number of periods before the server is again idle? Alternatively, given that the system is full, how many periods must we expect to elapse before it is again empty?

Examination of the form of our questions shows that we are seeking the expected value of the number of periods to enter a given state j for the first time from some starting state i. This is sometimes described as the *mean first passage time* from state i to state j, and we denote it by m_{ij}. Thus, for the queueing problem m_{00} is the expected number of periods between one idle period and the next. So far we have no guarantee that the mean first passage time is finite, and the consequences of infinite value would be unfortunate, not only for the server but for the analyst wishing to compare some of the measurable properties of particular systems, and choose from among the systems that with 'best' performance. In a regular chain, after all, there is a very high degree of connectivity among the states and transitions between states avoiding entry to the state of interest is always possible. Fortunately, we can demonstrate that the number of steps until first entry into the state of interest has an expected value which is finite.

Suppose that we are interested in m_{ij}. Our proof is in two parts corresponding to the cases $j \neq i$ and $j = i$. Assume first that $j \neq i$ and form a new Markov chain from our current regular one by making j into an absorbing state. The resultant Markov chain is an absorbing chain with a single ergodic set (composed of j) and the remaining states transient. For example, if the transition probability matrix for our regular chain is

$$
\begin{array}{c} \\ 1 \\ 2 \\ 3 \end{array}
\begin{array}{ccc} 1 & 2 & 3 \\ \end{array}
\begin{bmatrix} 1/3 & 1/3 & 1/3 \\ 1/2 & 1/4 & 1/4 \\ 1/4 & 0 & 3/4 \end{bmatrix}
$$

and we are interested in say m_{13}, then the new chain would have transition probability matrix given by

$$
\begin{array}{c} \\ 1 \\ 2 \\ 3 \end{array}
\begin{array}{ccc} 1 & 2 & 3 \\ \end{array}
\begin{bmatrix} 1/3 & 1/3 & 1/3 \\ 1/2 & 1/4 & 1/4 \\ 0 & 0 & 1 \end{bmatrix}.
$$

Only the transitions out of $j(= 3)$ are changed and the expected time to go from i to j in this new chain is therefore the same as in the old one. What we seek in the derived chain is thus the expected time to absorption in the trapping state j given the system starts in transient i, and this is always finite (and given by the appropriate element of the fundamental matrix N). Thus, for the numerical example

$$
Q = \begin{bmatrix} 1/3 & 1/3 \\ 1/2 & 1/4 \end{bmatrix}
$$

giving

$$
N = (I - Q)^{-1} = \begin{bmatrix} 9/4 & 1 \\ 3/2 & 2 \end{bmatrix},
$$

and

$$
B = NR = \begin{bmatrix} 9/4 & 1 \\ 3/2 & 2 \end{bmatrix} \begin{bmatrix} 1/3 \\ 1/4 \end{bmatrix} = \begin{bmatrix} 1 \\ 1 \end{bmatrix}.
$$

Thus, $m_{13} = m_{23} = 1$.

For the second case of $j = i$ then, m_{ii} is just the expected time to return to state i. We have reverted to our original regular chain, abandoning the derived absorbing one. The system can return to state i in one of two ways. There is probability p_{ii} that it is in state i after one period (this counts as a 'return'), and there is a probability p_{ij} that in the first period it makes a transition to a state $j \neq i$ and then has an expected number of steps m_{ji} to go from j to i for the first time. Thus,

$$m_{ii} = p_{ii} \cdot 1 + \sum_{j \neq i} p_{ij}(1 + m_{ji}).$$

We have already seen that for $j \neq i$ the expected first passage time from j to i is finite. The right-hand side of this last equation is therefore finite and hence m_{ii} is finite.

We denote by M the expected first passage matrix, i.e. $M = [m_{ij}]$. Denoting by M_D the matrix derived from M by setting all elements other than those of the diagonal equal to zero, we have that the expected first passage matrix satisfies the equation

$$M = P(M - M_D) + E, \quad \ldots \ldots \ldots \ldots \ldots \ldots \quad (7)$$

where E is an $N \times N$ matrix all of whose elements are one.

Using our now traditional argument where we look at first transition and appropriate continuations the first passage from i to j can happen in one step with probability p_{ij} or, with probability p_{ik}, transition is made to some state $k \neq j$ (using up one step) and from state k there is an expected number m_{kj} of transitions until j is first entered. Thus,

$$m_{ij} = p_{ij} \cdot 1 + \sum_{k \neq j} p_{ik}(1 + m_{kj})$$

$$= \sum_k p_{ik} m_{kj} + \sum_k p_{ik} - p_{ij} m_{jj}$$

$$= \sum_k p_{ik} m_{kj} - p_{ij} m_{jj} + 1.$$

Stated in matrix form this is exactly the matrix equation (7) above. Some of the expected first passage times are readily found. If $\pi = [\pi_1, \pi_2, \ldots, \pi_N]$ is the limiting state probability vector for the regular chain then $m_{ii} = 1/\pi_i$ for $1 \leqslant i \leqslant N$.

To prove this we multiply both sides of (7) by π to obtain

$$\pi M = \pi P(M - M_D) + \pi E$$
$$= \pi(M - M_D) + \pi E, \quad \text{since } \pi P = \pi,$$

and thus $\pi M_D = \pi E = [1 \quad 1 \quad 1 \quad 1 \ldots 1]$ since the row π into a column of ones from E gives the sum of the π_i which is of course 1. Thus, $\pi_i m_{ii} = 1$ and $m_{ii} = 1/\pi_i$.

8.8 Further Reading

Texts on probability and statistics commonly contain some material on Markov chains. Kemeny and Snell (1976) and Bhat (1972) are devoted exclusively to Markov chains and generalizations of the Markov model. Both texts go far beyond the material of this chapter, but are quite approachable and do offer more examples of applications.

Exercises for Chapter 8

In these exercises most of the concepts of this chapter are tested. Material directly relevant to the chapters which follow is limited to the solution of simultaneous linear equations (for steady state probabilities in regular chains) and the numerical methods for absorbing chains (i.e. the calculation of the fundamental matrix and absorption probabilities).

8.1   Given the transition probability matrix

$$P = \begin{bmatrix} 1/3 & 2/3 \\ 1/2 & 1/2 \end{bmatrix},$$

calculate some of the sequence $P^2, P^3, P^4, \ldots$. Can you guess what the limit of this sequence is? Find the limiting state probability vector for this transition matrix. By calculating some of the sequence $P^2, P^4, P^8, \ldots$ (where each entry is found by squaring the previous entry) compare the entries of these multi-step transition probability matrices with their known limit.

8.2   Repeat the operations of question 1 with

$$P = \begin{bmatrix} 1/4 & 3/4 \\ 1/2 & 1/2 \end{bmatrix}.$$

8.3   Repeat the operations of question 1 with

$$P = \begin{bmatrix} 0.4 & 0.3 & 0.3 \\ 0.4 & 0.2 & 0.4 \\ 0.7 & 0.2 & 0.1 \end{bmatrix}.$$

8.4   For the matrix P^* of Section 8.5, calculate some of the sequence P^{*2}, P^{*4}, $P^{*8}, \ldots$. Note that, in this sequence, the rows of a given matrix are *not* tending to a common set of values. Why not?

What will the limiting multi-step transition probability matrix be? (*Hint*: Note the use in questions 1 and 2 above of 2×2 matrices which are submatrices of P^*.)

8.5   In Section 8.3 the Chapman–Kolmogorov equation was established from the result that $\Phi(n) = P^n$. By arguing from first principles (as in the establishment of equation (1)) demonstrate the validity of the Chapman–Kolmogorov equation.

8.6   In Example 8.2 take $a = 1/4, b = 1/2$ and $m = 2$. By solving the appropriate set of linear equations find the limiting state probability vector for this chain. With the same arrival and service probabilities find the steady state probabilities for the cases where $m = 3$ and $m = 4$.

In each of these three cases, state the proportion of time the server is idle and the proportion of time the system is full. Given that the transition probability matrix is based on a time interval of one minute, state the expected time between successive idle minutes for the server.

For the case where $m = 2$ calculate the expected time from the state of a full system to the minute where the server is first idle.

8.7   Consider a queueing problem where arrivals are potentially 'bunched' e.g. in any one time interval we may have none, one or a paired arrival. Let the probability of a single arrival be a and the probability of a paired arrival be a^*. Suppose the limit on queue size is m (including the customer being served) and the service probability is b.

Making your assumptions explicit construct the transition probability matrix for the case where

(a) both members of a paired arrival are rejected if on their arrival there is room for only one more customer to queue, or

(b) one member of a paired arrival can join the queue (and the other be rejected) in the event of the queue size $(m-1)$.

Solve for the steady state probabilities where $a = 1/4$, $a^* = 1/8$, $b = 1/4$ and $m = 3$.

8.8   In a model of the weather suppose that a day may be classed as either rainy (R), dull but dry (D), or sunny (S). The matrix P below describes the probabilities of each type of day following from every other

$$
\begin{array}{c c}
 & \begin{array}{c c c} R & D & S \end{array} \\
P = \begin{array}{c} R \\ D \\ S \end{array} & \begin{bmatrix} 0.2 & 0.6 & 0.2 \\ 0.4 & 0.4 & 0.2 \\ 0.25 & 0.25 & 0.5 \end{bmatrix}
\end{array}.
$$

What proportion of days are sunny, rainy, and dull but dry? Given the assumptions inherent in a Markov model, would you consider a Markov model of weather to be a sensible proposition? If not, is there any extension (weakening) of the Markov model which could be appropriate?

8.9   We have already seen in Section 8.3 that the transition probability matrix

$$
P = \begin{bmatrix} 0 & 1 & 0 \\ 1/2 & 0 & 1/2 \\ 0 & 1 & 0 \end{bmatrix}
$$

does not give rise to multistep transition probability matrices with any 'convergent' properties. Indeed, powers of P alternate between two forms. By considering an arbitrary $\pi(0)$ vector and using $\pi(n) = \pi(0)P^n$ show that the state probability vector $\pi(n)$ also alternates between two forms.

Calculate π from $\pi = \pi P$ together with $\Sigma_i \pi_i = 1$ and hence show that $\pi = 1/2(\pi(n) + \pi(n+1))$.

8.10   For the transition probability matrices P and P^+ below, where an asterisk indicates a non-zero element, identify the ergodic sets in the corresponding Markov chains and re-arrange the rows and columns of P and P^+ so that these sets are more clearly distinguished in the matrices. As an aid to the classification of states it may be useful to construct a diagram for each chain, akin to that of Figure 8.1.

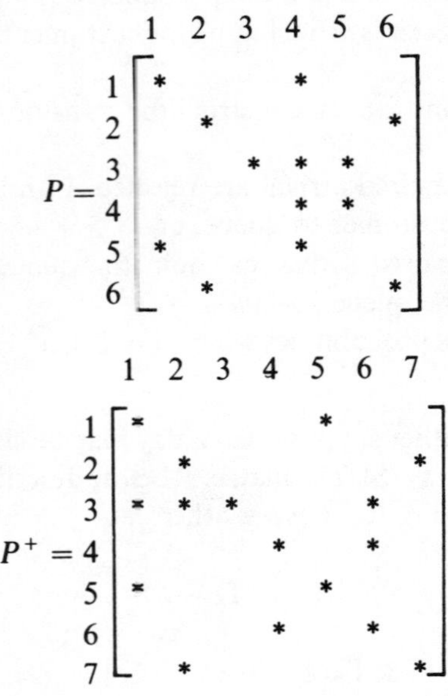

8.11   Consider an alternative set of rules for Example 8.4, the model of student progress. Again we are examining a three-year course, but in this version failure is not possible, except in the final year. Thus, in the first and second year a student may either pass or repeat the year, with probabilities 0.8 and 0.2, respectively. From the final year a student may graduate (with probability 0.8) or fail (with probability 0.2). Construct the transition probability matrix, calculate the fundamental matrix and thus find the expected number of years a student will spend in the system (until graduation or failure). It is obvious that the probability of graduation is 0.8 (and hence the failure probability is 0.2) Confirm these values using the fundamental matrix and other entries of the transition probability matrix in the usual way.

8.12   Consider a set of rules for Example 8.4 where at most one repetition of each year is allowed. Define carefully the possible states of a Markov model for this system and construct a transition probability matrix for it.

If the rules allow at most one repetition in a student's career define an appropriate transition probability matrix.

8.13   Two gamblers, Peter and Paul, begin a game with m dollars between them, e.g. Peter may have d dollars and Paul would have $m - d$ dollars (where $d < m$). The game consists of a sequence of coin-tosses where if a head results from the toss Peter pays a dollar to Paul, while a result of tails means that Paul pays a dollar to Peter. Only when one of the gamblers has all of the m dollars does the game stop.

On the assumption that the coin is fair, show that the game can be modelled as a Markov chain with transition probability matrix

$$
\begin{array}{c}
\qquad\quad 0 \quad\ m \quad\ 1 \quad\ 2 \quad\ 3 \quad m-2 \quad m-1 \\[4pt]
P =
\begin{array}{c}
0 \\ m \\ 1 \\ 2 \\ \vdots \\ m-1
\end{array}
\left[
\begin{array}{ccccccc}
1 & & & & & & \\
& 1 & & & & & \\
1/2 & & & 1/2 & & & \\
& & 1/2 & & 1/2 & & \\
& & & & & & \\
& 1/2 & & & & & 1/2
\end{array}
\right],
\end{array}
$$

where $p_{ij} = 1/2$, $j = i+1$, for $i = 1, 2, \ldots, m-1$, $p_{00} = p_{mm} = 1$, and all other matrix entries are zero. The state of the system is the number of dollars held by one of the players, say Paul.

For the case $m = 4$, calculate the fundamental matrix from the absorbing chain transition probability matrix and thus calculate the probability of victory for Paul if the game begins with a division (of the \$4) of three to Paul and one to Peter. What is the expected number of coin-tosses before the game ends if the \$4 is initially divided equally between Peter and Paul?

8.14   Consider a duel where two opponents, A and B, take it in turn to fire at one another. The first duellist to score a hit is the victor. The probability that A scores a hit with one shot is 1/3, while B has a probability 1/2 of hitting with one shot. Show that this contest can be modelled as an absorbing Markov chain with transition probability matrix

$$
\begin{array}{c}
\qquad\quad \text{AW} \quad \text{BW} \quad \text{AF} \quad \text{BF} \\[4pt]
P =
\begin{array}{c}
\text{AW} \\ \text{BW} \\ \text{AF} \\ \text{BF}
\end{array}
\left[
\begin{array}{cccc}
1 & 0 & 0 & 0 \\
0 & 1 & 0 & 0 \\
1/3 & 0 & 0 & 2/3 \\
0 & 1/2 & 1/2 & 0
\end{array}
\right],
\end{array}
$$

where AW (BW) is the state corresponding to a win by A (B) and AF (BF) is the state corresponding to the fire of a shot by A (B).

If A fires the first shot what is the likelihood that he will (eventually) win the duel? If B fires the first shot what is the likelihood that he will (eventually) win the duel? For both cases what is the expected number of shots fired before a winner emerges?

If the first person to fire is determined by the toss of a fair coin, what are the probabilities of victory for A and B?

Chapter 9

Infinite Stage Markovian Decision Processes

9.1 Introduction

In Chapter 7 we made a study of finite stage Markovian decision processes where the problem was to decide upon a policy to be applied at a (previously known) finite number of decision epochs with the objective of optimizing some measure of performance. Under certain circumstances the finite stage aspect may be too limiting a prospect for our purposes. We may be faced with a problem of uncertain duration, for example a daily re-order decision to be taken (seven days a week) for the next one, two or three months. Alternatively, our problem may be open-ended, and thus of effectively unbounded duration. In this case many decisions are to be taken and we may feel that the problem is better represented by an infinite stage model whose results will approximate to those of the finite (but considerable) stage system under study, or at least offer some insight into the structure of the optimal policy for the finite problem. This problem of approximation is itself of interest, but beyond our scope to study in technical detail, though we do validate one approximating property in the next section. It may even be the case that solution of the large finite stage problem is computationally wearisome, but the infinite approximation is a more feasible proposition.

Chapter 8 revealed some limiting properties of regular Markov chains, and perhaps may prompt us to speculate on the potential for optimal decisions independent of the stage. This was not the case in Chapter 7 where we saw that the optimal decision in a finite stage problem could, in general, depend on both state and stage. Our attention in this chapter is confined to policies which are *stationary*, i.e. a function of state but not stage.

For the finite stage problem our criterion for discriminating between the merits of different policies was the maximization of the expected reward (or minimization of the expected loss) associated with operating a policy.

If we consider now the infinite stage analogue of the first example of Chapter 7 (i.e. the problem with the same transition and reward matrices but no finite horizon when the transitions terminate) then the cumulative expected reward from using a given policy will not be finite. It will increase without bound as we accumulate the expected rewards from more and more transitions. The expected reward criterion is not then a meaningful basis for comparison of policies.

One method of obviating this difficulty would be to discount the rewards by some factor for each period from the start of the problem, and (as we show below) this will give for each policy an expected discounted reward which is finite. Comparison can then be made on the basis of this measure, the optimal policy being that which maximizes expected discounted reward (or minimizes expected discounted loss). In Section 9.4 we return to a discussion of discounting and study the solution procedures for these models.

In the next section we propose an alternative criterion which does not involve discounting, and examine appropriate solution procedures.

9.2 The Undiscounted Case

We have seen in Chapter 7 how we may derive for a regular Markov chain the limiting state probability vector, whose elements can be interpreted as the proportion of time the system spends in the given states 'in the long run'.

Suppose then we have a regular transition probability matrix $P^{(k)}$, an associated limiting state probability vector $\pi^{(k)}$ and a reward matrix $R^{(k)}$ for transition from state to state in one stage. In general these will be a function of the policy and we denote this dependence by the superfix K. For each state of the system a policy determines a unique response (action), so that if in state i we take option $k = K(i)$ there is an *immediate expected reward* denoted as before by $q^k(i)$, where $q^k(i) = \sum_{j=1}^N p_{ij}^k r_{ij}^k$. This is the expected reward received under policy K as a consequence of the use of the $K(i)$ option every time state i is entered. In the long run the system spends a proportion of time π_i^K in state i so that the *expected reward per transition* is $\sum_{i=1}^N \pi_i^K q^k(i) = g^{(k)}$, say. This is sometimes called the (expected) *gain* (per transition) from policy K.

If the system runs for a sufficiently large number of transitions under policy K then $g^{(k)}$ will be (approximately) the average reward per transition. Our criterion for the undiscounted case is to maximize the expected reward per transition, or to minimize the expected loss per transition.

Consider again the demand level problem of which we have already solved a finite stage version (in Section 7.1 of Chapter 7) and seen something of its limiting properties (in Chapter 8). We have two options (I and II) where the transition probability matrices are

$$
P^{\mathrm{I}} = \begin{array}{c} \\ \mathrm{H} \\ \mathrm{L} \end{array}\begin{array}{c} \mathrm{H} \quad\ \mathrm{L} \\ \begin{bmatrix} 1/2 & 1/2 \\ 1/4 & 3/4 \end{bmatrix} \end{array} \quad \text{and} \quad P^{\mathrm{II}} = \begin{array}{c} \\ \mathrm{H} \\ \mathrm{L} \end{array}\begin{array}{c} \mathrm{H} \quad\ \mathrm{L} \\ \begin{bmatrix} 4/5 & 1/5 \\ 1/2 & 1/2 \end{bmatrix} \end{array},
$$

and the immediate expected rewards are $q^{\mathrm{I}}(\mathrm{H}) = 15$, $q^{\mathrm{I}}(\mathrm{L}) = 39/4$, $q^{\mathrm{II}}(\mathrm{H}) = 16$ and $q^{\mathrm{II}}(\mathrm{L}) = 19/2$.

Since we have two options in both states this gives rise to four distinct policies as follows:

policy 1—take option I in state H, and option I in state L,
policy 2—take option I in state H, and option II in state L,
policy 3—take option II in state H, and option I in state L,
policy 4—take option II in state H, and option II in state L,

These four policies have associated transition probability matrices as follows:

$$P^{(1)}\,(\,=P^{\mathrm{I}}) = \begin{bmatrix} 1/2 & 1/2 \\ 1/4 & 3/4 \end{bmatrix}; \qquad P^{(2)} = \begin{bmatrix} 1/2 & 1/2 \\ 1/2 & 1/2 \end{bmatrix},$$

$$P^{(3)} = \begin{bmatrix} 4/5 & 1/5 \\ 1/4 & 3/4 \end{bmatrix} \quad \text{and} \quad P^{(4)}\,(\,=P^{\mathrm{II}}) = \begin{bmatrix} 4/5 & 1/5 \\ 1/2 & 1/2 \end{bmatrix}.$$

Thus, for policy 2 we the H row of P^{I} and the L row of P^{II}, while for policy 3 we use the H row of P^{II} and the L row of row P^{I}. The reader can confirm that the associated limiting state probability vectors are

$$\pi^{(1)} = (1/3 \quad 2/3); \qquad \pi^{(2)} = (1/2 \quad 1/2),$$
$$\pi^{(3)} = (5/9 \quad 4/9) \quad \text{and} \quad \pi^{(4)} = (5/7 \quad 2/7),$$

where $\pi^{(k)}$ is the limiting state probability vector for policy $K\,(=1, 2, 3$ and $4)$. If we denote the expected reward per transition under policy K by $g^{(k)}$, then

$$g^{(1)} = 1/3q^{\mathrm{I}}\,(\mathrm{H}) + 2/3q^{\mathrm{I}}\,(\mathrm{L}) = 11\tfrac{1}{2},$$
$$g^{(2)} = 1/2q^{\mathrm{I}}\,(\mathrm{H}) + 1/2q^{\mathrm{II}}(\mathrm{L}) = 12\tfrac{1}{4},$$
$$g^{(3)} = 5/9q^{\mathrm{II}}(\mathrm{H}) + 4/9q^{\mathrm{I}}\,(\mathrm{L}) = 13\tfrac{2}{9},$$
$$g^{(4)} = 5/7q^{\mathrm{II}}(\mathrm{H}) + 2/7q^{\mathrm{II}}(\mathrm{L}) = 14\tfrac{1}{7}.$$

Under our criterion of maximizing expected reward per transition (over an unbounded number of transition) the optimal policy is number 4, where we take the second option (II) in both states.

Reference to the first section of Chapter 7 will show that this is the optimal policy for the finite stage problem if there are at least two transitions before the stage at which the system stops. With only one transition to go the optimal response is not that of policy 4, but given that we are far enough away from the terminal stage our optimal response at these stages is just that given by the policy which maximizes expected reward per transition. In the next section we make a slightly more formal examination of the relationship between the finite stage problem (where expected rewards are accumulated) and the infinite state problem (where the average of rewards is used).

For a problem with N states and m options in each state there is a total of m^N policies. To find that policy which maximizes the expected reward per transition the scheme above would involve the solution of m^N sets of N linear equations (to give the limiting state probability vectors for all policies) and the calculation of the mN values for immediate expected reward (the $q^k(i)$ for $i = 1, 2, \ldots, N$ and $k = 1, 2, \ldots, m$). From these quantities the expected reward per transition for each policy could be calculated and the optimal policy found from the comparison of these quantities.

Even for innocuous values of m and N (e.g. $m = N = 10$) the number of policies can be dauntingly large (10^{10}) and there is a strong incentive, indeed need, to look for computational schemes other than enumeration and evaluation. This is pursued in the next section, and we complete this section with an examination of the stock control problems described as Example 8.3. Here we have only three policies to evaluate, but justify its inclusion because of the interesting reward and cost structure which we can incorporate.

Recall that the state description for the system is the number of items held in stock at the end of a period after demand has been satisfied but prior to any re-ordering to meet future demand. Thus, for policies I and II the states are 0, 1, 2 and 3 while for policy III the states are $-1, 0, 1$ and 2 (where -1 corresponds to a back-order). In the previous chapter we were concerned with the probabilistic aspects of the model and made only passing reference to the existence of particular types of costs. We associate with the system a selling price per item, a holding cost per item per period (calculated on the number of items held at the end of each period), a shortage cost per item (only for policy II) and a back-order cost per item (only for policy III). Let us denote the selling price per item by p, the holding cost per item per period by k, the shortage cost per item by s, and the back-order cost per item by r.

For each policy we can easily determine the limiting state probability vectors by solving, in each case, a set of four independent linear equations in four unknowns. Three of the equations come from equations akin to (5) of Chapter 8 and the fourth is the particular version of equation (6) from that same chapter, taking $N = 4$. The reader can readily confirm that these give

$$\pi^{\mathrm{I}} = (\pi^{\mathrm{I}}_0 \quad \pi^{\mathrm{I}}_1 \quad \pi^{\mathrm{I}}_2 \quad \pi^{\mathrm{I}}_3) \qquad = (\ 2/15 \quad 6/15 \quad 5/15 \quad 2/15),$$

$$\pi^{\mathrm{II}} = (\pi^{\mathrm{II}}_0 \quad \pi^{\mathrm{II}}_1 \quad \pi^{\mathrm{II}}_2 \quad \pi^{\mathrm{II}}_3) \qquad = (16/45 \quad 15/45 \quad 10/45 \quad 4/45),$$

and

$$\pi^{\mathrm{III}} = (\pi^{\mathrm{III}}_{-1} \quad \pi^{\mathrm{III}}_0 \quad \pi^{\mathrm{III}}_1 \quad \pi^{\mathrm{III}}_2) \qquad = (\ 2/15 \quad 6/15 \quad 5/15 \quad 2/15).$$

Under policy I we can meet all the demand without incurring shortage or back-orders, so we have:

$$\text{expected income from sales per period} = 0.4p + 0.4 \times 2p = 1.2p$$

$$\text{expected holding costs per period} = \pi^{\mathrm{I}}_0 \times 0 + \pi^{\mathrm{I}}_1 \times k + \pi^{\mathrm{I}}_2 \times 2k + \pi^{\mathrm{I}}_3 \times 3k$$
$$= 22k/15.$$

This gives an expected net income per period from policy I of $(1.2p\text{–}1.47k)$.

Under policy II we can only meet the demand for two items (i.e. suffer no shortage) if the stock level at the end of the previous period was not one. In the event of having this stock level (and hence no re-order under this policy) one item is supplied if demand is two and the other is regarded as a lost sale. Thus, for policy II:

expected income from sales per period

$$= p\{\text{demand} = 1\} \times \text{income from sale of 1}$$
$$\quad + p\{\text{stock level} \neq 1\} \times p\{\text{demand} = 2\} \times \text{income from sale of 2}$$
$$\quad + p\{\text{stock level} = 1\} \times p\{\text{demand} = 2\} \times \text{income from sale of 1}$$
$$= 0.4p + (16/45 + 10/45 + 4/45)0.4 \times 2p + 15/45 \times 0.4 \times p$$
$$= 1.07p;$$

expected holding costs per period $= \pi_0^{II} \times 0 + \pi_1^{II} \times k$
$$+ \pi_2^{II} \times 2k + \pi_3^{II} \times 3k$$
$$= 47k/45;$$

expected cost of lost sales per period $= p\{\text{stock level} = 1\} \times p\{\text{demand} = 2\}$
$$\times \text{lost sales costs}$$
$$= 15/45 \times 0.4 \times s = (2/15)s.$$

This gives an expected net income per period from policy II of $(1.07p - 1.04k - 0.13s)$.

Under policy III all demands are met but not necessarily in the period in which they are made, nevertheless:

expected income from sales per period $\quad = 0.4p + 0.4 \times 2p \quad = 1.2p;$

expected holding costs per period $\quad = \pi_1^{III} \times k + \pi_2^{III} \times 2k \; = 3k/5;$

expected back-ordering costs per period $\quad = p\{\text{stock level} = 1\}$
$$\times p\{\text{demand} = 2\}$$
$$\times \text{back-order cost}$$
$$= 5/15 \times 0.4 \times r = 2r/15.$$

This gives an expected net income per period from policy III of $(1.2p - 0.6k - 0.13r)$.

The costs associated with holding stock are often taken as directly related to the value of the stock, and in this example we take $k = 0.1p$. We then have the expected net income from policies I, II and III are $1.053k$, $0.963k - 0.13s$ and $1.14k - 0.13r$, respectively. Policy II is thus inferior to policy I regardless of the value of s (assuming all our costs and rewards are non-negative).

Policy I is preferred to policy III when $1.053k > 1.14k - 0.13r$, i.e. $r > 0.67k$. Thus, if the back-order cost is less than two-thirds of the selling price, policy III is optimal.

9.3 An Alternative Solution Scheme

Our functional equation for a finite stage problem is typically of the form

$$v_n(i) = \max_k \left\{ q^k(i) + \sum_{j=1}^N p_{ij}^k v_{n-1}(j) \right\}, \qquad 1 \leqslant i \leqslant N, \quad n \geqslant 2, \ldots \ldots (1)$$

as, for example, in equation (3) of Chapter 7. Here $v_n(i)$ is the maximum expected total reward which can be obtained starting in state i with n stages to go until the time horizon.

If we are using a policy for which the transition probability matrix is regular and there is an expected reward per transition g (which can be calculated via the limiting state probabilities and immediate expected rewards as usual), let us denote by $r_n(i)$ the expected reward which will be obtained starting in state i and using the policy in question over the remaining n stages. Note that no mention is made here of optimality. We are interested only in the total expected return over n

stages and the expected reward per transition associated with some policy. Given the regularity of the underlying chain the $r_n(i)$ can be approximated for sufficiently large values of n by $ng + r(i)$. In words, the total expected return over n stages is a linear function of the number of stages and the increment per stage—the slope of the function—is g.

We do not prove this property but demonstrate it for one of the (four) policies of the demand level example. Consider policy 1 for this problem, as stated in the previous section. This consists of taking option I in conditions of both high and low demand with a transition probability matrix given by

$$P^{(1)} = \begin{array}{c} \\ H \\ L \end{array} \begin{array}{cc} H & L \\ \begin{bmatrix} 1/2 & 1/2 \\ 1/4 & 3/4 \end{bmatrix} \end{array},$$

immediate expected rewards $q^{\mathrm{I}}(\mathrm{H}) = 15$, $q^{\mathrm{I}}(\mathrm{L}) = 39/4$, and an expected reward per transition $g = 11.5$. Let us denote by $r_n(i)$ the total expected reward obtained by using that policy over n stages $(n = 0, 1, 2, \ldots)$, starting in state $i (= \mathrm{H}, \mathrm{L})$. We have $r_0(\mathrm{H}) = r_0(\mathrm{L}) = 0$, $r_1(\mathrm{H}) = q^{\mathrm{I}}(\mathrm{H}) = 15$ and $r_1(\mathrm{L}) = q^{\mathrm{I}}(\mathrm{L}) = 39/4$. Then

$$r_2(\mathrm{H}) = q^{\mathrm{I}}(\mathrm{H}) + \tfrac{1}{2}r_1(\mathrm{H}) + \tfrac{1}{2}r_1(\mathrm{L}) = 27.38$$

and

$$r_2(\mathrm{L}) = q^{\mathrm{I}}(\mathrm{L}) + \tfrac{1}{4}r_1(\mathrm{H}) + \tfrac{3}{4}r_1(\mathrm{L}) = 20.81,$$

since the expected reward over two stages is just the immediate expected reward (out of the appropriate state) plus the expectation from the continuation—here over one more transition.

In general

$$r_n(\mathrm{H}) = q^{\mathrm{I}}(\mathrm{H}) + \tfrac{1}{2}r_{n-1}(\mathrm{H}) + \tfrac{1}{2}r_{n-1}(\mathrm{L})$$

and

$$r_n(\mathrm{L}) = q^{\mathrm{I}}(\mathrm{L}) + \tfrac{1}{4}r_{n-1}(\mathrm{H}) + \tfrac{3}{4}r_{n-1}(\mathrm{L}), \quad \text{for } n \geqslant 2.$$

In Table 9.1 we list for $n = 0, 1, \ldots, 7$ the values of ng, $r_n(\mathrm{H})$, $r_n(\mathrm{L})$ and the two differences $(r_n(\mathrm{H}) - ng)$ and $(r_n(\mathrm{L}) - ng)$.

Table 9.1 A summary of calculations for the policy of taking option I in both states

n	$r_n(\mathrm{H})$	$r_n(\mathrm{L})$	ng	$r_n(\mathrm{H}) - ng$	$r_n(\mathrm{L}) - ng$
0	0	0	0	0	0
1	15	9.75	11.5	3.5	-1.75
2	27.38	20.81	23	4.38	-2.19
3	39.10	32.20	34.5	4.60	-2.30
4	50.65	43.68	46	4.65	-2.32
5	62.17	55.17	57.5	4.67	-2.33
6	73.67	66.67	69	4.67	-2.33
7	85.17	78.17	80.5	4.67	-2.33

The calculations of this table are to two decimal places and we see that, with this accuracy, the differences $(r_n(H) - ng)$ and $(r_n(L) - ng)$ have 'converged' to 4.67 and -2.33, respectively. Recall that $r_n(i) = ng + r(i)$ (where = denotes 'approximately equal to') and our values for $r(H)$ and $r(L)$ are thus 4.67 and -2.33, respectively. Note that $r_n(H) - r_n(L) = ng + r(H) - ng - r(L) = r(H) - r(L) = 7.00$, and this can be interpreted as the relative advantage of starting the n-stage problem in state H as opposed to state L. As a fraction of the expected reward over n stages it is diminishing as n increases.

Our alternative computational scheme to find that policy which maximizes the expected reward per transition substitutes the linear approximation for $v_n(i)$ $(= ng + v(i))$ and $v_{n-1}(j)\,(= (n-1)g + v(j))$ in the finite stage equation (1) above. For large enough values of n these approximations can be made arbitrarily accurate without necessarily being exact. This substitution gives:

$$ng + v(i) = \max_k \left\{ q^k(i) + \sum_{j=1}^{N} p_{ij}^k((n-1)g + v(j)) \right\}, \qquad 1 \leqslant i \leqslant N,$$

i.e.

$$ng + v(i) = \max_k \left\{ q^k(i) + (n-1)g + \sum_{j=1}^{N} p_{ij}^k v(j) \right\}, \qquad 1 \leqslant i \leqslant N,$$

i.e.

$$g + v(i) = \max_k \left\{ q^k(i) + \sum_{j=1}^{N} p_{ij}^k v(j) \right\}, \qquad 1 \leqslant i \leqslant N. \quad \ldots \ldots (2)$$

Here we have a set of N equations (one for each state of the system) and a total of $(N+1)$ unknowns, i.e. $v(1), v(2), \ldots, v(N)$ and g. We have already seen that $r_n(i) - r_n(j) = r(i) - r(j)$ for large enough values of n, so that the difference $(r(i) - r(j))$ relates to the relative advantage or otherwise of starting in state i rather than state j. This is true for the optimal policy as well as for the particular one evaluated above. Adding a constant, C say, to each $v(i)$ for $i = 1, 2, \ldots, N$ and denoting $v(i) + C = v^*(i)$, then the g which satisfies

$$g + v^*(i) = \max_k \left\{ q^k(i) + \sum_{j=1}^{N} p_{ij}^k v^*(j) \right\}, \qquad 1 \leqslant i \leqslant N,$$

also satisfies (2), as the reader can confirm by substitution in (and cancellation from) the equation above. We also have $v^*(i) - v^*(j) = v(i) + C - v(j) - C = v(i) - v(j)$, so that adding a constant to each $v(i)$ does not change the measure of relative advantage which emerges from the solution to (2). Our method of solving (2) exploits these properties by choosing to set one of the $v(i)$ variables equal to zero, say $v(N) = 0$. This is equivalent to adding the quantity $C = -v(N)$ to all of the $v(1), \ldots, v(N)$.

With this assignment, (2) then becomes a set of N equations in N unknowns. The first algorithm to solve this set of equations was proposed by Howard (1960). There are two main components to the algorithm which are called the value determination operation (**VDO**) and the policy improvement routine (**PIR**).

Given a policy the VDO determines the 'implications' for the expected reward per transition and $v(\cdot)$ values while the PIR 'improves' the current policy (if that is possible) using the values determined. The algorithm stops when no improvement is found and this can be shown to be the optimal policy, i.e. that which maximizes expected reward per transition.

In detail the steps of the procedure are

Step 1: Choose an initial policy $d_0(\cdot)$, i.e. for each state i where $1 \leqslant i \leqslant N$ select an option $d_0(i)$ from the set of options. Put $n = 0$.

Step 2: By setting, say, $v_n(N) = 0$ solve the N equations below for g_n and $v_n(1), \ldots, v_n(N-1)$:

$$g_n + v_n(1) = q^{d_0(1)}(1) + \sum_{j=1}^{N} p_{1j}^{d_0(1)} v_n(j)$$
$$\vdots$$
$$g_n + v_n(N) = q^{d_0(N)}(N) + \sum_{j=1}^{N} p_{Nj}^{d_0(N)} v_n(j).$$

Step 3: Using the $v_n(\cdot)$ values found in Step 2 find for each state (that is, for $i = 1, 2, \ldots, N$) the option k which maximizes $\{q^k(i) + \sum_{j=1}^{N} p_{ij}^k v_n(j)\}$. Denote the policy thus found by $d_{n+1}(\cdot)$, that is $d_{n+1}(i)$ is the option k which maximizes the test expression.

Step 4: If the policy has not changed in the last cycle, that is if $d_{n+1}(i) = d_n(i)$ for $1 \leqslant i \leqslant N$, then stop, for the optimal policy has been found. Else return with the new found policy to Step 2 (taking $n = n+1$) and solve the simultaneous equations generated by that policy.

Step 2 is the VDO and Step 3 the PIR.

The optimal policy will be found in a finite number of cycles, but we leave this unproven. Complications can arise at Step 2 if, for example, the N equations are not independent, but for the problems we examine this will not occur. In particular, if each possible policy for the system under study has an associated transition probability matrix which is regular, then no problems arise. We illustrate the procedure by solving the demand level problem for which the optimal policy has already been found by enumeration and evaluation.

The first step of the algorithm is the choice of some initial policy. Let us set $d_0(H) = I$ and $d_0(L) = I$. The linear equations we have to solve are thus:

$$g_0 + v_0(H) = q^I(H) + p_{HH}^I v_0(H) + p_{HL}^I v_0(L),$$
$$g_0 + v_0(L) = q^I(L) + p_{LH}^I v_0(H) + p_{LL}^I v_0(L),$$

where we have the three unknowns g_0, $v_0(H)$ and $v_0(L)$. We set one of the $v_0(\cdot)$ equal to zero, say $v_0(L) = 0$, and the equations then become (on substitution of the appropriate numerical values)

$$g_0 + v_0(H) = 15 \ \ + 0.5 v_0 \ (H),$$
$$g_0 \qquad = 9.75 + 0.25 v_0(H),$$

which have as solution $g_0 = 11.5$, $v_0(H) = 7$ and, of course, $v_0(L) = 0$.

To find an improved policy $d_1(\cdot)$ we use the test expression $\{q^k(i) + \sum_j p_{ij}^k v_0(j)\}$ for both states ($i = $ H and L) where in each state we have two options ($k = $ I or II).

Thus, for state H we evaluate option I, giving

$$q^{\mathrm{I}}(\mathrm{H}) + p_{\mathrm{HH}}^{\mathrm{I}} v_0(\mathrm{H}) + p_{\mathrm{HL}}^{\mathrm{I}} v_0(\mathrm{L}) = 15 + 0.5 \times 7 = 18.5,$$

against option II which gives

$$q^{\mathrm{II}}(\mathrm{H}) + p_{\mathrm{HH}}^{\mathrm{II}} v_0(\mathrm{H}) + p_{\mathrm{HL}}^{\mathrm{II}} v_0(\mathrm{L}) = 16 + 0.8 \times 7 = 21.6.$$

The better option is obviously the second and we have $d_1(\mathrm{H}) = \mathrm{II}$.

Similarly, for the state L we evaluate

$$\max \begin{pmatrix} \mathrm{I} : \ q^{\mathrm{I}}(\mathrm{L}) + p_{\mathrm{LH}}^{\mathrm{I}} v_0(\mathrm{H}) + p_{\mathrm{LL}}^{\mathrm{I}} v_0(\mathrm{L}) = 9.75 + 0.25 \times 7 = 11.5 \\ \mathrm{II}: \ q^{\mathrm{II}}(\mathrm{L}) + p_{\mathrm{LH}}^{\mathrm{II}} v_0(\mathrm{H}) + p_{\mathrm{LL}}^{\mathrm{II}} v_0(\mathrm{L}) = 9.5 + 0.5 \times 7 = 13 \end{pmatrix}$$

and thus $d_1(\mathrm{L}) = \mathrm{II}$.

Our improved policy is thus to take option II in both states. With this policy (not identical to that of the previous cycle) we return to the VDO of Step 2. The equations we solve are

$$g_1 + v_1(\mathrm{H}) = q^{\mathrm{II}}(H) + p_{\mathrm{HH}}^{\mathrm{II}} v_1(H) + p_{\mathrm{HL}}^{\mathrm{II}} v_1(\mathrm{L}),$$
$$g_1 + v_1(\mathrm{L}) = q^{\mathrm{II}}(\mathrm{L}) + p_{\mathrm{LH}}^{\mathrm{II}} v_1(\mathrm{H}) + p_{\mathrm{LL}}^{\mathrm{II}} v_1(\mathrm{L}),$$

and this can be achieved by setting, for example, $v_1(\mathrm{L}) = 0$. This gives on substitution of known values for immediate expected rewards and transition probabilities

$$g_1 + v_1(\mathrm{H}) = 16 + 0.8 v_1(\mathrm{H}),$$
$$g_1 \qquad\quad = 9.5 + 0.5 v_1(\mathrm{H}),$$

which solve to give $g_1 = 14.14$, $v_1(\mathrm{H}) = 9.29$ and $v_1(\mathrm{L}) = 0$.

Using the $v_1(\cdot)$ values in the PIR section of the algorithm (Step 3) we find for state H:

$$\max \begin{pmatrix} \mathrm{I} : \ q^{\mathrm{I}}(\mathrm{H}) + p_{\mathrm{HH}}^{\mathrm{I}} v_1(\mathrm{H}) + p_{\mathrm{HL}}^{\mathrm{I}} v_1(\mathrm{L}) = 15 + 0.5 \times 9.29 = 19.65 \\ \mathrm{II}: \ q^{\mathrm{II}}(\mathrm{H}) + p_{\mathrm{HH}}^{\mathrm{II}} v_1(\mathrm{H}) + p_{\mathrm{HL}}^{\mathrm{II}} v_1(\mathrm{L}) = 16 + 0.8 \times 9.29 = 23.43 \end{pmatrix}$$

$$= 24.43 \text{ with } d_2(\mathrm{H}) = \mathrm{II};$$

and for state L;

$$\max \begin{pmatrix} \mathrm{I} : \ q^{\mathrm{I}}(\mathrm{L}) + p_{\mathrm{LH}}^{\mathrm{I}} v_1(\mathrm{H}) + p_{\mathrm{LL}}^{\mathrm{I}} v_1(\mathrm{L}) = 9.75 + 0.25 \times 9.29 = 12.07 \\ \mathrm{II}: \ q^{\mathrm{II}}(\mathrm{L}) + p_{\mathrm{LH}}^{\mathrm{II}} v_1(\mathrm{H}) + p_{\mathrm{LL}}^{\mathrm{II}} v_1(\mathrm{L}) = 9.5 \ + 0.50 \times 9.29 = 14.15 \end{pmatrix}$$

$$= 14.15 \text{ with } d_1(\mathrm{L}) = \mathrm{II}.$$

Since $d_2(\cdot) = d_1(\cdot)$ we stop with the optimal policy of taking option II in both states. This is the same policy as found by the enumeration procedure, and the value for the expected reward per transition ($g_1 = 14.14$) agrees with that found earlier. If we perform the calculations analogous to those involved in the construction of Table 9.1, but this time use the (optimal) policy of taking option II in both states H and L we obtain Table 9.2.

Table 9.2 A summary of calculations for the optimal policy of taking option II in both states

n	$v_n(\text{H})$	$v_n(\text{L})$	ng	$v_n(\text{H}) - ng$	$v_n(\text{L}) - ng$
0	0	0	0	0	0
1	16	9.5	14.14	1.86	-4.64
2	30.7	22.25	28.29	2.41	-6.04
3	45.01	35.98	42.43	2.58	-6.45
4	59.20	49.99	56.57	2.63	-6.58
5	73.36	64.10	70.71	2.65	-6.61
6	87.51	78.23	84.86	2.65	-6.63
7	101.65	92.36	99.00	2.65	-6.64

Again the differences $(v_n(\text{H}) - ng)$ and $(v_n(\text{L}) - ng)$ rapidly converge to the values shown after very few stages. If we examine $(v_n(\text{H}) - v_n(\text{L}))$ then this too is exhibiting a tendency to converge and we see that $(v_7(\text{H}) - v_7(\text{L})) = 101.65 - 92.36 = 9.29$ and this is just the $(v(\text{H}) - v(\text{L}))$ value found by the algorithm. The distinction between suffixes should be kept in mind. Prior to the policy iteration algorithm above the suffix on, for example, $v_n(i)$ referred to the number of stages to go in a multi-stage problem (as indeed it does in Table 9.2). In the context of the algorithm the suffix indicates the cycle number, i.e. the number of times the process has been through Steps 2, 3 and 4. When no improvement has taken place, say on the nth cycle, then we have an optimal policy and we denote the associated expected reward per transition by g and the v values by $v(\cdot)$ without a suffix.

Some comments on the algorithm are in order. The first step of the process is the construction of an initial policy. If the analyst is modelling a system currently in operation, then it may be sensible to start the calculations with the current policy, knowing that improvements on this will be found by the algorithm (if such improvements exist). The number of cycles to optimality will be finite but will obviously be a function of the initial policy. Thus, for the calculations above the initial policy of $d_0(\text{H}) = d_0(\text{L}) = \text{I}$ is improved to $d_1(\text{H}) = d_1(\text{L}) = \text{II}$ and one further cycle confirms this as the optimal policy. If we had started with $d_0(\text{H}) = d_0(\text{L}) = \text{II}$ then in the first cycle the optimality of this policy would have been manifest since no improvement would have taken place. The calculations would involve only one cycle as opposed to the two cycles which we needed. It would therefore seem reasonable, if the computational effort per cycle is substantial, to start with a 'good' policy in the hope that few iterations will be needed to reach optimality.

In our solution we took in the first cycle $v_0(\text{L}) = 0$ and in the second $v_1(\text{L}) = 0$, to leave in both cases two simultaneous linear equations in two unknowns. It is not necessary that the same state be used in every cycle, e.g. we could have taken $v_0(\text{H}) = 0$ in the first cycle and $v_1(\text{L}) = 0$ in the second. The g value would be unchanged by these variations and the relative value, i.e. $(v_n(\text{H}) - v_n(\text{L}))$ for $n = 1, 2, \ldots$, also unchanged. For example, if we take $v_0(\text{H}) = 0$ then the first set of simultaneous equations will solve to give $g_0 = 11.5$, $v_0(\text{H}) = 0$ and $v_0(\text{L}) =$

-7. The relative advantage of H over L $(= v_0(\text{H}) - v_0(\text{L}))$ is the same (value 7) in both this solution and our earlier one.

We now examine the solution of an infinite stage version of the third example of Chapter 7 (see Section 7.3). This is intended to reinforce some aspects of the solution mechanism, and demonstrate again the sub-optimality of myopic or greedy policies. In the finite stage version of this problem there are rewards associated with the terminal conditions of the machine, but these are obviously not applicable to a problem where the operation of the machine continues indefinitely, and all the relevant data for the problem is contained in the P^{I}, R^{I}, P^{II} and R^{II}. In fact we only use the transition probability matrices (reproduced below for ease of reference) and the immediate expected rewards for each state under either option.

The appropriate data is

$$
\begin{array}{cccc}
 & \text{FO} & \text{PO} & \text{BD} \\
\end{array}
$$

$$
P^{\text{I}} = \begin{array}{c} \text{FO} \\ \text{PO} \\ \text{BD} \end{array}
\begin{bmatrix} 0.6 & 0.2 & 0.2 \\ 0 & 0.6 & 0.4 \\ 0.5 & 0.5 & 0 \end{bmatrix}
\begin{array}{l} q^{\text{I}}(\text{FO}) = 14 \\ q^{\text{I}}(\text{PO}) = 6, \\ q^{\text{I}}(\text{BD}) = -3 \end{array}
$$

$$
\begin{array}{cccc}
 & \text{FO} & \text{PO} & \text{BD} \\
\end{array}
$$

$$
P^{\text{II}} = \begin{array}{c} \text{FO} \\ \text{PO} \\ \text{BD} \end{array}
\begin{bmatrix} 0.8 & 0.2 & 0 \\ 0 & 0.8 & 0.2 \\ 0.7 & 0.3 & 0 \end{bmatrix}
\begin{array}{l} q^{\text{II}}(\text{FO}) = 13.6 \\ q^{\text{II}}(\text{PO}) = 6.4 \\ q^{\text{II}}(\text{BD}) = -4 \end{array}
$$

There are two options in each of three stages giving $2^3 = 8$ policies. With no prior knowledge of the system, we still have to provide an initial policy for the application of Howard's algorithm. Whilst decrying myopic decision rules as (sometimes) sub-optimal they may nevertheless provide a starting point for improvement. As an initial policy we therefore take for each state that option which gives greater immediate expected reward. This gives $d_0(\text{FO}) = \text{I}$, $d_0(\text{PO}) = \text{II}$ and $d_0(\text{BD}) = \text{I}$.

Corresponding to Step 2 of the algorithm the equations to be solved are:

$$g_0 + v_0(\text{FO}) = 14 + 0.6v_0(\text{FO}) + 0.2v_0(\text{PO}) + 0.2v_0(\text{BD})$$
$$g_0 + v_0(\text{PO}) = 6.4 + 0.8v_0(\text{PO}) + 0.2v_0(\text{BD})$$
$$g_0 + v_0(\text{BD}) = -3 + 0.5v_0(\text{FO}) + 0.5v_0(\text{PO}).$$

Taking $v_0(\text{BD}) = 0$ we obtain $v_0(\text{FO}) = 18.92$, $v_0(\text{PO}) = -0.08$ and $g_0 = 6.42$. In seeking improvements to the existing policy we examine, for state FO:

$$
\max\left(\begin{array}{l} \text{I: } 14 + 0.6v_0(\text{FO}) + 0.2v_0(\text{PO}) + 0.2v_0(\text{BD}) = 25.34 \\ \text{II: } 13.6 + 0.8v_0(\text{FO}) + 0.2v_0(\text{PO}) \phantom{ + 0.2v_0(\text{BD})} = 28.72 \end{array} \right)
$$

$= 28.72$, giving $d_1(\text{FO}) = \text{II}$;

for state PO:

$$\max\begin{pmatrix} \text{I: } 6 \ \ +0.6v_0(\text{PO})+0.4v_0(\text{BD}) = 5.95 \\ \text{II: } 6.4+0.8v_0(\text{PO})+0.2v_0(\text{BD}) = 6.34 \end{pmatrix}$$

$= 6.34$, giving $d_1(\text{PO}) = \text{II}$;

and for state BD:

$$\max\begin{pmatrix} \text{I. } -3+0.5v_0(\text{FO})+0.5v_0(\text{PO}) = 6.42 \\ \text{II: } -4+0.7v_0(\text{FO})-0.3v_0(\text{PO}) = 9.22 \end{pmatrix}$$

$= 9.22$, giving $d_1(\text{BD}) = \text{II}$.

Since the policy has changed in this cycle we return to Step 2 where the equations to be solved are now:

$$\begin{aligned} g_1 + v_1(\text{FO}) &= 13.6+0.8v_1(\text{FO})+0.2v_1(\text{PO}) \\ g_1 + v_1(\text{PO}) &= \ \ 6.4 \qquad\qquad +0.8v_1(\text{PO})+0.2v_1(\text{BD}) \\ g_1 + v_1(\text{BD}) &= \ \ -4+0.7v_1(\text{FO})+0.3v_1(\text{PO}). \end{aligned}$$

Taking $v_1(\text{BD}) = 0$ we obtain $v_1(\text{FO}) = 20.42$, $v_1(\text{PO}) = -7.79$ and $g_1 = 7.95$. With these values we again examine, for state FO:

$$\max\begin{pmatrix} \text{I: } 14 \ \ +0.6v_1(\text{FO})+0.2v_1(\text{PO})+0.2v_1(\text{BD}) = 24.69 \\ \text{II: } 13.6+0.8v_1(\text{FO})+0.2v_1(\text{PO}) \qquad\qquad = 28.38 \end{pmatrix}$$

$= 28.38$, giving $d_2(\text{FO}) = \text{II}$;

for state PO:

$$\max\begin{pmatrix} \text{I: } 6 \ \ +0.6v_1(\text{PO})+0.4v_1(\text{BD}) = 1.33 \\ \text{II: } 6.4+0.8v_1(\text{PO})+0.2v_1(\text{BD}) = 0.17 \end{pmatrix}$$

$= 1.33$, giving $d_2(\text{PO}) = \text{I}$;

and for state BD:

$$\max\begin{pmatrix} \text{I: } -3+0.5v_1(\text{FO})+0.5v_1(\text{PO}) = 3.32 \\ \text{II: } -4+0.7v_1(\text{FO})+0.3v_1(\text{PO}) = 7.95 \end{pmatrix}$$

$= 7.95$ giving $d_2(\text{BD}) = \text{II}$.

Again the policy has changed $(d_2 \neq d_1)$ and hence a return to Step 2 is in order. The equations to be solved are now:

$$\begin{aligned} g_2 + v_2(\text{FO}) &= \ \ 13.6+0.8v_2(\text{FO})+0.2v_2(\text{PO}) \\ g_2 + v_2(\text{PO}) &= \ \ \ \ 6 \qquad\qquad +0.6v_2(\text{PO})+0.4v_2(\text{BD}) \\ g_2 + v_2(\text{BD}) &= \ \ -4 \ \ +0.7v_2(\text{FO})+0.3v_2(\text{PO}). \end{aligned}$$

Setting $v_2(\text{BD}) = 0$ gives $v_2(\text{FO}) = 20.21$, $v_2(\text{PO}) = -5.93$ and $g_2 = 8.37$. Using these v values in Step 3 to look for policy improvement gives a policy d_3 such that $d_3 = d_2$. The process stops with optimal policy $d(\text{FO}) = \text{II}$, $d(\text{PO}) = \text{I}$ and $d(\text{BD}) = \text{II}$. This yields an expected reward per transition of $g = 8.37$. Note that the sequence of g values in the solution process is offering an improvement at each cycle, i.e. $g_2 > g_1 > g_0$, confirming our contention that the policy deduced from the test quantities is indeed an improvement over that which started the cycle, for all cycles except the last (where the policy repeats and is hence optimal).

One interesting feature of this policy is that for no state does it agree with the option which maximizes immediate expected reward! The value for the expected reward per transition can be confirmed by finding the limiting state probability vector for the transition probability matrix associated with the optimal policy. Thus, we solve for π_{FO}, π_{PO} and π_{BD} using two equations from

$$(\pi_{FO} \quad \pi_{PO} \quad \pi_{BD}) = (\pi_{FO} \quad \pi_{PO} \quad \pi_{BD}) \begin{bmatrix} 0.8 & 0.2 & 0 \\ 0 & 0.6 & 0.4 \\ 0.7 & 0.3 & 0 \end{bmatrix},$$

together with $\pi_{FO} + \pi_{PO} + \pi_{BD} = 1$.

The transition probability matrix uses the FO row of P^{II}, the PO row of P^{I} and the BD row from P^{II}, as dictated by the optimal policy. The reader can confirm that the limiting state probability vector is $[1/2 \quad 5/14 \quad 1/7]$.

Given our interpretation of these probabilities as the proportion of time spent in the different states, then the expected reward per transition is just given by

$$g = \pi_{FO} q^{II}(FO) + \pi_{PO} q^{I}(PO) + \pi_{BD} q^{II}(BD) = 8.37, \text{ as before.}$$

In Chapter 7 where the finite stage version of this was solved as far as stage 3, the policy optimal in the infinite stage case had not yet emerged. We had

$$D_3 = \begin{bmatrix} II \\ II \\ II \end{bmatrix}$$

and the reader may confirm that

$$D_4 = \begin{bmatrix} II \\ II \\ II \end{bmatrix}.$$

It is not until the system is five transitions distant from the time horizon of the problem that the policy above emerges as optimal for that stage, and we have

$$D_5 = \begin{bmatrix} II \\ I \\ II \end{bmatrix}.$$

Further calculations would show that

$$D_n = \begin{bmatrix} II \\ I \\ II \end{bmatrix}$$

for $n \geq 5$. Recall that the finite stage problem had values associated with the terminal condition of the machine, though at time periods distant enough from the deadline we would expect the influence of these values to be insignificant or extinct.

9.4 The Discounted Case

In this chapter we are concerned with the problem of discriminating between policies when a system is operating over an infinite number of stages and the sum of the expected rewards can thus be unbounded. In this section we study the consequences of discounting future rewards by some factor and offer two solution techniques to cope with the functional equation which arises.

Consider again the general finite horizon problem. In this case the functional equation is of the form

$$v_n(i) = \max_k \left\{ q^k(i) + \sum_{j=1}^{N} p_{ij}^k v_{n-1}(j) \right\} \qquad 1 \leqslant i \leqslant N, \quad n \geqslant 1,$$

with some 'boundary condition' on $v_0(\cdot)$, i.e. values for this function. In words, the maximum expected reward which can be gained when the system is in state i and there are n periods left in which to operate is found by maximizing the sum of the immediate expected reward and the residual reward expected after transition (consequent upon some decision). The $v_{n-1}(j)$ can be thought of as the worth of being in state j with $(n-1)$ periods remaining. The worth of being in state i with n periods to go—$v_n(i)$—is therefore composed of rewards which are received at different points in time—the $q^k(i)$ immediately and the $v_{n-1}(j)$ over subsequent transitions.

In many problems, especially those which encompass a substantial time-span, it is sometimes reasonable to discount rewards received over to time to some 'equivalent' value at one point in time—normally the present. Instead of an even-handed aggregation of rewards this discounting process discriminates in favour of rewards to be received in the near future and against those which are further into the future. As an illustration consider the problem where the decisionmaker is interested in choosing between options where the assessment of an option's worth is in terms of the profits which it brings over the next five years, discounted back to the present. If the discount rate is, say, 0.8, then a succession of profits of 5, 10, 8, 10 and 12 (where all figures are in millions of dollars, say) would be evaluated as having a discounted value of $5 + 0.8(10) + 0.8^2(8) + 0.8^3(10) + 0.8^4(12) = \$28.16$ million. Note that the discount rate is applied in a compound manner. If the sequence of profits is 5, 8, 10, 10, 12 then this has the (inferior) discounted total of 27.84. Since the second- and third-year figures of this set are just the third- and second-year figures of the first set, then the option which produces the larger profit at an earlier date (i.e. the first example) will have superior discounted value.

In general we will use a factor α, where $0 < \alpha < 1$, by which we discount per period expected rewards back to some initial period. In this context we define $v_n(i)$

as the *maximum discounted expected reward starting in state i with n transitions to go, where the discounting is back to the time period in which the first of the n decisions is taken.* The functional equation is then

$$v_n(i) = \max_k \left\{ q^k(i) + \alpha \sum_{j=1}^{N} p_{ij}^k v_{n-1}(j) \right\} \qquad 1 \leq i \leq N, \quad n \geq 1 \ldots \ldots (3)$$

On the right-hand side of the equation we have the immediate expected reward $q^k(i)$ received in the period of the first decision (and therefore not subject to discounting). With probability p_{ij}^k the system is in state j and the best that can then be achieved is a discounted expected reward of $v_{n-1}(j)$, where the discounting is to the period in which the first of these $(n-1)$ decisions is made. As part of the evaluation of total discounted reward over n periods the $v_{n-1}(j)$ must be discounted by one more period—hence the mutiplication by α.

By virtue of the discount factor the $v_n(i)$ is bounded for all values of n (unlike the undiscounted case). For suppose M is the maximum expected reward which can be received in any transition regardless of state (e.g. take $M = \max_k \max_i q^k(i)$), then

$$v_n(i) \leq M + \alpha M + \alpha^2 M + \alpha^3 M + \ldots + \alpha^{n-1} M$$
$$= M(1 - \alpha^n)/(1 - \alpha) < M/(1 - \alpha),$$
$$\text{if } \alpha > 0.$$

Now $v_{n+1}(i) \geq v_n(i)$ and hence the sequence $\{(v_n(i)\}$ is an increasing sequence, but bounded above by $M/(1-\alpha)$. Under these circumstances it can be shown that $\lim_{n \to \infty}\{v_n(i)\}$ exists and we denote this by $v(i)$. This is the expected discounted reward when the system operates over an unbounded number of transitions and an optimal policy is used.

In the functional equation (3) above if we take the limit as n tends to infinity of both sides of the equation we have

$$v(i) = \max_k \left\{ q^k(i) + \alpha \sum_{j=1}^{N} p_{ij}^k v(j) \right\}, \qquad 1 \leq i \leq N, \ldots \ldots \ldots (4)$$

How then are we to solve (4) for $v(i)$ $(i = 1, \ldots, N)$ and the optimal policy? It is of course possible to ignore the functional equation (4) and rely on a process of enumeration and evaluation, but ample evidence of the ineffectiveness of this procedure for problems of a non-trivial size had already been seen.

One method of solution is similar to that used in Section 7.5 of Chapter 7 where we saw a functional equation (equation (5) of that chapter) similar to (4) in that it too had no explicit reference to a stage variable. The optimal discounted reward function $v(i)$ is subject to a 'successive approximation' technique, namely starting with an initial set of values $v_0(i)$ for $i = 1, \ldots, N$ we calculate

$$v_1(i) = \max_k \left\{ q^k(i) + \alpha \sum_{j=1}^{N} p_{ij}^k v_0(j) \right\}, \qquad 1 \leq i \leq N,$$

and then

$$v_n(i) = \max_k \left\{ q^k(i) + \alpha \sum_{j=1}^{N} p_{ij}^k v_{n-1}(j) \right\}, \qquad 1 \leqslant i \leqslant N, \ldots \ldots (5)$$

for $n = 2, 3, \ldots$.

Under certain circumstances the value of $v_n(i)$ will become a better approximation to $v(i)$ with increasing n (for all states i) and we consequently might hope that the policy deduced from (5) would, for large enough values of n, agree with the optimal policy of (4), or at worst bear a close relationship to it. Any problem which leads to the solution of (5) for very large values of n lands us again with the computational burdens which we had hoped to alleviate by consideration of the infinite stage version of the problem. However, if the initial $v_0(i)$ values are reasonably close to the optimum solution then it may require only a few iterations to satisfy us that the policy generated is good, if not optimal. One major advantage of this scheme is that it does not involve the solution of sets of simultaneous equations.

Consider the demand level example which we have solved in a finite stage form in Chapter 7 and in an infinite stage form in Sections 9.2 and 9.3 of this chapter. Let us take a discount rate of 0.8 per period. The method just described needs an appropriate set (here pair) of values $v_0(i)$ (for $i = $ H, L). For this problem we have four immediate expected rewards, $q^{\mathrm{I}}(\mathrm{H}) = 15$, $q^{\mathrm{I}}(\mathrm{L}) = 9.75$, $q^{\mathrm{II}}(\mathrm{H}) = 16$ and $q^{\mathrm{II}}(\mathrm{L}) = 9.5$. As a lower bound we can therefore obtain at least 9.5 (thousand dollars) per period. The total discounted expected profit is thus at least $9.5 + 0.8(9.5) + 0.8^2(9.5) + \ldots = 9.5/(1 - 0.8) = 47.5$ thousand dollars.

It is possible to argue in a more sophisticated manner for lower bounds but this starting value is sufficient for our needs. Thus, we take $v_0(\mathrm{H}) = v_0(\mathrm{L}) = 47.5$, and apply the recurrence relationship to find $v_1(\cdot), v_2(\cdot), \ldots$. Figures 9.1 and 9.2 show the values of $v_n(\mathrm{H})$ and $v_n(\mathrm{L})$, respectively, calculated up to $n = 40$. The true values for $v(\mathrm{H})$ and $v(\mathrm{L})$ (which we later calculate by an exact mechanism) are 73.158 and 64.605, respectively (to an accuracy of three places of decimals). Our solution by successive approximation is within 1 % of this by $n = 17$, within 0.1 % by $n = 27$ and within 0.01 % by $n = 37$. At $n = 40$ the values are accurate to within approximately 0.005 %. Perhaps more important, the optimal policy (which is to take option II in both states) emerges very early in the calculations. The degree to which this is true in general will be a function of the starting values (for $v_0(\cdot)$) and the size of the problem (namely number of states and number of options), as well as some other considerations which we ignore.

As an alternative procedure we can adapt the policy iteration technique (or 'approximation in policy space') from the previous section. In seeking the solution to (4) above we follow the procedure below (compare with the description of Howard's algorithm or the material of the last section of Chapter 7).

Step 1:   Choose an initial policy $d_0(\cdot)$, i.e. for each state i where $1 \leqslant i \leqslant N$ select an option $d_0(i)$ from the set of options. Put $n = 0$.

236

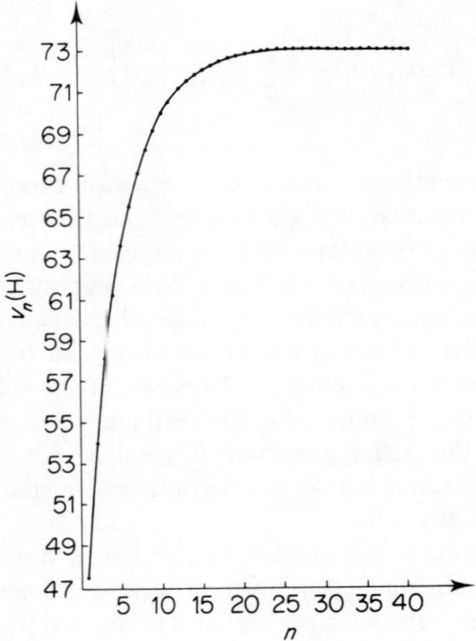

Figure 9.1 The value of $v_n(H)$, the optimal
discounted expected reward over n periods
starting in state H, versus n

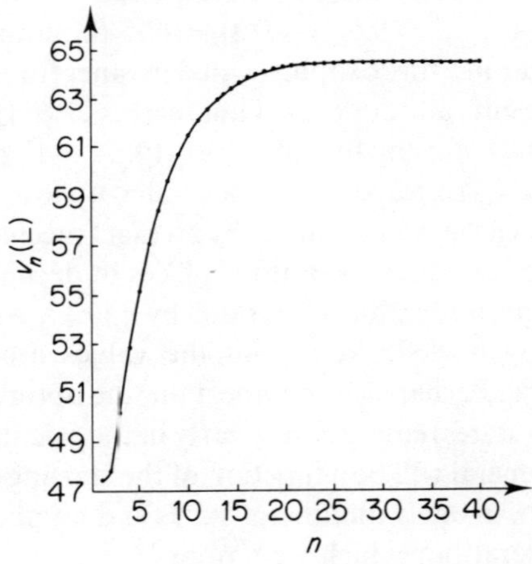

Figure 9.2 The value of $v_n(L)$, the optimal discounted expected reward over n
periods starting in state L, versus n

Step 2:   Solve the N equations for the N unknowns $v_n(1), \ldots, v_n(N)$

$$v_n(i) = q^k(i) + \alpha \sum_{j=1}^{N} p_{ij}^k v_n(j), \qquad 1 \leqslant i \leqslant N,$$

taking $k = d_n(i)$.

Step 3:   Using the $v_n(.)$ found in Step 2 find for each state (that is, for $1 \leqslant i \leqslant N$) the option k which maximizes

$$q^k(i) + \alpha \sum_{j=1}^{N} p_{ij}^k v_n(j).$$

Denote the policy found by $d_{n+1}(\cdot)$, that is, $d_{n+1}(i)$ is the option k which maximizes the test expression for state i.

Step 4:   If the policy has not changed in the last cycle, i.e. if $d_{n+1}(i) = d_n(i)$ for $1 \leqslant i \leqslant N$, then stop, for the optimal policy has been found. Else return with the new found policy to Step 2 (taking $n = n+1$) and solve the simultaneous equations generated by that policy.

If we apply this method to the demand level problem as above with an initial policy given by $d_0(H) = d_0(L) = I$ then our simultaneous equations are

$$v_0(H) = 15 \quad + 0.8(0.5v_0(H) + 0.5v_0(L)),$$
$$v_0(L) = 9.75 + 0.8(0.25v_0(H) + 0.75v_0(L)),$$

with solution $v_0(H) = 61.875$ and $v_0(L) = 55.3125$.

In looking for an improved policy we calculate, for state H:

$$\max\begin{cases} \text{I:} \quad q^{\text{I}}(H) + 0.8(0.5v_0(H) + 0.5v_0(L)) = 61.875, \\ \text{II:} \quad q^{\text{II}}(H) + 0.8(0.8v_0(H) + 0.2v_0(L)) = 64.45, \end{cases}$$

and thus take $d_1(H) = II$, while for state L we calculate

$$\max\begin{cases} \text{I:} \quad q^{\text{I}}(L) + 0.8(0.25v_0(H) + 0.75v_0(L)) = 55.3125, \\ \text{II:} \quad q^{\text{II}}(L) + 0.8(0.5v_0(H) + 0.5v_0(L)) = 56.375, \end{cases}$$

and thus we take $d_1(L) = II$.

Using this new policy we solve the equations

$$v_1(H) = 16 \quad + 0.8(0.8v_1(H) + 0.2v_1(L)),$$
$$v_1(L) = 9.5 + 0.8(0.5v_1(H) + 0.5v_1(L))$$

to obtain $v_1(H) = 73.158$ and $v_1(L) = 64.605$.

If we perform the calculation of Step 3 we find that the policy which emerges is unchanged, i.e. $d_2 = d_1$ and we therefore stop with the optimal policy, which is to take option II in both states.

9.5 Further Reading

Howard (1960) is one of the earliest works in this area and remains one of the most readable. The dynamic programming references at the end of Chapter 7 mostly contain some material on Markovian decision processes. Derman (1970) gives an advanced presentation while White (1978) emphasises the variety of functional equations which can arise in finite state problems, and studies the algorithms used for solving them. In Hartley et al. (1980) is to be found the 'state-of-the-art', as far as solution procedures are concerned. A wide range of problems and exercises are to be found in Wagner (1972). Puterman (1978) presents an advanced set of surveys, applications and theoretical papers.

Exercises for Chapter 9

Most of these exercises are applications of Howard's algorithm and the algorithm given in Section 9.4 for the discounted case.

9.1   Demand for a product in a given week may be high (H) or low (L) and in seeking to influence the level of demand we may use different amounts of advertising. In any week we can choose from three advertising campaigns and we know that the transition probability matrices (describing system behaviour from one week to the next) associated with these campaigns are:

$$P^{\mathrm{I}} = \begin{array}{c} \mathrm{H} \\ \mathrm{L} \end{array} \begin{bmatrix} 1/2 & 1/2 \\ 1/4 & 3/4 \end{bmatrix}; \quad P^{\mathrm{II}} = \begin{array}{c} \mathrm{H} \\ \mathrm{L} \end{array} \begin{bmatrix} 4/5 & 1/5 \\ 1/2 & 1/2 \end{bmatrix}; \quad P^{\mathrm{III}} = \begin{array}{c} \mathrm{H} \\ \mathrm{L} \end{array} \begin{bmatrix} 2/3 & 1/3 \\ 1/3 & 2/3 \end{bmatrix}$$

The corresponding net reward matrices for these transitions using the different advertising campaigns are:

$$R^{\mathrm{I}} = \begin{array}{c} \mathrm{H} \\ \mathrm{L} \end{array} \begin{bmatrix} 40 & 20 \\ 30 & 16 \end{bmatrix}; \quad R^{\mathrm{II}} = \begin{array}{c} \mathrm{H} \\ \mathrm{L} \end{array} \begin{bmatrix} 36 & 16 \\ 26 & 12 \end{bmatrix}; \quad R^{\mathrm{III}} = \begin{array}{c} \mathrm{H} \\ \mathrm{L} \end{array} \begin{bmatrix} 30 & 24 \\ 30 & 15 \end{bmatrix}.$$

If we wish to maximize the (long-run) expected reward per period use the policy iteration method (with an initial policy of using the first option under either demand) to find the optimal policy. Find the limiting state probabilities for this policy and thus confirm the figure previously found for the expected reward per period.

9.2   Consider the following infinite stage Markovian decision process, where there are three options in each of the two states. The transition probability matrices and immediate expected rewards are:

Option	Transition probabilities		Immediate expected reward
I	0.6	0.4	12
	0.5	0.5	8
II	0.7	0.3	11
	0.6	0.4	6
III	0.8	0.2	10
	0.4	0.6	9

With an initial policy which takes option I in both states, use Howard's algorithm to find the policy which maximizes the average expected reward per transition (over an unbounded number of transitions). Find the limiting state probabilities for this policy and thus confirm the value found for the average expected reward per period.

9.3 Consider the three-state, two-action problem with transition probability matrices P^I, P^{II} and immediate expected rewards $q^k(i)$ using action k ($=$ I or II) when in state i ($= A$, B or C). The problem data is:

$$P^I = \begin{matrix} & A & B & C \\ A & \\ B & \\ C & \end{matrix} \begin{bmatrix} 0.4 & 0.2 & 0.4 \\ 0.2 & 0.1 & 0.7 \\ 0.6 & 0.1 & 0.3 \end{bmatrix} \qquad \begin{matrix} q^I(A) = 10 \\ q^I(B) = 5, \\ q^I(C) = 2 \end{matrix}$$

$$P^{II} = \begin{matrix} & A & B & C \\ A & \\ B & \\ C & \end{matrix} \begin{bmatrix} 0.3 & 0.3 & 0.4 \\ 0.3 & 0.4 & 0.3 \\ 0.4 & 0.3 & 0.3 \end{bmatrix} \qquad \begin{matrix} q^{II}(A) = 12 \\ q^{II}(B) = 2, \\ q^{II}(C) = 3 \end{matrix}$$

and the criterion is to maximize the expected reward per transition over an unbounded number of transitions. Using Howard's policy iteration algorithm confirm that the optimal policy $d(\cdot)$ is given by $d(A) = II$, $d(B) = I$ and $d(C) = I$.

Find the limiting state probability vector for this optimal policy and thus confirm the value found for the expected reward per transition.

9.4 Consider the problem where we have two states (H and L) and three options which can be taken in either state. The transition probability and reward matrices are given below:

$$P^{(1)} = \begin{matrix} H \\ L \end{matrix} \begin{bmatrix} 1/2 & 1/2 \\ 1/2 & 1/2 \end{bmatrix}; \qquad R^{(1)} = \begin{matrix} H \\ L \end{matrix} \begin{bmatrix} 20 & 15 \\ 10 & 10 \end{bmatrix},$$

$$P^{(2)} = \begin{matrix} H \\ L \end{matrix} \begin{bmatrix} 3/4 & 1/4 \\ 1/4 & 3/4 \end{bmatrix}; \qquad R^{(2)} = \begin{matrix} H \\ L \end{matrix} \begin{bmatrix} 16 & 12 \\ 8 & 12 \end{bmatrix},$$

$$P^{(3)} = \begin{matrix} H \\ L \end{matrix} \begin{bmatrix} 2/3 & 1/3 \\ 1/3 & 2/3 \end{bmatrix}; \qquad R^{(3)} = \begin{matrix} H \\ L \end{matrix} \begin{bmatrix} 20 & 8 \\ 16 & 10 \end{bmatrix}.$$

Starting with a policy of using decision 2 in both states, use the policy iteration technique to find that policy which maximizes the expected reward per period for the case of an infinite number of transitions.

Find the limiting state probabilities for this policy and confirm the figure previously found for the expected reward per period.

9.5   Consider the decision problem in a Markov chain where the reward matrix R is given by

$$
R = \begin{array}{c} \\ 1 \\ 2 \\ 3 \end{array}
\begin{array}{ccc} 1 & 2 & 3 \end{array}
\begin{bmatrix} \sigma & \sigma-1 & \sigma-2 \\ \sigma-1 & \sigma & \sigma-2 \\ \sigma-2 & \sigma-1 & \sigma \end{bmatrix}
$$

and two transition probability matrices corresponding to options I and II are

$$
P^{\mathrm{I}} = \begin{array}{c} \\ 1 \\ 2 \\ 3 \end{array}
\begin{array}{ccc} 1 & 2 & 3 \end{array}
\begin{bmatrix} 1/3 & 1/3 & 1/3 \\ 1/2 & 0 & 1/2 \\ 1/4 & 1/4 & 1/2 \end{bmatrix}
$$

and

$$
P^{\mathrm{II}} = \begin{array}{c} \\ 1 \\ 2 \\ 3 \end{array}
\begin{bmatrix} 1/5 & 2/5 & 2/5 \\ 1/4 & 1/2 & 1/4 \\ 1/2 & 0 & 1/2 \end{bmatrix}.
$$

If the process is to be controlled over three transitions and no reward or loss is associated with any of the terminal states, find the policy which maximizes the expected reward over these three periods.

If we are interested in maximizing the expected reward per transition for the case where we allow an unbounded number of transitions, use the policy iteration technique to find the optimal policy. Relate the g and $v(i)$ found from this process to those implied by the finite three transition case.

9.6   Using the data of Exercise 7.1, find the policy which minimizes the expected cost per period for the case where the number of periods is unbounded.

9.7   Using the data of Exercise 7.5, find the policy which maximizes the expected reward per period for the case where the number of periods is unbounded. The information on the value of terminal states is no longer relevant.

9.8   A production process can use up to two identical machines, each of which generates a profit of $100 per day when in operation. Given that the process starts the day with a number I of machines, the number J of machines available for use the following day depends on the maintenance policy adopted by the company. The company has to make a daily choice on maintenance, and the effect of each option $K (= 1, 2, 3)$ is summarized in the three transition probability matrices given below. The entries here are the probability of going from I to J under K:

$$J$$

$$
P^{(1)} = I \begin{array}{c} 0 \\ 1 \\ 2 \end{array} \begin{bmatrix} 1 & 0 & 0 \\ 1/2 & 1/2 & 0 \\ 1/4 & 1/2 & 1/4 \end{bmatrix},
$$

$$J$$

$$
P^{(2)} = I \begin{array}{c} 0 \\ 1 \\ 2 \end{array} \begin{bmatrix} 1/4 & 1/2 & 1/4 \\ 1/4 & 1/4 & 1/2 \\ 1/4 & 1/4 & 1/2 \end{bmatrix},
$$

$$J$$

$$
P^{(3)} = I \begin{array}{c} 0 \\ 1 \\ 2 \end{array} \begin{bmatrix} 0 & 1/2 & 1/2 \\ 1/4 & 1/4 & 1/2 \\ 0 & 1/2 & 1/2 \end{bmatrix}.
$$

The daily cost of option 1 is zero. Option 2 costs \$30 per day and option 3, \$50 per day. Given that the company is interested in maximizing the average expected profit per period in the long run, use the policy improvement technique (with an initial policy of taking option 1 in every state) to find an optimal policy.

Find the limiting state probability vector for your optimal policy, and thus confirm the value found for the average expected profit per period.

9.9   Demand for a product on a given day can be high (H), medium (M) or low (L) and these demands give rise to daily profits of \$2000, \$1500 and \$1000, respectively. The transition probability matrix P below describes the dependence of demand (on any day) on the demand of the previous day:

$$
\begin{array}{ccc} L & M & H \end{array}
$$

$$
P = \begin{array}{c} L \\ M \\ H \end{array} \begin{bmatrix} 1/3 & 1/3 & 1/3 \\ 1/2 & 1/4 & 1/4 \\ 1/4 & 1/4 & 1/2 \end{bmatrix}.
$$

The vendor has the option of advertising the product during the evening broadcasts of the local radio station and this has the effect of modifying the probabilities for that transition to those of Q below:

$$Q = \begin{array}{c} \\ L \\ M \\ H \end{array} \begin{array}{ccc} L & M & H \\ \begin{bmatrix} 1/4 & 1/4 & 1/2 \\ 1/3 & 1/3 & 1/3 \\ 1/6 & 1/3 & 1/2 \end{bmatrix} \end{array}.$$

The advertising fee is \$120 but this is only payable if:

   (i) a low demand is improved to medium or high; or
  (ii) a medium demand is maintained or improved to high; or
 (iii) a high demand is maintained.

Given that the vendor is interested in maximizing the average expected profit per period in the long run, use the policy improvement technique to find the optimal policy. Find the limiting state probability vector for your optimal policy and thus confirm the value found for the average expected profit per period.

9.10   An item has a target delivery date (say day 0) with penalties incurred by the manufacturer for early or late delivery. These are at a rate of c per day early and k per day late. The production process for the item is faulty, and given that an item is put into production the probability of an acceptable item is p. The production process takes place overnight, and (at most) one unit of the item is produced in one session. Defining $v(n)$ to be the minimum expected cost of delivery given that by day n (n days prior to day 0) the item is not yet ready show that

$$v(0) = pk + 2pk(1-p) + 3pk(1-p)^2 + \ldots.$$

Given that $(1 + 2\alpha + 3\alpha^2 + \ldots)$ sums to $(1-\alpha)^{-2}$ for $|\alpha| < 1$, show that

$$v(0) = k/p.$$

Show that for $n > 1$

$$v(n) = \min\left(p(n-1)c + (1-p)v(n-1), v(n-1)\right)$$
$$= p\min\{(n-1)c, v(n-1)\} + (1-p)v(n-1).$$

If the item is not yet ready by day n show that attempted production is worthwhile on day n if

$$(n-1)c < v(n-1).$$

Show that once attempted production is worthwhile it will remain so until an item is produced. (*Hint*: Assume $v(n) > nc$, $v(n-1) \leqslant (n-1)c$ and generate a contradiction.)

   For $k = 100, c = 100$ and $p = 1/2$ show that production is worthwhile for day 4 and later.

9.11   Using the policy iteration technique solve the problem of Exercise 9.6 above (i.e. Exercise 7.1) where future costs are discounted at a rate of 0.9 per period, and the criterion is to minimize the expected discounted cost.

9.12   Using the policy iteration technique solve the problem of Exercise 9.7 above (i.e. Exercise 7.5) where future rewards are discounted at a rate of 0.8 per period, and the criterion is to maximize the expected discounted reward.

9.13   Solve the problem of Exercise 9.4 above when a discount rate of 0.8 per period is applied.

Chapter 10

Decisions in Absorbing Chains

10.1 Introduction and First Example

In this our final chapter we return to the absorbing Markov chain structures first seen in Chapter 8, and consider some problems which can be formulated and solved in this setting. Unlike the regular Markov chains and associated decision processes of Chapter 9 we do not offer a variety of algorithms for solution. Instead, we concentrate on the formulation of the problems in an absorbing Markov chain framework and the assessment of expectations uses information directly from the fundamental matrix N and the stochastic matrix B of absorption probabilities (from each transient starting state).

As our first example consider a gamble which may be played in one of two ways. Two balls are drawn from a bag which contains two black and two white balls. If the draw results in two black balls the gamble terminates and we receive a prize of $30, while if two white balls are drawn the game terminates and we pay a penalty of $10. In the first method of play the balls are drawn simultaneously (for a fee of $3 per draw) until one of the two terminating events occurs. The drawn balls are of course replaced before the next draw is made. In the second method we start with a draw of two balls but in the event of one black and one white ball being drawn we make a further draw from the two balls remaining in the bag (i.e. without replacing any of the balls drawn initially). If this draw results in a black ball we receive the prize as before but should the draw be white then all drawn balls are replaced in the bag and the process is started over again. For each draw of the two balls simultaneously we pay $3, as before, while for the privilege of holding onto the drawn balls and making a draw from the two remaining in the bag we pay $5 each time this happens. On the assumption that we wish to maximize our expected income from playing the game which of the two methods is to be preferred?

Let us denote by BB and WW, the receipt of the reward (associated with two blacks) and the payment of the penalty (associated with two whites), respectively. For the first method denote by D a draw from the bag (always involving two balls from a total of four in this method). In constructing the transition probability matrix for this method we have the two absorbing states BB and WW, and a single transient state D. The matrix is of the form

$$\begin{array}{c} \\ \begin{array}{c}\text{BB}\\ \text{WW}\\ \text{D}\end{array}\end{array}\overset{\begin{array}{ccc}\text{BB}&\text{WW}&\text{D}\end{array}}{\begin{bmatrix} 1 & 0 & 0 \\ 0 & 1 & 0 \\ 1/6 & 1/6 & 2/3 \end{bmatrix}} = P^{\text{I}}, \text{ say.}$$

On a single draw of the two balls the probability of the two blacks being drawn is 1/6, and this is also the probability of the two white being drawn. In the event of a pair consisting of one black and one white the balls are replaced and another draw takes place. The gamble terminates at **BB** or **WW**, hence the probabilities for those rows.

For the second method we have two types of draws which we denote by D_1 and D_2. The first of these is the simultaneous draw of two balls from the four in the bag (i.e. just the same as D in the first method) while the second corresponds to the draw of one ball from two remaining in the bag—inevitably one black and one white (since a black and a white have already been drawn and not replaced). As before **BB** and **WW** denote, respectively, the prize-winning and penalty-paying states. The transition probability matrix for this process is of the form

$$\begin{array}{c}\text{BB}\\ \text{WW}\\ \text{D}_1\\ \text{D}_2\end{array}\overset{\begin{array}{cccc}\text{BB}&\text{WW}&\text{D}_1&\text{D}_2\end{array}}{\begin{bmatrix} 1 & 0 & 0 & 0 \\ 0 & 1 & 0 & 0 \\ 1/6 & 1/6 & 0 & 2/3 \\ 1/2 & 0 & 1/2 & 0 \end{bmatrix}} = P^{\text{II}}, \text{ say.}$$

The **BB** and **WW** rows, as before, are of this form since the states are trapping states. Transitions out of D_1 (which are akin to those out of D in P^{I}) correspond to draws of two blacks (going to **BB**), two whites (going to **WW**) and a pair consisting of one black and one white, where we now go to a draw of the second type (D_2) rather than replace the balls and repeat the draw as is done in the first method. On the second draw where we sample one ball from a pair consisting of one black and one white, we win a prize (i.e. make transition to **BB**) if a black is drawn (and this obviously has probability 1/2) and make a transition to D_1 (i.e. replace all balls and start again) if a white is drawn (and this obviously has probability 1/2).

In P^1 the matrix of transient transitions is given by $Q = [2/3]$, so that the fundamental matrix $N = (I - Q)^{-1} = [1/3]^{-1} = [3]$ and $B = NR = [3][1/6 \quad 1/6] = [1/2 \quad 1/2]$. The expected number of transitions (draws) before the gamble terminates is thus 3 and the prize and penalty are equally likely (as seems reasonable from the symmetry of the problem description). The expected income from this procedure is thus $1/2 \times 30 + 1/2 \times (-10) - 3 \times 3 = \$1$.

For the alternative procedure the matrix of transient to transient transitions is given by

$$Q = \begin{bmatrix} 0 & 2/3 \\ 1/2 & 0 \end{bmatrix}$$

and thus

$$N = (I - Q)^{-1} = \begin{bmatrix} 1 & -2/3 \\ -1/2 & 1 \end{bmatrix}^{-1} = \begin{bmatrix} 3/2 & 1 \\ 3/4 & 3/2 \end{bmatrix}.$$

Given the process starts with a draw of the first type (D_1), which it must, the expected number of D_1 draws is 3/2 and the expected number of D_2 draws is 1. The matrix of absorption probabilities is found thus

$$B = NR = \begin{bmatrix} 3/2 & 1 \\ 3/4 & 3/2 \end{bmatrix}\begin{bmatrix} 1/6 & 1/6 \\ 1/2 & 0 \end{bmatrix} = \begin{bmatrix} 3/4 & 1/4 \\ 7/8 & 1/8 \end{bmatrix}.$$

Thus, given that the process starts with a D_1 draw, which it must, the probability of a prize is 3/4 and the probability that the penalty is paid is 1/4. The expected income from this method is $3/4 \times 30 + 1/4 \times (-10) - 3/2 \times 3 - 1 \times 5 = \$10.5$, and this second method is therefore to be preferred.

10.2 A Second Example

In this example we examine a problem in credit control and illustrate another use to which the initial and derived data of an absorbing chain may be put.

For many organizations a significant proportion of total income may be tied up in accounts yet to be settled and the behaviour of the accounts is thus worthy of study. Money receivable is categorized by its delinquency i.e. we have a set of ages i $(i = 0, 1, \ldots, n-1)$. We use i equal to zero for the current category and assume that the age one period later than $(n-1)$ is the 'bad debt' category. Money of this age is automatically written off. The number of ages for a model will vary with the practice of particular organizations. We denote by PD the 'paid' classification and BD the 'bad debt' classification.

There are at least two methods of categorizing accounts. In one the age (or delinquency) of an account is the age of the 'oldest dollar' in the account. Alternatively the age of all money in the account can be taken into consideration by some sort of averaging procedure. We will not concern ourselves with the details of these accounting procedures, but note that no sensible system of categorizing should make an account age more quickly than time itself is passing, i.e. no money can go from age i at time t to any age older than $(i+1)$ at time $(t+1)$. We make the assumption that the transition probability matrix for the problem is constant over time (i.e. is the same at all transitions), and while in practice it can be constructed from historical data we offer in P below a reasonable set of likelihoods for a problem where accounts more than two periods overdue are written off as bad debts. We assume that the time periods here are, say, months:

$$P = \begin{array}{c} \\ \text{PD} \\ \text{BD} \\ 0 \\ 1 \\ 2 \end{array} \begin{array}{c} \text{PD} \quad \text{BD} \quad\; 0 \quad\;\; 1 \quad\;\; 2 \\ \begin{bmatrix} 1 & 0 & 0 & 0 & 0 \\ 0 & 1 & 0 & 0 & 0 \\ 0.9 & 0 & 0 & 0.1 & 0 \\ 0.4 & 0 & 0 & 0.3 & 0.3 \\ 0.2 & 0.1 & 0 & 0.6 & 0.1 \end{bmatrix} \end{array}.$$

Thus, our model has two absorbing and three transient states. The interpretation of the entries of P is fairly straightforward. Thus, a dollar which is one month old has a probability 0.4 of being paid off in the next month, a probability 0.3 of ageing one month in a month and a probability 0.3 of being the same age one month later! To the reader who is perturbed by this last property we direct his attention to the rather elliptical remarks on the definition of age given above. Perhaps a more accessible interpretation is to say that of the dollars which are of age one month 40% will be paid off, 30% will go toward that set of dollars which is defined to be of age 2 and 30% will go toward that set of dollars which is defined to be of age 1.

Regardless of these difficulties, we can perform our usual manipulations on the components of P to find the fundamental matrix N and the matrix of absorption probabilities B. Thus, since

$$Q = \begin{bmatrix} 0 & 0.1 & 0 \\ 0 & 0.3 & 0.3 \\ 0 & 0.6 & 0.1 \end{bmatrix}, \quad \text{we have } (I - Q) = \begin{bmatrix} 1 & -0.1 & 0 \\ 0 & 0.7 & -0.3 \\ 0 & -0.6 & 0.9 \end{bmatrix},$$

and

$$N = (I - Q)^{-1} = \begin{bmatrix} 1 & 0.20 & 0.07 \\ 0 & 2 & 0.67 \\ 0 & 1.33 & 1.56 \end{bmatrix},$$

and

$$B = NR = \begin{bmatrix} 1 & 0.20 & 0.07 \\ 0 & 2 & 0.67 \\ 0 & 1.33 & 1.56 \end{bmatrix} \begin{bmatrix} 0.9 & 0 \\ 0.4 & 0 \\ 0.2 & 0.1 \end{bmatrix} = \begin{bmatrix} 0.99 & 0.01 \\ 0.93 & 0.07 \\ 0.84 & 0.16 \end{bmatrix}.$$

Thus, of money entering the current account 99% will eventually be paid and the average time to payment is $(1 + 0.20 + 0.07) = 1.27$ months. Only 1% of money in the current account is written off. Accounts which are, for example, two time periods overdue will yield an 84% success rate of payment and the average time taken for the eventual status of account already 2 months old to become clear (i.e. paid or written off) is $1.33 + 1.56 = 2.89$ months.

In addition to these routine deductions there are other questions which can be tackled. For example, suppose at a given point in time we have certain amounts in each of the ages what is the eventual fate of these monies if we allow a sufficient number of transition for (most of) the money in the accounts to be either paid or written-off? In particular if we have a total of $600000 due, of which $450000 is current, $100000 is one month overdue and $50000 is two months overdue, how much of this money will eventually be paid and how much written-off?

Using the B matrix above, we see that 99% of money in the current account is paid while the one month old and two month old accounts yield 93% and 84%, respectively. Thus, we can expect a total payment of $0.99 \times 450 + 0.93 \times 100 + 0.84 \times 50 = \$580.5$ thousand out of the $600 thousand due.

This arithmetic and that for the written-off case can be more succinctly put in matrix form thus:

$$[450 \quad 100 \quad 50] \begin{bmatrix} 0.99 & 0.01 \\ 0.93 & 0.07 \\ 0.84 & 0.16 \end{bmatrix} = [580.5 \quad 19.5]$$

Thus, $19.5 thousand will eventually be written off.

Alternative credit policies are easily evaluated. If pressure on customers to pay early is relaxed the impact of this can be assessed from the transition probability matrix for the modified problem—given that we have the ability to construct it. The value of this model in practical terms is dependent as much on its ability to answer readily and with little computation, questions about the effect of changes in credit policy as on its ability to describe the process.

10.3 A Third Example with Variations

You are offered a gamble involving a fair coin where there is a prize p to be won when you achieve three successive heads on tosses of the coin. For each toss of the coin you pay a fee of $1. How much must the prize be worth before you would accept the gamble, given that we use an expected money criterion?

We can model this as an absorbing Markov chain where in the state H^3 (denoting three successive heads) the game stops and the prize p is received. For our transient states we keep track of the number of successive heads so far, and this can be 0, 1 or 2. The transition probability matrix P is given by

$$P = \begin{array}{c} \\ H^3 \\ S \\ H \\ H^2 \end{array} \begin{array}{c} \begin{array}{cccc} H^3 & S & H & H^2 \end{array} \\ \begin{bmatrix} 1 & 0 & 0 & 0 \\ 0 & 1/2 & 1/2 & 0 \\ 0 & 1/2 & 0 & 1/2 \\ 1/2 & 1/2 & 0 & 0 \end{bmatrix} \end{array},$$

where S is the state with no heads accumulated so far, and H, H^2 are the states with one and two heads accumulated respectively.

State H^3 is absorbing and no transitions out of it are possible. In state S (where we have no heads in our present run) then this is the state again after one toss (if a tail turns up on that toss) or we can make a transition to state H (if a head turn up on this toss). Since head and tail are equally likely this gives the elements of the S row. Out of state H we can either make a transition to state S (in the event of a tail) or state H^2 (in the event of a head). From state H^2 we can either be absorbed into H^3 (in the event of a head) or go back to state S (in the event of a tail).

For this transition probability matrix we have

$$N = (I - Q)^{-1} = \begin{bmatrix} 1/2 & -1/2 & 0 \\ -1/2 & 1 & -1/2 \\ -1/2 & 0 & 1 \end{bmatrix}^{-1} = \begin{bmatrix} 8 & 4 & 2 \\ 6 & 4 & 2 \\ 4 & 2 & 2 \end{bmatrix}.$$

Thus, starting in state S (as we do) the expected number of tosses which take place when we have accumulated zero heads in succession is 8, the expected number when we already have one head is 4, and the expected number when we have had two successive heads is 2. The expected number of tosses until absorption in H^3 is $(8 + 4 + 2) = 14$. Since H^3 is the only absorbing state, then transition into this state is inevitable. If each toss of the coin costs \$1 then the prize must be greater than \$14 before participation in the gamble can be expected to yield a profit.

Consider a more complicated version of the problem where the cost of coin-tossing and the criterion for a prize remain as above, but in the event of two successive tails in the sequence of tosses the game stops, and the fees paid for the coin tosses are 'sunk'. What now is the size of prize for which this gamble is worth taking?

The absorbing states are now H^3 (three heads in a row) and T^2 (two tails in a row). As before we have a starting state S where no relevant sequence has been accumulated, and states T, H and H^2 where we have one tail, one head and two heads accumulated, respectively. The transition probability matrix, again assuming a fair coin, is given by

$$
P = \begin{array}{c}
 \\ H^3 \\ T^2 \\ S \\ H \\ H^2 \\ T
\end{array}
\begin{array}{c}
\begin{array}{cccccc}
H^3 & T^2 & S & H & H^2 & T
\end{array} \\
\left[\begin{array}{cccccc}
1 & 0 & 0 & 0 & 0 & 0 \\
0 & 1 & 0 & 0 & 0 & 0 \\
0 & 0 & 0 & 1/2 & 0 & 1/2 \\
0 & 0 & 0 & 0 & 1/2 & 1/2 \\
1/2 & 0 & 0 & 0 & 0 & 1/2 \\
0 & 1/2 & 0 & 1/2 & 0 & 0
\end{array}\right]
\end{array} .
$$

Note that in this case after the initial occupation of state S (at the start) this state is never entered again. If, for example, we are in state H then transition is to H^2 or T, depending on the next toss of the coin. The fundamental matrix is given by

$$
N = \begin{array}{c}
 \\ S \\ H \\ H^2 \\ T
\end{array}
\begin{array}{c}
\begin{array}{cccc}
S & H & H^2 & T
\end{array} \\
\left[\begin{array}{cccc}
1 & 1.2 & 0.6 & 1.4 \\
0 & 1.6 & 0.8 & 1.2 \\
0 & 0.4 & 1.2 & 0.8 \\
0 & 0.8 & 0.4 & 1.6
\end{array}\right]
\end{array}
$$

and

$$
B = NR = \begin{array}{c}
 \\ S \\ H \\ H^2 \\ T
\end{array}
\begin{array}{c}
\begin{array}{cc}
H^3 & T^2
\end{array} \\
\left[\begin{array}{cc}
0.3 & 0.7 \\
0.4 & 0.6 \\
0.6 & 0.4 \\
0.2 & 0.8
\end{array}\right]
\end{array} .
$$

Thus, from the starting state the expected number of tosses until absorption is $(1 + 1.2 + 0.6 + 1.4) = 4.2$, while the absorption probabilities from this starting state are 0.3 for H^3 (and the prize) and 0.7 for T^2. If the prize is \$$p$ and the cost per toss

250

is \$1 the net expected reward from the game is $0.3p - 4.2$. For this to be positive the prize must therefore be greater than \$14. This is exactly the condition arrived at in the first problem! Despite the possibility of no prize in this second option (compared to the certainty of a prize in the first) the minimum prize for which either gamble will break even (in expected terms) is \$14. The reader may verify that for a prize in excess of this amount the first gamble has superior expected outcome.

Exercises for Chapter 10

Included in this selection are versions of the problem which first appeared in Section 1.5 of Chapter 1, in the discussion on Example 1.4.

10.1   A system can be described by four states A_1, A_2, T_1 and T_2. Consider the process which can start in either of the states T_1 or T_2 and has transition probability matrices (describing system behaviour from one time period to the next) P_u and P_v under policies u and v, respectively, where

$$P_u = \begin{array}{c} A_1 \\ A_2 \\ T_1 \\ T_2 \end{array} \begin{array}{cccc} A_1 & A_2 & T_1 & T_2 \\ \left[\begin{array}{cccc} 1 & 0 & 0 & 0 \\ 0 & 1 & 0 & 0 \\ 1/4 & 1/4 & 1/4 & 1/4 \\ 1/2 & 1/4 & 1/4 & 0 \end{array}\right] \end{array} ; \qquad P_v = \begin{array}{c} A_1 \\ A_2 \\ T_1 \\ T_2 \end{array} \begin{array}{cccc} A_1 & A_2 & T_1 & T_2 \\ \left[\begin{array}{cccc} 1 & 0 & 0 & 0 \\ 0 & 1 & 0 & 0 \\ 1/2 & 1/3 & 0 & 1/6 \\ 1/3 & 1/3 & 1/6 & 1/6 \end{array}\right] \end{array} .$$

When in transient state T_1 there is an outlay of 1 unit per time period whilst in state T_2 the outlay is 2 units per time period. If the state becomes A_1 the process stops and a reward of 40 units is received whilst if the process enters A_2 the process stops and a penalty of 40 units is paid.

The process starts in T_1 and T_2 with probabilities p and $1-p$, respectively. If the objective is to maximize expected income find the decision rule which chooses the optimal policy as a function of p.

If the objective is to minimize the expected duration in the transient states before absorption (regardless of costs and rewards) show that the policy v is optimal for all possible values of p.

10.2   A system can be described by four states A_1, A_2, T_1 and T_2. Consider the process which can start in either of the states T_1 or T_2 and has transition probability matrices (describing system behaviour from one time period to the next) P_u and P_v under policies u and v, respectively, where

$$P_u = \begin{array}{c} A_1 \\ A_2 \\ T_1 \\ T_2 \end{array} \begin{array}{cccc} A_1 & A_2 & T_1 & T_2 \\ \left[\begin{array}{cccc} 1 & 0 & 0 & 0 \\ 0 & 1 & 0 & 0 \\ 1/5 & 1/5 & 2/5 & 1/5 \\ 2/5 & 1/5 & 2/5 & 0 \end{array}\right] \end{array} ; \qquad P_v = \begin{array}{c} A_1 \\ A_2 \\ T_1 \\ T_2 \end{array} \begin{array}{cccc} A_1 & A_2 & T_1 & T_2 \\ \left[\begin{array}{cccc} 1 & 0 & 0 & 0 \\ 0 & 1 & 0 & 0 \\ 1/2 & 1/4 & 1/4 & 0 \\ 1/4 & 1/4 & 1/4 & 1/4 \end{array}\right] \end{array} ,$$

When in either of the transient states T_1 or T_2 there is an outlay of 1 unit per time period. If the state becomes A_1 the process stops and a reward of r units is received whilst if the process enters A_2 the process stops and a reward of $2r$ units is received.

If the process starts in T_1 or T_2 with equal probability and the objective is to maximize expected income, find the decision rule which chooses the optimal policy as a function of r.

If instead the objective is to maximize the probability of absorption in A_2 and the process starts in T_1 and T_2 with probabilities p and $1-p$, respectively (instead of T_1 and T_2 being equiprobable), find the decision rule which chooses the optimal policy as a function of p.

10.3   Consider a system with five states, A_1, A_2, T_1, T_2 and T_3 and a transition probability matrix

$$
P = \begin{array}{c} \\ A_1 \\ A_2 \\ T_1 \\ T_2 \\ T_3 \end{array}
\begin{array}{ccccc}
A_1 & A_2 & T_1 & T_2 & T_3 \\
\left[\begin{array}{ccccc}
1 & 0 & 0 & 0 & 0 \\
0 & 1 & 0 & 0 & 0 \\
1/6 & 1/6 & 1/3 & 0 & 1/3 \\
1/4 & 0 & 1/4 & 1/4 & 1/4 \\
0 & 1/3 & 1/6 & 1/2 & 0
\end{array}\right]
\end{array},
$$

When in a transient state there is an outlay of $1/4$ unit per time period. Upon absorption in A_1 a reward of 10 units is received, whilst absorption in A_2 means a penalty of 10 units is paid. Given that the system starts in T_1, T_2 and T_3 with probabilities $1/4$, p and $3/4-p$, respectively, (where $0 \leqslant p \leqslant 3/4$) find the total expected income in operating the system.

Suppose we are allowed to choose a value of p upon payment of a penalty of $5p^2$ units. Find (approximately) the value of p we would choose to maximize our total expected income.

For this Markov chain the fundamental matrix has all entries strictly positive. Would you expect this to be so for all absorbing Markov chains of this simple type, and if so, why?

10.4   A businessman is starting a new company which he hopes to sell once it has reached a predetermined size. The company is initially small in size and can grow to medium or large. Denote these three conditions by S, M and L, respectively.

After one year a small company can still be small, grow to a medium size or go bankrupt. In the same time a medium sized company can expand to large, contract to small or remain the same size. A large company can remain large, contract to medium or be found a buyer (since this is the size at which the owner wishes to sell). Denoting the states of bankruptcy and sale by B and C respectively, the transition probability matrix for the process is given by P below:

$$P = \begin{array}{c} \\ C \\ B \\ S \\ M \\ L \end{array}
\begin{array}{ccccc} C & B & S & M & L \\ \end{array}
\left[\begin{array}{ccccc}
1 & 0 & 0 & 0 & 0 \\
0 & 1 & 0 & 0 & 0 \\
0 & p & q & r & 0 \\
0 & 0 & p & q & r \\
r & 0 & 0 & p & q
\end{array} \right].$$

In P the probabilities are such that $p + q + r = 1$, since P is a stochastic matrix.

Calculate the fundamental matrix and the matrix of absorption probabilities for the cases where

(i) $p = r = 0.1$ and $q = 0.8$,
(ii) $p = r = 0.2$ and $q = 0.6$.

Note that the probability of eventual sale is the same for the two cases. Is this intuitively reasonable? Note that in case (ii) the expected number of years to absorption (i.e. sale or bankruptcy) is one-half the same statistic for case (i). Given the relative p (or r) values for the two cases, is this intuitively reasonable?

10.5   By calculating the fundamental matrix and the matrix of absorption probabilities from the P matrix of Exercise 10.4 show that the probability of eventual sale is 0.25 when $p = r$ (i.e. confirm the numerical cases above). Under the same conditions show that the expected number of years until sale or bankruptcy is $3/2p$.

10.6   Consider an amended version of the problem of Exercise 10.4 in which new companies are protected from bankruptcy in their first year of operation (by an agency such as a bank). From its starting state (denoted by ST) a company can progress in one year, to either small (S) or medium (M) size and the transition probability matrix describing this and all other transitions is given by P below:

$$P = \begin{array}{c} \\ C \\ B \\ ST \\ S \\ M \\ L \end{array}
\begin{array}{cccccc} C & B & ST & S & M & L \\ \end{array}
\left[\begin{array}{cccccc}
1 & 0 & 0 & 0 & 0 & 0 \\
0 & 1 & 0 & 0 & 0 & 0 \\
0 & 0 & 0 & p+q & r & 0 \\
0 & p & 0 & q & r & 0 \\
0 & 0 & 0 & p & q & r \\
r & 0 & 0 & 0 & p & q
\end{array} \right].$$

For the case where $p = r = 0.1$ and $q = 0.8$, calculate the fundamental matrix and matrix of absorption probabilities, and compare the results with those of Exercise 10.4.

10.7   The businessman of Exercise 10.4 is faced with the choice of operating either with the transition probabilities of case (i) or case (ii). Successful sale of the business will bring him $5 million and his profit per year is $100 000, $250 000 or $1 million in states small, medium and large, respectively. On bankruptcy he has no additional income, but is assumed to retain his previously earned profits. If the criterion he uses is total expected income over the lifetime of the company, which option should he use, and why? What is the expected worth to the businessman of the protection offered in Exercise 10.6?

References

Aitchison, J. (1970), *Choice Against Chance: An Introduction to Statistical Decision Theory*, Addison-Wesley, London.

Bell, D. E., Keeney, R. L. and Raiffa, H. (1977), *Conflicting Objectives in Decisions*, Wiley, Chichester.

Bellman, R. E. (1957), *Dynamic Programming*, Princeton University Press, Princeton.

Bellman, R. E. and Dreyfus, S. E. (1962), *Applied Dynamic Programming*, Princeton University Press, Princeton.

Bhat, U. N. (1972), *Elements of Applied Stochastic Processes*, Wiley, New York.

Derman, C. (1970), *Finite State Markovian Decision Processes*, Academic Press, New York.

Edwards, W. (1977), 'How to Use Multiattribute Utility Measurement for Social Decisionmaking', *IEEE Trans. on Systems, Man and Cybernetics*, **SMC-7,** 5.

Edwards, W. and Tversky, A. (1967), *Decision Making*, Penguin, Harmondsworth.

Hampton, J. M., Moore, P. G. and Thomas, H. (1973), 'Subjective Probability and its Measurement', *J. R. Statist. Soc. A*, **136,** Part 1.

Hartley, R., Thomas, L. C. and White, D. J. (1980), *Recent Developments in Markov Decision Processes*, Academic Press, London.

Howard, R. A. (1960), *Dynamic Programming and Markov Processes*, Wiley, London.

Howard, R. A. (1980), 'An Assessment of Decision Analysis', *Op. Res.*, **28,** 1.

Hull, J., Moore, P. G. and Thomas, H. (1973), 'Utility and its Measurement', *J. R. Statist. Soc. A*, **136,** Part 2. [Also in Kaufman and Thomas (1977).]

Johnson, E. M. (1977), 'The Technology of Utility Assessment', *IEEE Trans. on Systems, Man and Cybernetics*, **SMC-7**, 5.

Kaufman, G. M. and Thomas, H. (1977), *Modern Decision Analysis*, Penguin, Harmondsworth.

Keeney, R. L. and Raiffa, H. (1976), *Decisions with Multiple Objectives: Preference and Value Tradeoffs*, Wiley, New York.

Kemeny, J. G. and Snell, J. L. (1976), *Finite Markov Chains*, Springer-Verlag, New York.

Krischer, J. P. (1980), 'An Annotated Bibliography of Decision Analytic Applications to Health Care', *Op. Res.*, **28,** 1.

LaValle, I. H. (1978), *Fundamentals of Decision Analysis*, Holt, Rinehart and Winston, New York.

Lindley, D. V. (1971), *Making Decisions*, Wiley, London.

Luce, R. D. and Raiffa, H. (1957), *Games and Decisions*, Wiley, New York.

Moore, P. G., Thomas, H., Bunn, D. W. and Hampton, J. (1976), *Case Studies in Decision Analysis*, Penguin, Harmondsworth.

Nemhauser, G. L. (1966), *Introduction to Dynamic Programming*, Wiley, New York.

Puterman, M. L. (1978), *Dynamic Programming and its Applications*, Academic Press, New York.

Raiffa, H. (1968), *Decision Analysis*, Addison-Wesley, Reading, Mass.

Ramsey, F. P. (1926), 'Truth and Probability', in *The Foundation of Mathematics and other Logical Essays*, Kegan Paul (1931).

Savage, L. J. (1954), *The Foundations of Statistics*, Wiley, New York.

Spetzler, C. S. and Staël von Holstein, C.-A.S. (1975), 'Probability Encoding in Decision Analysis', *Management Sci.*, **22,** 3.

Tversky, A. and Kahneman, D. (1974), 'Judgement Under Uncertainty: Heuristics and Biases', *Science*, **185**. [Also in Kaufman and Thomas (1977).]

von Neumann, J. and Morgenstern, O. (1947), *Theory of Games and Economic Behaviour*, Princeton University Press, Princeton (2nd edition).

Wagner, H. M. (1972), *Principles of Operations Research*, Prentice-Hall, London.

White D. J. (1969), *Dynamic Programming*, Oliver and Boyd, Edinburgh and London.

White, D. J. (1976), *Fundamentals of Decision Theory*, North-Holland/American Elsevier, New York.

White, D. J. (1978), *Finite Dynamic Programming*, Wiley, Chichester.

Index